b18782413

Haruka

-Beyond the Stream of Time-

2

HAYNER PL/ALTON SQUARE

Story & Art by **Tohko Mizuno**

AKRAM

THE LEADER OF THE DEMON CLAN WHO IS TRYING TO DESTROY THE CAPITAL. HE NEEDS AKANE'S POWER IN ORDER TO FULFILL HIS PLANS. HE HAS BLOND HAIR, BLUE EYES, PORCELAIN-WHITE SKIN, AND ALWAYS WEARS HIS FAVORITE COLOR, RED.

PRINCESS FUJI

A DESCENDANT OF THE STAR CLAN WHO HAS SERVED THE PRIESTESS OF THE DRAGON GOD FOR GENERATIONS. SHE IS DEDICATED TO HER MISSION.

TACHIBANA-NO-TOMOMASA

A MAJOR GENERAL AND NOBLEMAN OF THE CAPITAL. HE IS ATTRACTIVE AND HAS A BEAUTIFUL VOICE. HE HAS YET TO RECEIVE HIS DRAGON JEWEL.

THE DRAGON GOD HAS CHOSEN *YOU* TO BE ITS PRIESTESS.

PLEASE, USE THAT POWER FOR THE CAPITAL... WE ARE BESET BY AN EVIL KNOWN AS THE DEMON CLAN.

A RECAP OF THE STORY THUS FAR

APRIL 2000. AKANE WAS JUST A NORMAL HIGH SCHOOL GIRL UNTIL ONE DAY SHE, ALONG WITH HER FRIENDS TENMA AND SHIMON, WAS SUDDENLY SUMMONED BACK IN TIME TO A WORLD RESEMBLING JAPAN DURING THE HEIAN ERA (794-1185 CE). HARBORING HATRED FOR THE PEOPLE OF THE CAPITAL, THE MEMBERS OF THE DEMON CLAN ARE TRYING TO DESTROY THE LAND. AKRAM, THE LEADER OF THE DEMON CLAN, SUMMONED AKANE, THE PRIESTESS OF THE DRAGON GOD, IN ORDER TO USE THE POWER OF THE DRAGON GOD FOR HIS PLANS.

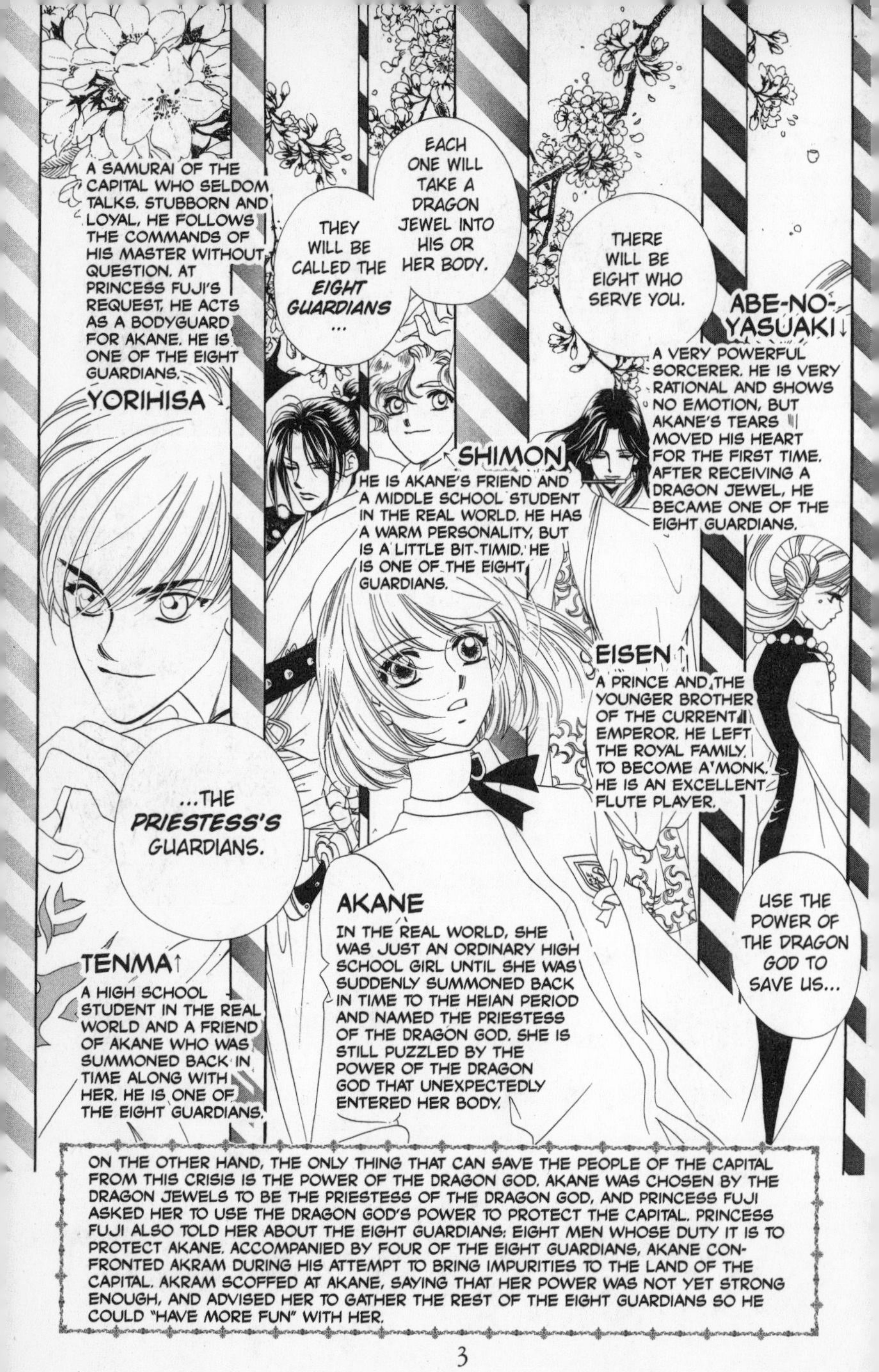
ABE-NO-YASUAKI↓
A VERY POWERFUL SORCERER. HE IS VERY RATIONAL AND SHOWS NO EMOTION, BUT AKANE'S TEARS MOVED HIS HEART FOR THE FIRST TIME. AFTER RECEIVING A DRAGON JEWEL, HE BECAME ONE OF THE EIGHT GUARDIANS.
THERE WILL BE EIGHT WHO SERVE YOU.
EACH ONE WILL TAKE A DRAGON JEWEL INTO HIS OR HER BODY.
THEY WILL BE CALLED THE *EIGHT GUARDIANS*...
A SAMURAI OF THE CAPITAL WHO SELDOM TALKS. STUBBORN AND LOYAL, HE FOLLOWS THE COMMANDS OF HIS MASTER WITHOUT QUESTION. AT PRINCESS FUJI'S REQUEST, HE ACTS AS A BODYGUARD FOR AKANE. HE IS ONE OF THE EIGHT GUARDIANS.
YORIHISA→
SHIMON
HE IS AKANE'S FRIEND AND A MIDDLE SCHOOL STUDENT IN THE REAL WORLD. HE HAS A WARM PERSONALITY, BUT IS A LITTLE BIT TIMID. HE IS ONE OF THE EIGHT GUARDIANS.
EISEN↑
A PRINCE AND THE YOUNGER BROTHER OF THE CURRENT EMPEROR. HE LEFT THE ROYAL FAMILY TO BECOME A MONK. HE IS AN EXCELLENT FLUTE PLAYER.
USE THE POWER OF THE DRAGON GOD TO SAVE US...
AKANE
IN THE REAL WORLD, SHE WAS JUST AN ORDINARY HIGH SCHOOL GIRL UNTIL SHE WAS SUDDENLY SUMMONED BACK IN TIME TO THE HEIAN PERIOD AND NAMED THE PRIESTESS OF THE DRAGON GOD. SHE IS STILL PUZZLED BY THE POWER OF THE DRAGON GOD THAT UNEXPECTEDLY ENTERED HER BODY.
...THE *PRIESTESS'S* GUARDIANS.
TENMA↑
A HIGH SCHOOL STUDENT IN THE REAL WORLD AND A FRIEND OF AKANE WHO WAS SUMMONED BACK IN TIME ALONG WITH HER. HE IS ONE OF THE EIGHT GUARDIANS.

ON THE OTHER HAND, THE ONLY THING THAT CAN SAVE THE PEOPLE OF THE CAPITAL FROM THIS CRISIS IS THE POWER OF THE DRAGON GOD. AKANE WAS CHOSEN BY THE DRAGON JEWELS TO BE THE PRIESTESS OF THE DRAGON GOD, AND PRINCESS FUJI ASKED HER TO USE THE DRAGON GOD'S POWER TO PROTECT THE CAPITAL. PRINCESS FUJI ALSO TOLD HER ABOUT THE EIGHT GUARDIANS: EIGHT MEN WHOSE DUTY IT IS TO PROTECT AKANE. ACCOMPANIED BY FOUR OF THE EIGHT GUARDIANS, AKANE CONFRONTED AKRAM DURING HIS ATTEMPT TO BRING IMPURITIES TO THE LAND OF THE CAPITAL. AKRAM SCOFFED AT AKANE, SAYING THAT HER POWER WAS NOT YET STRONG ENOUGH, AND ADVISED HER TO GATHER THE REST OF THE EIGHT GUARDIANS SO HE COULD "HAVE MORE FUN" WITH HER.

Haruka
–Beyond the Stream of Time–

❷

CONTENTS

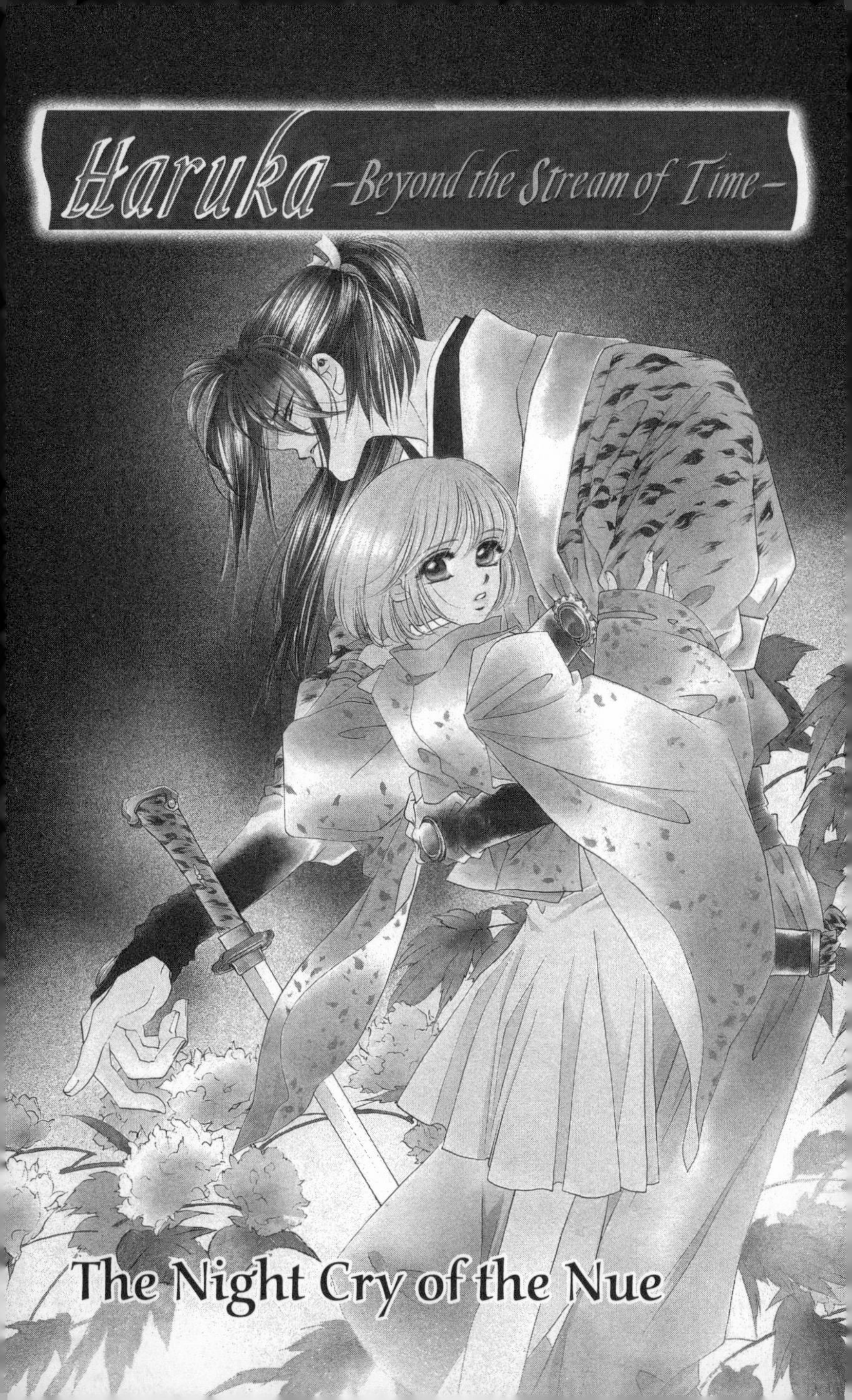
Haruka -Beyond the Stream of Time-
The Night Cry of the Nue

THE EIGHT GUARDIANS: WHAT YOU WISH THEY'D SAY <Inori>

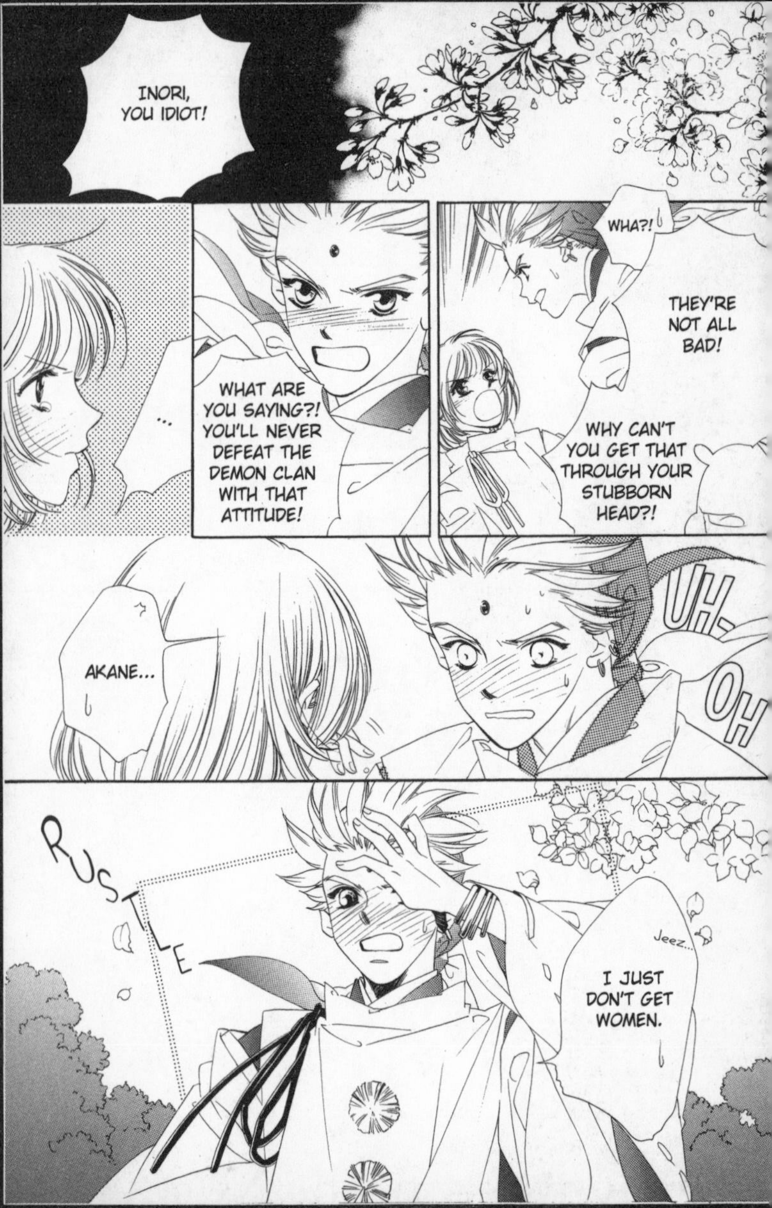
INORI, YOU IDIOT!
WHA?!
THEY'RE NOT ALL BAD!
WHY CAN'T YOU GET THAT THROUGH YOUR STUBBORN HEAD?!
WHAT ARE YOU SAYING?! YOU'LL NEVER DEFEAT THE DEMON CLAN WITH THAT ATTITUDE!
...
UH-OH
AKANE...
RUSTLE
Jeez...
I JUST DON'T GET WOMEN.

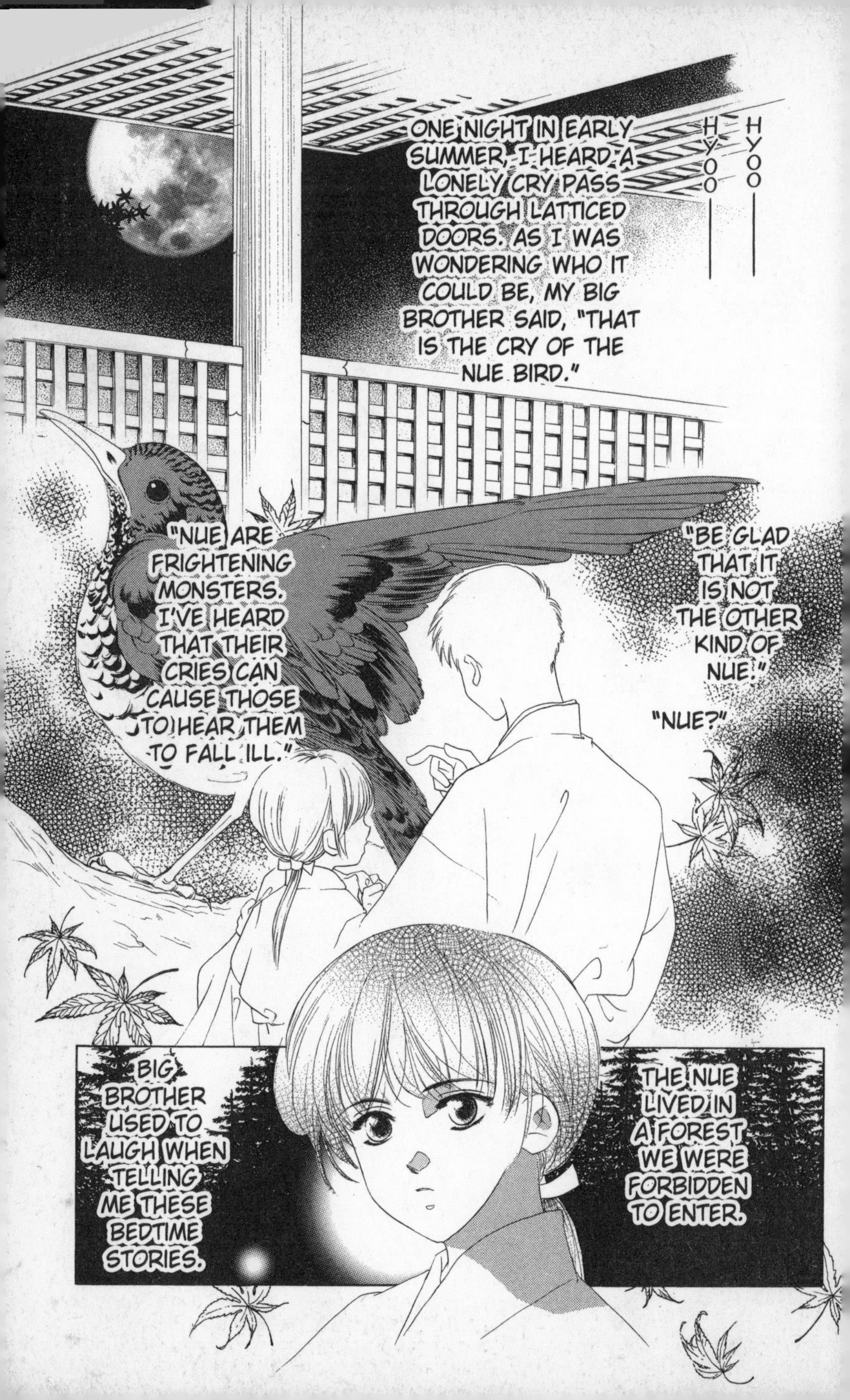
HYOO
HYOO
ONE NIGHT IN EARLY SUMMER, I HEARD A LONELY CRY PASS THROUGH LATTICED DOORS. AS I WAS WONDERING WHO IT COULD BE, MY BIG BROTHER SAID, "THAT IS THE CRY OF THE NUE BIRD."
"BE GLAD THAT IT IS NOT THE OTHER KIND OF NUE."
"NUE?"
"NUE ARE FRIGHTENING MONSTERS. I'VE HEARD THAT THEIR CRIES CAN CAUSE THOSE TO HEAR THEM TO FALL ILL."
THE NUE LIVED IN A FOREST WE WERE FORBIDDEN TO ENTER.
BIG BROTHER USED TO LAUGH WHEN TELLING ME THESE BEDTIME STORIES.

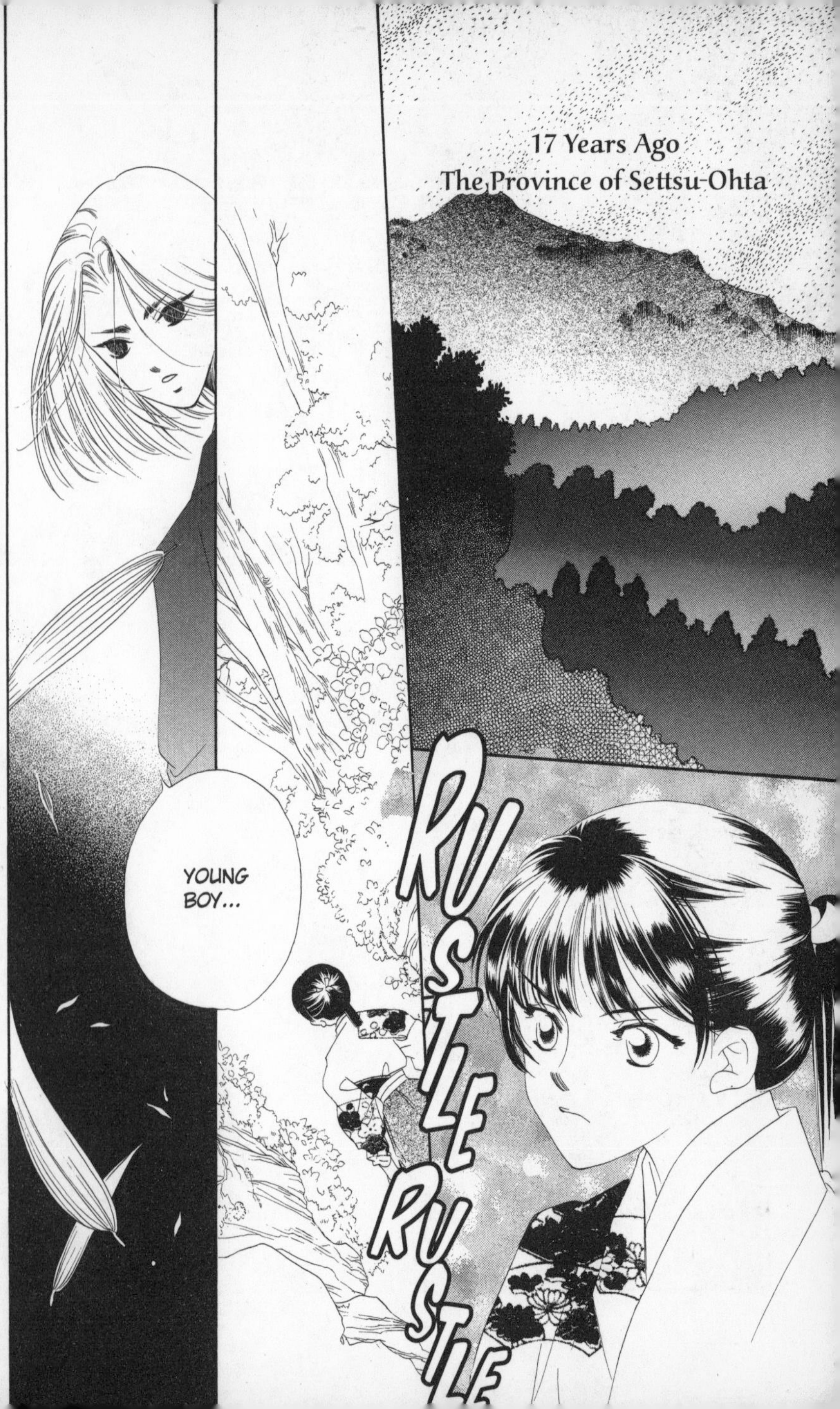
17 Years Ago
The Province of Settsu-Ohta
RUSTLE RUSTLE
YOUNG BOY...

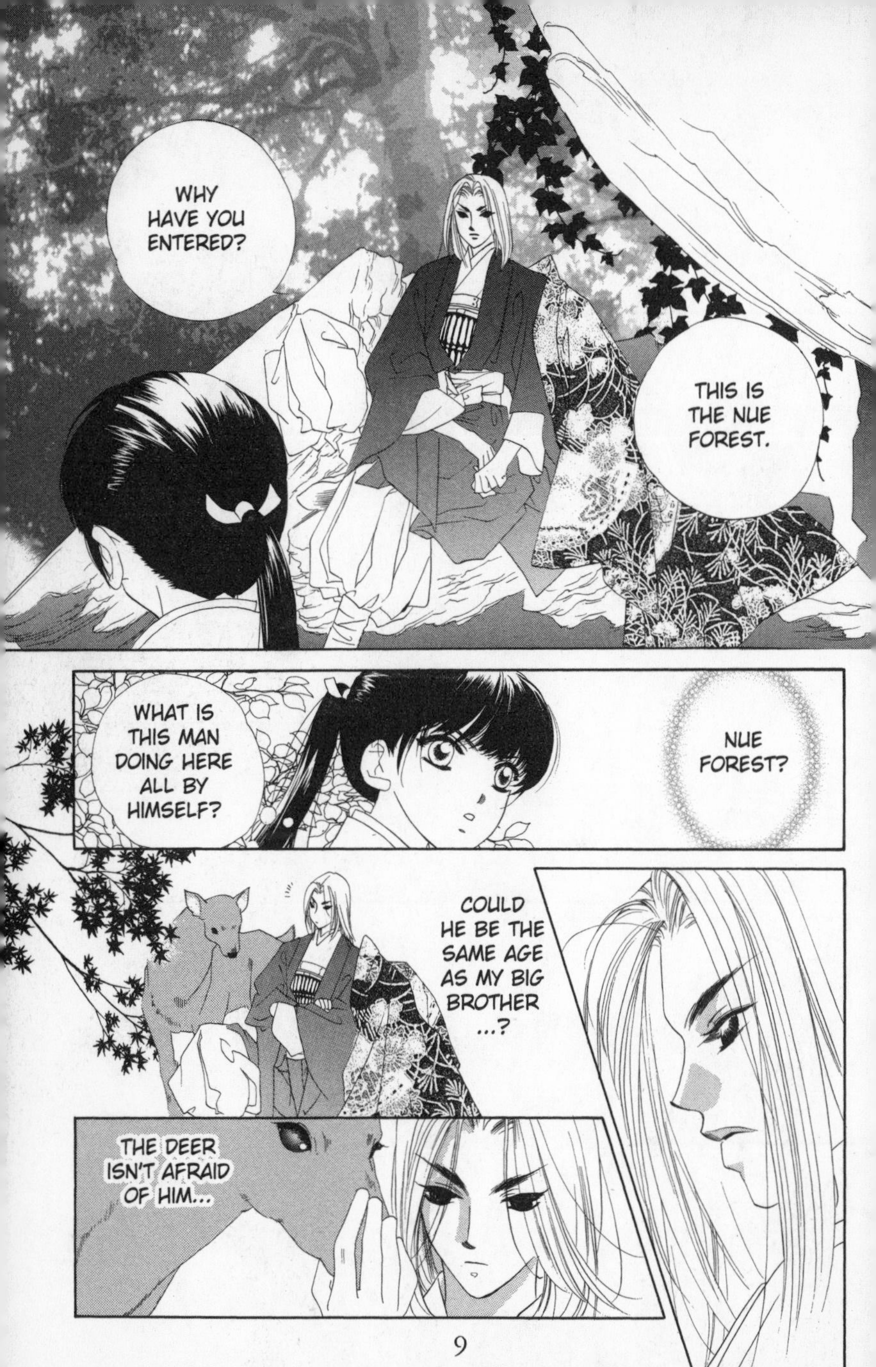
WHY HAVE YOU ENTERED?
THIS IS THE NUE FOREST.
NUE FOREST?
WHAT IS THIS MAN DOING HERE ALL BY HIMSELF?
COULD HE BE THE SAME AGE AS MY BIG BROTHER ...?
THE DEER ISN'T AFRAID OF HIM...

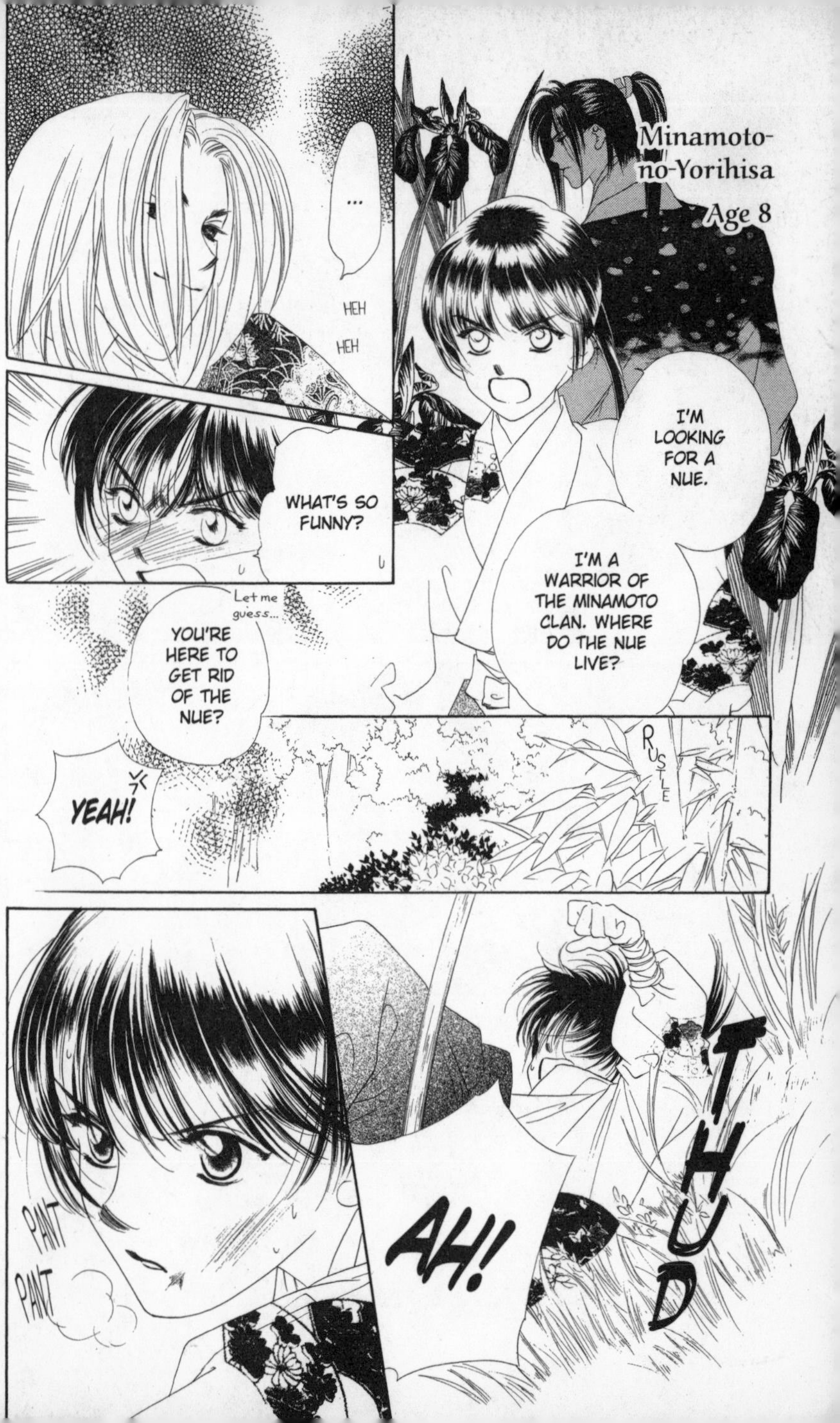

Minamoto-no-Yorihisa
Age 8
I'M LOOKING FOR A NUE.
I'M A WARRIOR OF THE MINAMOTO CLAN. WHERE DO THE NUE LIVE?
...
HEH
HEH
WHAT'S SO FUNNY?
Let me guess...
YOU'RE HERE TO GET RID OF THE NUE?
YEAH!
RUSTLE
THUD
AH!
PANT
PANT

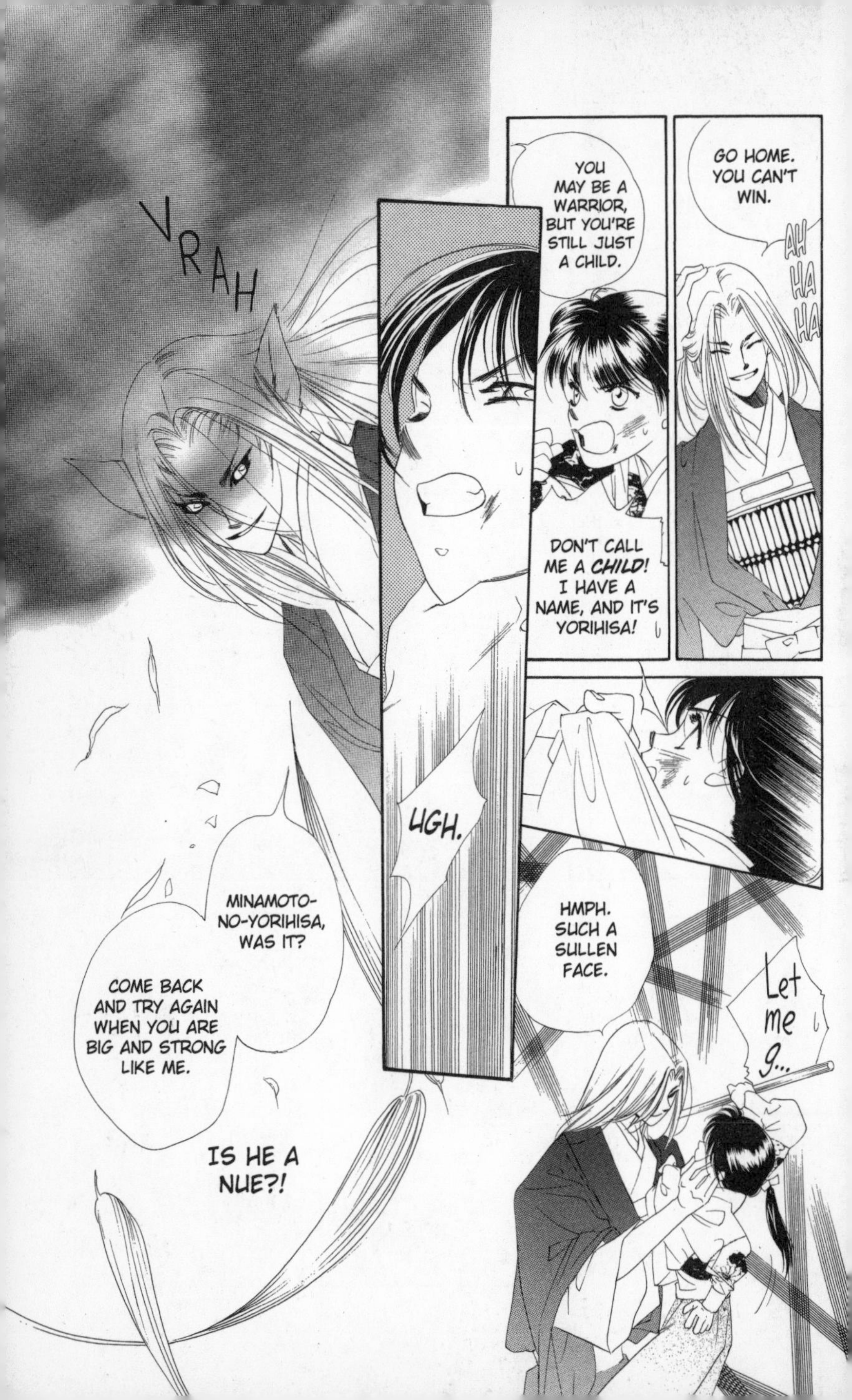
GO HOME. YOU CAN'T WIN.
AH HA HA HA
YOU MAY BE A WARRIOR, BUT YOU'RE STILL JUST A CHILD.
DON'T CALL ME A ***CHILD!*** I HAVE A NAME, AND IT'S YORIHISA!
UGH.
HMPH. SUCH A SULLEN FACE.
Let me g...
VRAH
MINAMOTO-NO-YORIHISA, WAS IT?
COME BACK AND TRY AGAIN WHEN YOU ARE BIG AND STRONG LIKE ME.
IS HE A NUE?!

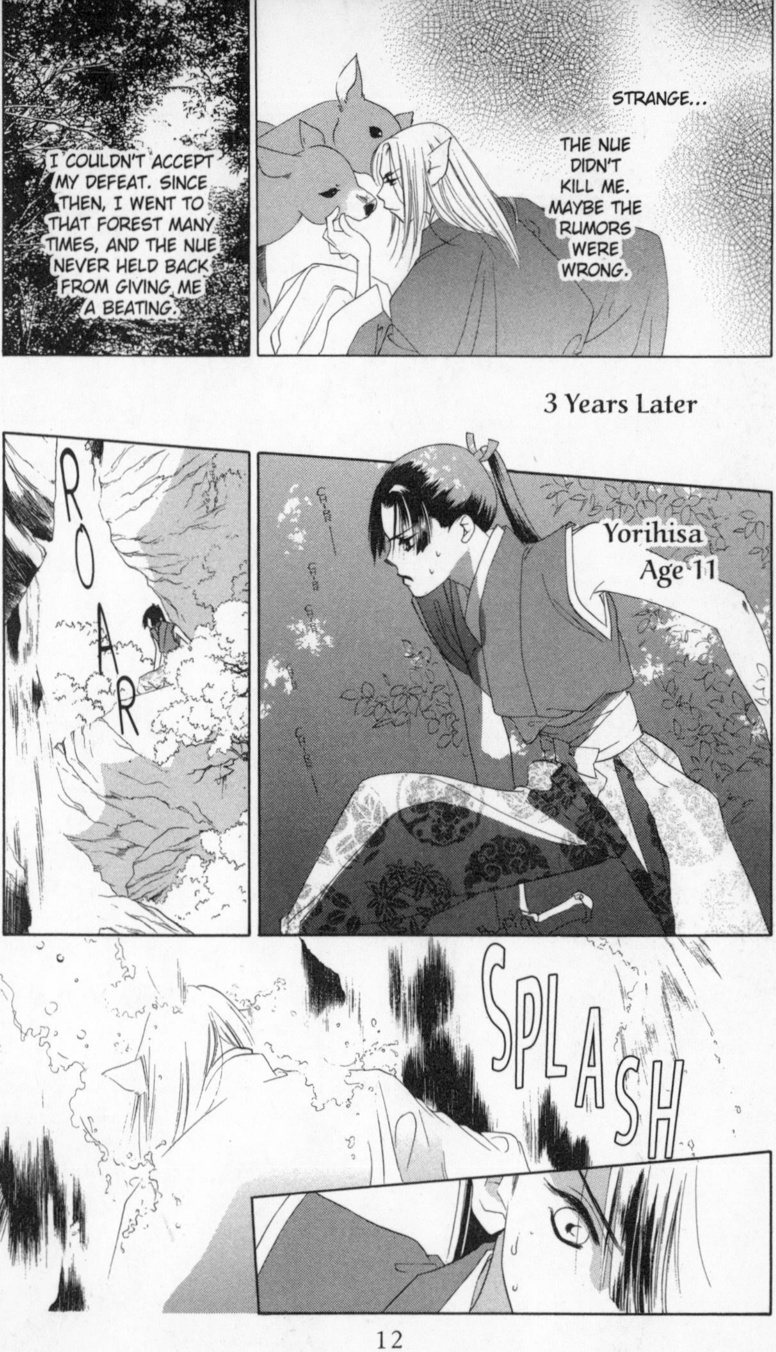

STRANGE...
THE NUE DIDN'T KILL ME. MAYBE THE RUMORS WERE WRONG.
I COULDN'T ACCEPT MY DEFEAT. SINCE THEN, I WENT TO THAT FOREST MANY TIMES, AND THE NUE NEVER HELD BACK FROM GIVING ME A BEATING.
3 Years Later
Yorihisa Age 11
ROAR
SPLASH

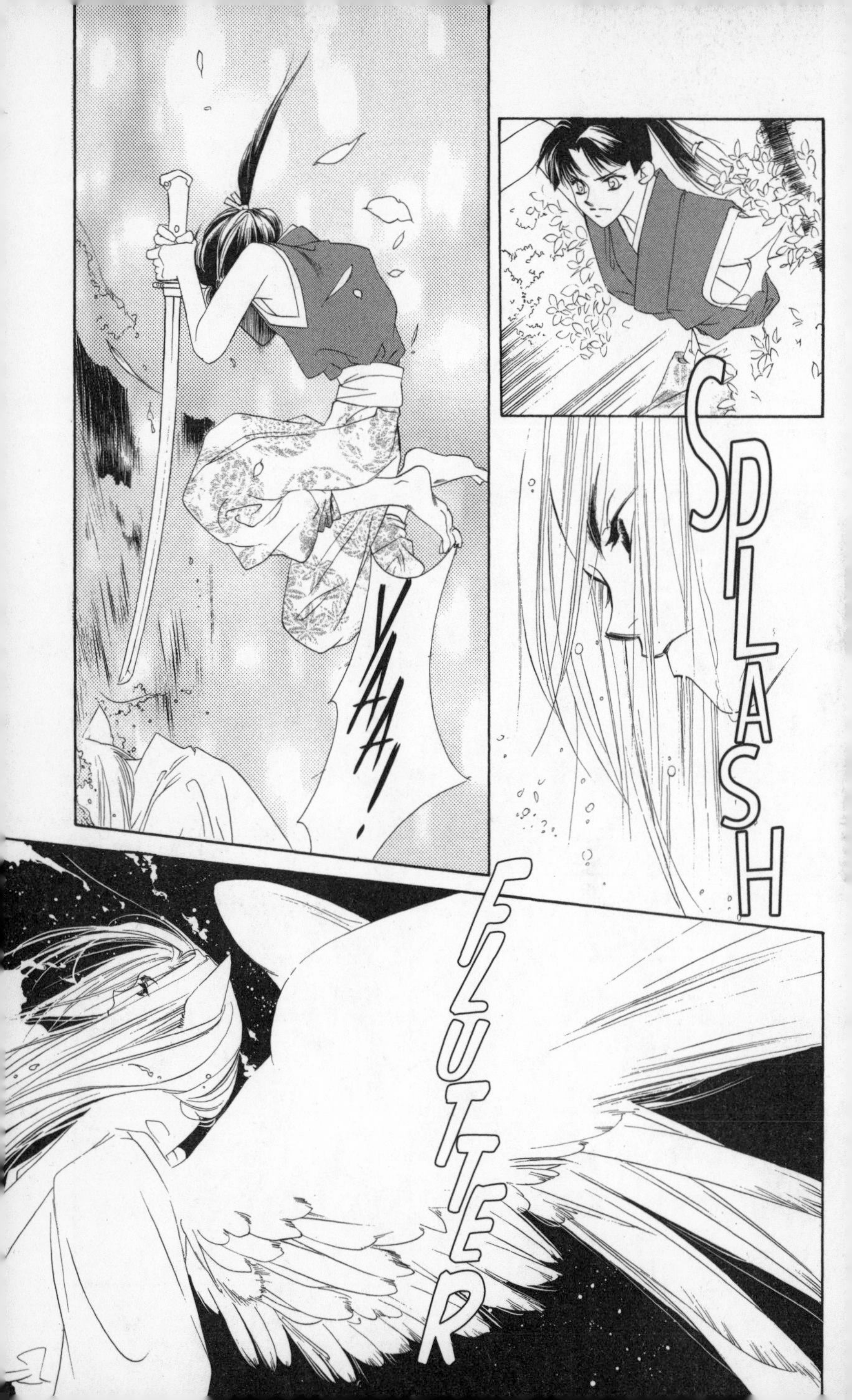
SPLASH
YAAA!
FLUTTER

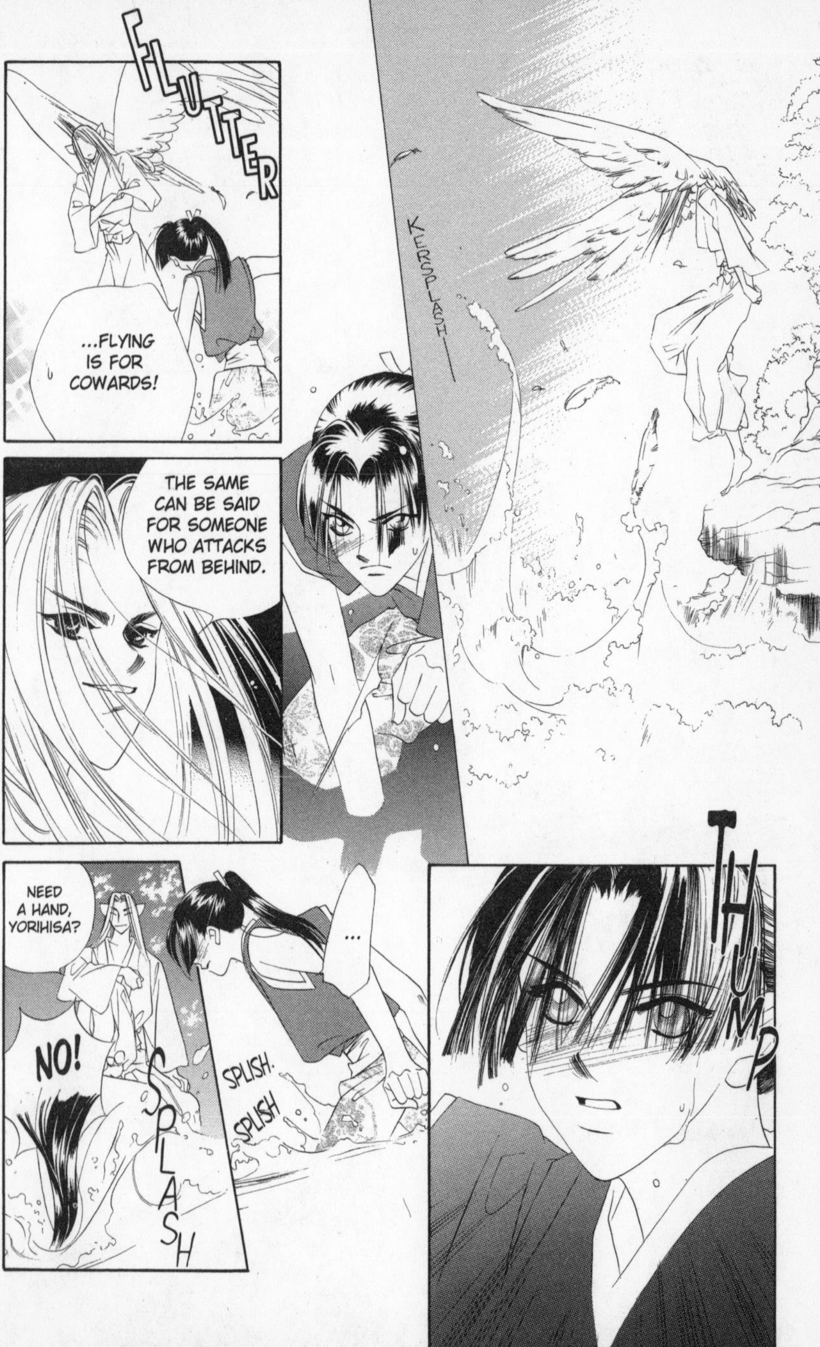
KERSPLASH
FLUTTER
...FLYING IS FOR COWARDS!
THE SAME CAN BE SAID FOR SOMEONE WHO ATTACKS FROM BEHIND.
THUMP
...
NEED A HAND, YORIHISA?
SPLISH SPLISH
SPLASH
NO!

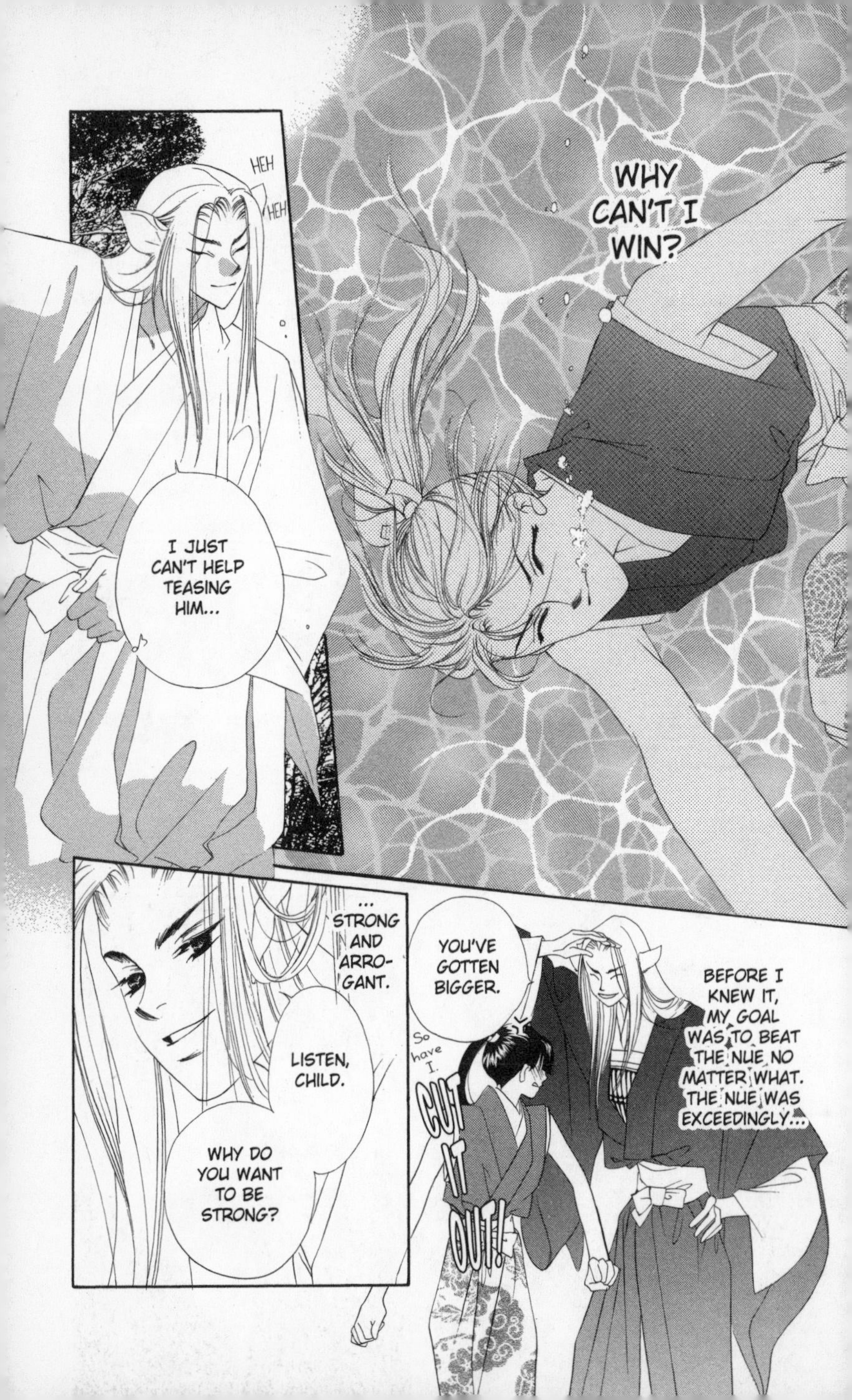
WHY CAN'T I WIN?
HEH HEH
I JUST CAN'T HELP TEASING HIM...
BEFORE I KNEW IT, MY GOAL WAS TO BEAT THE NUE NO MATTER WHAT. THE NUE WAS EXCEEDINGLY...
YOU'VE GOTTEN BIGGER.
So have I.
CUT IT OUT!
... STRONG AND ARRO-GANT.
LISTEN, CHILD.
WHY DO YOU WANT TO BE STRONG?

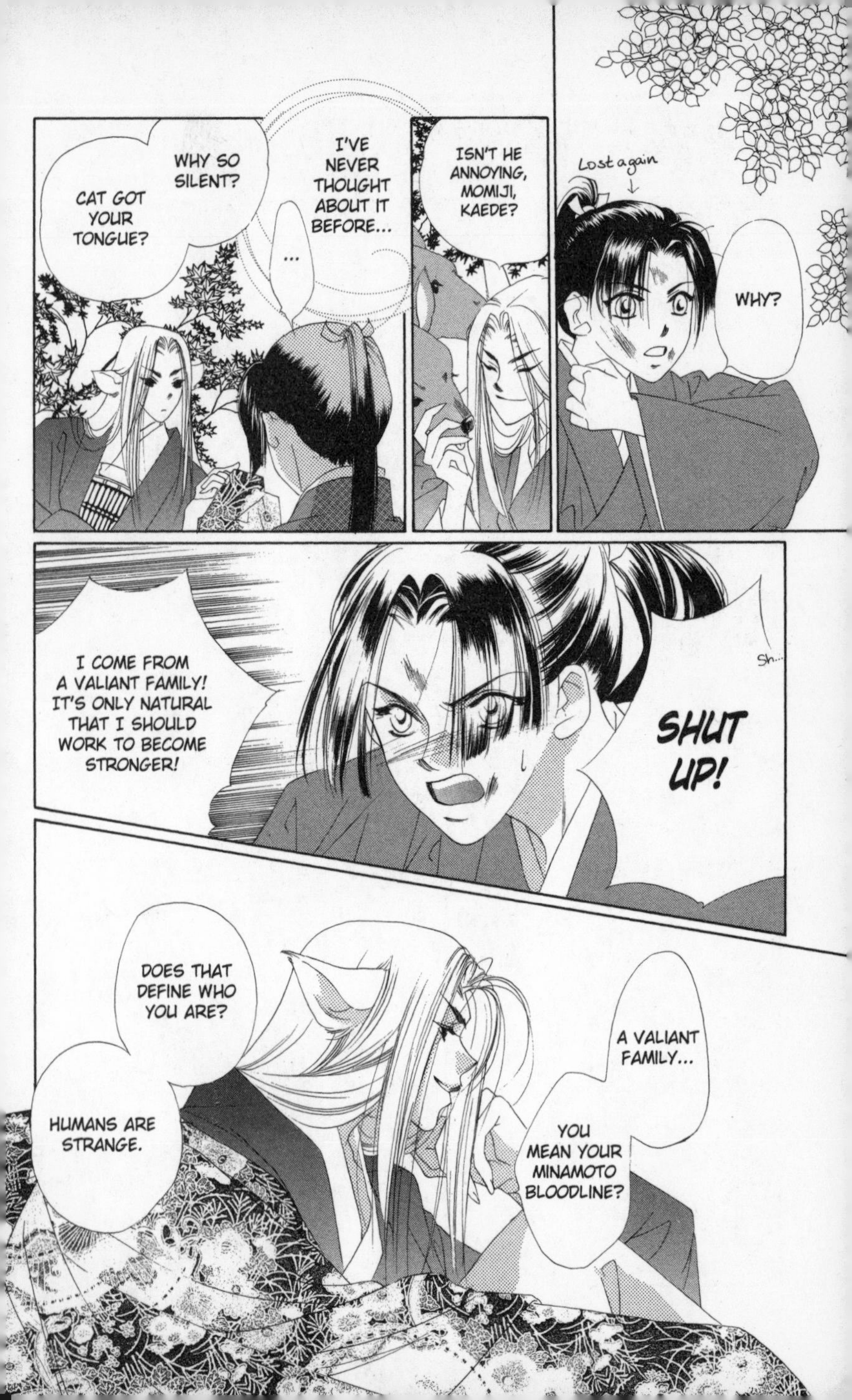
Lost again
WHY?
ISN'T HE ANNOYING, MOMIJI, KAEDE?
I'VE NEVER THOUGHT ABOUT IT BEFORE...
...
WHY SO SILENT?
CAT GOT YOUR TONGUE?
Sh...
SHUT UP!
I COME FROM A VALIANT FAMILY! IT'S ONLY NATURAL THAT I SHOULD WORK TO BECOME STRONGER!
A VALIANT FAMILY...
YOU MEAN YOUR MINAMOTO BLOODLINE?
DOES THAT DEFINE WHO YOU ARE?
HUMANS ARE STRANGE.

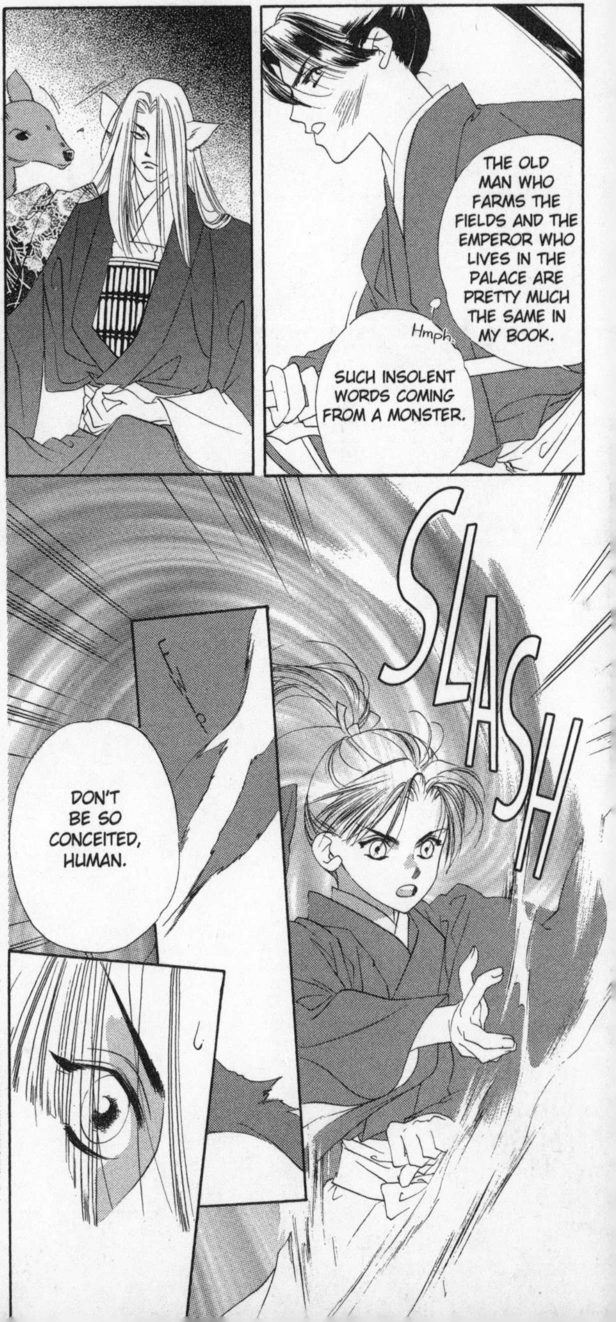
THE OLD MAN WHO FARMS THE FIELDS AND THE EMPEROR WHO LIVES IN THE PALACE ARE PRETTY MUCH THE SAME IN MY BOOK.
Hmph.
SUCH INSOLENT WORDS COMING FROM A MONSTER.
SLASH
DON'T BE SO CONCEITED, HUMAN.

A modern ending
Yorihisa + Akane

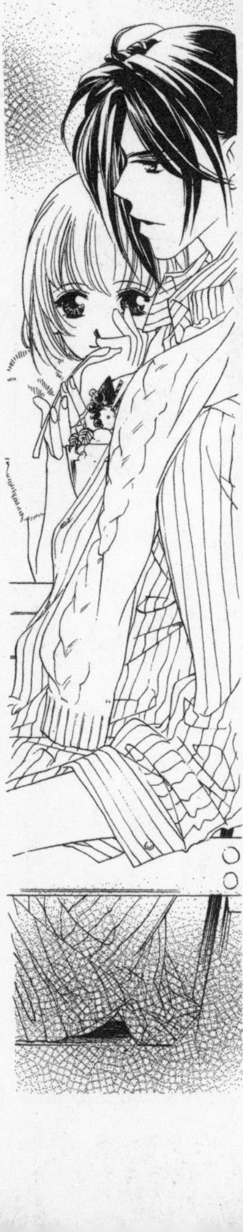

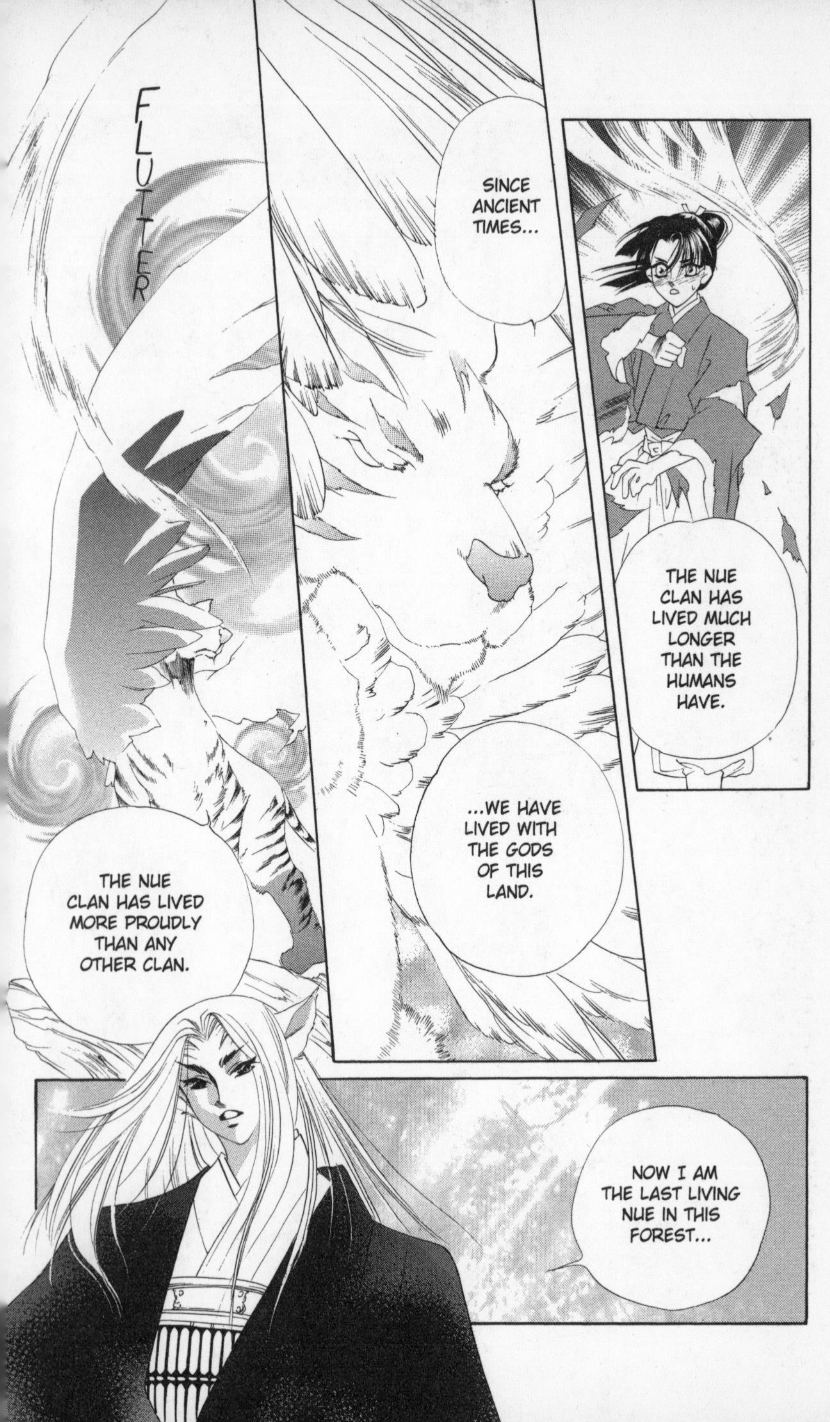
THE NUE CLAN HAS LIVED MUCH LONGER THAN THE HUMANS HAVE.
SINCE ANCIENT TIMES...
...WE HAVE LIVED WITH THE GODS OF THIS LAND.
FLUTTER
THE NUE CLAN HAS LIVED MORE PROUDLY THAN ANY OTHER CLAN.
NOW I AM THE LAST LIVING NUE IN THIS FOREST...

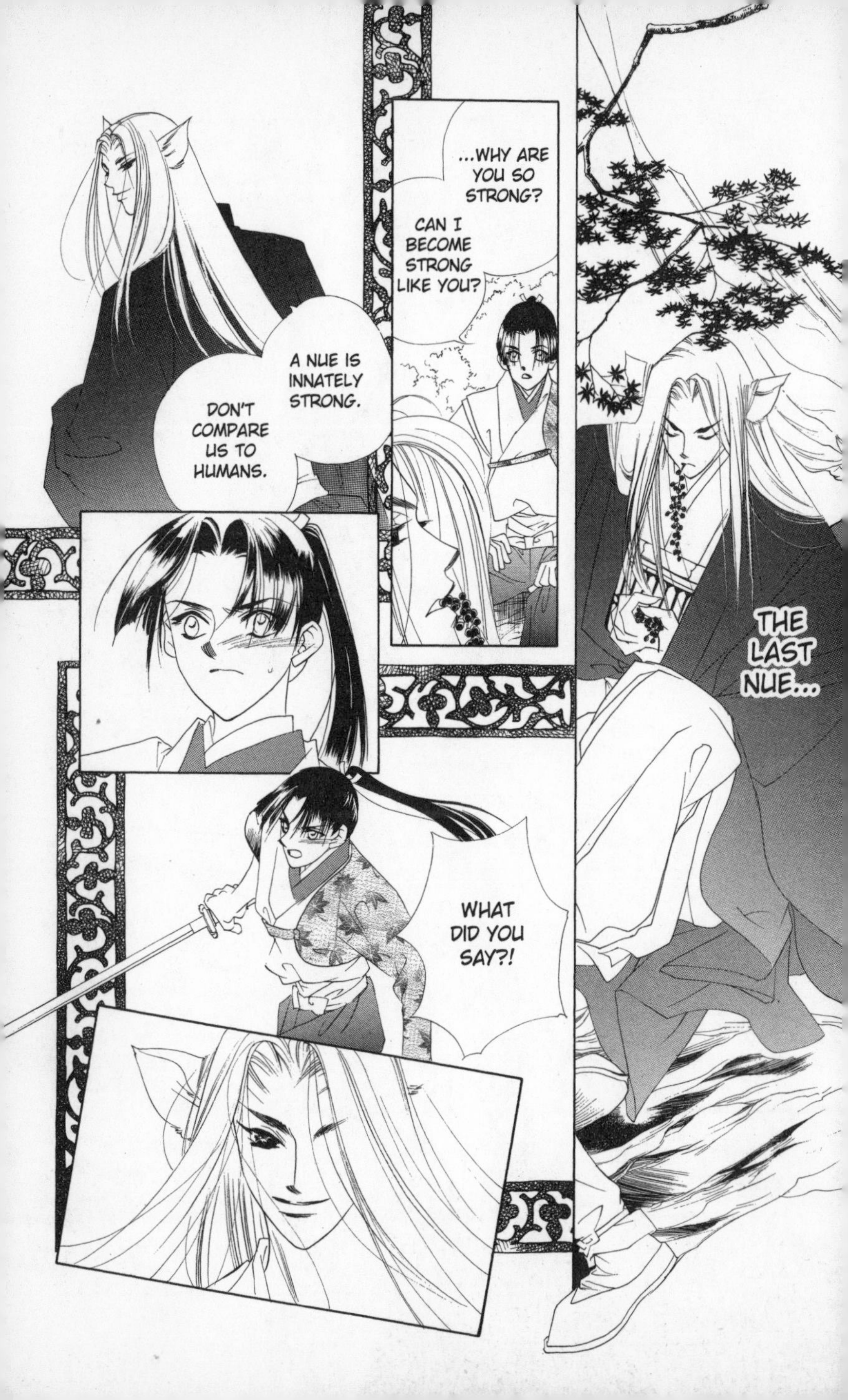
THE LAST NUE...
...WHY ARE YOU SO STRONG?
CAN I BECOME STRONG LIKE YOU?
A NUE IS INNATELY STRONG.
DON'T COMPARE US TO HUMANS.
WHAT DID YOU SAY?!

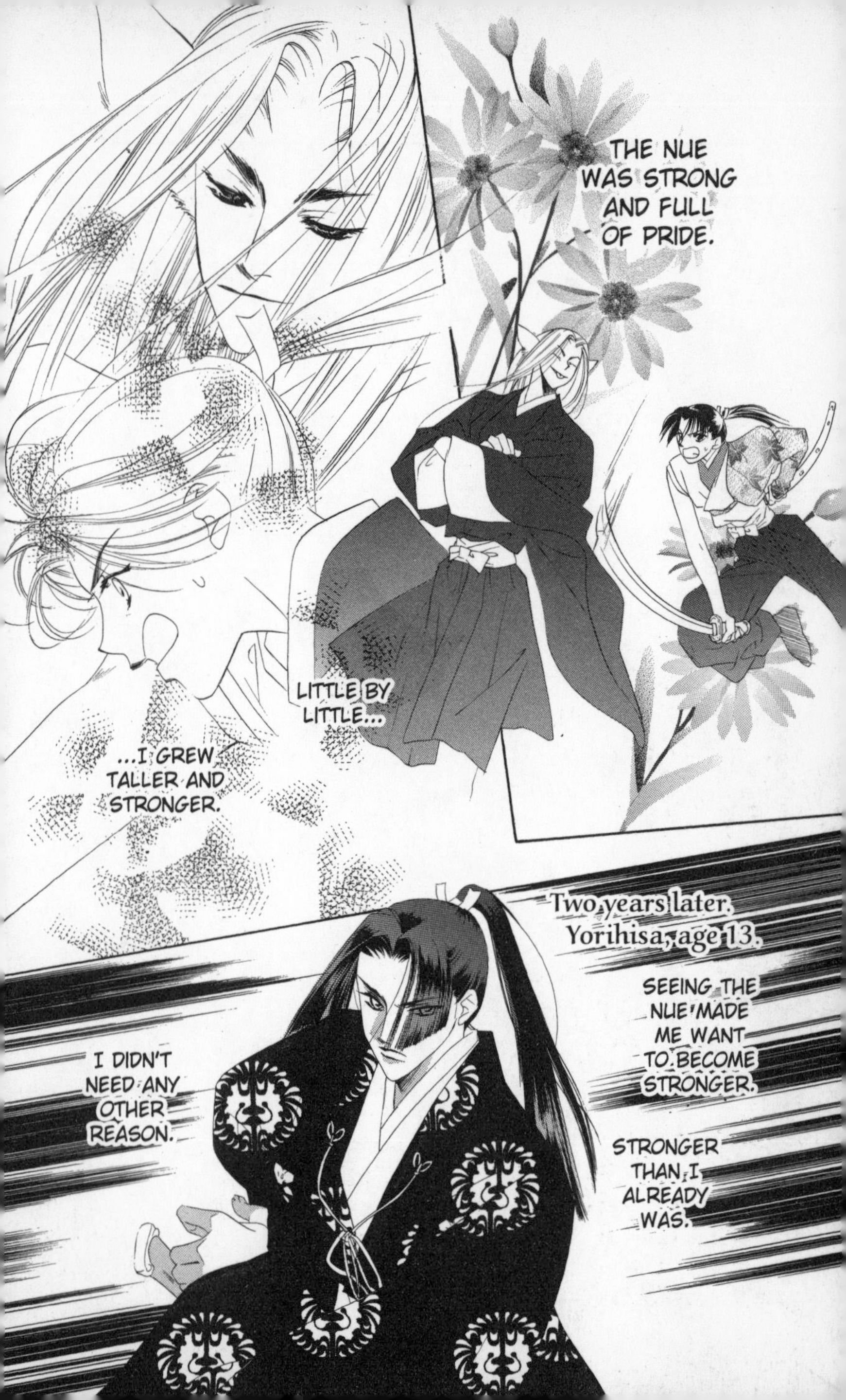
THE NUE WAS STRONG AND FULL OF PRIDE.
LITTLE BY LITTLE...
...I GREW TALLER AND STRONGER.
Two years later. Yorihisa, age 13.
SEEING THE NUE MADE ME WANT TO BECOME STRONGER.
STRONGER THAN I ALREADY WAS.
I DIDN'T NEED ANY OTHER REASON.

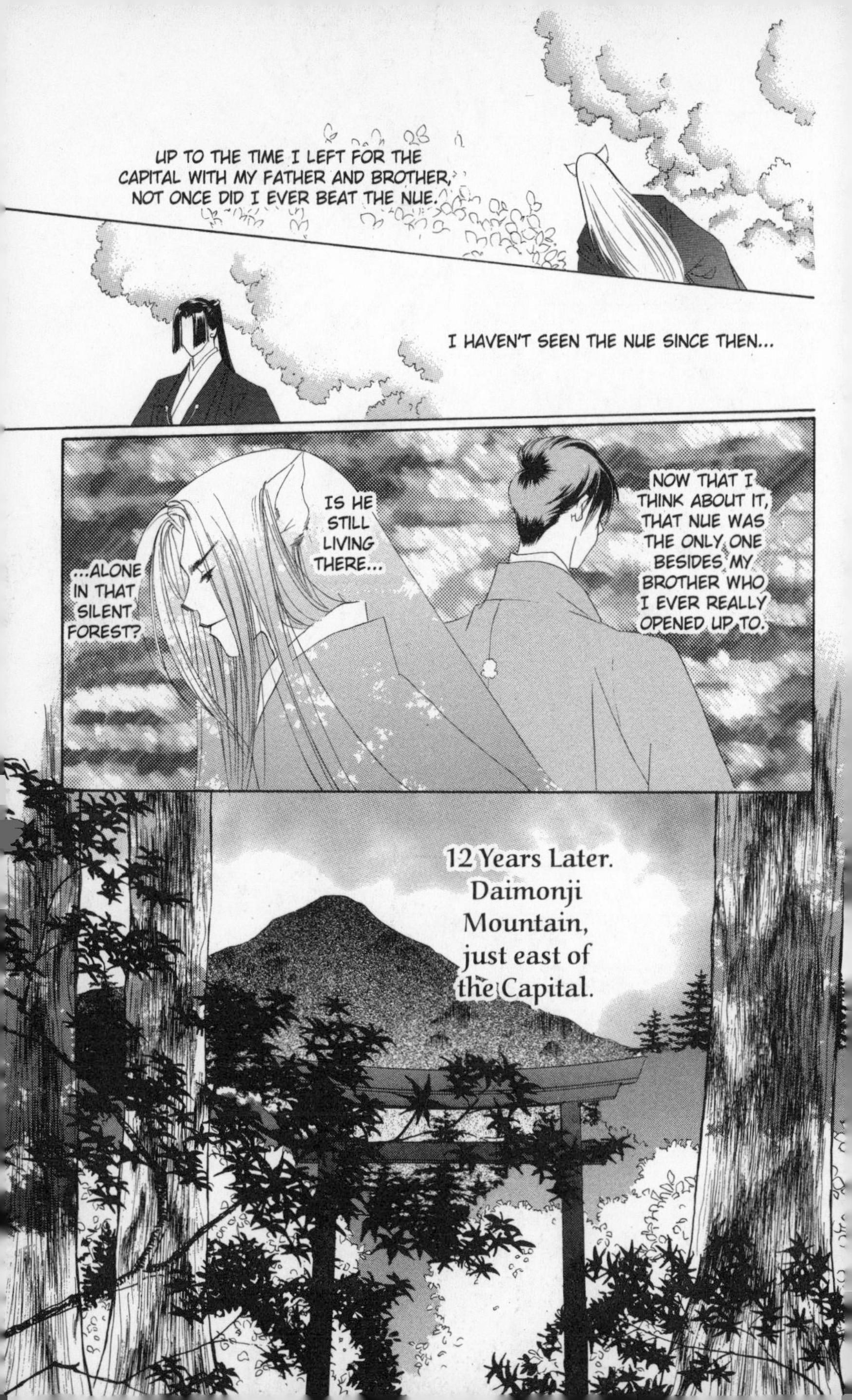

UP TO THE TIME I LEFT FOR THE CAPITAL WITH MY FATHER AND BROTHER, NOT ONCE DID I EVER BEAT THE NUE.
I HAVEN'T SEEN THE NUE SINCE THEN...
NOW THAT I THINK ABOUT IT, THAT NUE WAS THE ONLY ONE BESIDES MY BROTHER WHO I EVER REALLY OPENED UP TO.
IS HE STILL LIVING THERE...
...ALONE IN THAT SILENT FOREST?
12 Years Later. Daimonji Mountain, just east of the Capital.

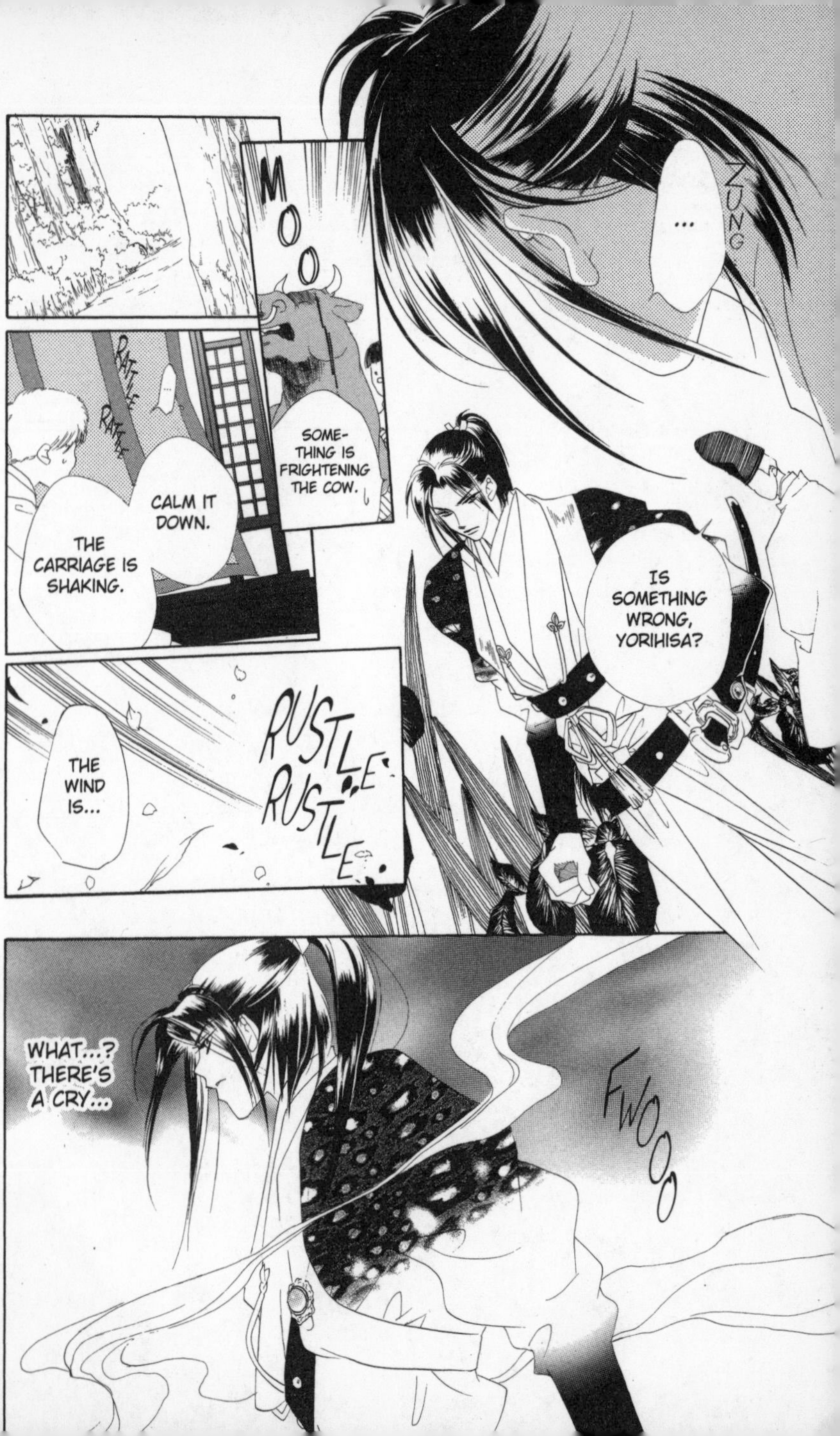
ZUNG
...
IS SOMETHING WRONG, YORIHISA?
MOOO
SOME-THING IS FRIGHTENING THE COW.
RATTLE RATTLE
...
CALM IT DOWN.
THE CARRIAGE IS SHAKING.
RUSTLE RUSTLE
THE WIND IS...
FWOOO
WHAT...? THERE'S A CRY...

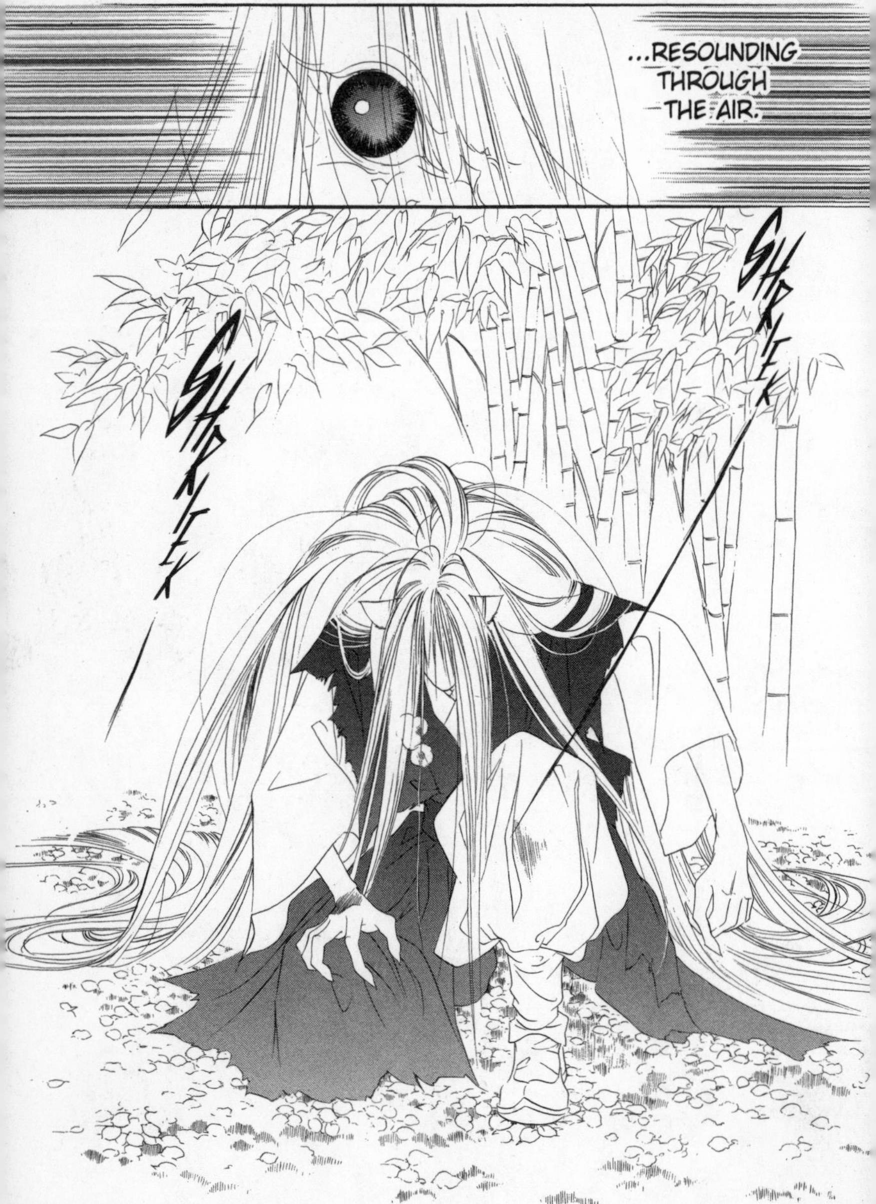
...RESOUNDING THROUGH THE AIR.
SHRIEEK
SHRIEEK

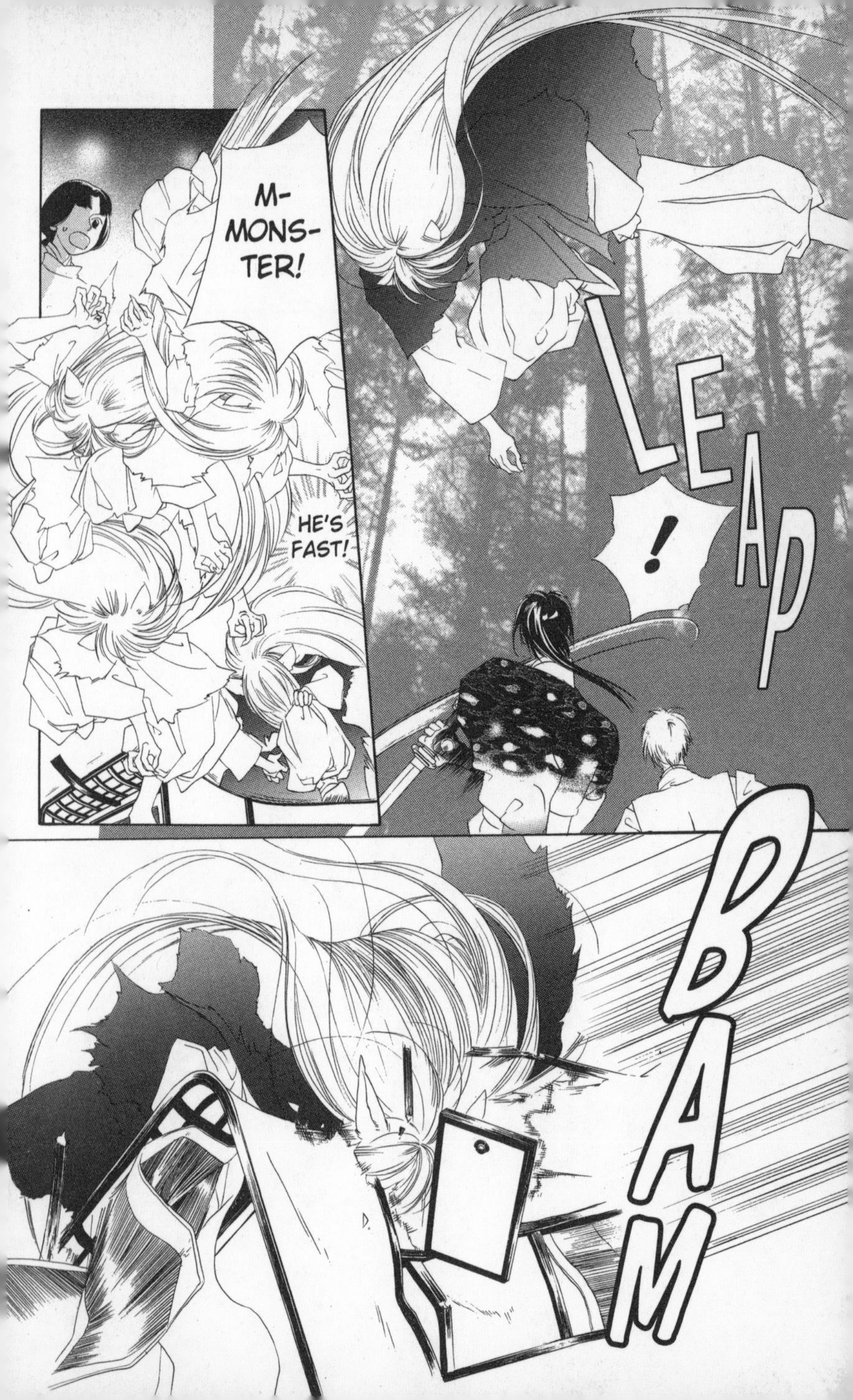
LEAP
!
M-MONSTER!
HE'S FAST!
BAM

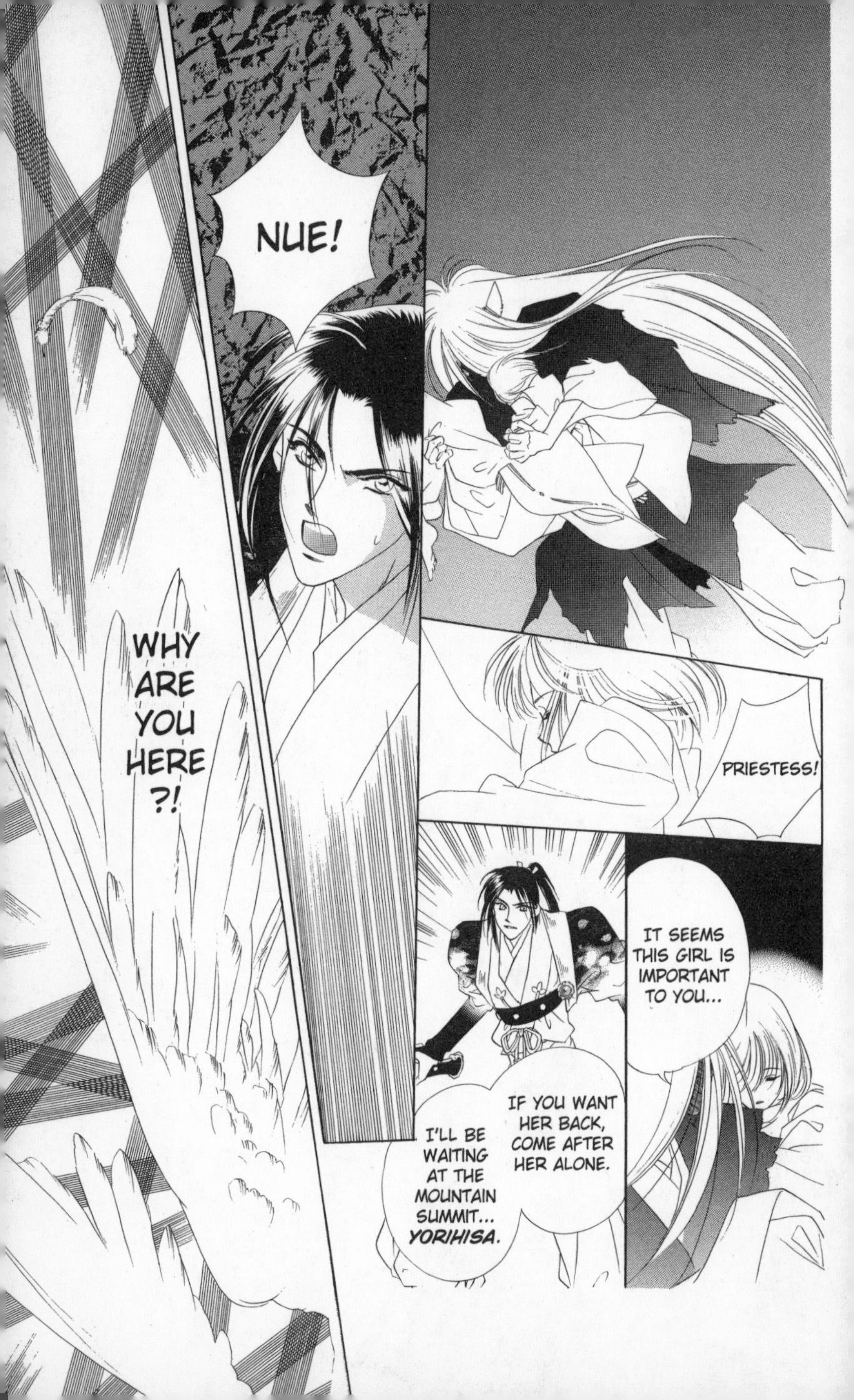
PRIESTESS!
IT SEEMS THIS GIRL IS IMPORTANT TO YOU...
IF YOU WANT HER BACK, COME AFTER HER ALONE.
I'LL BE WAITING AT THE MOUNTAIN SUMMIT... *YORIHISA*.
NUE!
WHY ARE YOU HERE?!

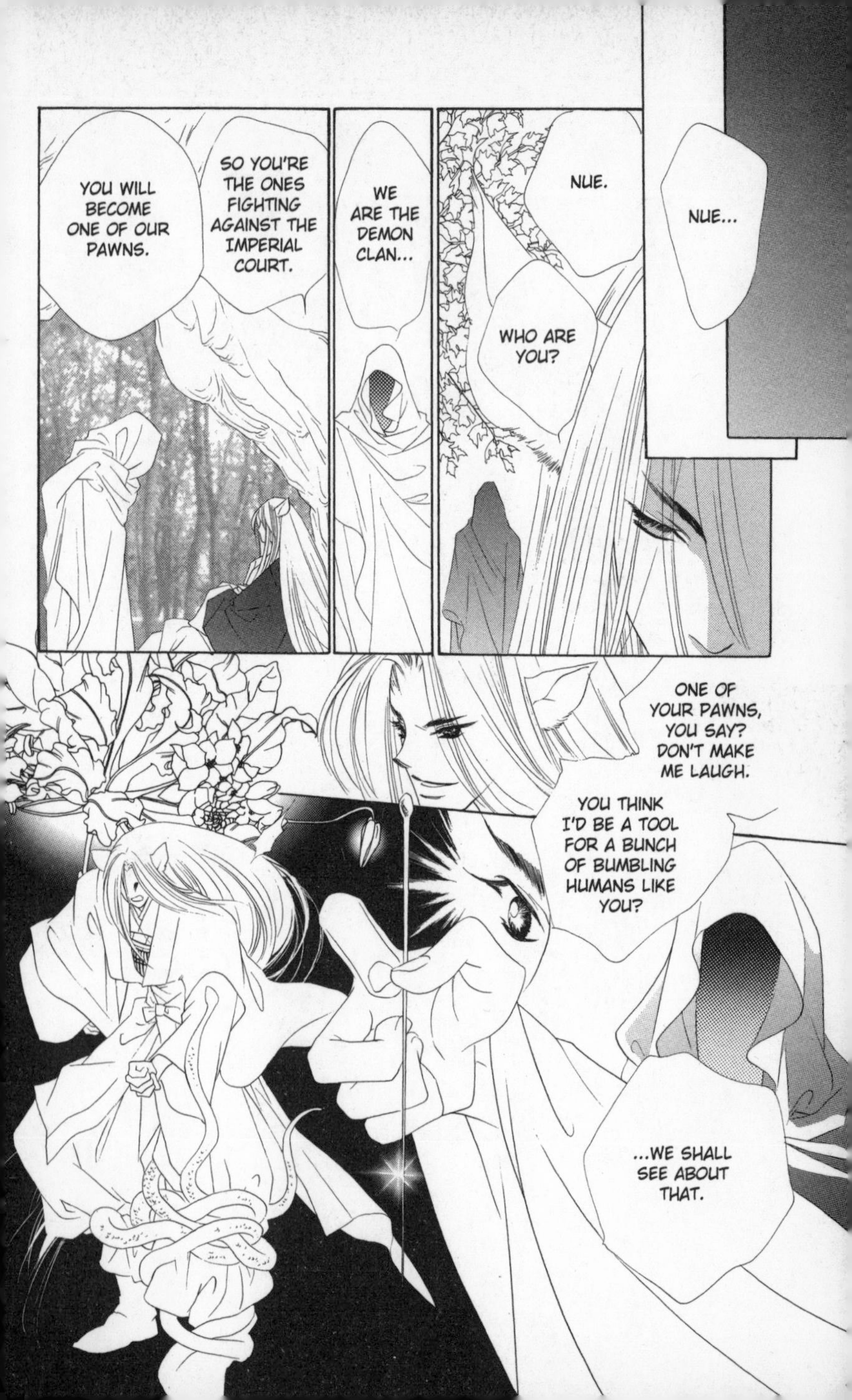
NUE...
NUE.
WHO ARE YOU?
WE ARE THE DEMON CLAN...
SO YOU'RE THE ONES FIGHTING AGAINST THE IMPERIAL COURT.
YOU WILL BECOME ONE OF OUR PAWNS.
ONE OF YOUR PAWNS, YOU SAY? DON'T MAKE ME LAUGH.
YOU THINK I'D BE A TOOL FOR A BUNCH OF BUMBLING HUMANS LIKE YOU?
...WE SHALL SEE ABOUT THAT.

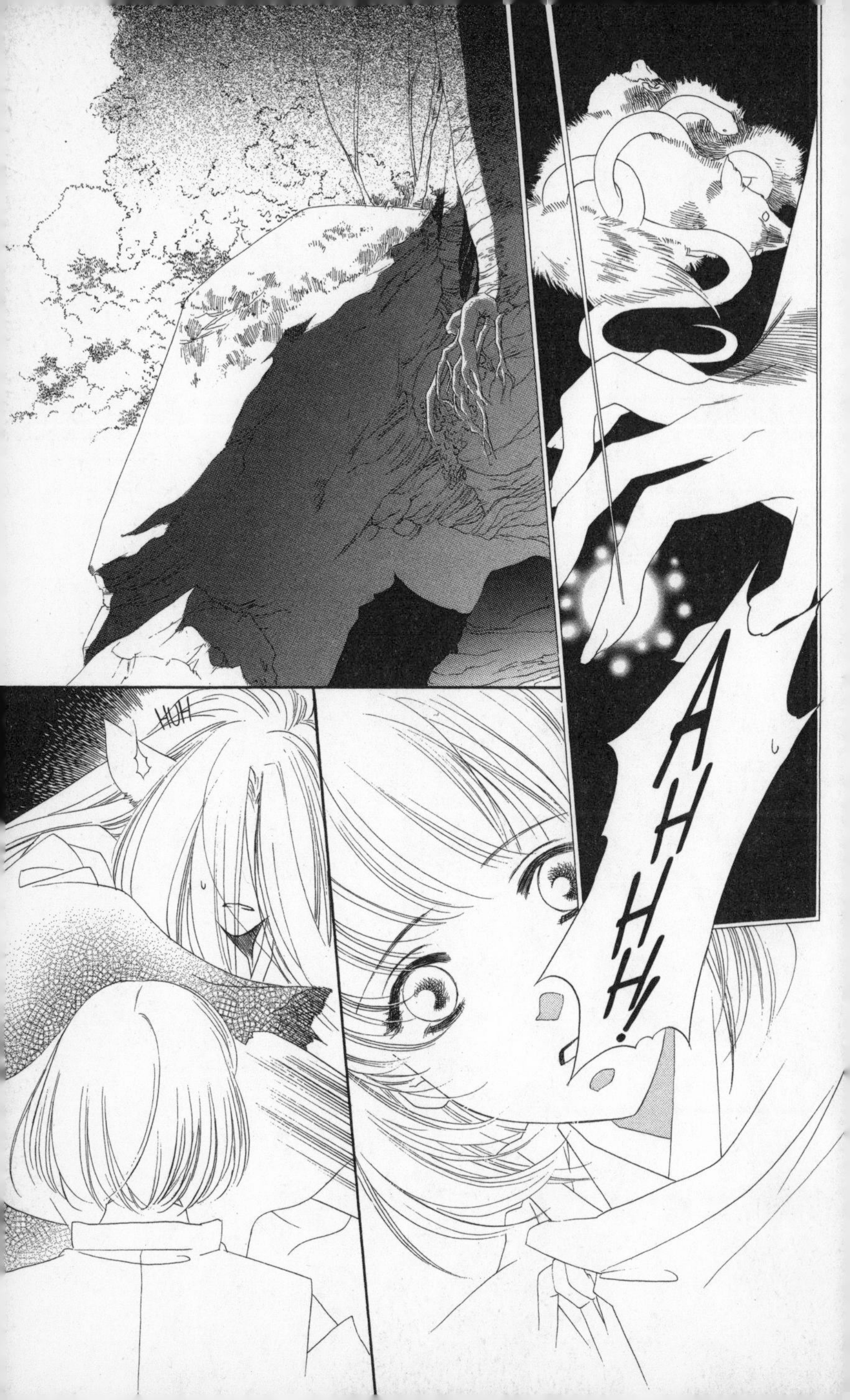

AHHHH!
HUH

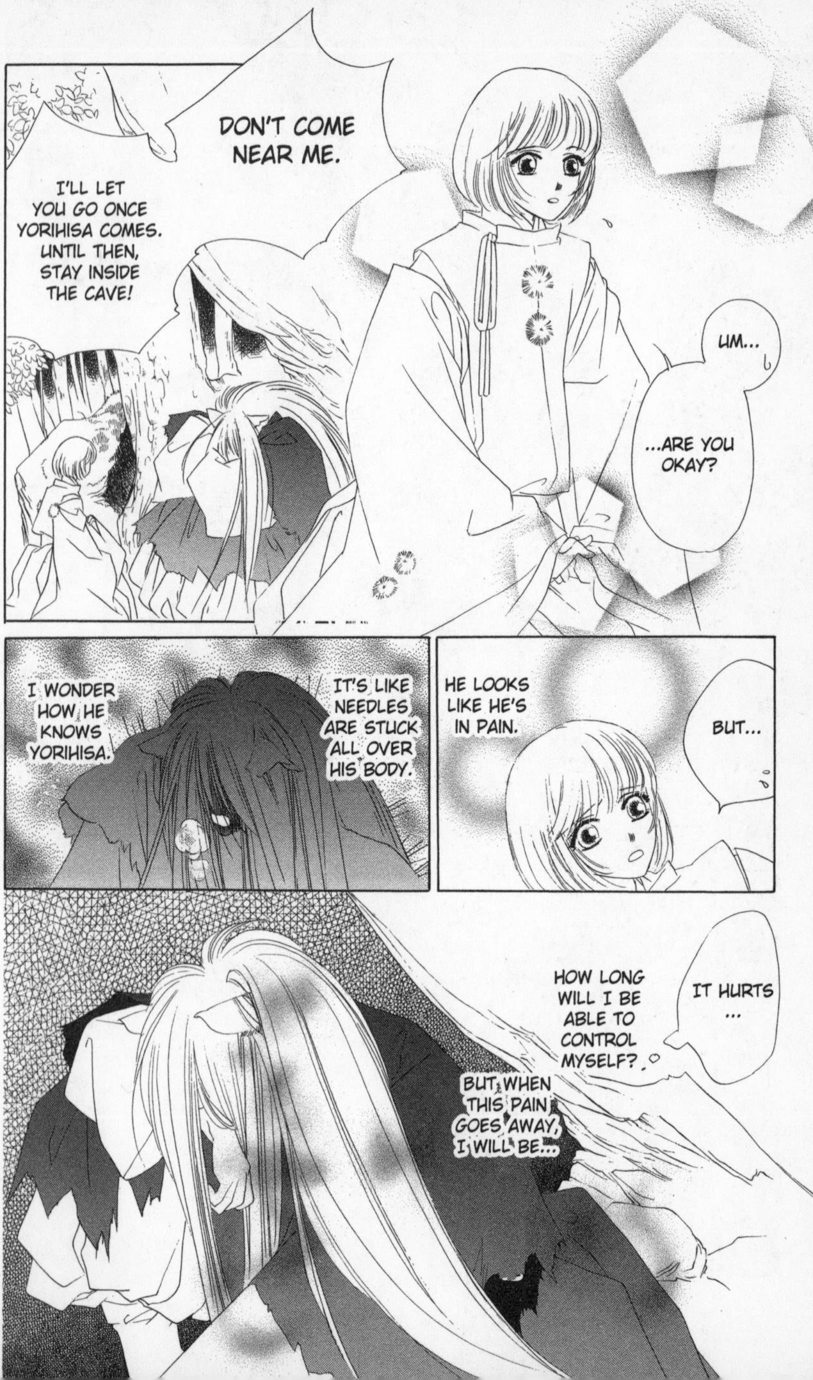
UM...
...ARE YOU OKAY?
DON'T COME NEAR ME.
I'LL LET YOU GO ONCE YORIHISA COMES. UNTIL THEN, STAY INSIDE THE CAVE!
BUT...
HE LOOKS LIKE HE'S IN PAIN.
IT'S LIKE NEEDLES ARE STUCK ALL OVER HIS BODY.
I WONDER HOW HE KNOWS YORIHISA.
IT HURTS ...
HOW LONG WILL I BE ABLE TO CONTROL MYSELF?
BUT WHEN THIS PAIN GOES AWAY, I WILL BE...

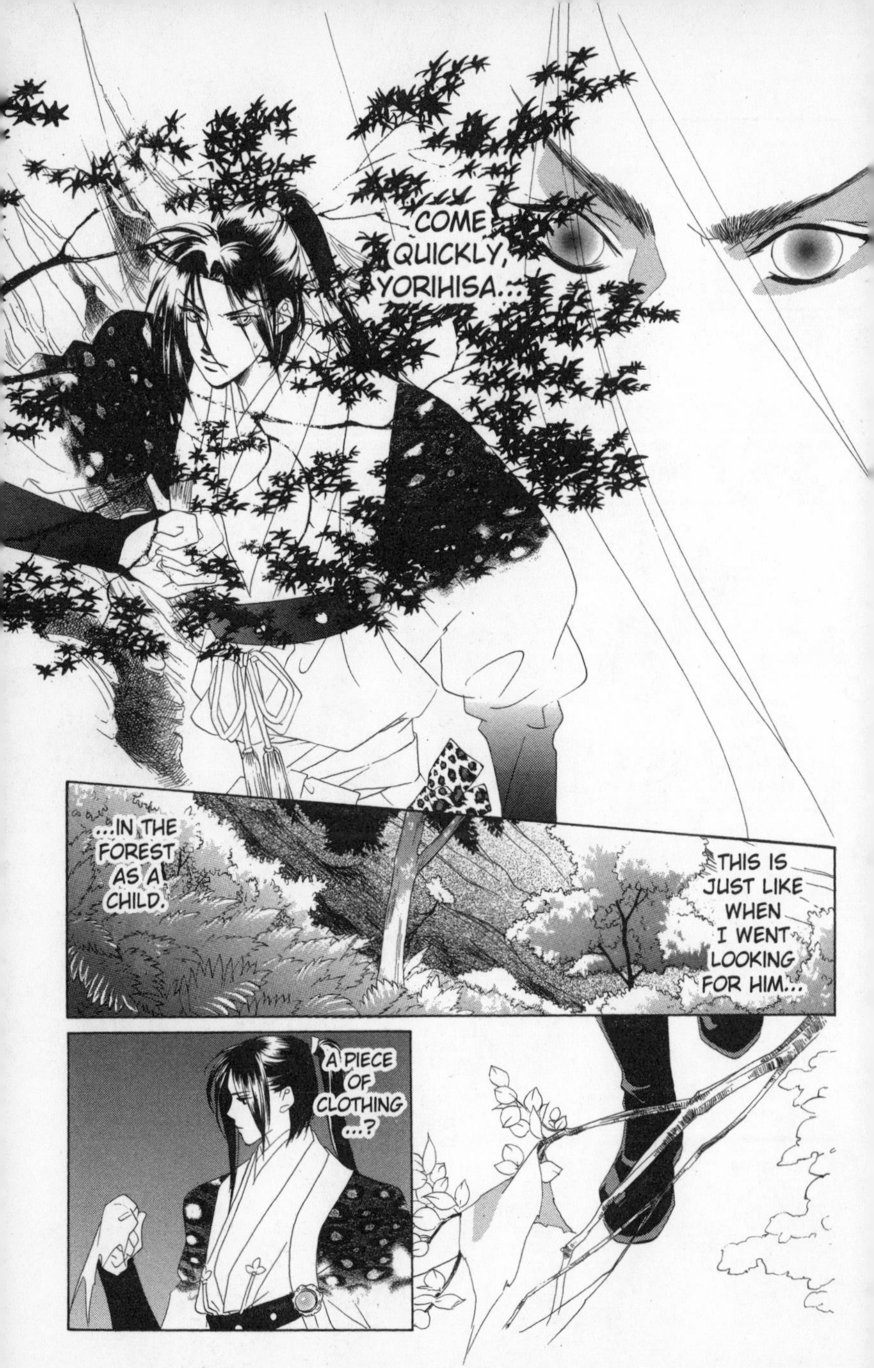
COME QUICKLY, YORIHISA...
THIS IS JUST LIKE WHEN I WENT LOOKING FOR HIM...
...IN THE FOREST AS A CHILD.
A PIECE OF CLOTHING ...?

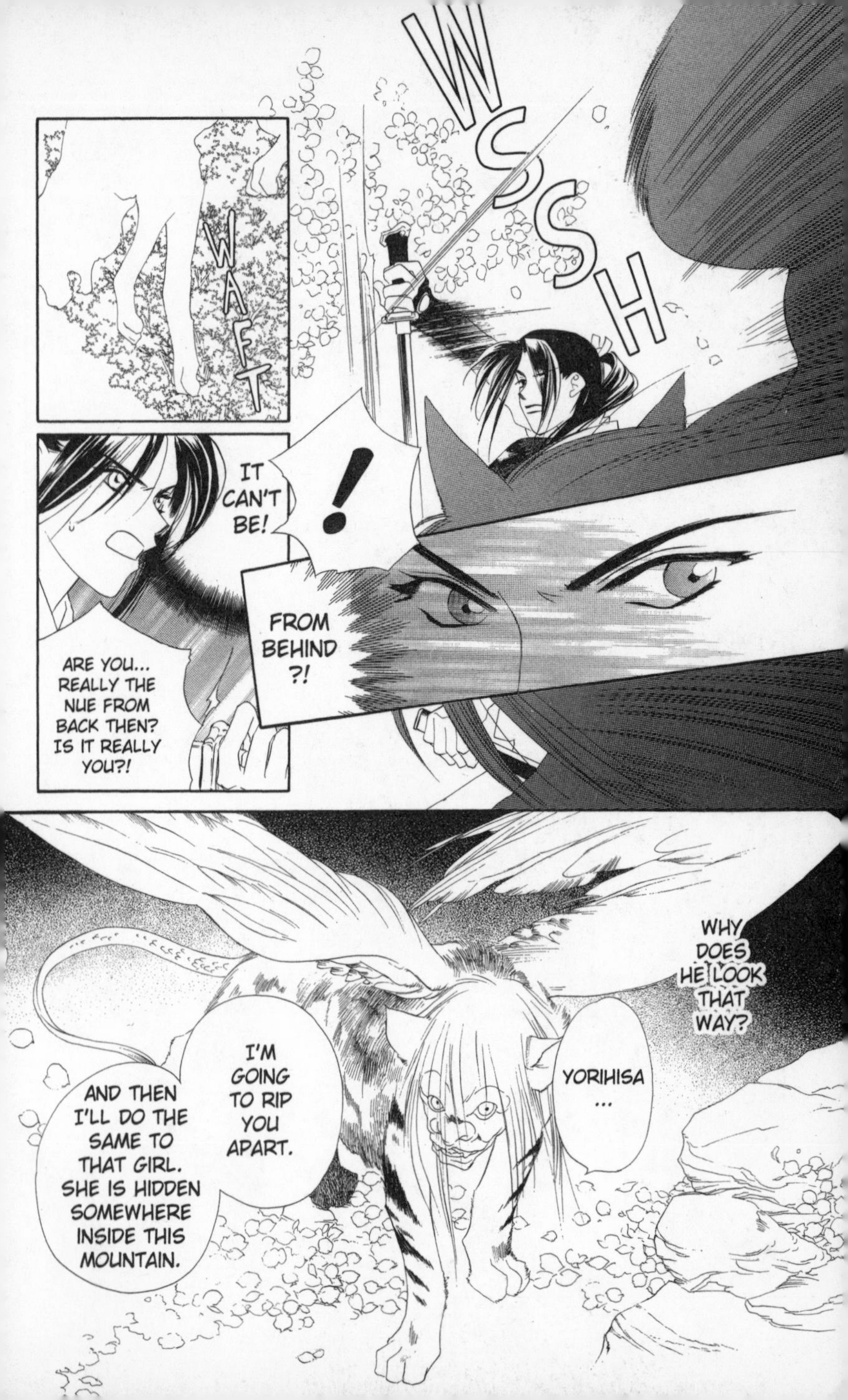
WSSH
!
FROM BEHIND?!
WAFT
IT CAN'T BE!
ARE YOU... REALLY THE NUE FROM BACK THEN? IS IT REALLY YOU?!
WHY DOES HE LOOK THAT WAY?
YORIHISA...
I'M GOING TO RIP YOU APART.
AND THEN I'LL DO THE SAME TO THAT GIRL. SHE IS HIDDEN SOMEWHERE INSIDE THIS MOUNTAIN.

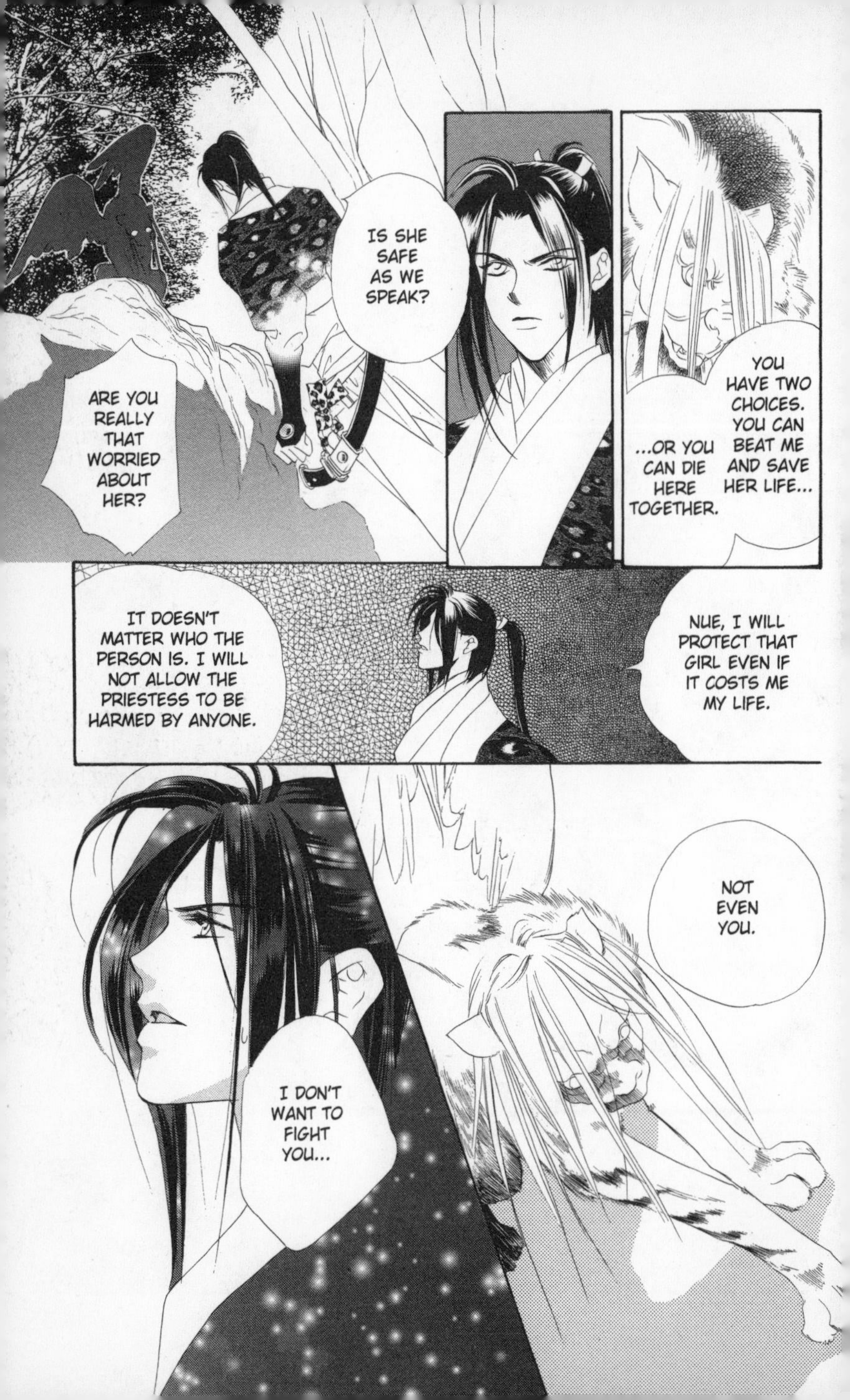
YOU HAVE TWO CHOICES. YOU CAN BEAT ME AND SAVE HER LIFE...
...OR YOU CAN DIE HERE TOGETHER.
IS SHE SAFE AS WE SPEAK?
ARE YOU REALLY THAT WORRIED ABOUT HER?
NUE, I WILL PROTECT THAT GIRL EVEN IF IT COSTS ME MY LIFE.
IT DOESN'T MATTER WHO THE PERSON IS. I WILL NOT ALLOW THE PRIESTESS TO BE HARMED BY ANYONE.
NOT EVEN YOU.
I DON'T WANT TO FIGHT YOU...

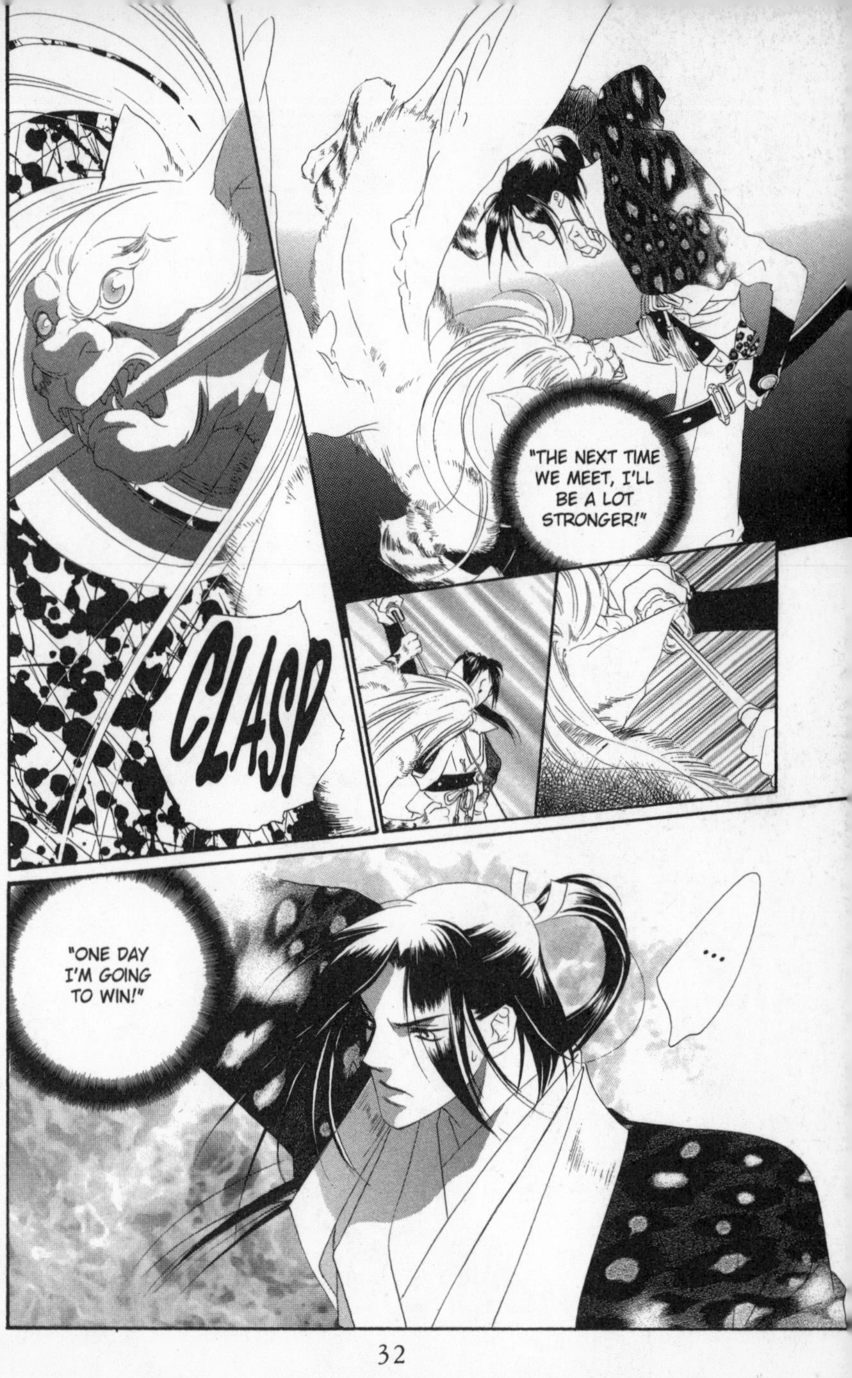
"THE NEXT TIME WE MEET, I'LL BE A LOT STRONGER!"
CLASP
"ONE DAY I'M GOING TO WIN!"
...

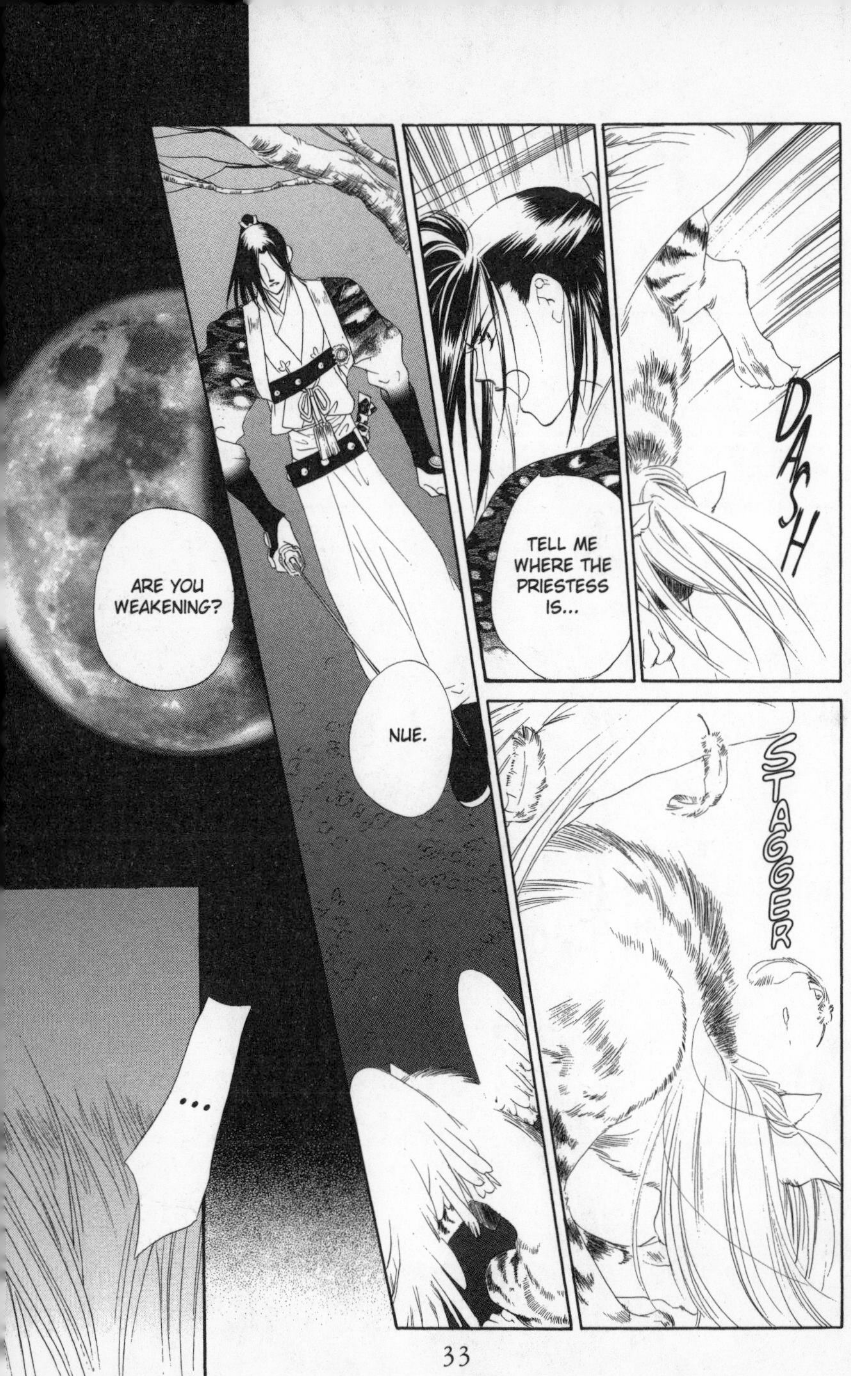
DASH
TELL ME WHERE THE PRIESTESS IS...
STAGGER
ARE YOU WEAKENING?
NUE.
...

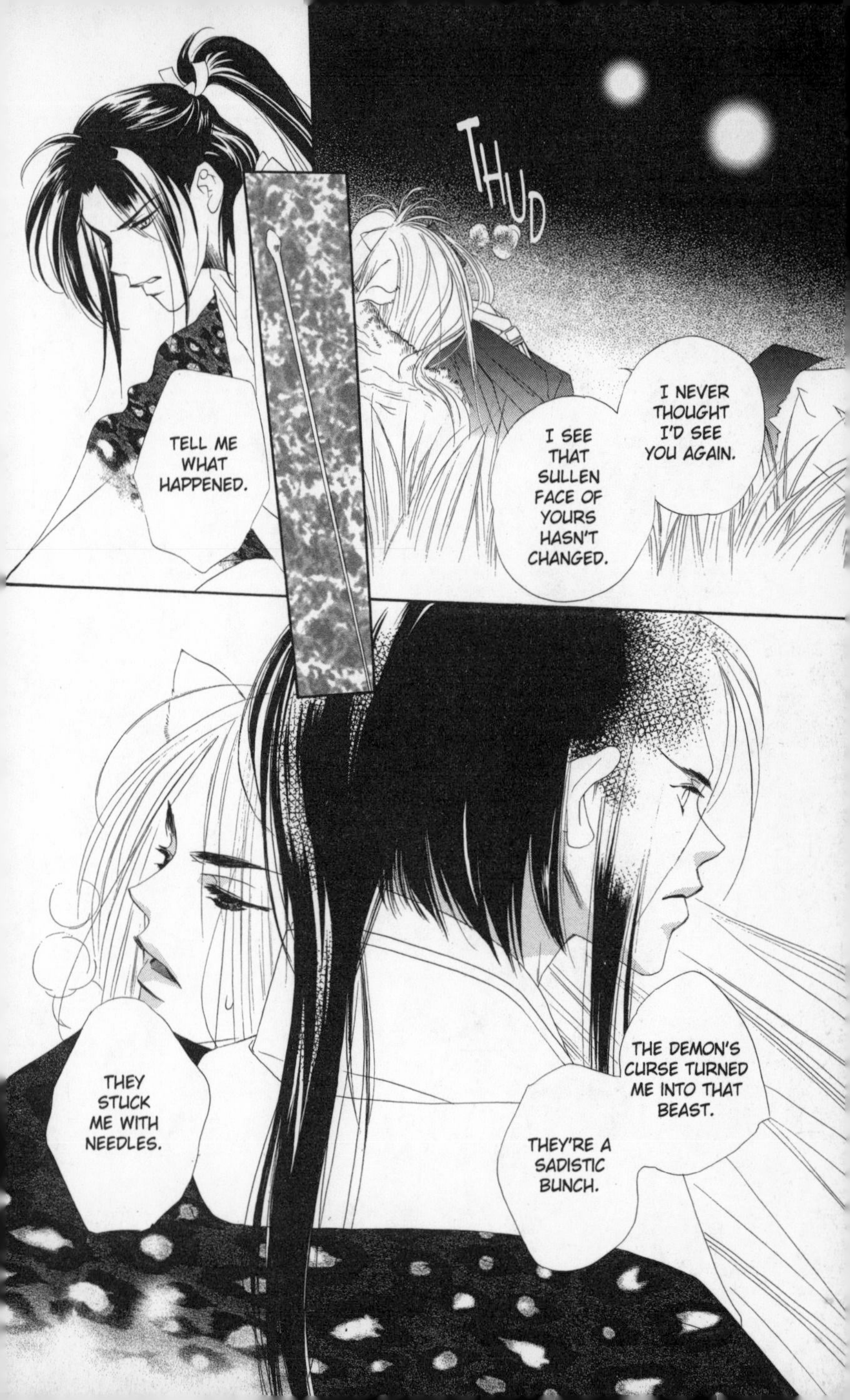
THUD
I NEVER THOUGHT I'D SEE YOU AGAIN.
I SEE THAT SULLEN FACE OF YOURS HASN'T CHANGED.
TELL ME WHAT HAPPENED.
THE DEMON'S CURSE TURNED ME INTO THAT BEAST.
THEY'RE A SADISTIC BUNCH.
THEY STUCK ME WITH NEEDLES.

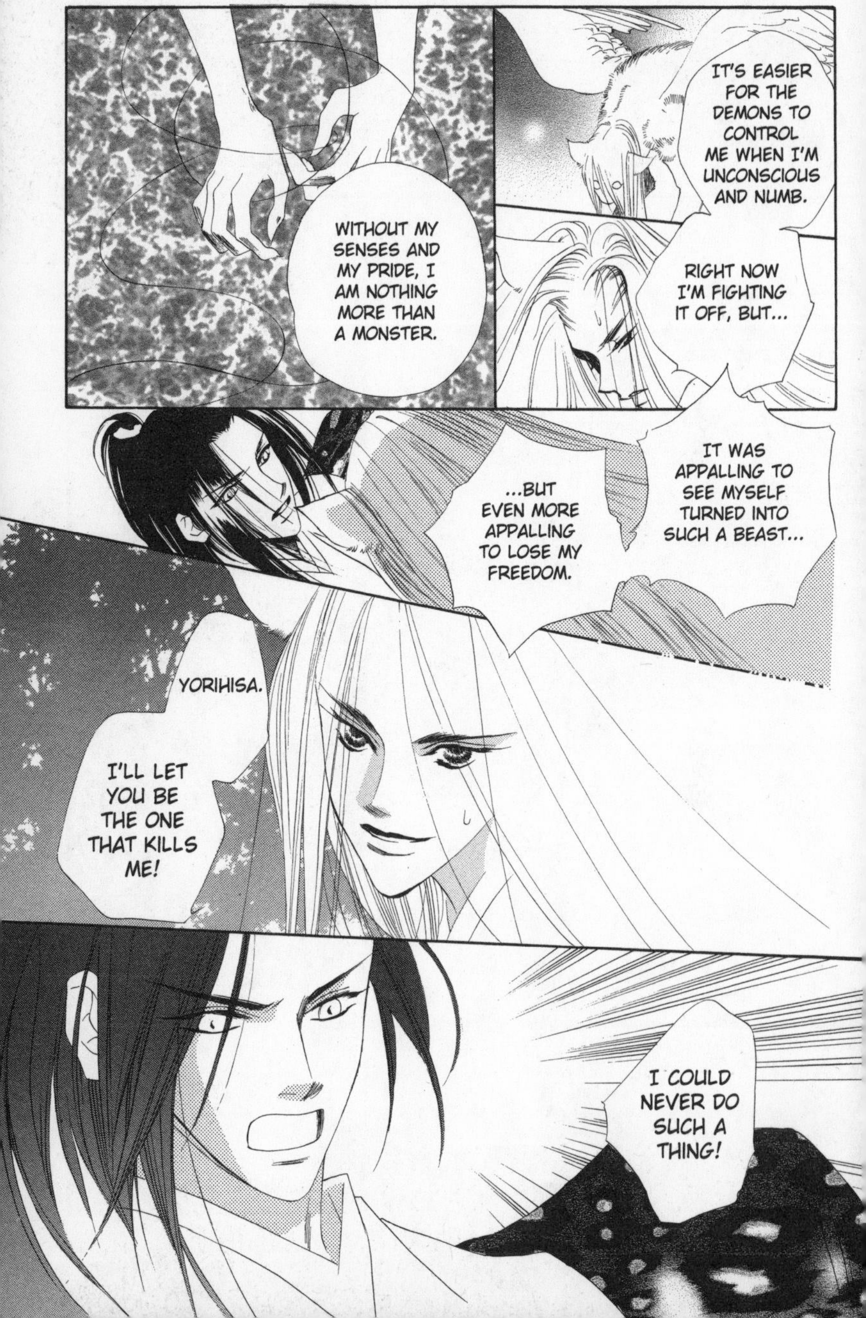
IT'S EASIER FOR THE DEMONS TO CONTROL ME WHEN I'M UNCONSCIOUS AND NUMB.
RIGHT NOW I'M FIGHTING IT OFF, BUT...
WITHOUT MY SENSES AND MY PRIDE, I AM NOTHING MORE THAN A MONSTER.
IT WAS APPALLING TO SEE MYSELF TURNED INTO SUCH A BEAST...
...BUT EVEN MORE APPALLING TO LOSE MY FREEDOM.
YORIHISA.
I'LL LET YOU BE THE ONE THAT KILLS ME!
I COULD NEVER DO SUCH A THING!

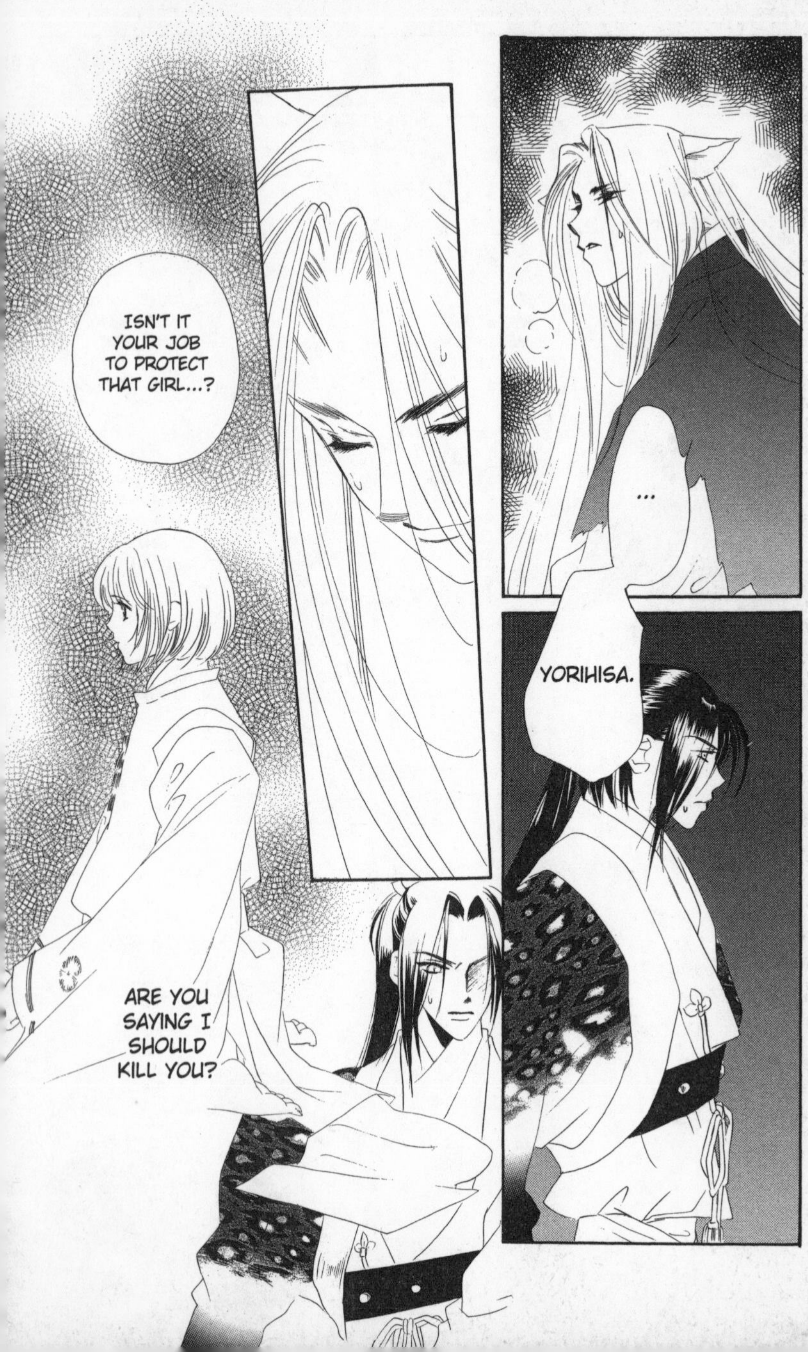
...
YORIHISA.
ISN'T IT YOUR JOB TO PROTECT THAT GIRL...?
ARE YOU SAYING I SHOULD KILL YOU?

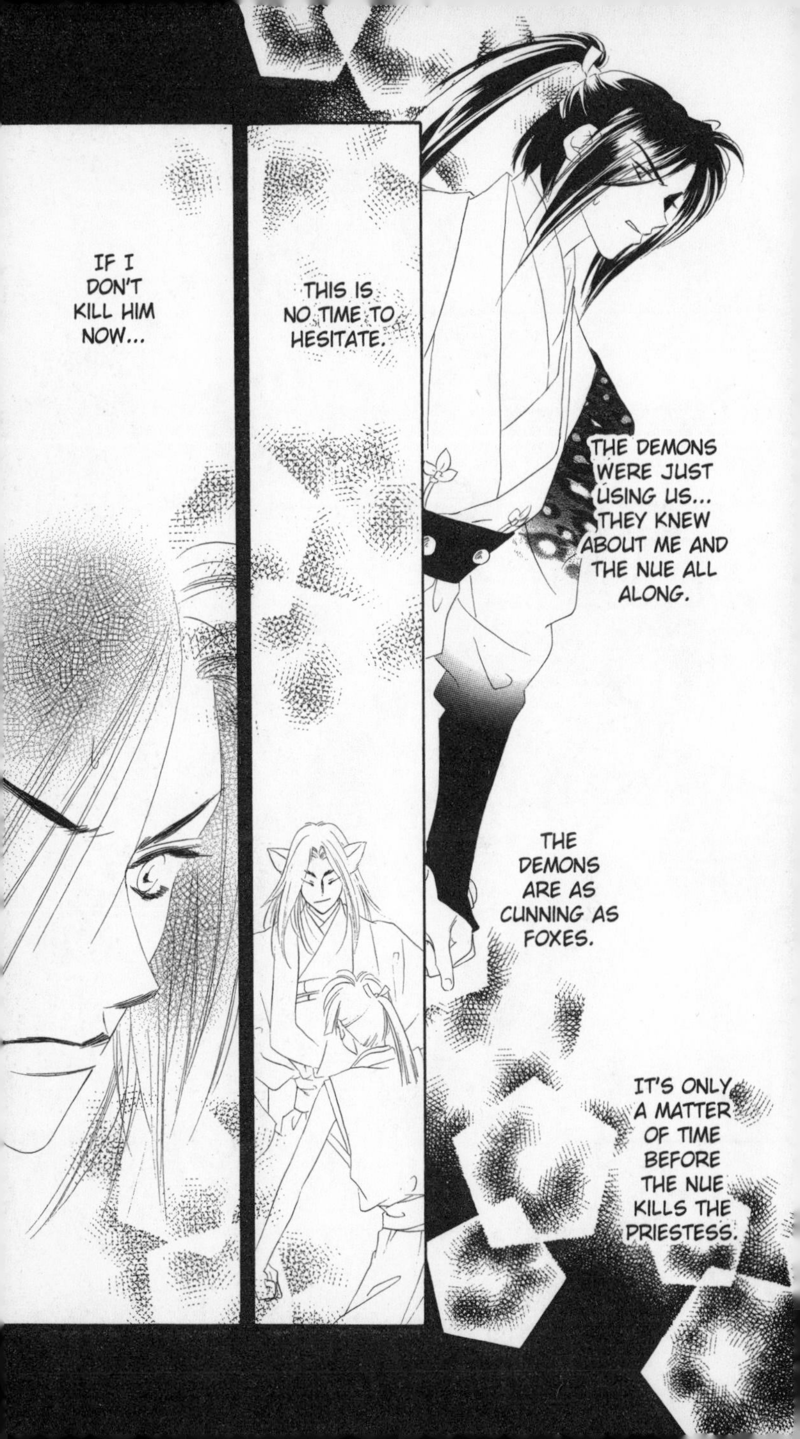
THE DEMONS WERE JUST USING US... THEY KNEW ABOUT ME AND THE NUE ALL ALONG.
THE DEMONS ARE AS CUNNING AS FOXES.
IT'S ONLY A MATTER OF TIME BEFORE THE NUE KILLS THE PRIESTESS.
THIS IS NO TIME TO HESITATE.
IF I DON'T KILL HIM NOW...

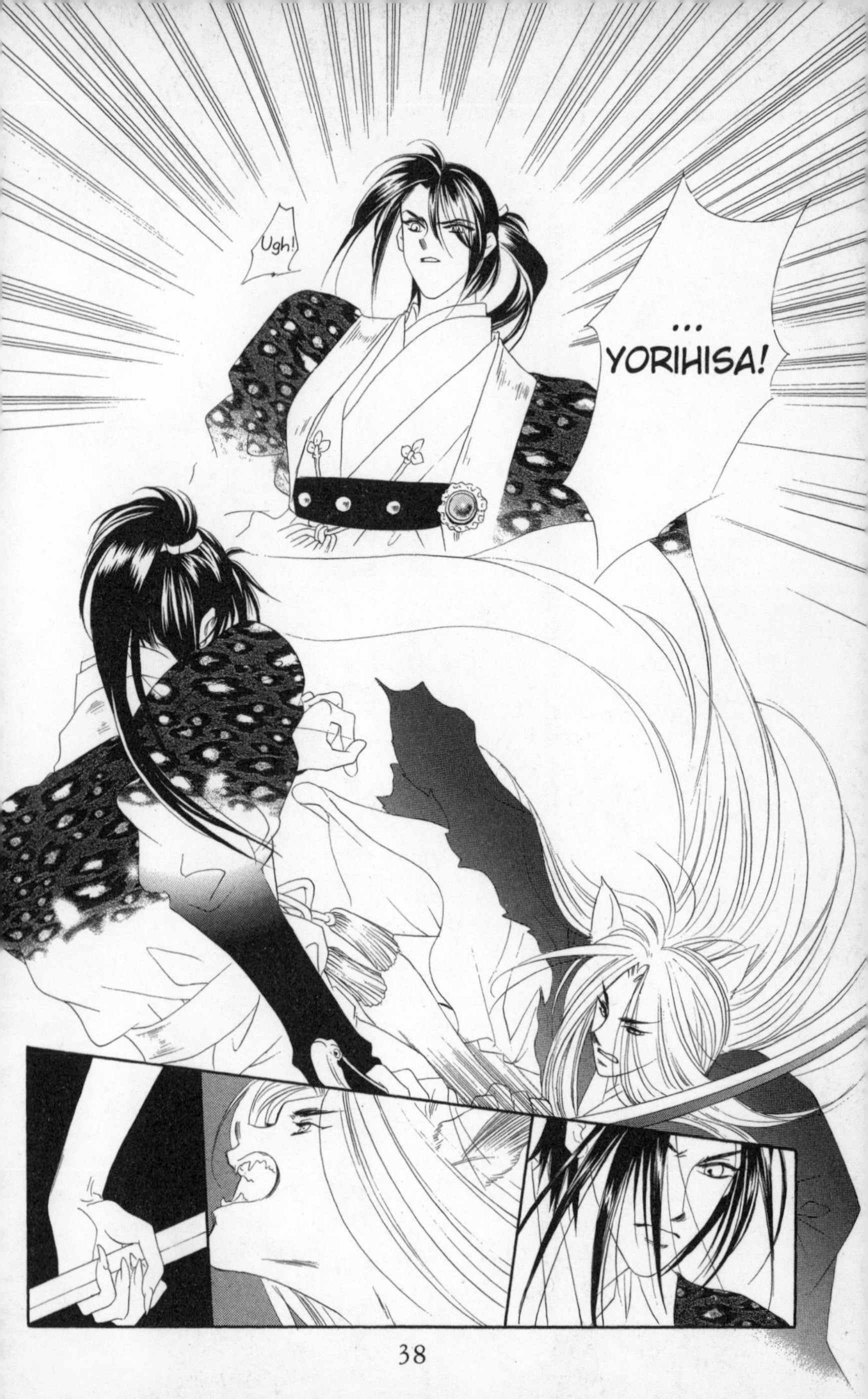
... YORIHISA!
Ugh!

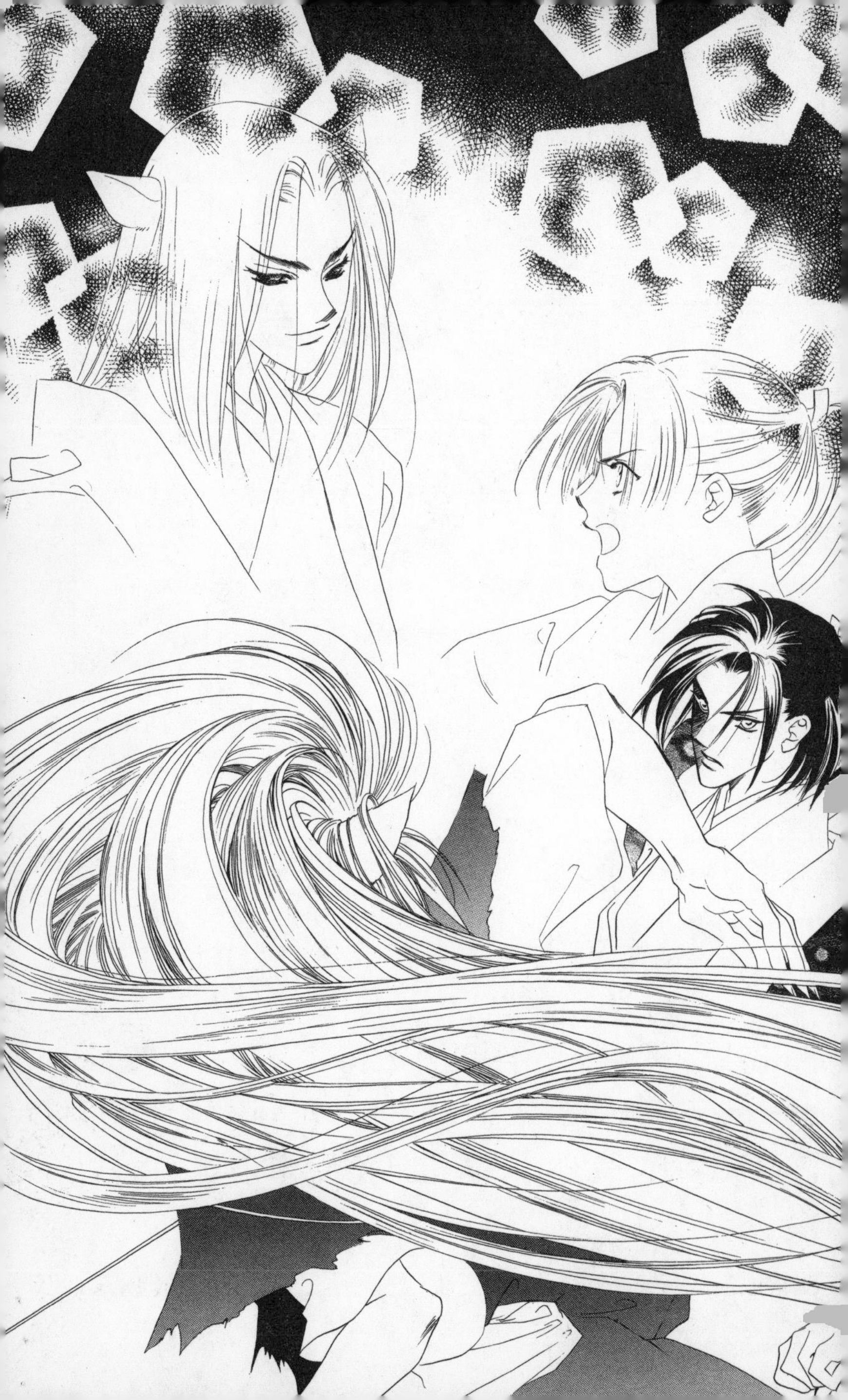

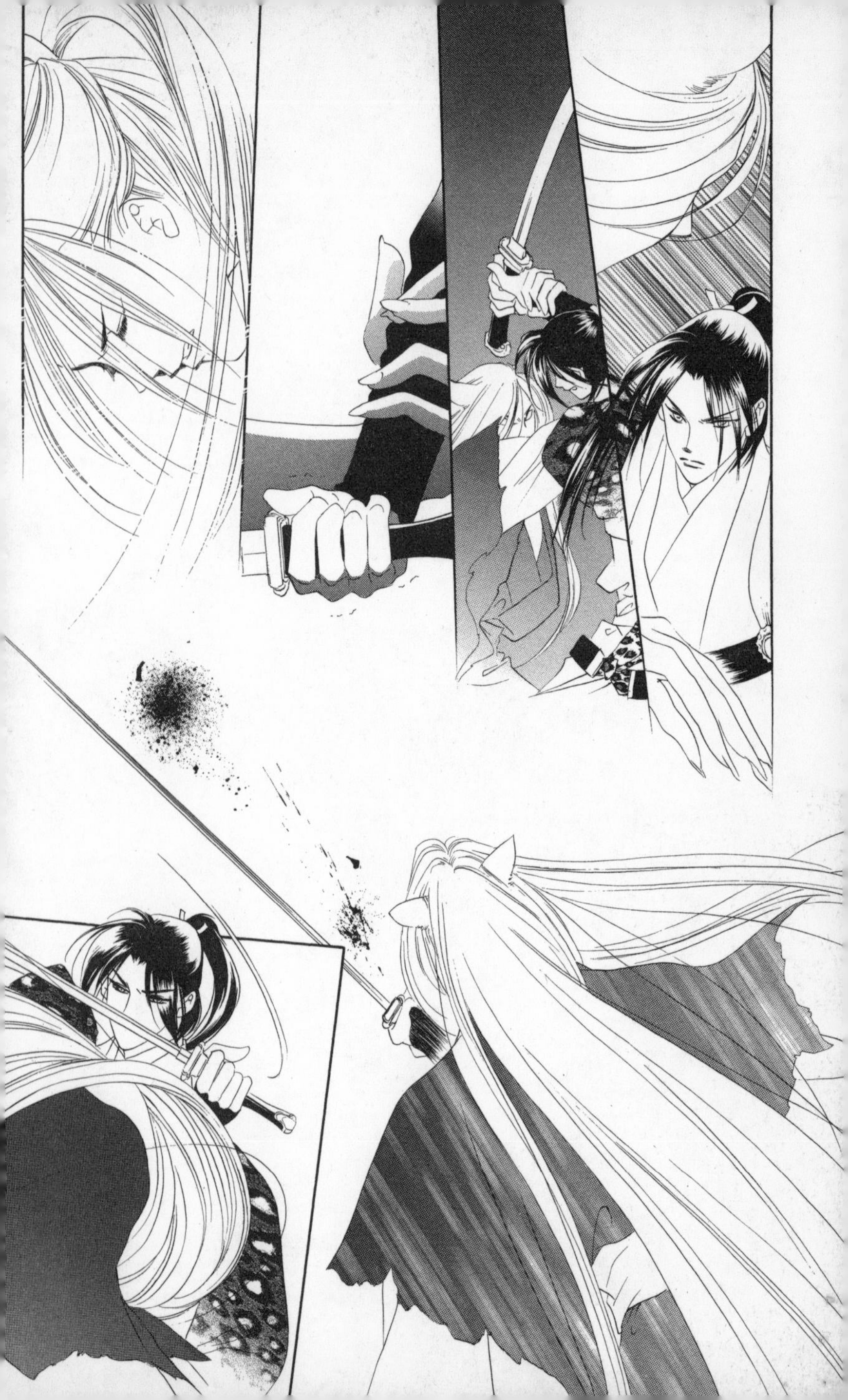

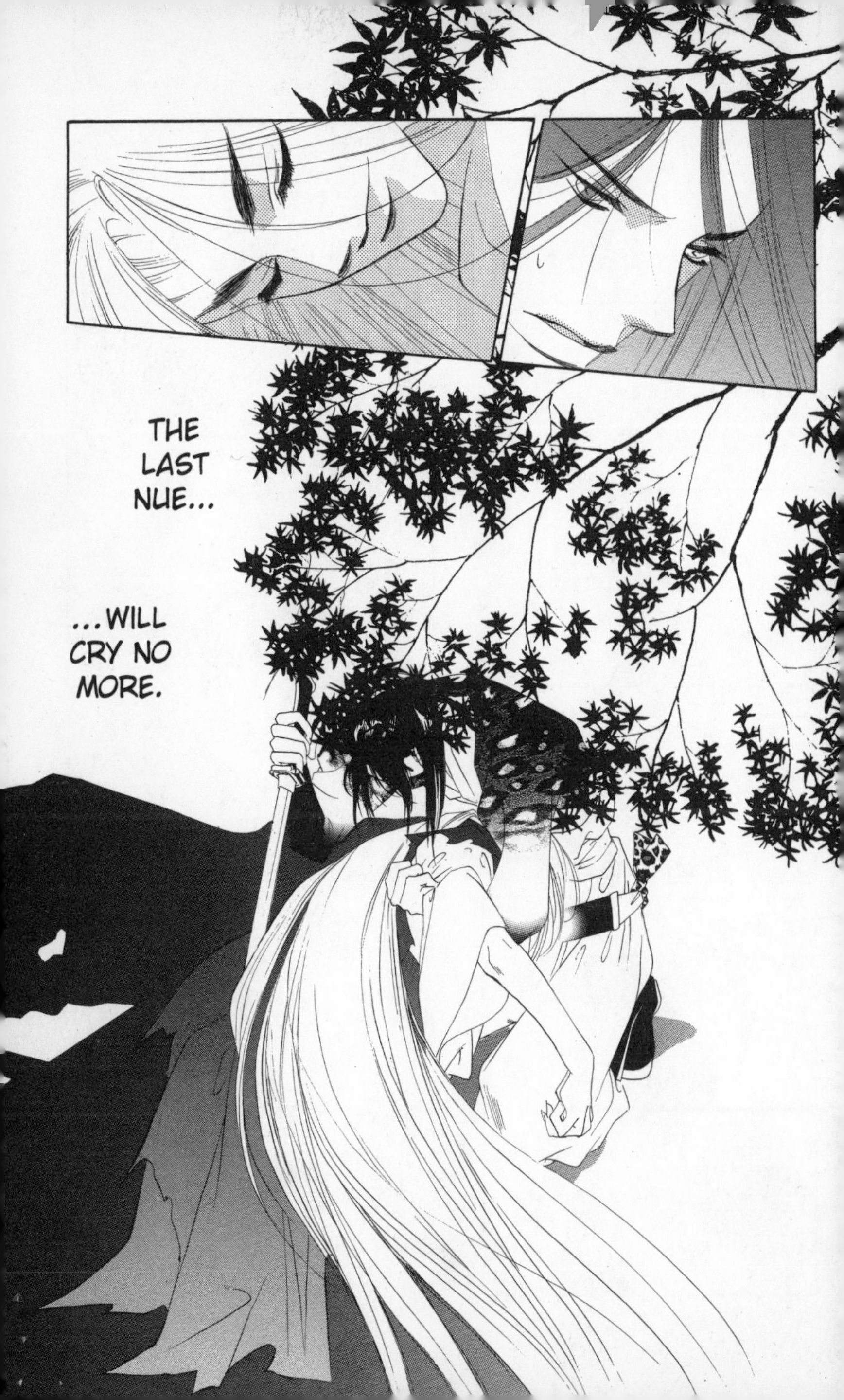
THE LAST NUE...
...WILL CRY NO MORE.

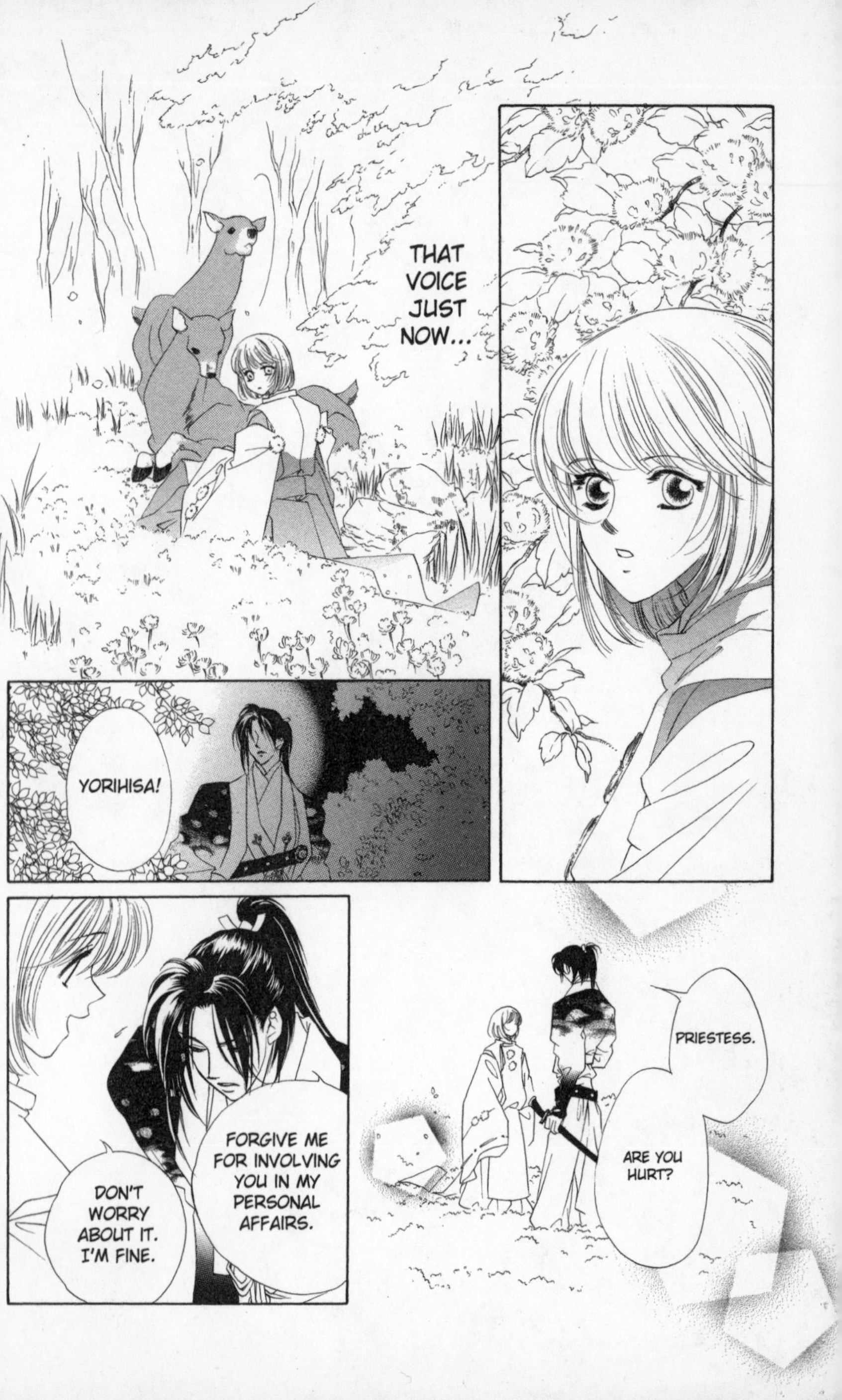
THAT VOICE JUST NOW...
YORIHISA!
PRIESTESS.
ARE YOU HURT?
FORGIVE ME FOR INVOLVING YOU IN MY PERSONAL AFFAIRS.
DON'T WORRY ABOUT IT. I'M FINE.

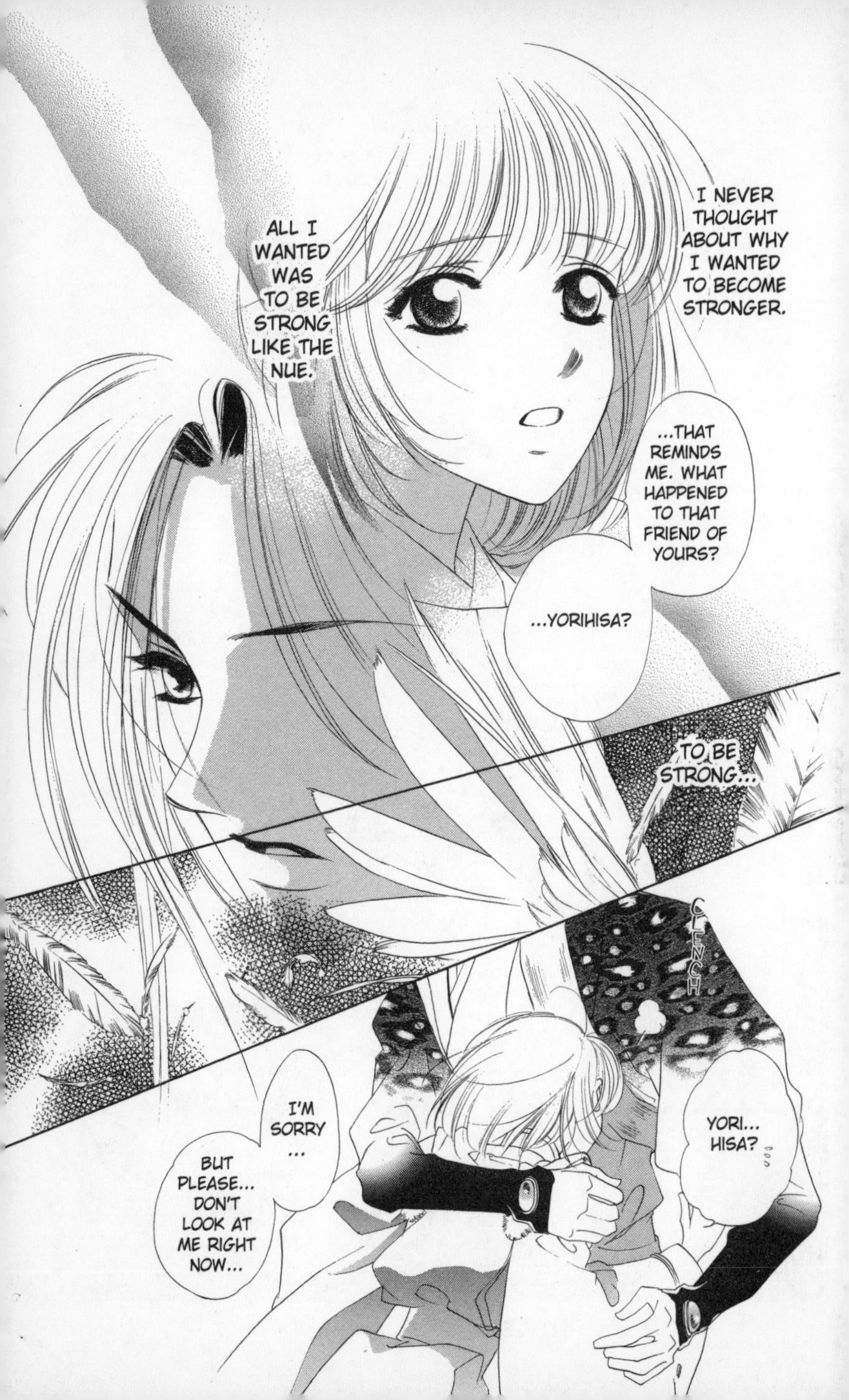
I NEVER THOUGHT ABOUT WHY I WANTED TO BECOME STRONGER.
ALL I WANTED WAS TO BE STRONG LIKE THE NUE.
...THAT REMINDS ME. WHAT HAPPENED TO THAT FRIEND OF YOURS?
...YORIHISA?
TO BE STRONG...
CLENCH
YORI... HISA?
I'M SORRY...
BUT PLEASE... DON'T LOOK AT ME RIGHT NOW...

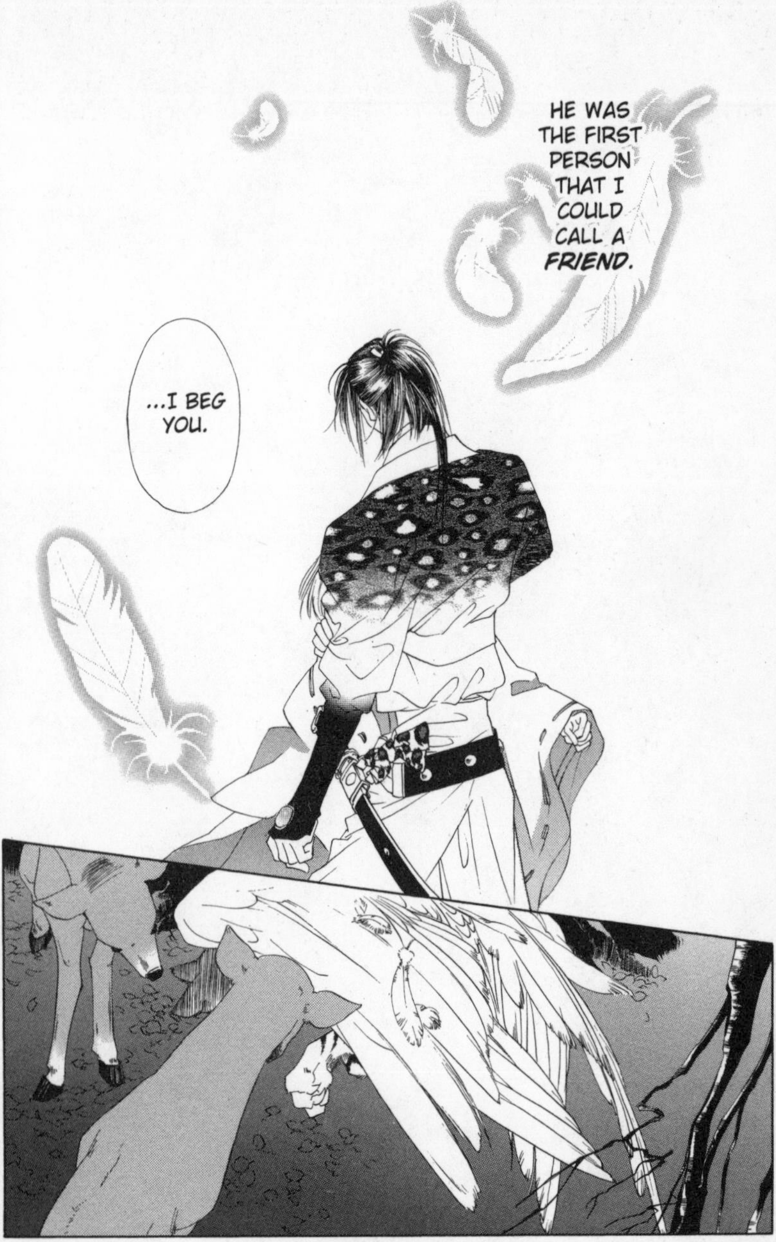
HE WAS THE FIRST PERSON THAT I COULD CALL A FRIEND.
...I BEG YOU.

THE NIGHT CRY OF THE NUE/END

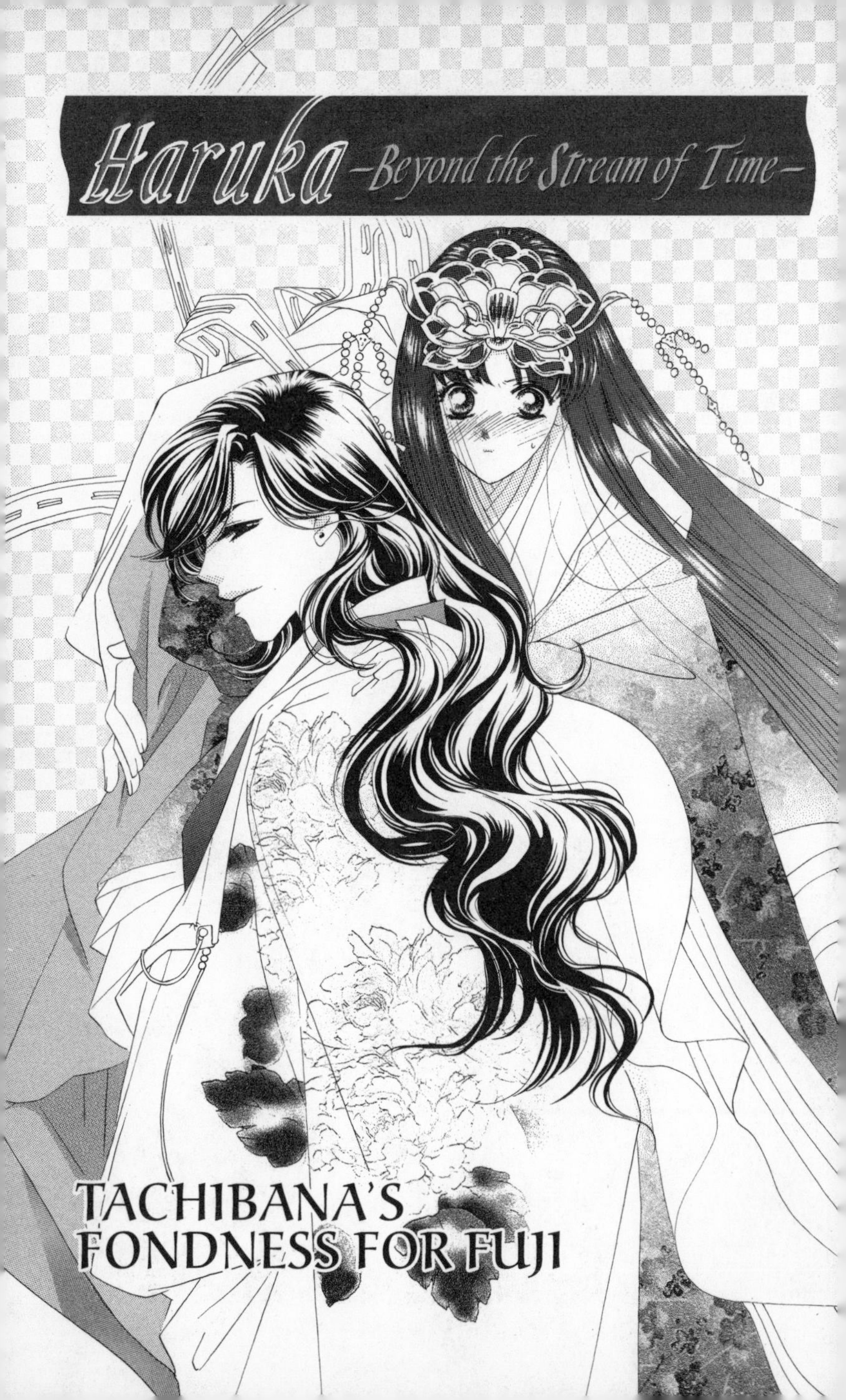
Haruka -Beyond the Stream of Time-
TACHIBANA'S FONDNESS FOR FUJI

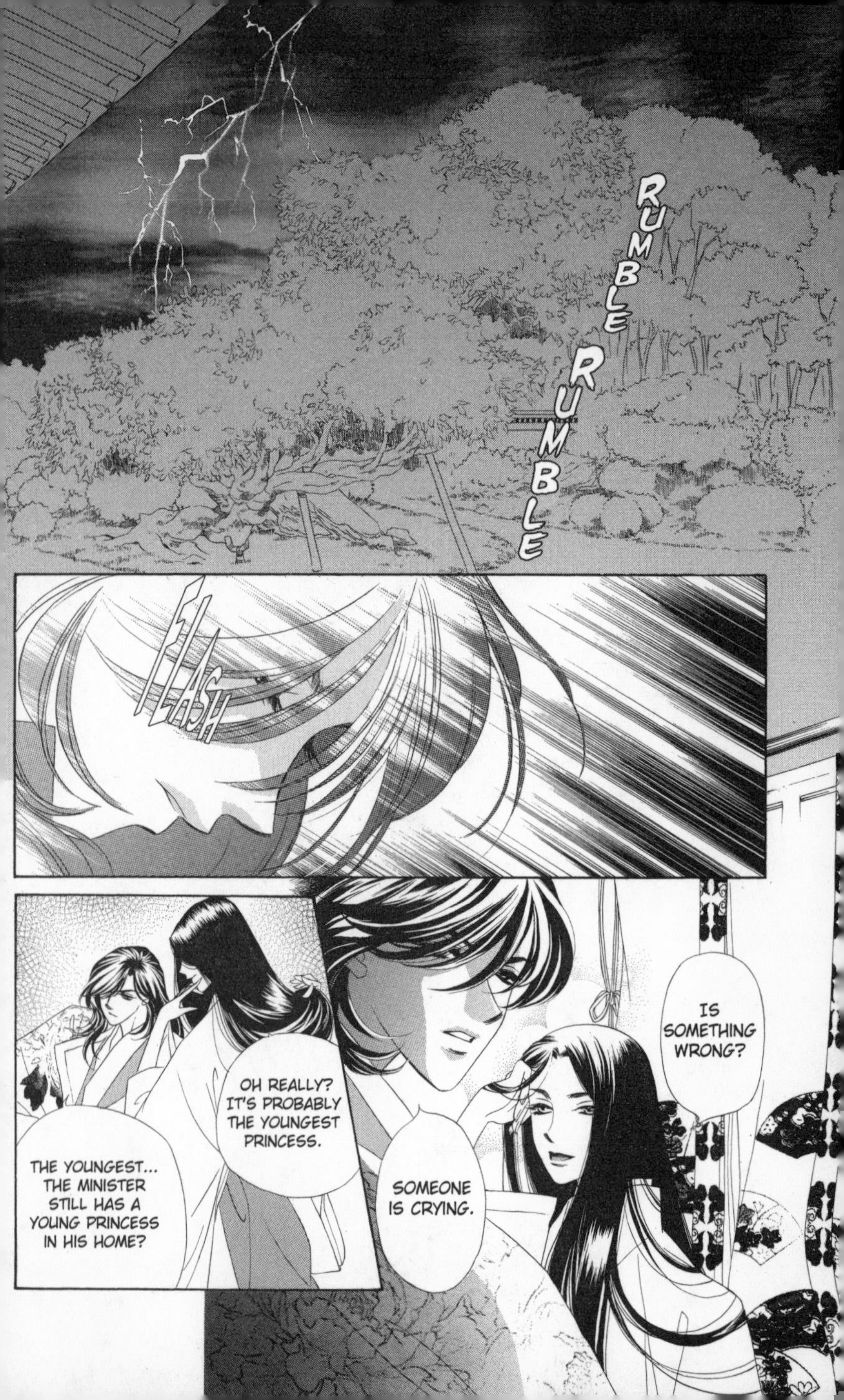
RUMBLE
RUMBLE
FLASH
IS SOMETHING WRONG?
SOMEONE IS CRYING.
OH REALLY? IT'S PROBABLY THE YOUNGEST PRINCESS.
THE YOUNGEST... THE MINISTER STILL HAS A YOUNG PRINCESS IN HIS HOME?

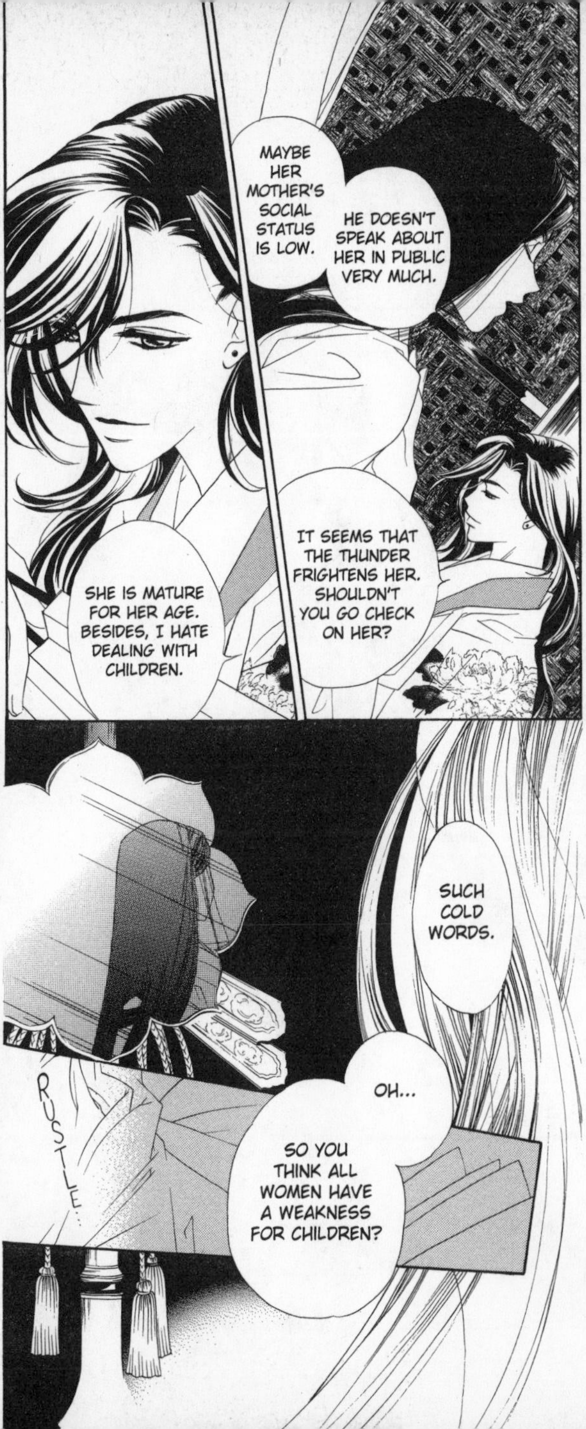
HE DOESN'T SPEAK ABOUT HER IN PUBLIC VERY MUCH.
MAYBE HER MOTHER'S SOCIAL STATUS IS LOW.
IT SEEMS THAT THE THUNDER FRIGHTENS HER. SHOULDN'T YOU GO CHECK ON HER?
SHE IS MATURE FOR HER AGE. BESIDES, I HATE DEALING WITH CHILDREN.
SUCH COLD WORDS.
OH...
SO YOU THINK ALL WOMEN HAVE A WEAKNESS FOR CHILDREN?
RUSTLE...

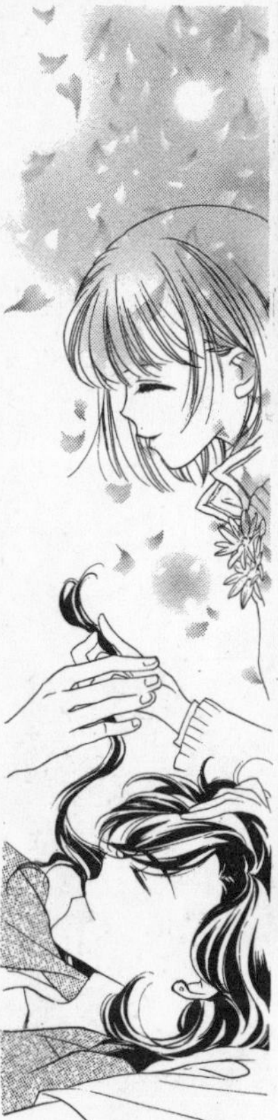

A modern ending
Tomomasa + Akane

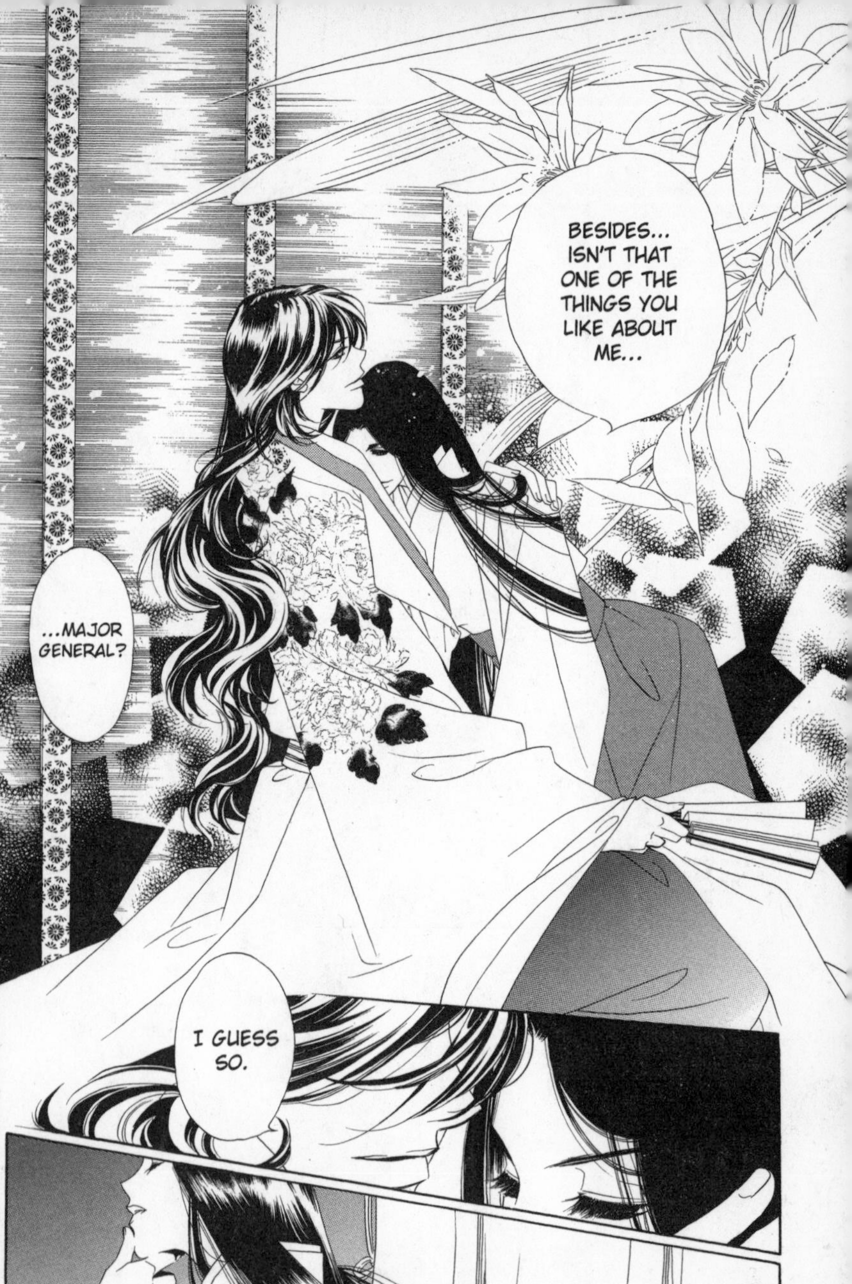
BESIDES... ISN'T THAT ONE OF THE THINGS YOU LIKE ABOUT ME...
...MAJOR GENERAL?
I GUESS SO.

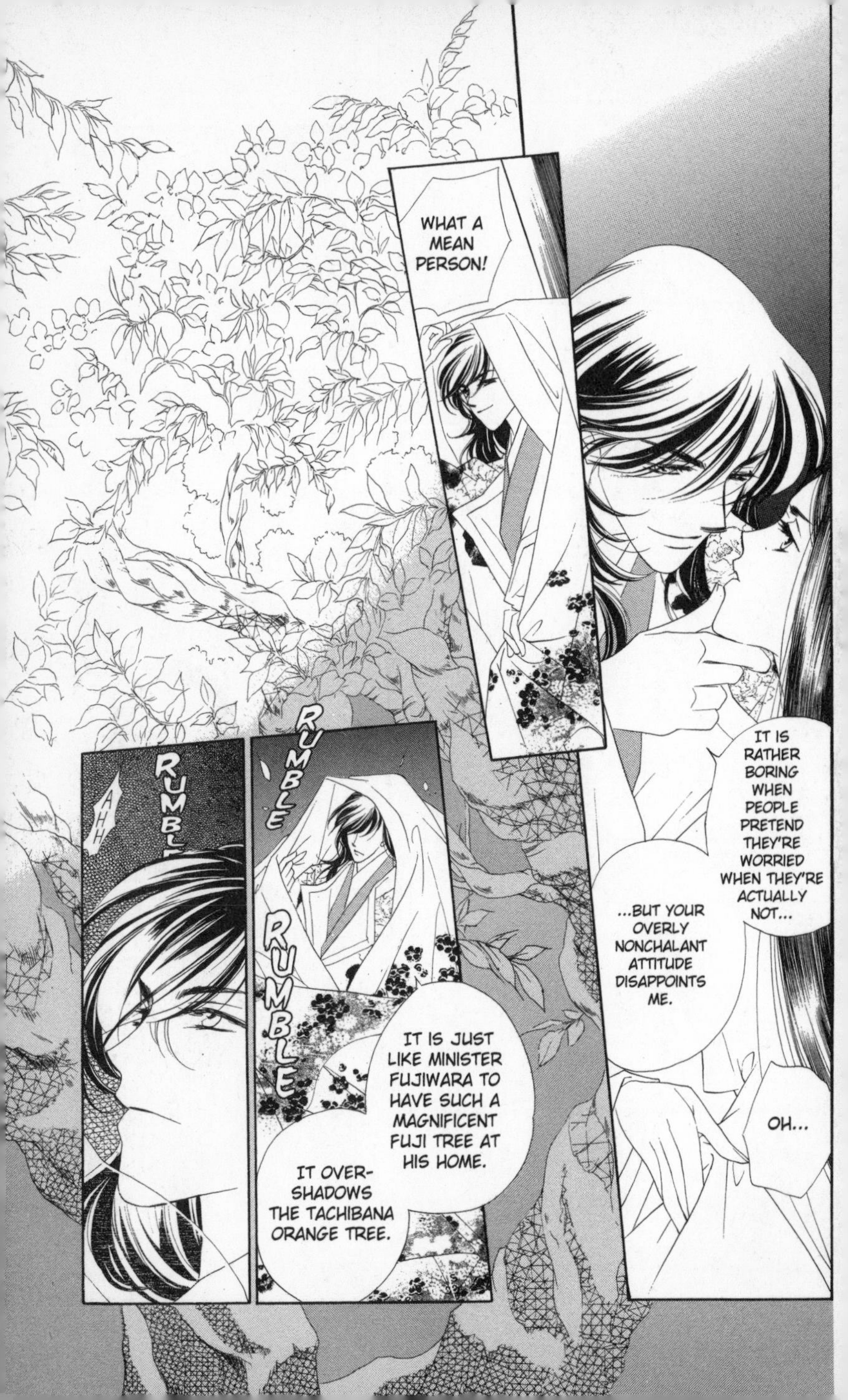
WHAT A MEAN PERSON!
IT IS RATHER BORING WHEN PEOPLE PRETEND THEY'RE WORRIED WHEN THEY'RE ACTUALLY NOT...
...BUT YOUR OVERLY NONCHALANT ATTITUDE DISAPPOINTS ME.
OH...
RUMBLE
RUMBLE
IT IS JUST LIKE MINISTER FUJIWARA TO HAVE SUCH A MAGNIFICENT FUJI TREE AT HIS HOME.
IT OVER-SHADOWS THE TACHIBANA ORANGE TREE.
AHH
RUMBLE

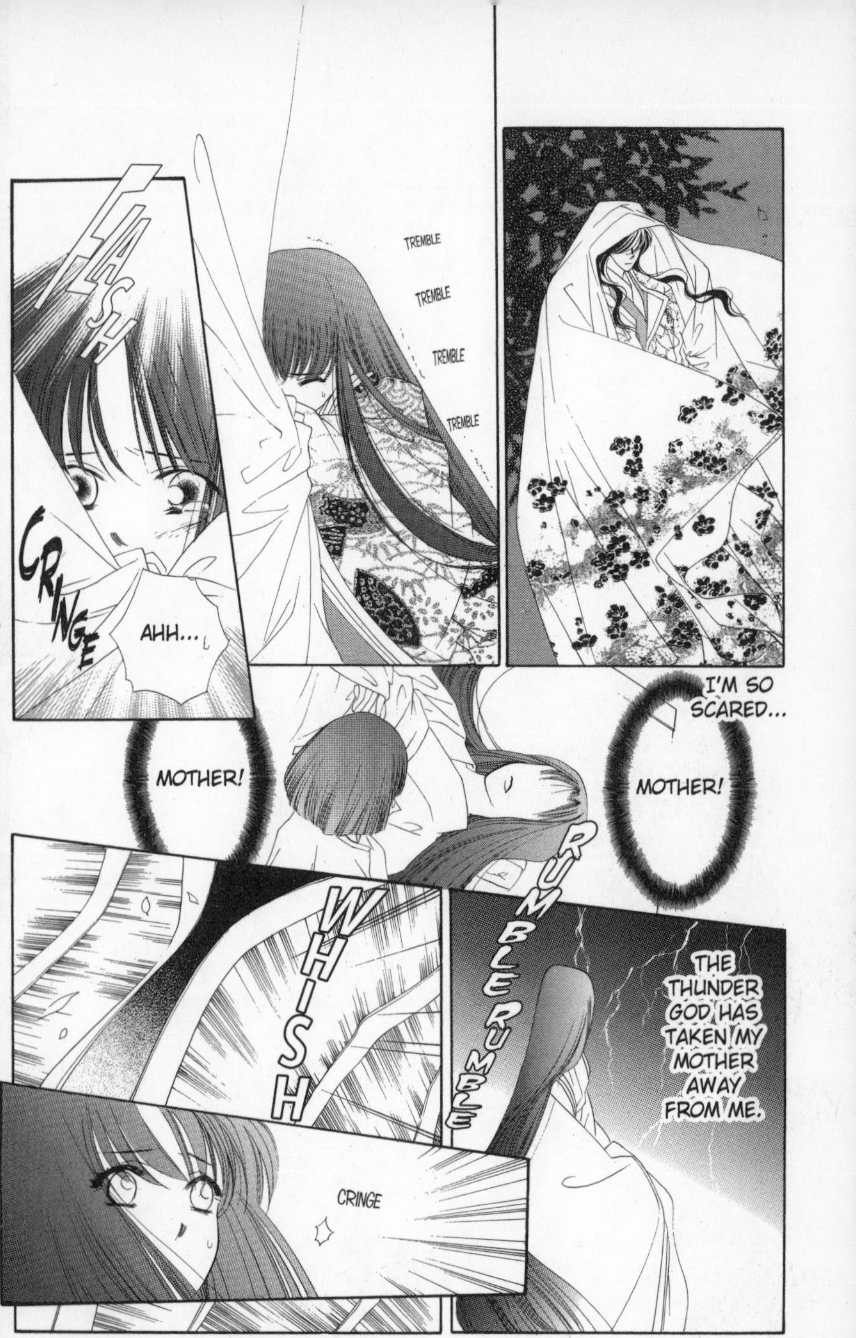

I'M SO SCARED...
TREMBLE
TREMBLE
TREMBLE
TREMBLE
FLASH
CRINGE
AHH...
MOTHER!
MOTHER!
RUMBLE RUMBLE
THE THUNDER GOD HAS TAKEN MY MOTHER AWAY FROM ME.
WHISH
CRINGE

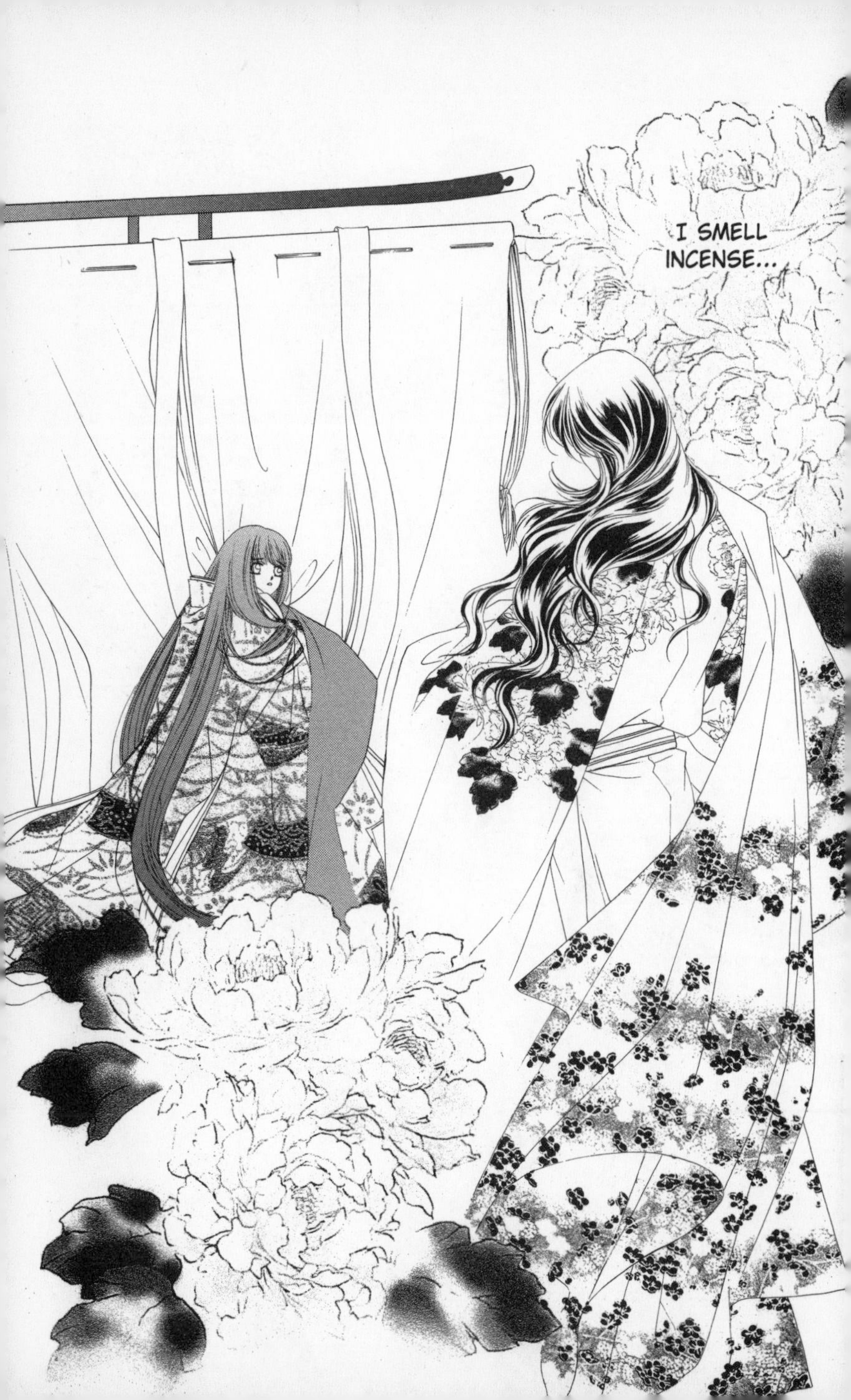
I SMELL INCENSE...

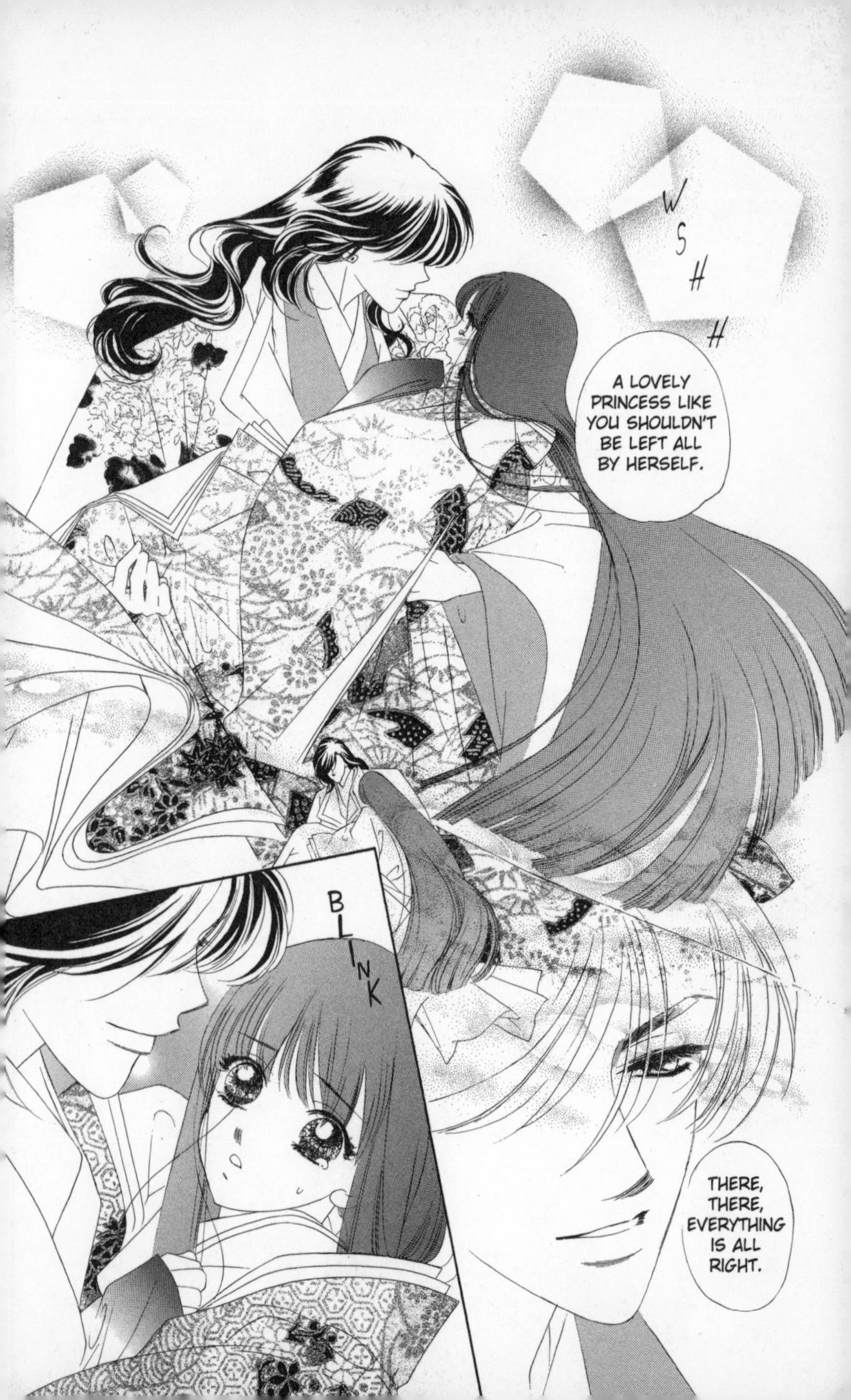
WSHH
A LOVELY PRINCESS LIKE YOU SHOULDN'T BE LEFT ALL BY HERSELF.
BLINK
THERE, THERE, EVERYTHING IS ALL RIGHT.

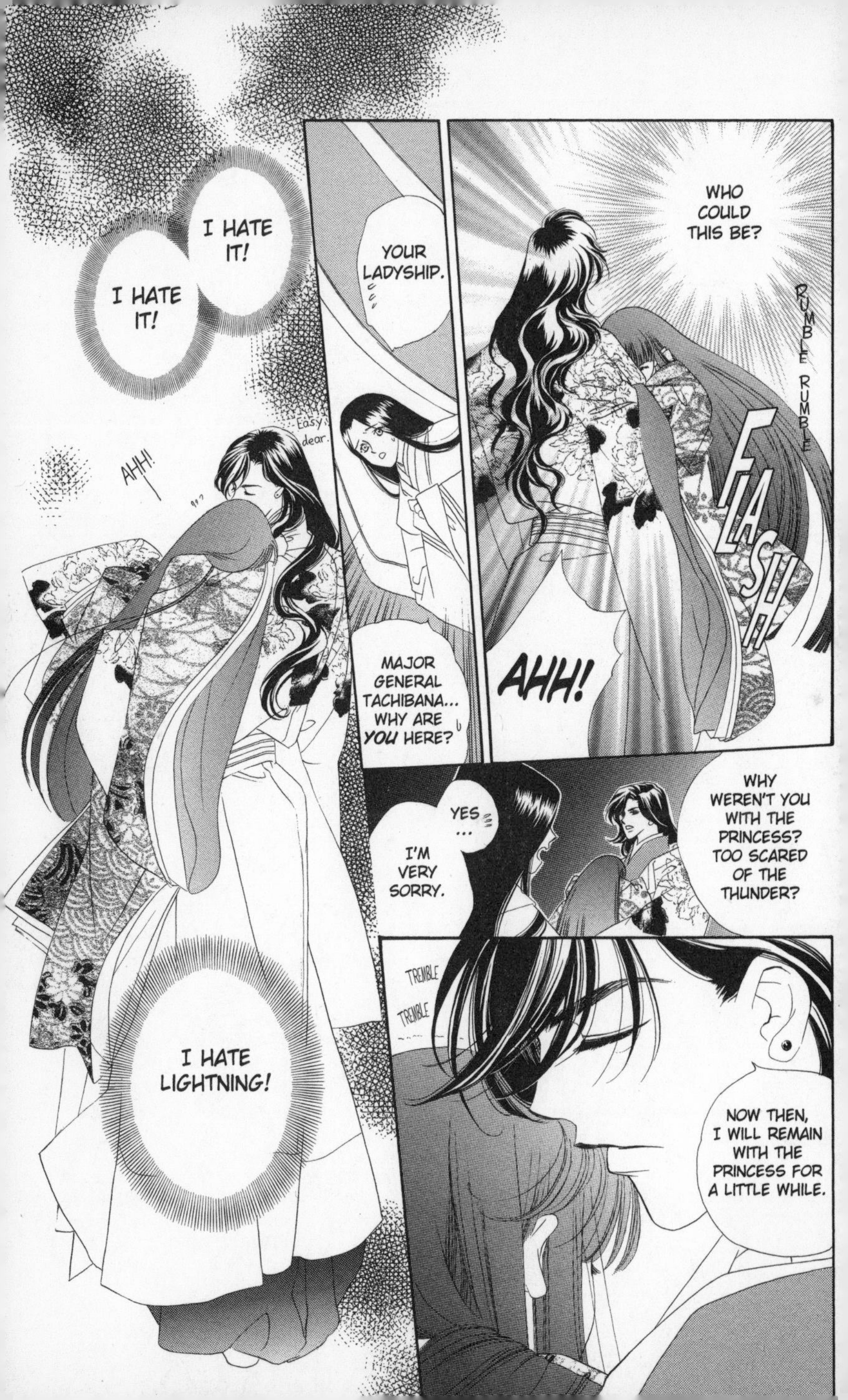

WHO COULD THIS BE?
RUMBLE RUMBLE
FLASH
AHH!
YOUR LADYSHIP.
MAJOR GENERAL TACHIBANA... WHY ARE *YOU* HERE?
WHY WEREN'T YOU WITH THE PRINCESS? TOO SCARED OF THE THUNDER?
YES...
I'M VERY SORRY.
TREMBLE TREMBLE
NOW THEN, I WILL REMAIN WITH THE PRINCESS FOR A LITTLE WHILE.
I HATE IT!
I HATE IT!
Easy, dear.
AHH!
I HATE LIGHTNING!

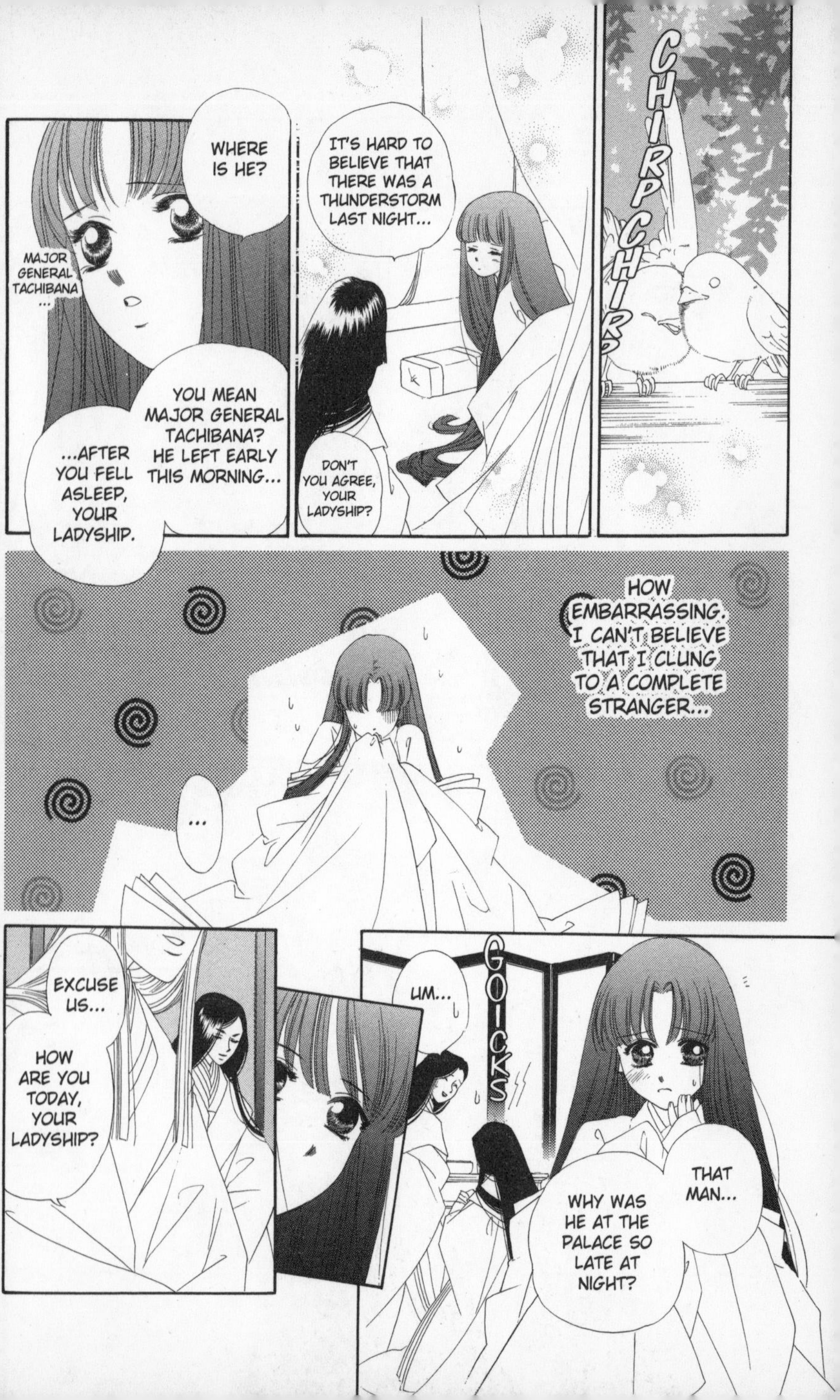
CHIRP CHIRP
IT'S HARD TO BELIEVE THAT THERE WAS A THUNDERSTORM LAST NIGHT...
DON'T YOU AGREE, YOUR LADYSHIP?
WHERE IS HE?
MAJOR GENERAL TACHIBANA...
YOU MEAN MAJOR GENERAL TACHIBANA? HE LEFT EARLY THIS MORNING...
...AFTER YOU FELL ASLEEP, YOUR LADYSHIP.
HOW EMBARRASSING. I CAN'T BELIEVE THAT I CLUNG TO A COMPLETE STRANGER...
...
UM...
GOICKS
THAT MAN...
WHY WAS HE AT THE PALACE SO LATE AT NIGHT?
EXCUSE US...
HOW ARE YOU TODAY, YOUR LADYSHIP?

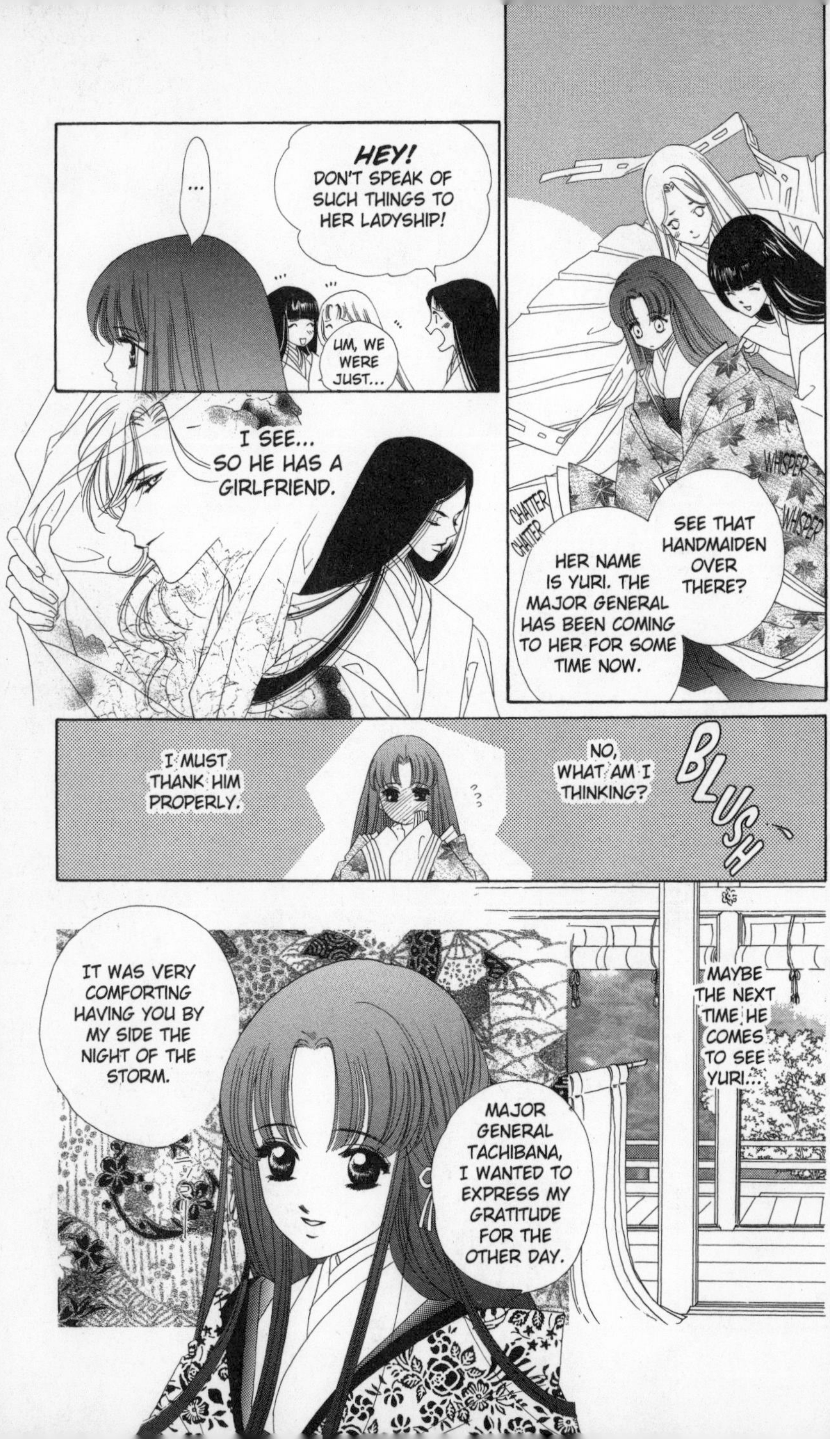
WHISPER
WHISPER
CHATTER
CHATTER
SEE THAT HANDMAIDEN OVER THERE?
HER NAME IS YURI. THE MAJOR GENERAL HAS BEEN COMING TO HER FOR SOME TIME NOW.
HEY! DON'T SPEAK OF SUCH THINGS TO HER LADYSHIP!
UM, WE WERE JUST...
...
I SEE... SO HE HAS A GIRLFRIEND.
BLUSH
NO, WHAT AM I THINKING?
I MUST THANK HIM PROPERLY.
MAYBE THE NEXT TIME HE COMES TO SEE YURI...
MAJOR GENERAL TACHIBANA, I WANTED TO EXPRESS MY GRATITUDE FOR THE OTHER DAY.
IT WAS VERY COMFORTING HAVING YOU BY MY SIDE THE NIGHT OF THE STORM.

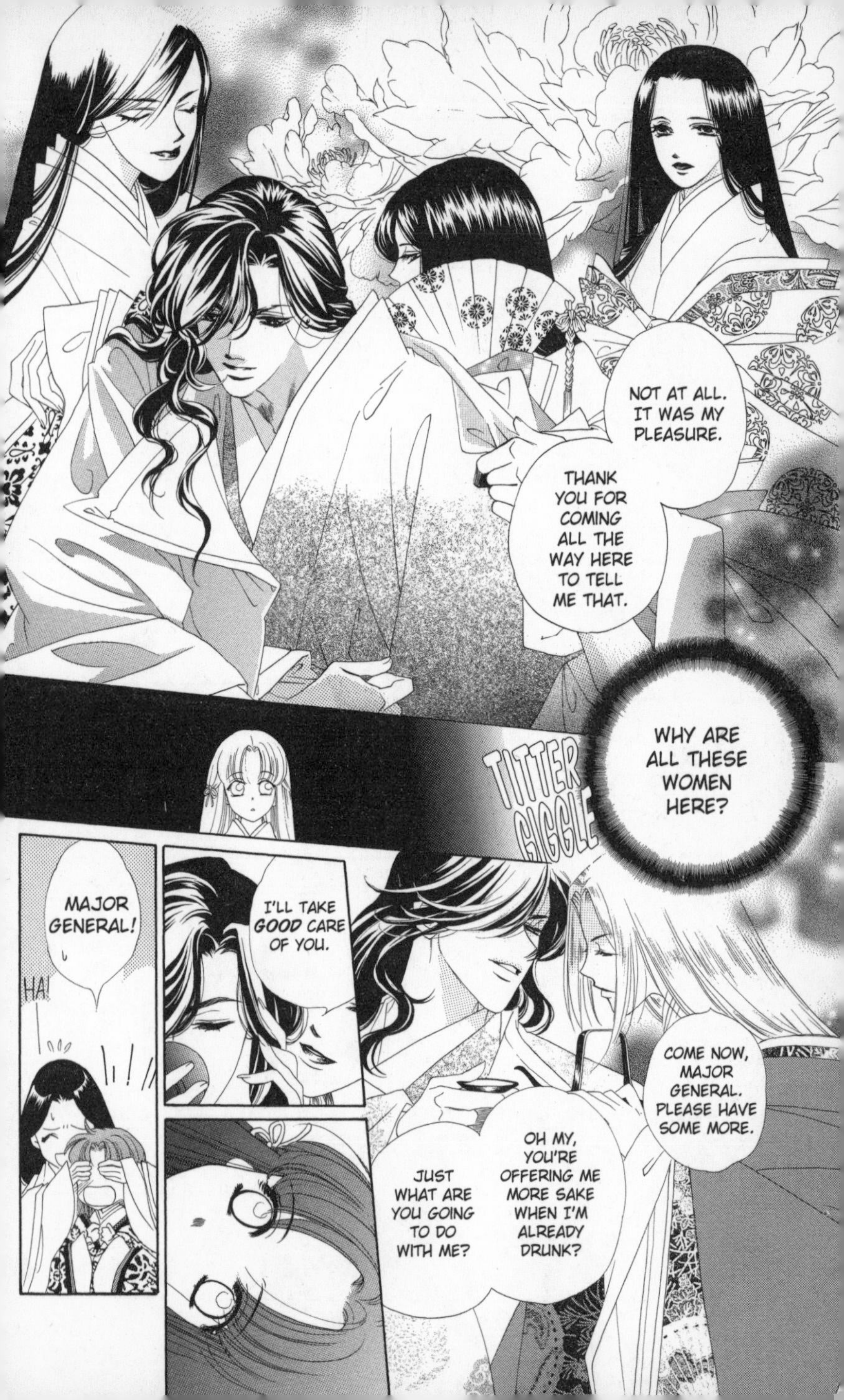
NOT AT ALL. IT WAS MY PLEASURE.
THANK YOU FOR COMING ALL THE WAY HERE TO TELL ME THAT.
WHY ARE ALL THESE WOMEN HERE?
TITTER
GIGGLE
COME NOW, MAJOR GENERAL. PLEASE HAVE SOME MORE.
OH MY, YOU'RE OFFERING ME MORE SAKE WHEN I'M ALREADY DRUNK?
JUST WHAT ARE YOU GOING TO DO WITH ME?
I'LL TAKE GOOD CARE OF YOU.
MAJOR GENERAL!
HA!

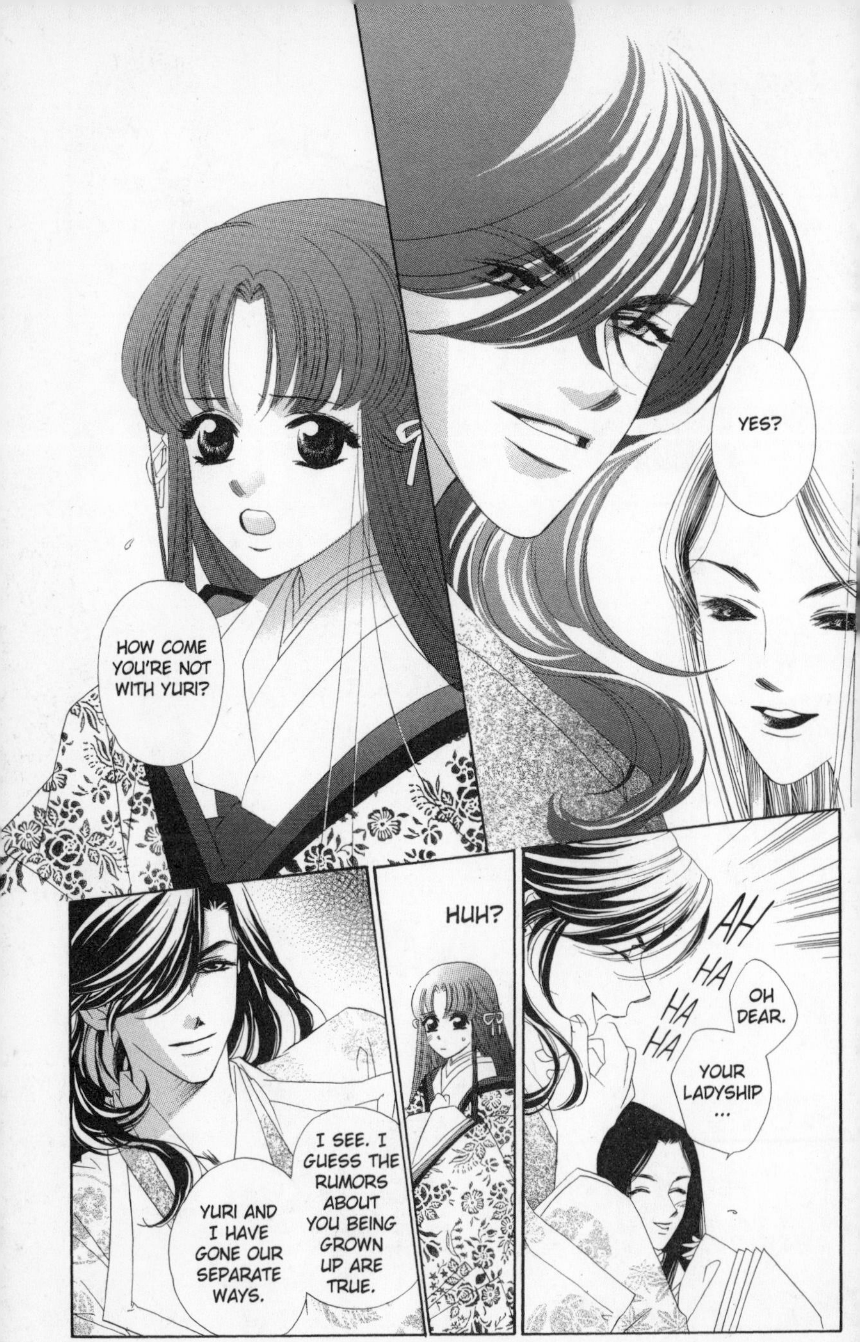
YES?
HOW COME YOU'RE NOT WITH YURI?
AH HA HA HA HA
OH DEAR.
YOUR LADYSHIP ...
HUH?
I SEE. I GUESS THE RUMORS ABOUT YOU BEING GROWN UP ARE TRUE.
YURI AND I HAVE GONE OUR SEPARATE WAYS.

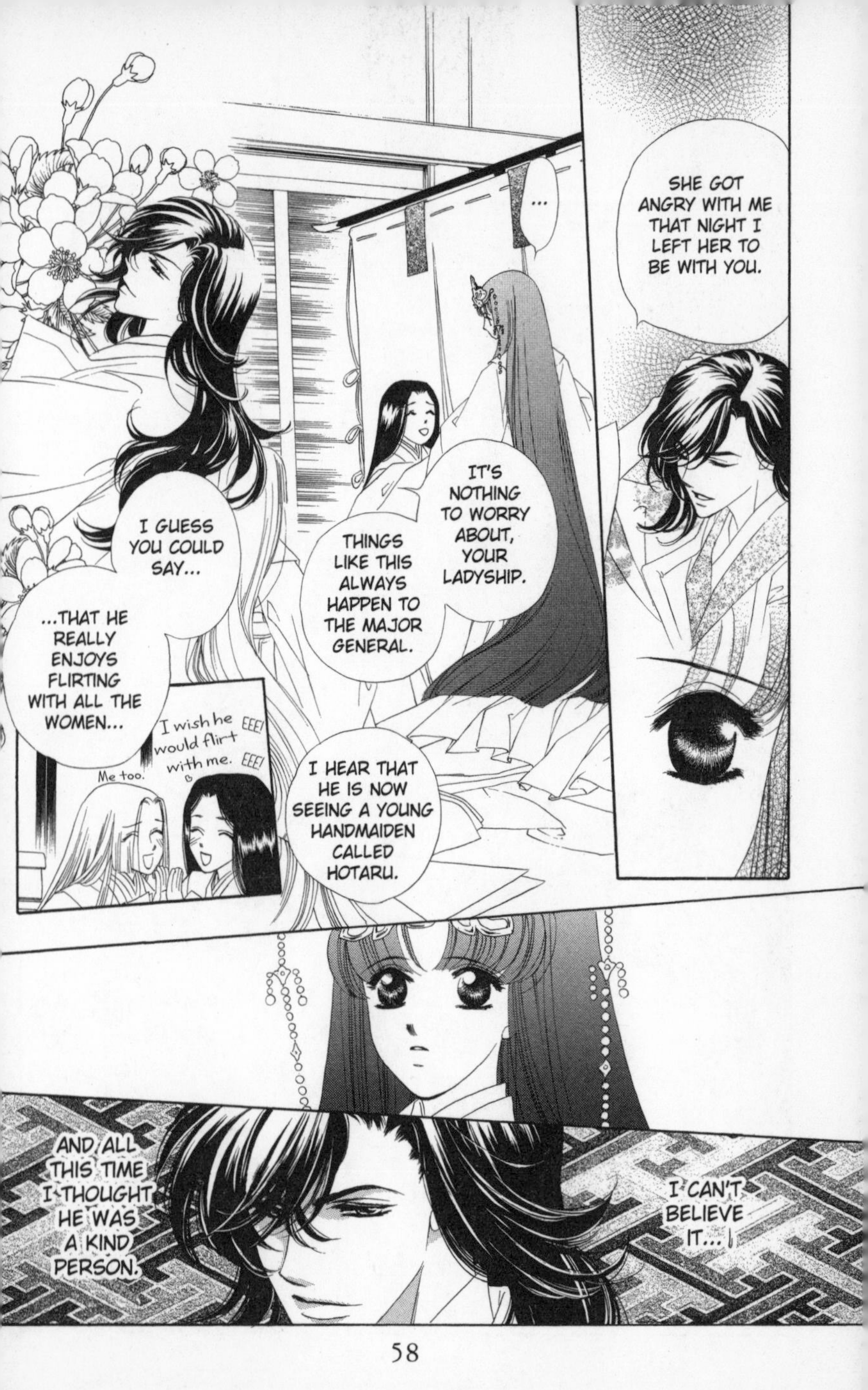
SHE GOT ANGRY WITH ME THAT NIGHT I LEFT HER TO BE WITH YOU.
...
IT'S NOTHING TO WORRY ABOUT, YOUR LADYSHIP.
THINGS LIKE THIS ALWAYS HAPPEN TO THE MAJOR GENERAL.
I GUESS YOU COULD SAY...
...THAT HE REALLY ENJOYS FLIRTING WITH ALL THE WOMEN...
EEE! EEE!
I wish he would flirt with me.
Me too.
I HEAR THAT HE IS NOW SEEING A YOUNG HANDMAIDEN CALLED HOTARU.
I CAN'T BELIEVE IT...
AND ALL THIS TIME I THOUGHT HE WAS A KIND PERSON.

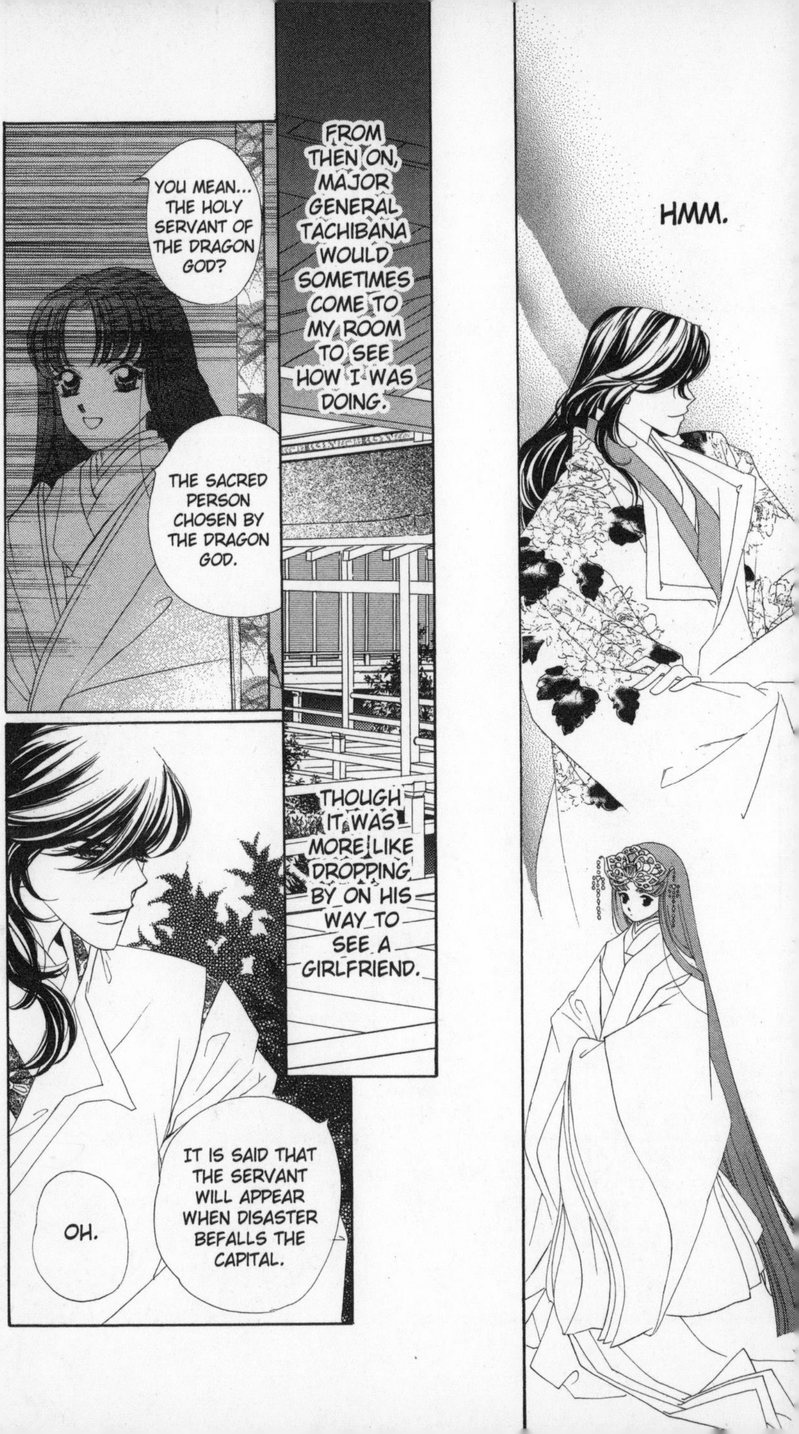
HMM.
FROM THEN ON, MAJOR GENERAL TACHIBANA WOULD SOMETIMES COME TO MY ROOM TO SEE HOW I WAS DOING.
THOUGH IT WAS MORE LIKE DROPPING BY ON HIS WAY TO SEE A GIRLFRIEND.
YOU MEAN... THE HOLY SERVANT OF THE DRAGON GOD?
THE SACRED PERSON CHOSEN BY THE DRAGON GOD.
IT IS SAID THAT THE SERVANT WILL APPEAR WHEN DISASTER BEFALLS THE CAPITAL.
OH.

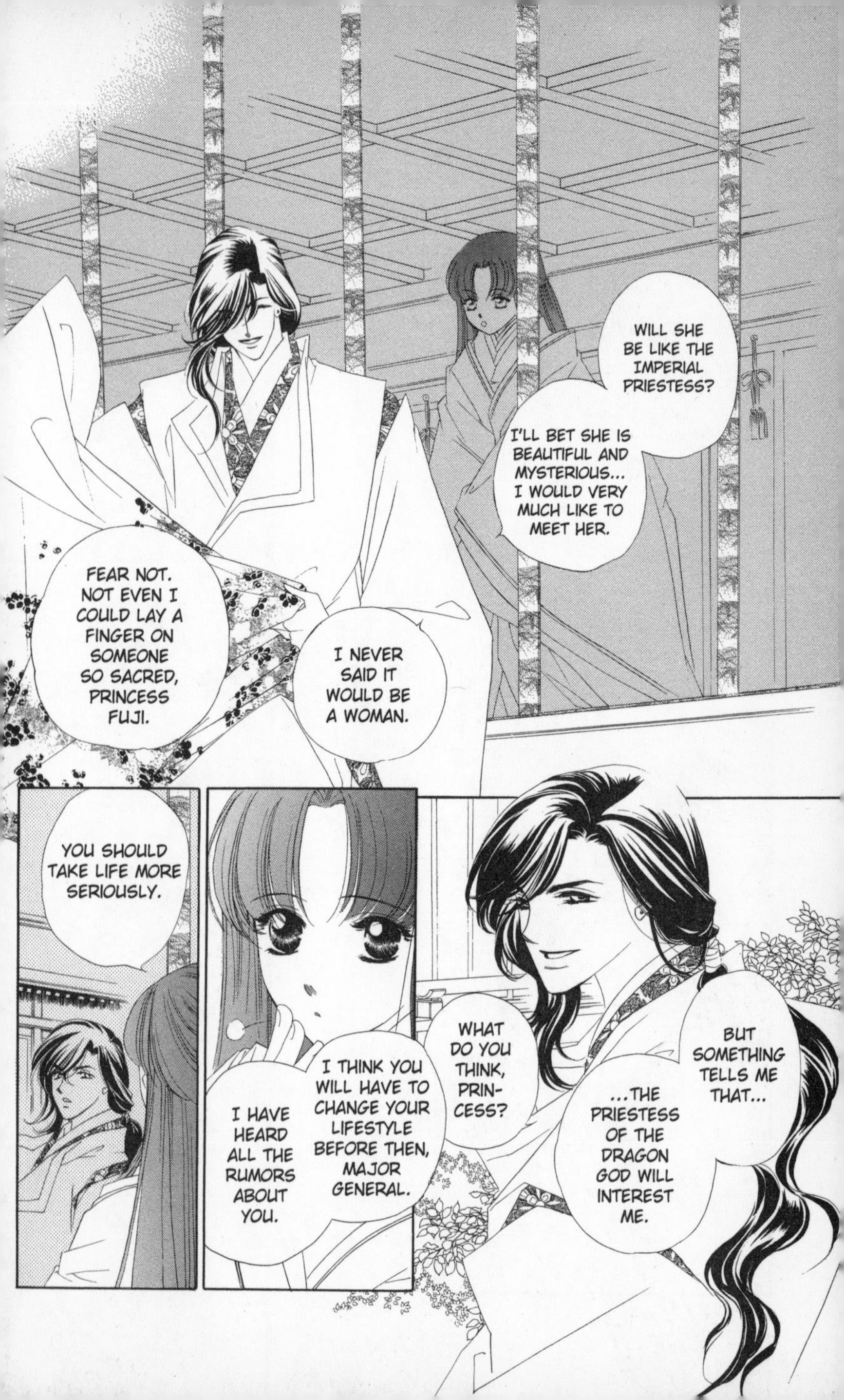
WILL SHE BE LIKE THE IMPERIAL PRIESTESS?
I'LL BET SHE IS BEAUTIFUL AND MYSTERIOUS... I WOULD VERY MUCH LIKE TO MEET HER.
I NEVER SAID IT WOULD BE A WOMAN.
FEAR NOT. NOT EVEN I COULD LAY A FINGER ON SOMEONE SO SACRED, PRINCESS FUJI.
BUT SOMETHING TELLS ME THAT...
...THE PRIESTESS OF THE DRAGON GOD WILL INTEREST ME.
WHAT DO YOU THINK, PRIN-CESS?
I THINK YOU WILL HAVE TO CHANGE YOUR LIFESTYLE BEFORE THEN, MAJOR GENERAL.
I HAVE HEARD ALL THE RUMORS ABOUT YOU.
YOU SHOULD TAKE LIFE MORE SERIOUSLY.

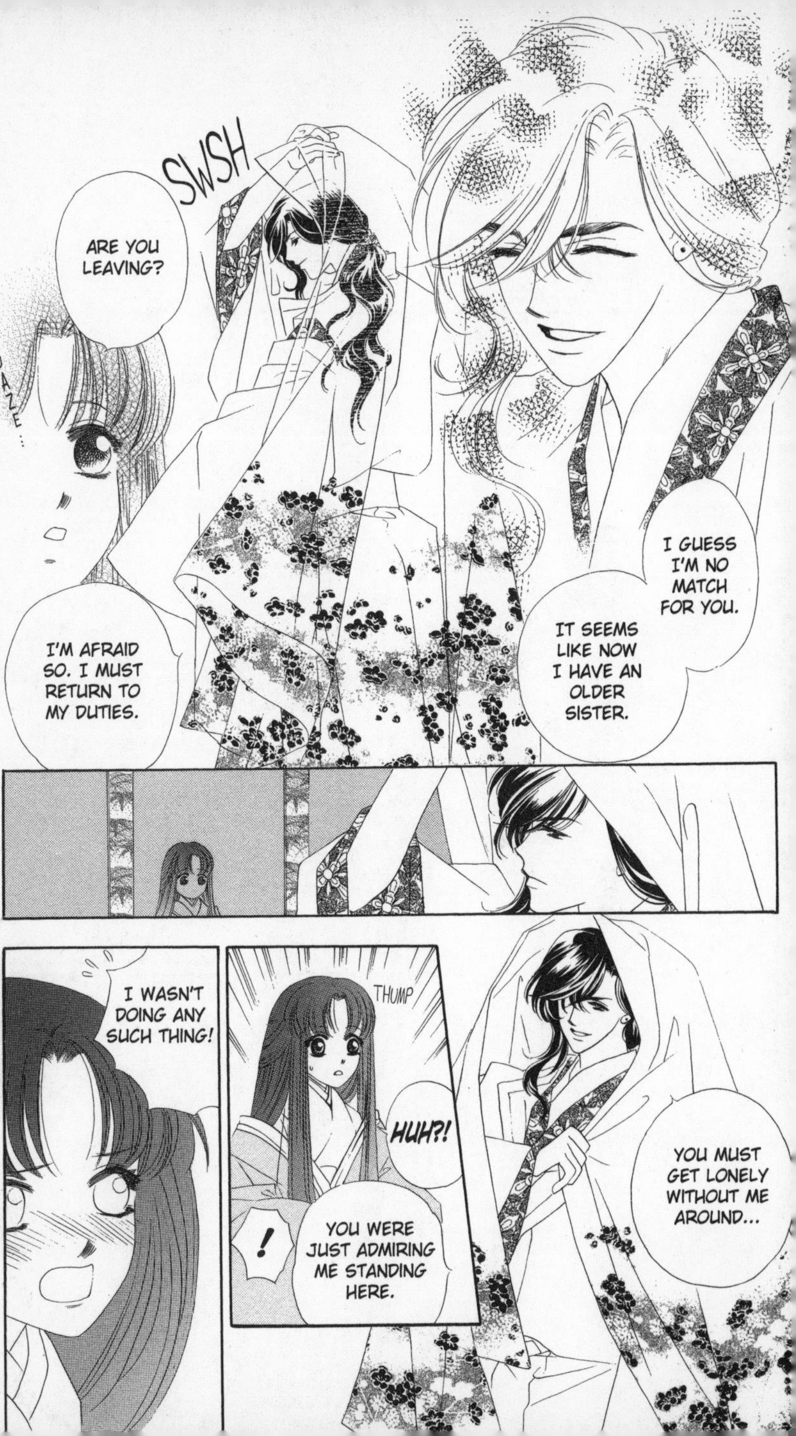
I GUESS I'M NO MATCH FOR YOU.
IT SEEMS LIKE NOW I HAVE AN OLDER SISTER.
SWSH
ARE YOU LEAVING?
GAZE...
I'M AFRAID SO. I MUST RETURN TO MY DUTIES.
YOU MUST GET LONELY WITHOUT ME AROUND...
THUMP
HUH?!
!
YOU WERE JUST ADMIRING ME STANDING HERE.
I WASN'T DOING ANY SUCH THING!

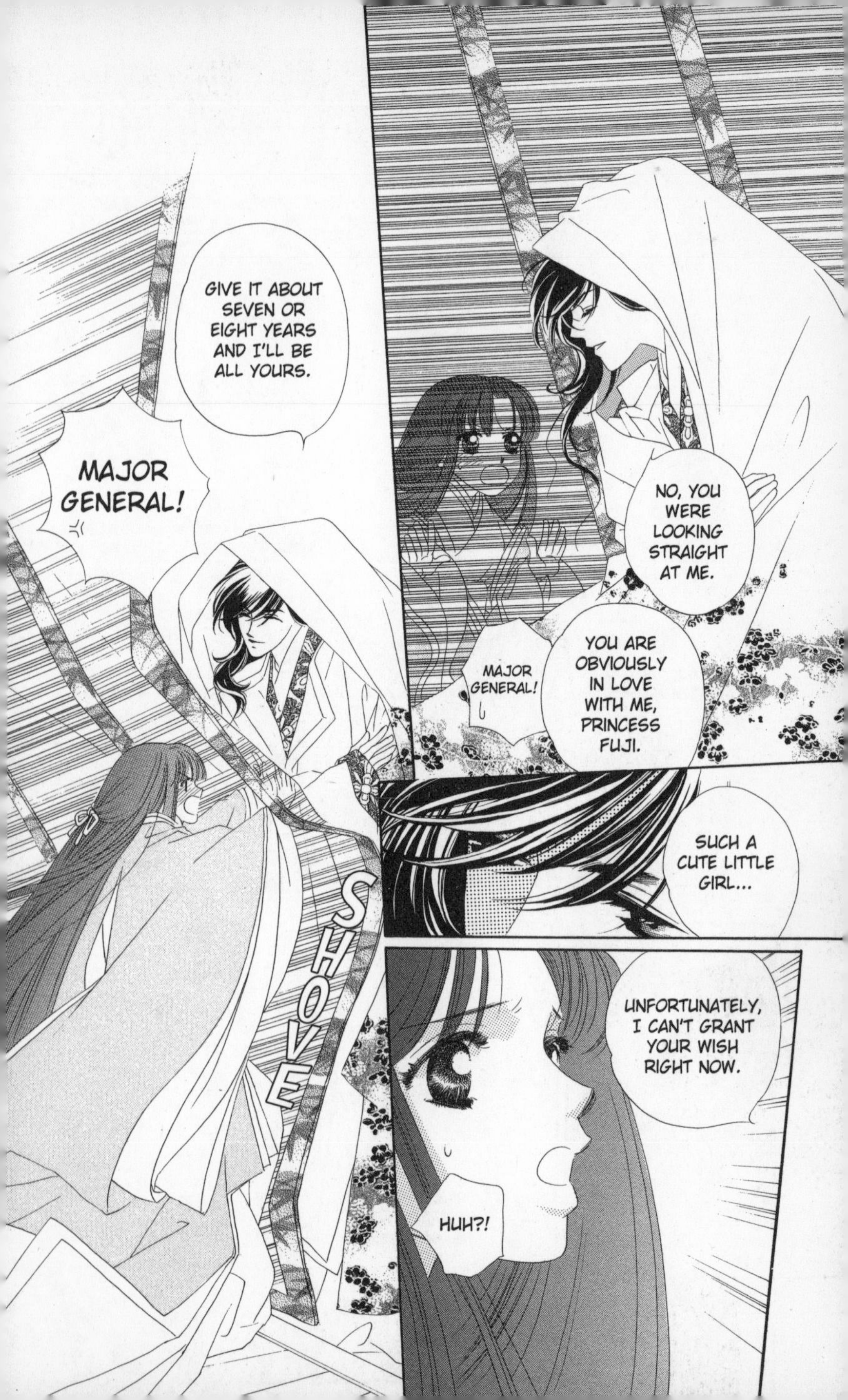
NO, YOU WERE LOOKING STRAIGHT AT ME.
YOU ARE OBVIOUSLY IN LOVE WITH ME, PRINCESS FUJI.
MAJOR GENERAL!
SUCH A CUTE LITTLE GIRL...
UNFORTUNATELY, I CAN'T GRANT YOUR WISH RIGHT NOW.
HUH?!
GIVE IT ABOUT SEVEN OR EIGHT YEARS AND I'LL BE ALL YOURS.
MAJOR GENERAL!
SHOVE

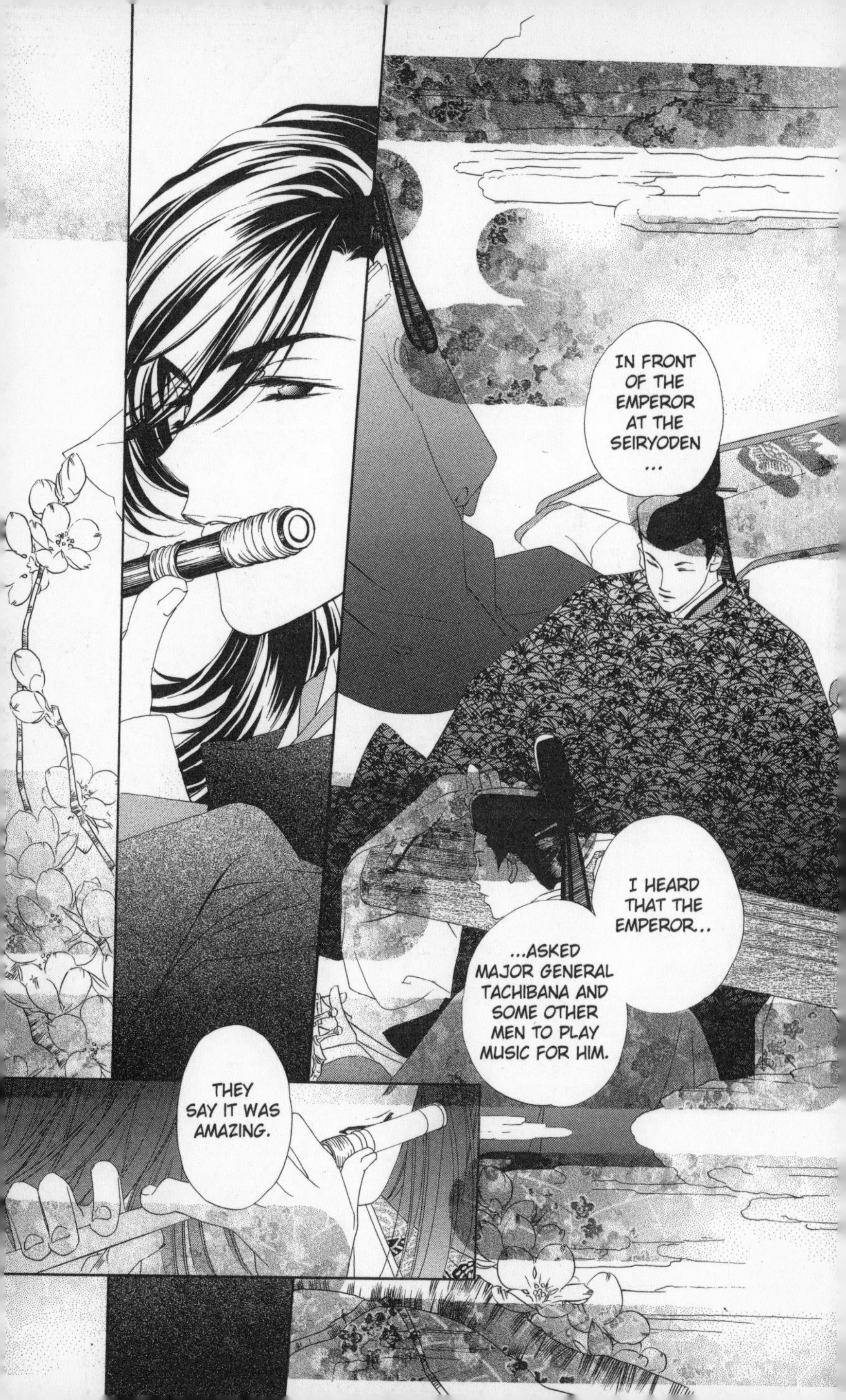
IN FRONT OF THE EMPEROR AT THE SEIRYODEN...
I HEARD THAT THE EMPEROR...
...ASKED MAJOR GENERAL TACHIBANA AND SOME OTHER MEN TO PLAY MUSIC FOR HIM.
THEY SAY IT WAS AMAZING.

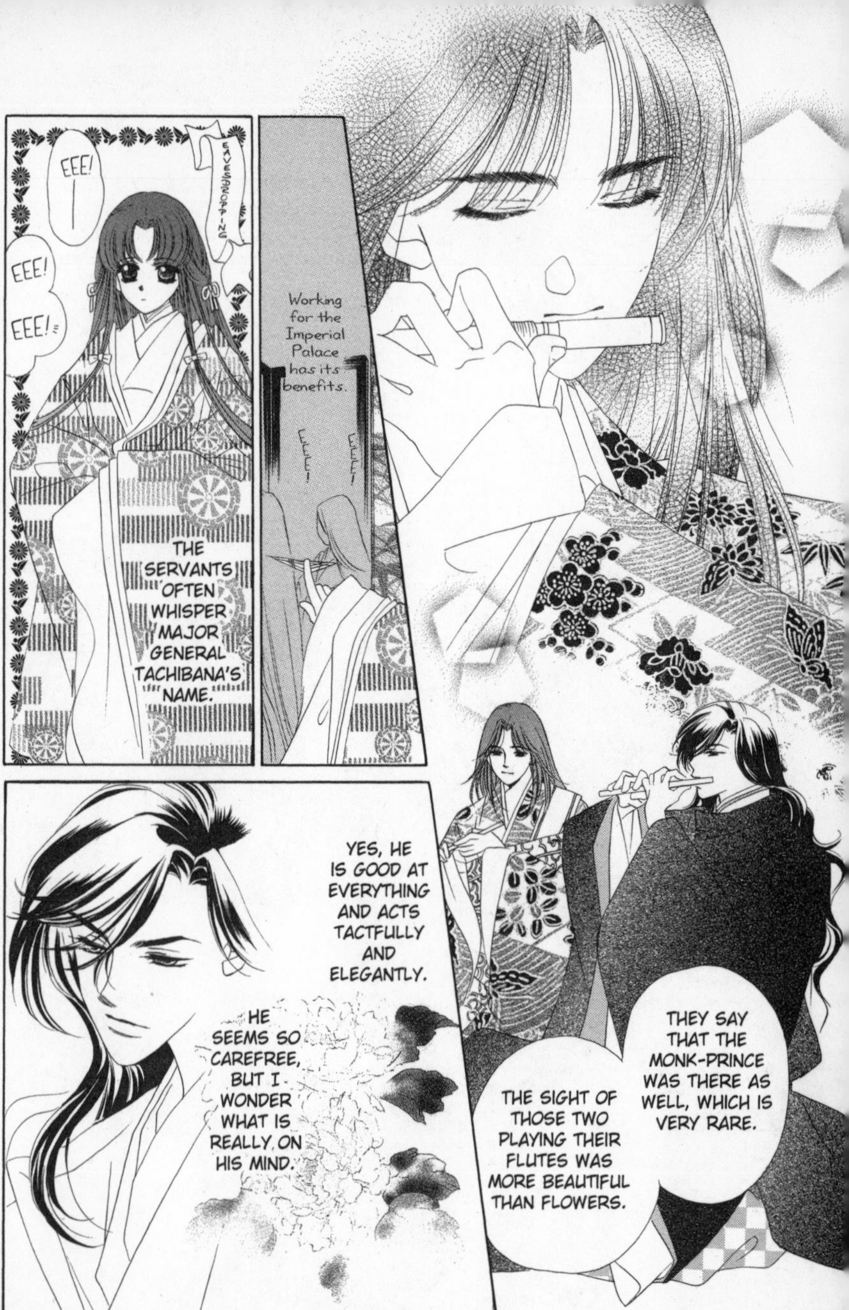
THEY SAY THAT THE MONK-PRINCE WAS THERE AS WELL, WHICH IS VERY RARE.
THE SIGHT OF THOSE TWO PLAYING THEIR FLUTES WAS MORE BEAUTIFUL THAN FLOWERS.
Working for the Imperial Palace has its benefits.
EEE!
EEE!
EAVESDROPPING
EEE!
EEE!
EEE!
THE SERVANTS OFTEN WHISPER MAJOR GENERAL TACHIBANA'S NAME.
YES, HE IS GOOD AT EVERYTHING AND ACTS TACTFULLY AND ELEGANTLY.
HE SEEMS SO CAREFREE, BUT I WONDER WHAT IS REALLY ON HIS MIND.

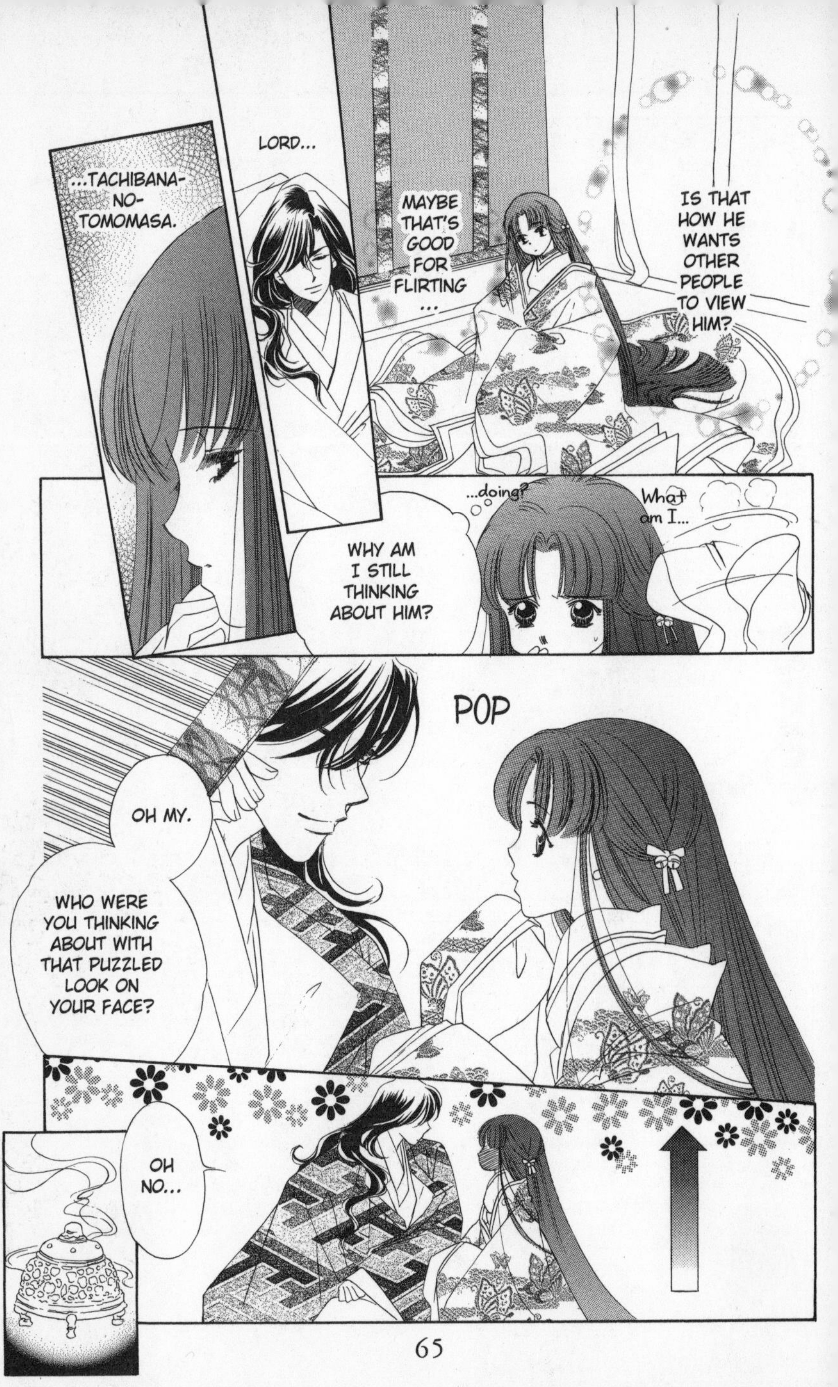
IS THAT HOW HE WANTS OTHER PEOPLE TO VIEW HIM?
MAYBE THAT'S GOOD FOR FLIRTING...
LORD...
...TACHIBANA-NO-TOMOMASA.
What am I...
...doing?
WHY AM I STILL THINKING ABOUT HIM?
POP
OH MY.
WHO WERE YOU THINKING ABOUT WITH THAT PUZZLED LOOK ON YOUR FACE?
OH NO...

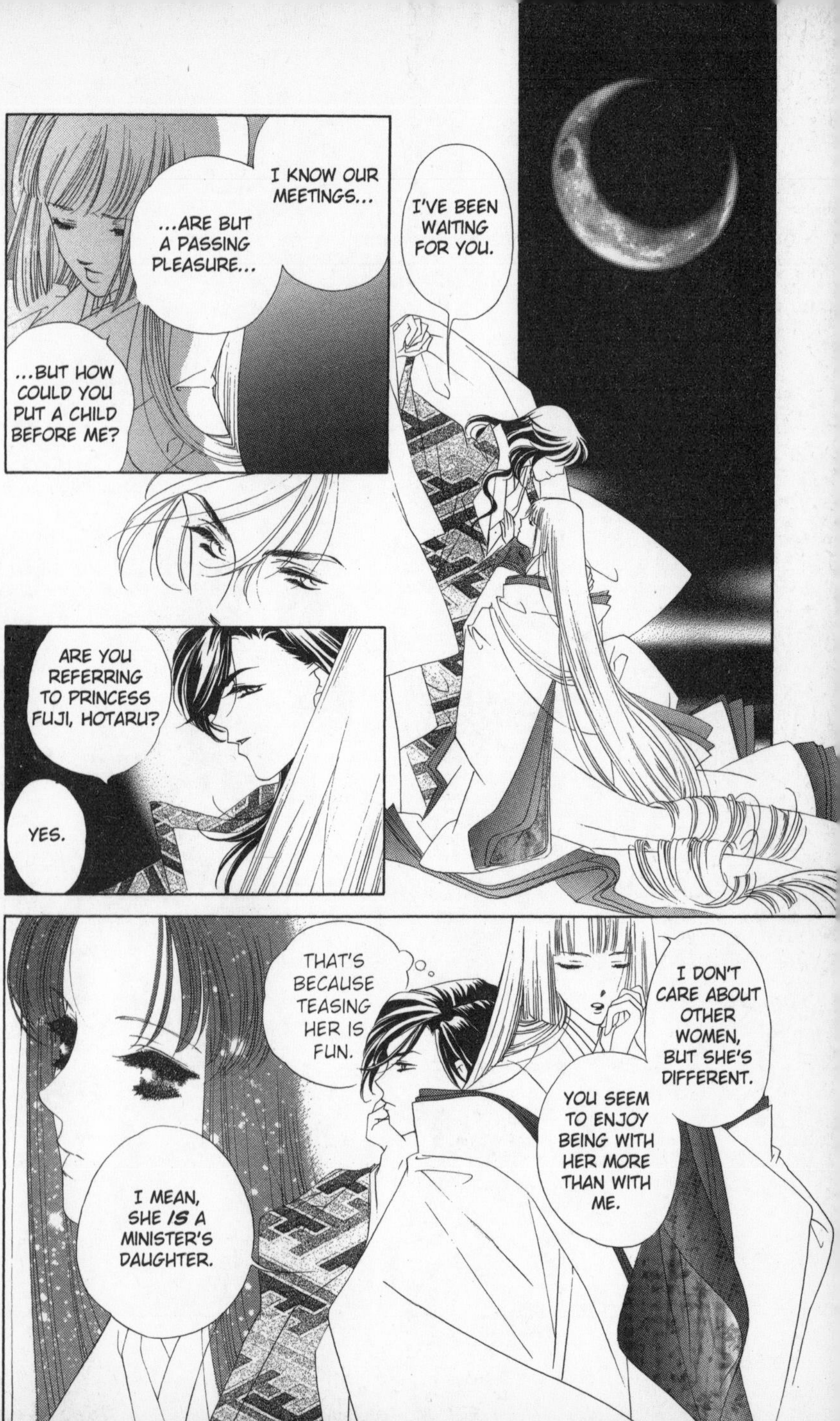
I'VE BEEN WAITING FOR YOU.
I KNOW OUR MEETINGS...
...ARE BUT A PASSING PLEASURE...
...BUT HOW COULD YOU PUT A CHILD BEFORE ME?
ARE YOU REFERRING TO PRINCESS FUJI, HOTARU?
YES.
I DON'T CARE ABOUT OTHER WOMEN, BUT SHE'S DIFFERENT.
YOU SEEM TO ENJOY BEING WITH HER MORE THAN WITH ME.
THAT'S BECAUSE TEASING HER IS FUN.
I MEAN, SHE *IS* A MINISTER'S DAUGHTER.

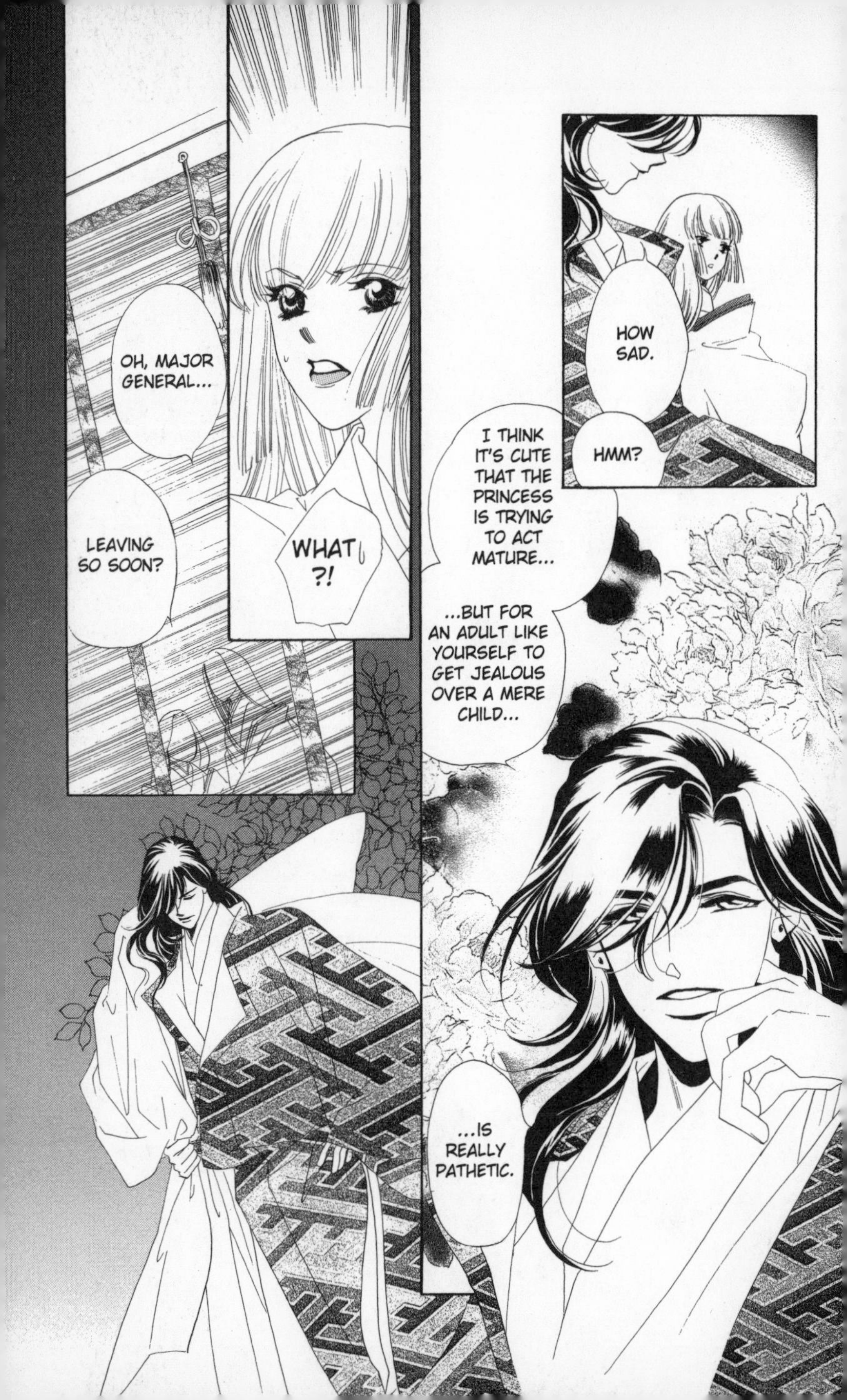
HOW SAD.
HMM?
I THINK IT'S CUTE THAT THE PRINCESS IS TRYING TO ACT MATURE...
...BUT FOR AN ADULT LIKE YOURSELF TO GET JEALOUS OVER A MERE CHILD...
...IS REALLY PATHETIC.
WHAT ?!
OH, MAJOR GENERAL...
LEAVING SO SOON?

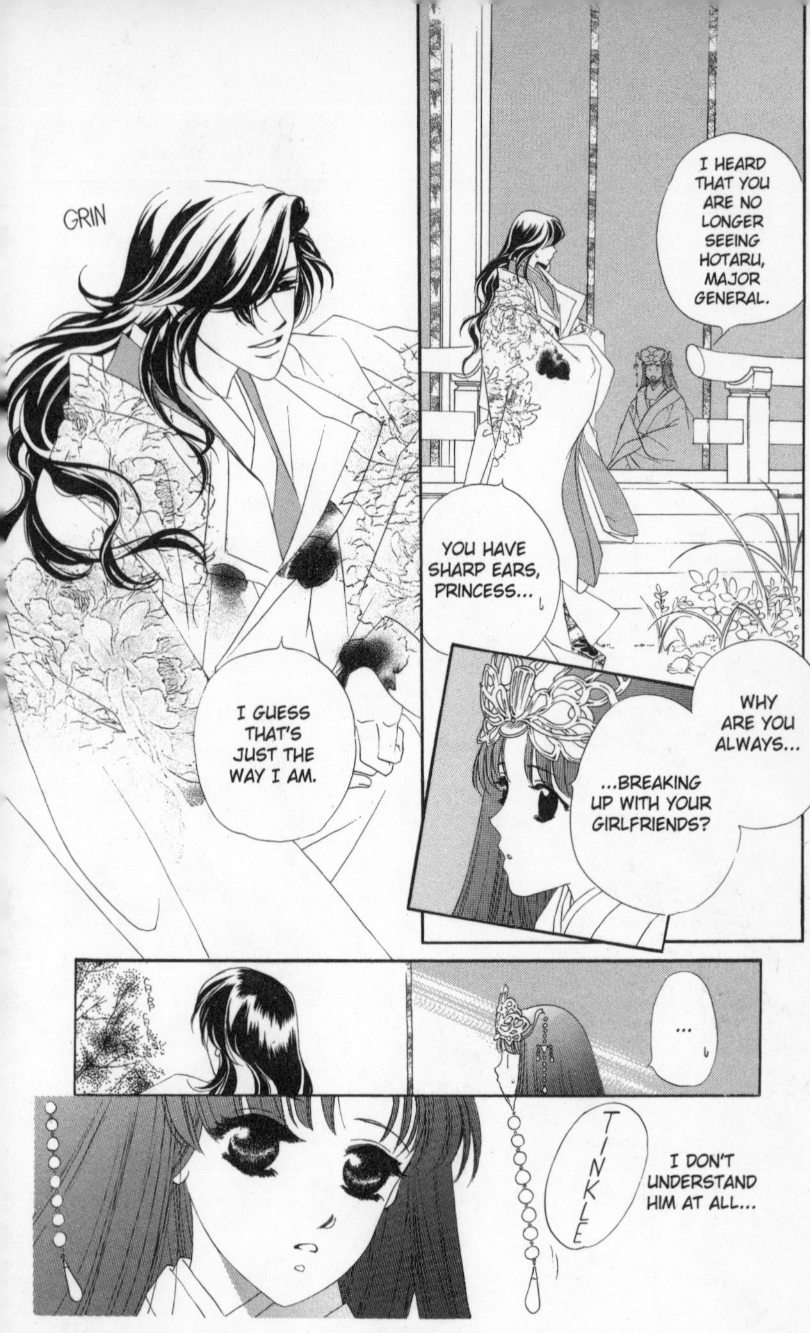
I HEARD THAT YOU ARE NO LONGER SEEING HOTARU, MAJOR GENERAL.
YOU HAVE SHARP EARS, PRINCESS...
WHY ARE YOU ALWAYS...
...BREAKING UP WITH YOUR GIRLFRIENDS?
GRIN
I GUESS THAT'S JUST THE WAY I AM.
...
TINKLE
I DON'T UNDERSTAND HIM AT ALL...

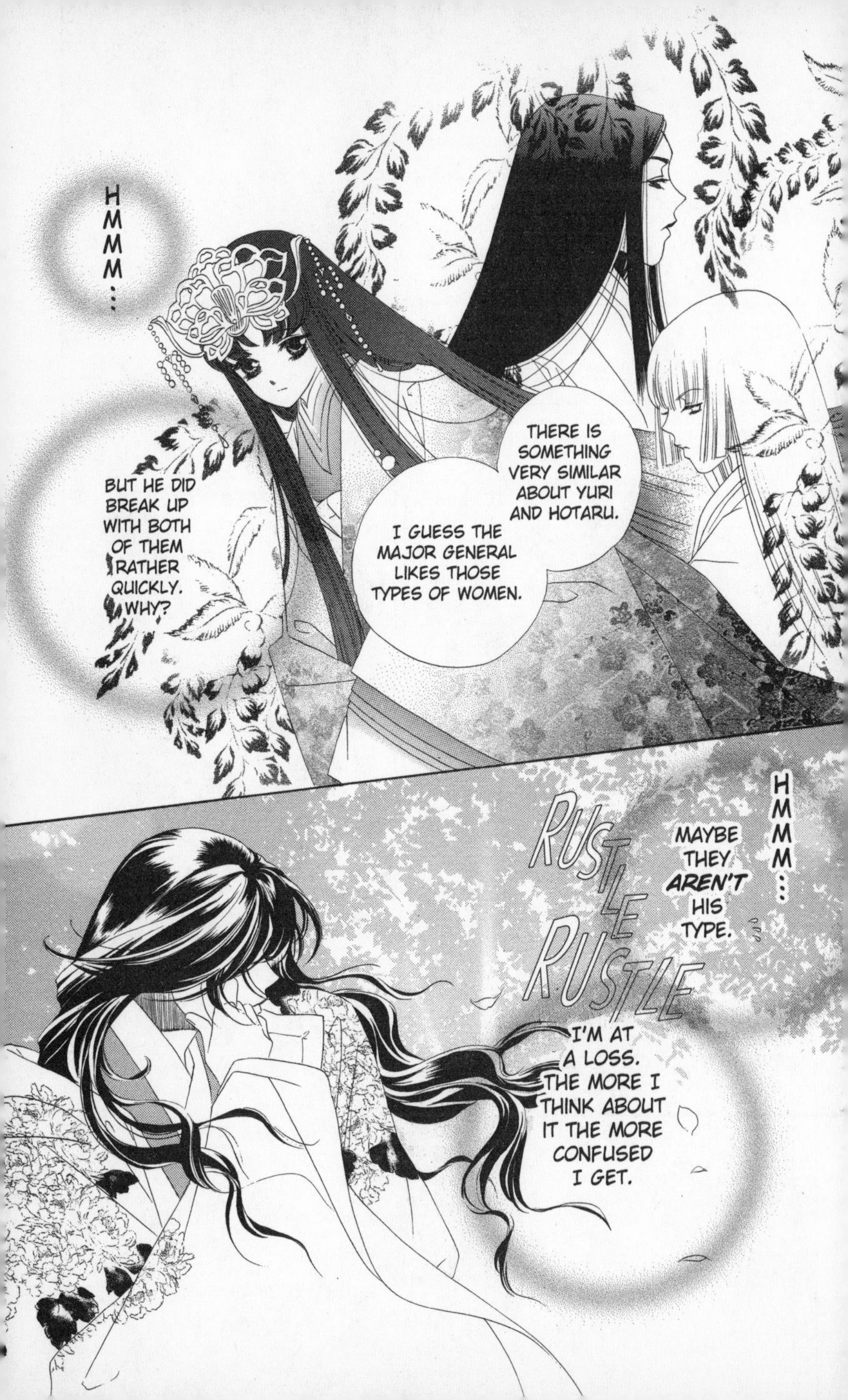
THERE IS SOMETHING VERY SIMILAR ABOUT YURI AND HOTARU.
I GUESS THE MAJOR GENERAL LIKES THOSE TYPES OF WOMEN.
BUT HE DID BREAK UP WITH BOTH OF THEM RATHER QUICKLY. WHY?
HMMM...
HMMM...
MAYBE THEY AREN'T HIS TYPE.
RUSTLE RUSTLE
I'M AT A LOSS. THE MORE I THINK ABOUT IT THE MORE CONFUSED I GET.

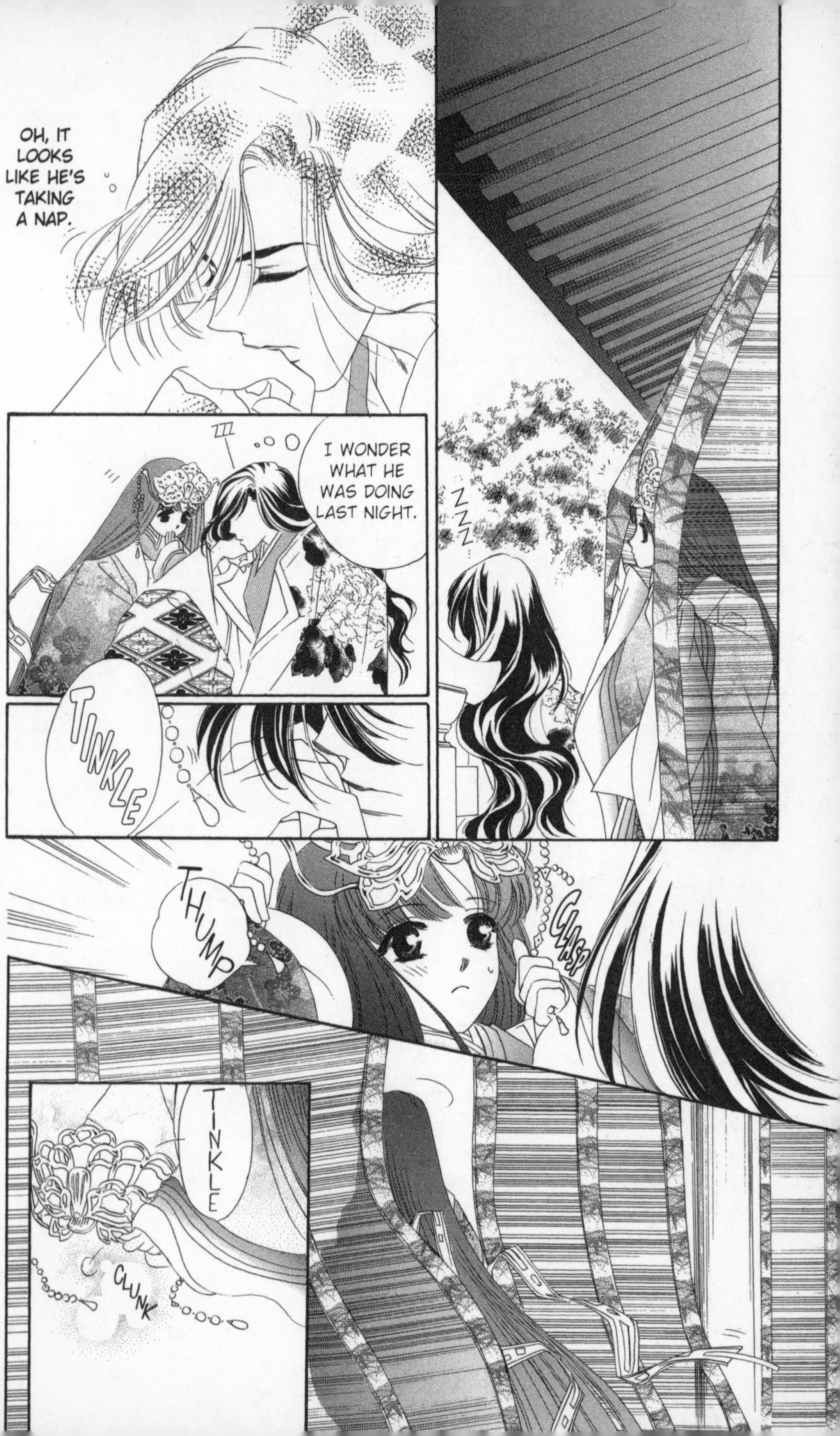
ZZZ
OH, IT LOOKS LIKE HE'S TAKING A NAP.
ZZZ
I WONDER WHAT HE WAS DOING LAST NIGHT.
TINKLE
CLASP
THUMP
TINKLE
CLUNK

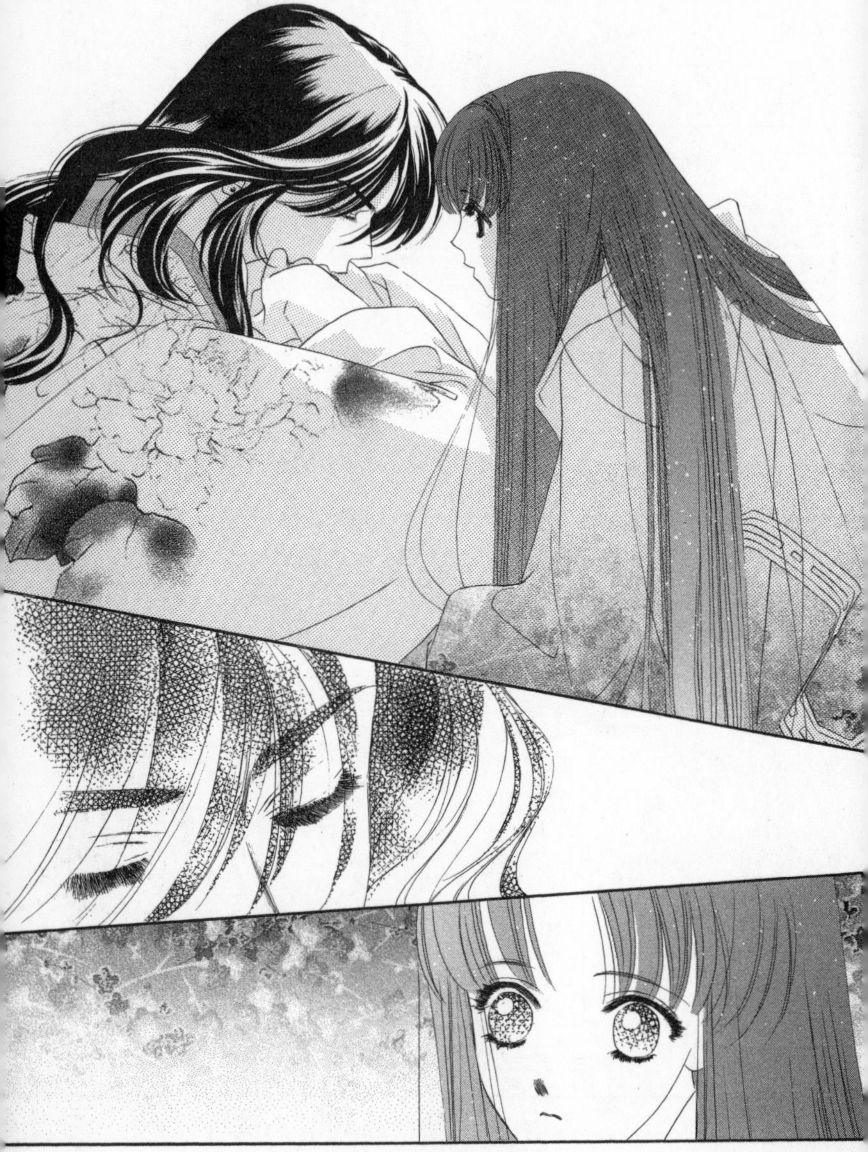

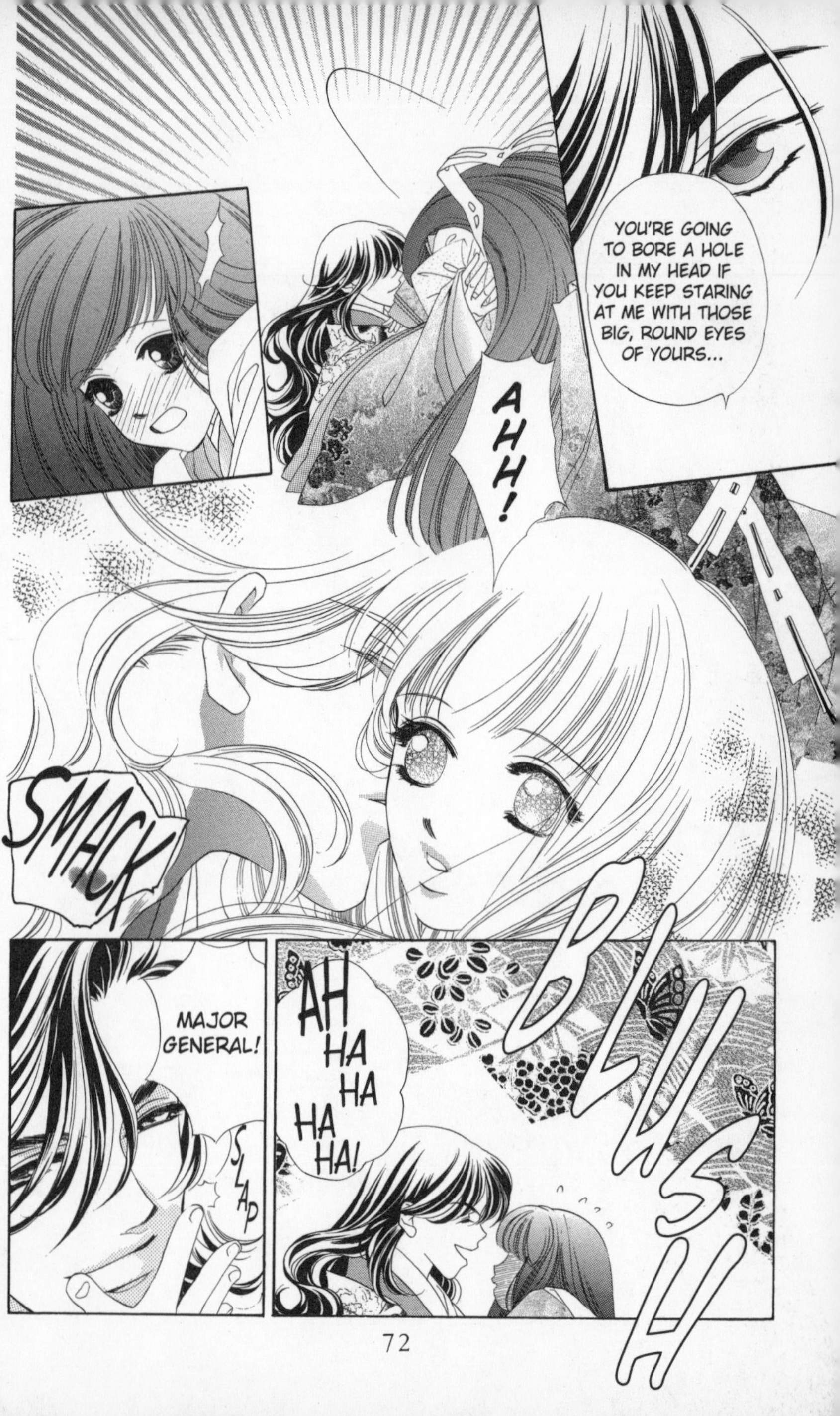
YOU'RE GOING TO BORE A HOLE IN MY HEAD IF YOU KEEP STARING AT ME WITH THOSE BIG, ROUND EYES OF YOURS...
AHHH!
SMACK
BLUSH
AH HA HA HA HA!
MAJOR GENERAL!
SLAP

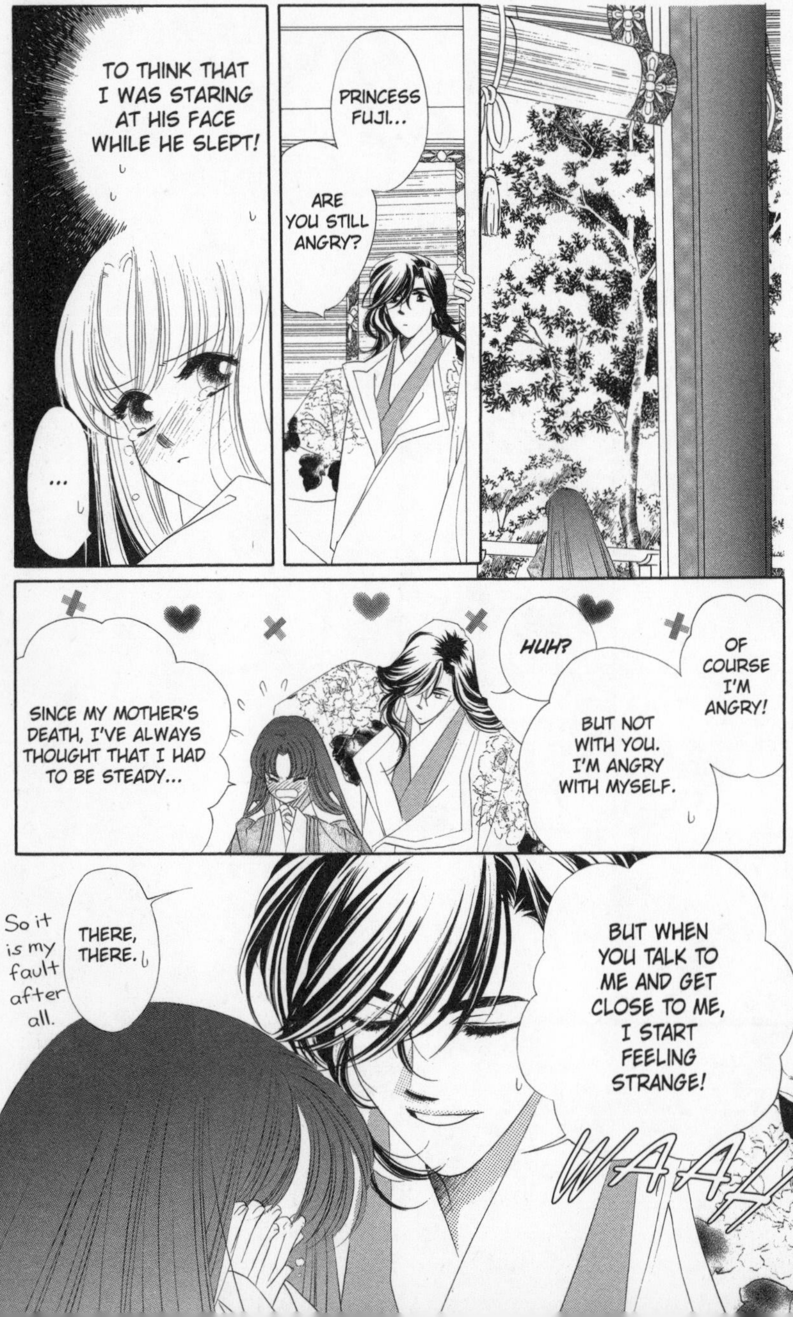
PRINCESS FUJI...
ARE YOU STILL ANGRY?
TO THINK THAT I WAS STARING AT HIS FACE WHILE HE SLEPT!
...
OF COURSE I'M ANGRY!
HUH?
BUT NOT WITH YOU. I'M ANGRY WITH MYSELF.
SINCE MY MOTHER'S DEATH, I'VE ALWAYS THOUGHT THAT I HAD TO BE STEADY...
BUT WHEN YOU TALK TO ME AND GET CLOSE TO ME, I START FEELING STRANGE!
WAAH
THERE, THERE.
So it is my fault after all.

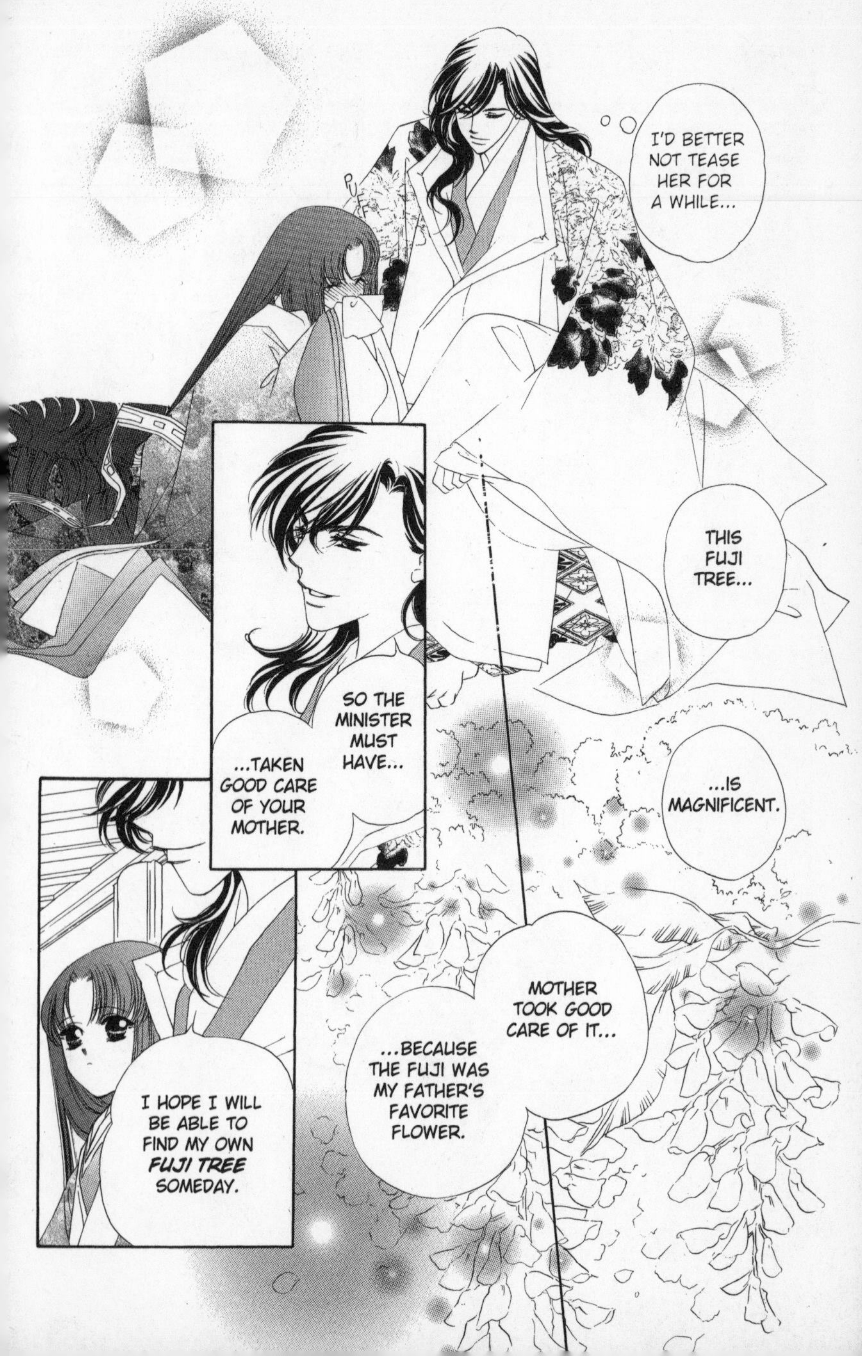
I'D BETTER NOT TEASE HER FOR A WHILE...
PUFF
THIS FUJI TREE...
...IS MAGNIFICENT.
SO THE MINISTER MUST HAVE...
...TAKEN GOOD CARE OF YOUR MOTHER.
MOTHER TOOK GOOD CARE OF IT...
...BECAUSE THE FUJI WAS MY FATHER'S FAVORITE FLOWER.
I HOPE I WILL BE ABLE TO FIND MY OWN *FUJI TREE* SOMEDAY.

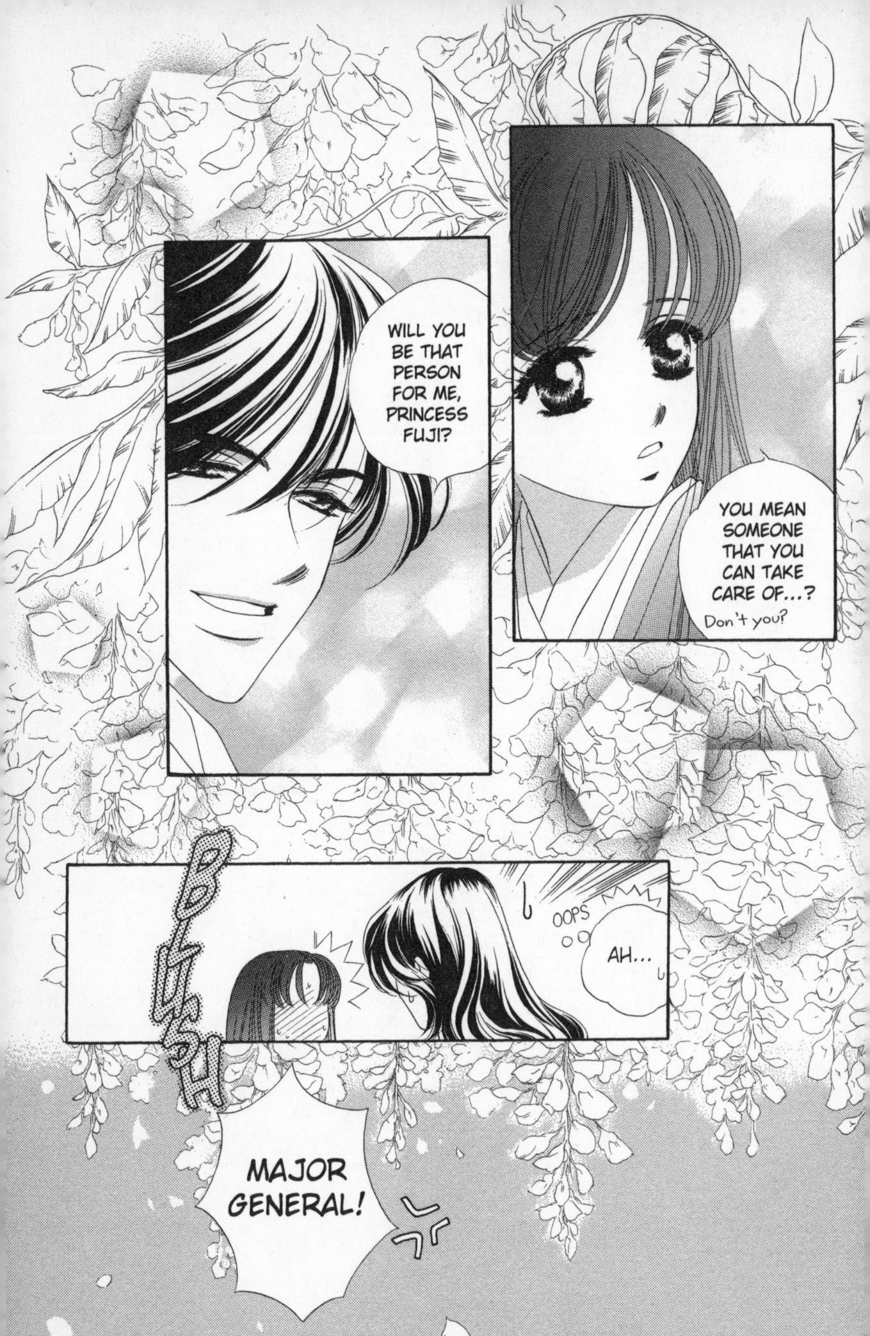
YOU MEAN SOMEONE THAT YOU CAN TAKE CARE OF...?
Don't you?
WILL YOU BE THAT PERSON FOR ME, PRINCESS FUJI?
OOPS
AH...
BLUSH
MAJOR GENERAL!

TACHIBANA'S FONDNESS FOR FUJI/END

THE EIGHT GUARDIANS: WHAT YOU WISH THEY'D SAY

<Tachibana-no-Tomomasa>

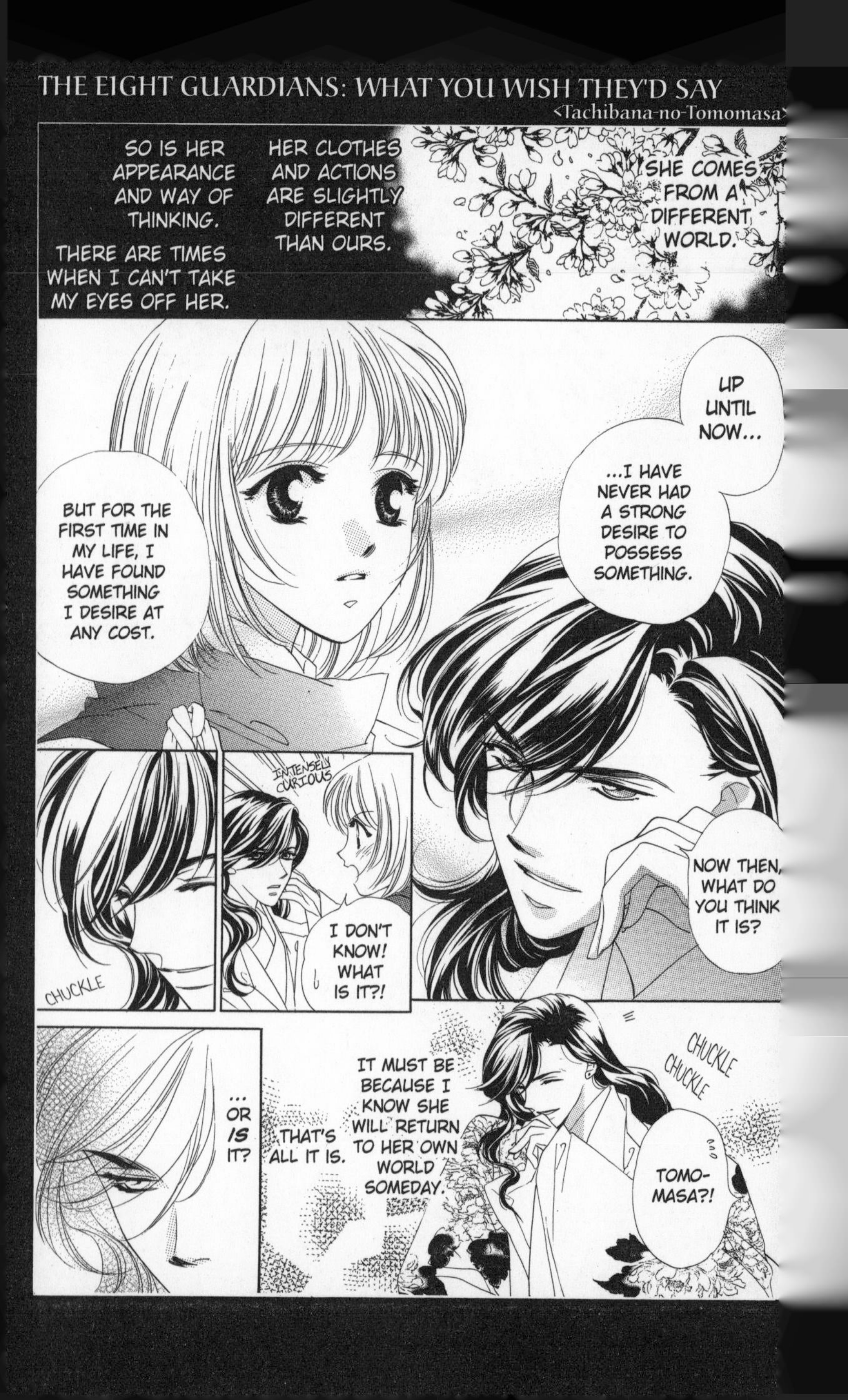
SHE COMES FROM A DIFFERENT WORLD.
HER CLOTHES AND ACTIONS ARE SLIGHTLY DIFFERENT THAN OURS.
SO IS HER APPEARANCE AND WAY OF THINKING.
THERE ARE TIMES WHEN I CAN'T TAKE MY EYES OFF HER.
UP UNTIL NOW...
...I HAVE NEVER HAD A STRONG DESIRE TO POSSESS SOMETHING.
BUT FOR THE FIRST TIME IN MY LIFE, I HAVE FOUND SOMETHING I DESIRE AT ANY COST.
NOW THEN, WHAT DO YOU THINK IT IS?
INTENSELY CURIOUS
I DON'T KNOW! WHAT IS IT?!
CHUCKLE
CHUCKLE CHUCKLE
TOMO-MASA?!
IT MUST BE BECAUSE I KNOW SHE WILL RETURN TO HER OWN WORLD SOMEDAY.
THAT'S ALL IT IS.
...OR *IS* IT?

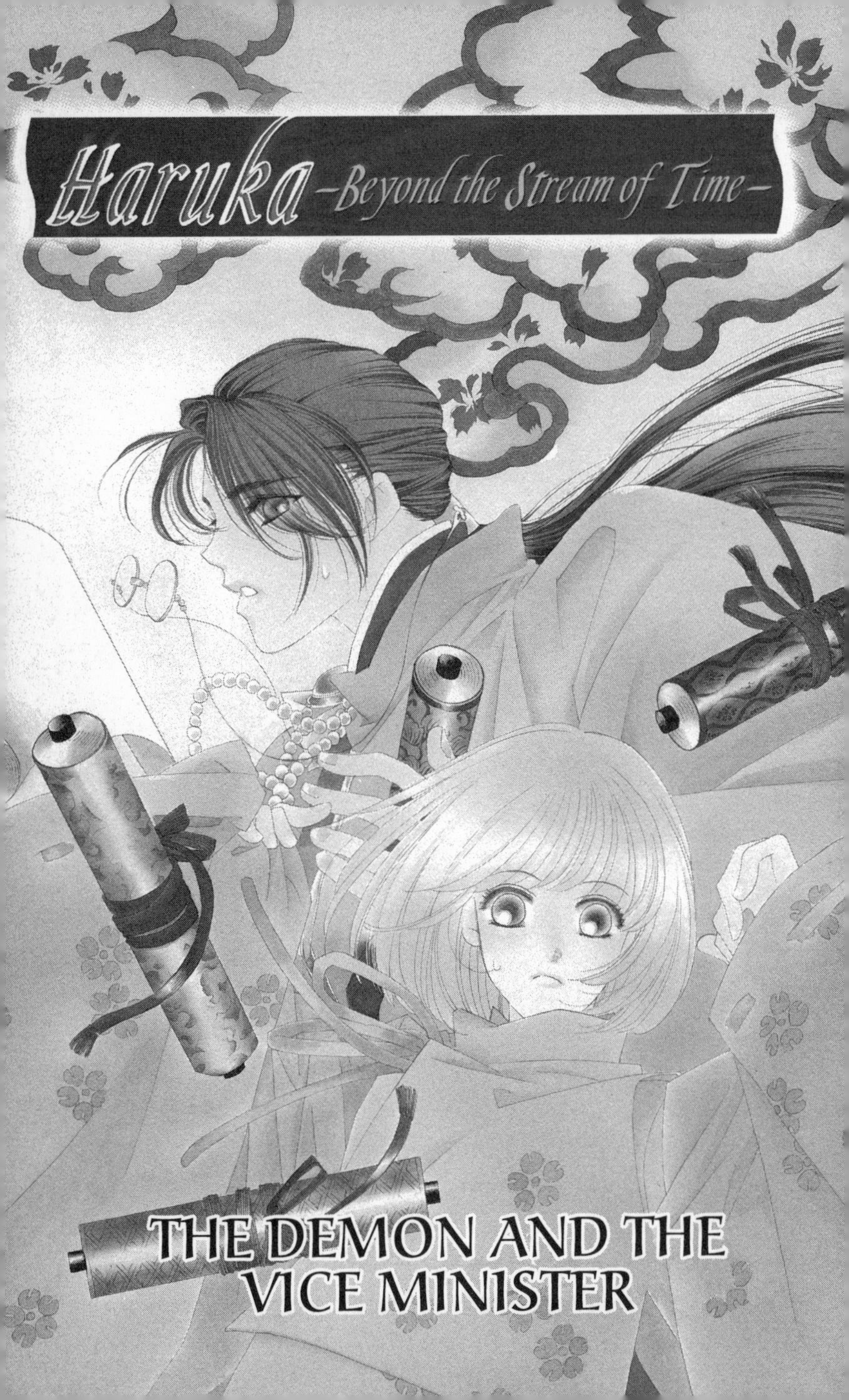
Haruka -Beyond the Stream of Time-
THE DEMON AND THE VICE MINISTER

THE EIGHT GUARDIANS: WHAT YOU WISH THEY'D SAY

<Tenma Morimura>

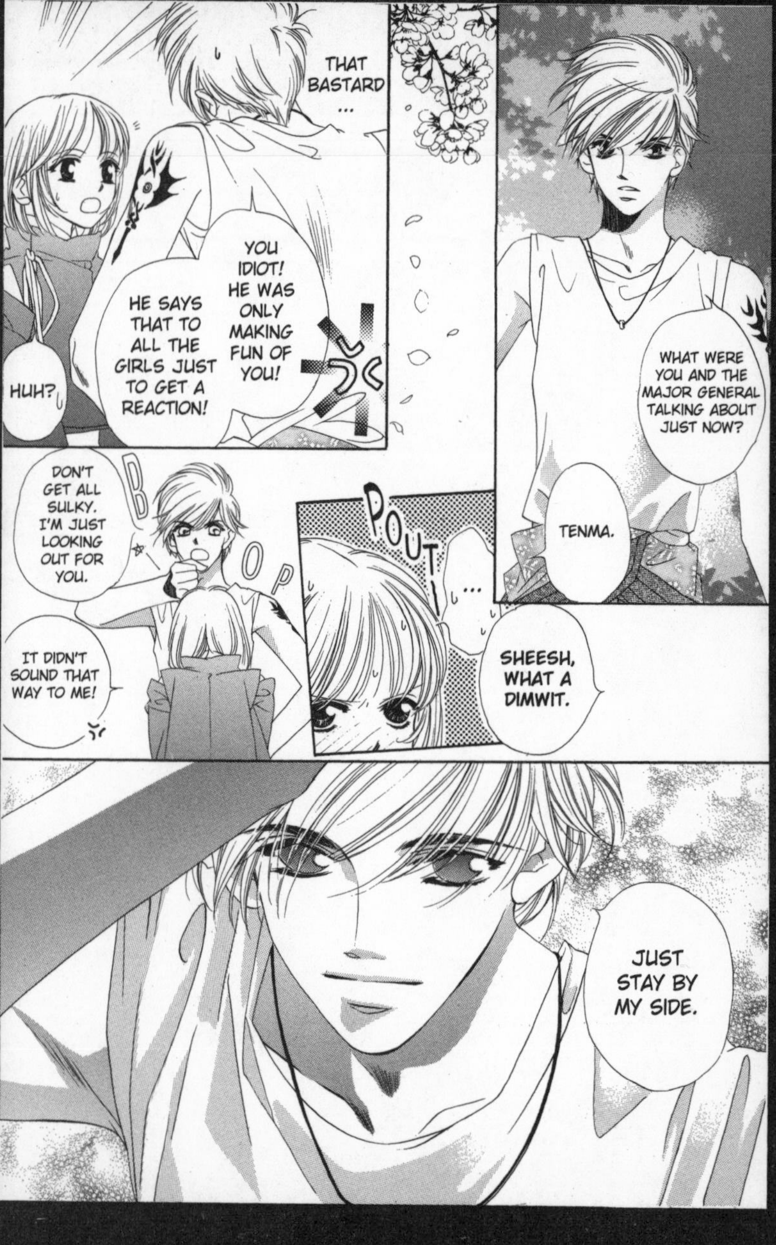

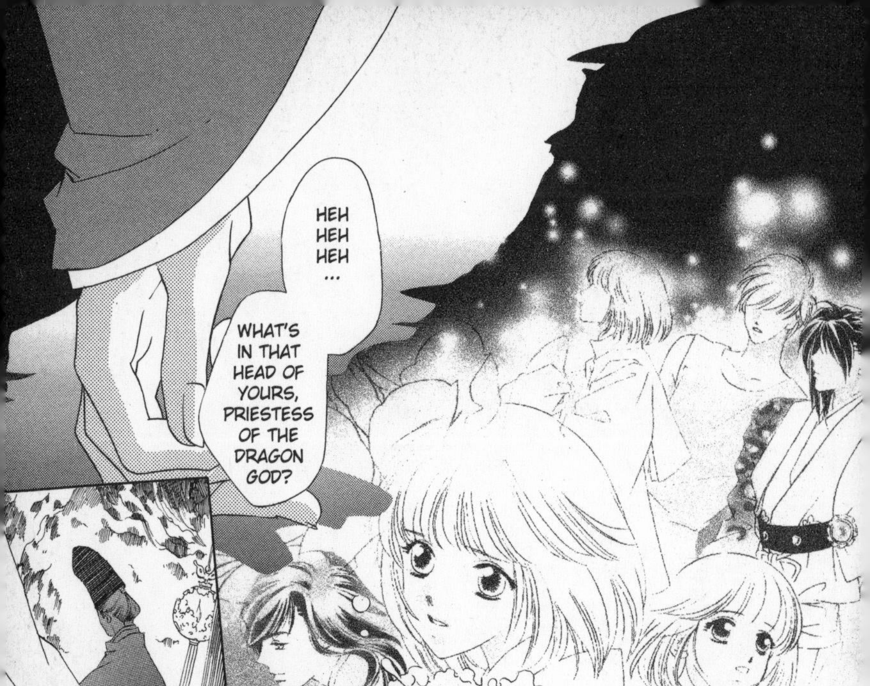
HEH HEH HEH ...
WHAT'S IN THAT HEAD OF YOURS, PRIESTESS OF THE DRAGON GOD?
HOW CAN SUCH TERRIFIED EYES BE SO CAPTIVATING?
IT MAKES ME WANT TO BREAK YOU EVEN MORE.
MASTER.

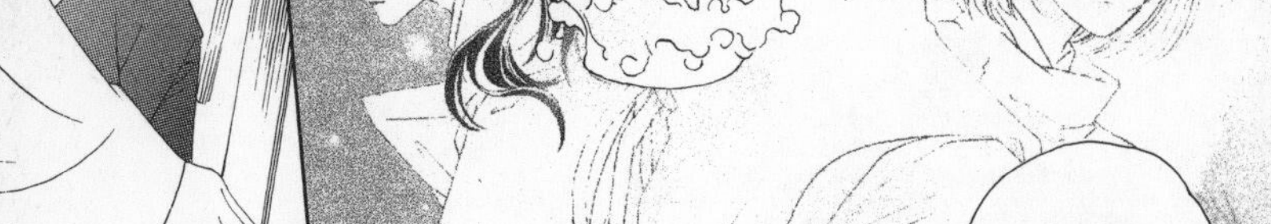
A modern ending
Shimon + Akane.

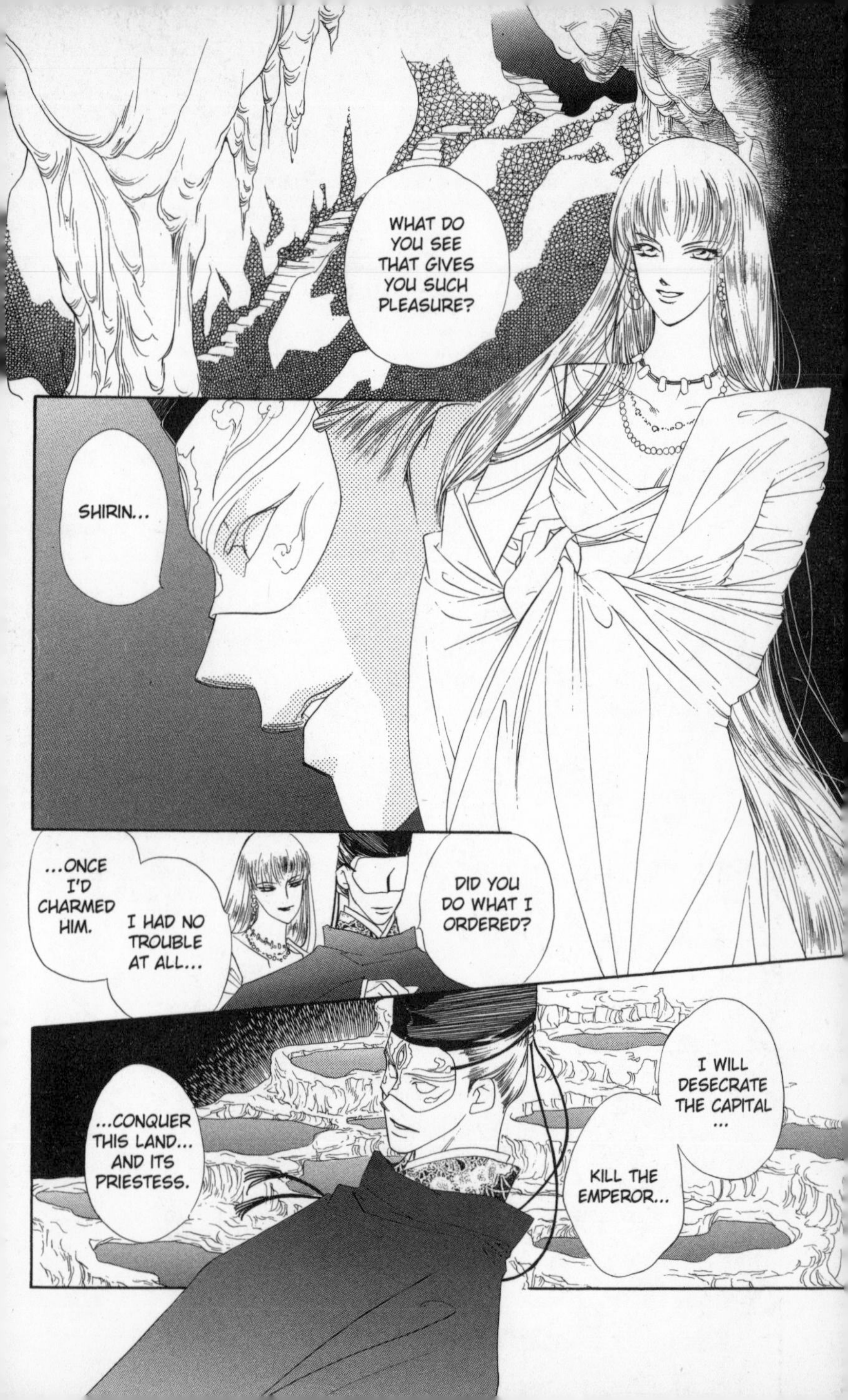
WHAT DO YOU SEE THAT GIVES YOU SUCH PLEASURE?
SHIRIN...
DID YOU DO WHAT I ORDERED?
I HAD NO TROUBLE AT ALL...
...ONCE I'D CHARMED HIM.
I WILL DESECRATE THE CAPITAL ...
KILL THE EMPEROR...
...CONQUER THIS LAND... AND ITS PRIESTESS.

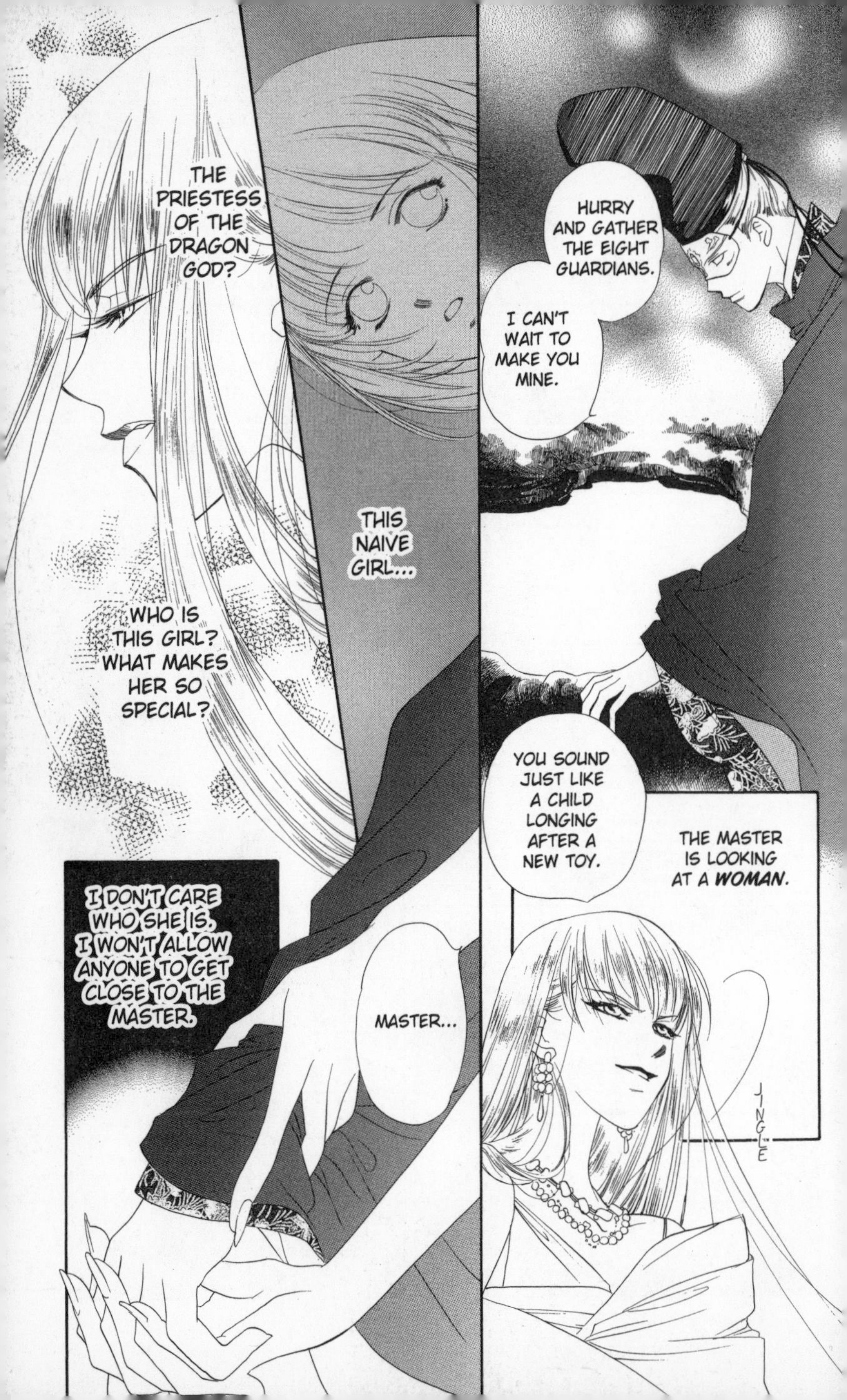
HURRY AND GATHER THE EIGHT GUARDIANS.
I CAN'T WAIT TO MAKE YOU MINE.
YOU SOUND JUST LIKE A CHILD LONGING AFTER A NEW TOY.
THE MASTER IS LOOKING AT A ***WOMAN***.
JINGLE
THE PRIESTESS OF THE DRAGON GOD?
THIS NAIVE GIRL...
WHO IS THIS GIRL? WHAT MAKES HER SO SPECIAL?
I DON'T CARE WHO SHE IS. I WON'T ALLOW ANYONE TO GET CLOSE TO THE MASTER.
MASTER...

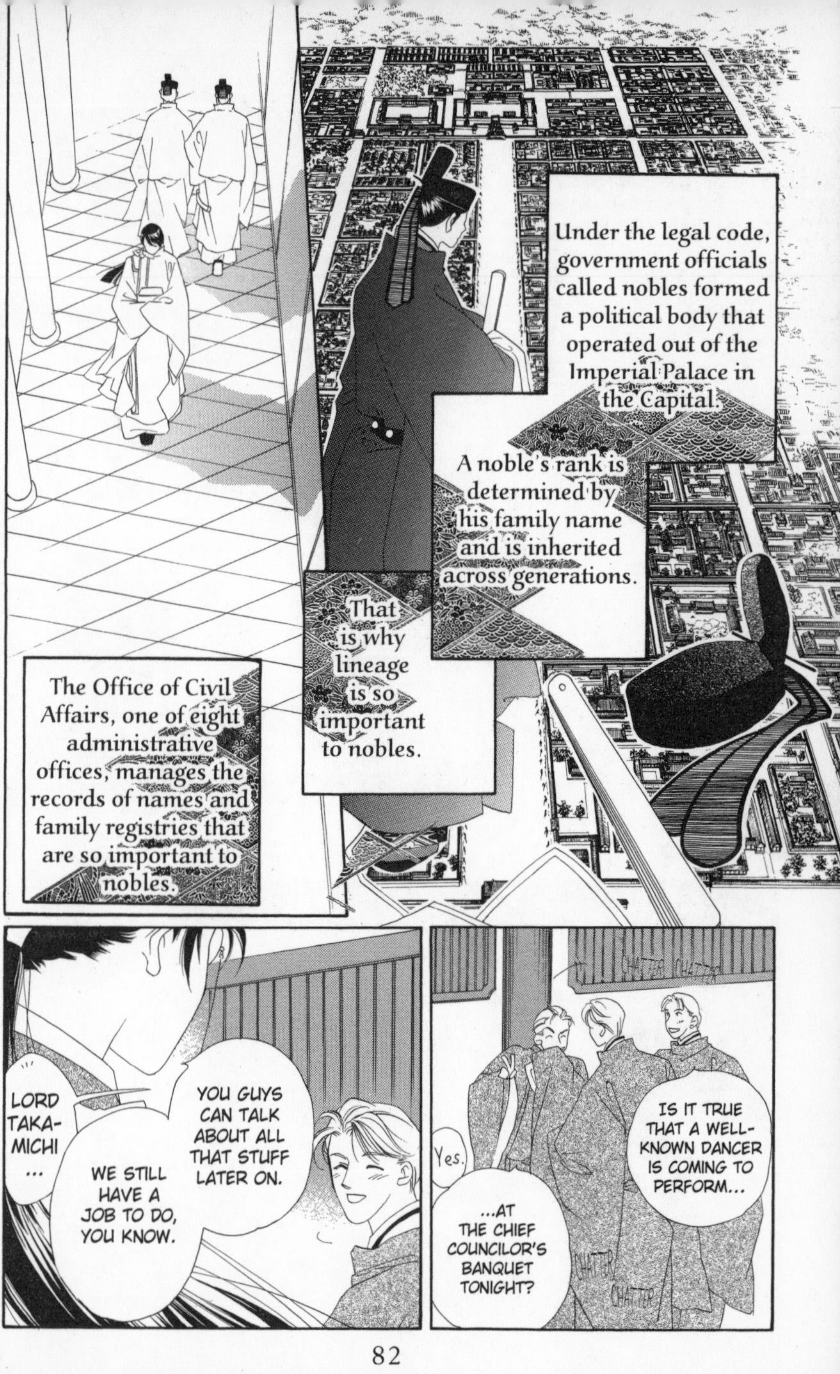
Under the legal code, government officials called nobles formed a political body that operated out of the Imperial Palace in the Capital.
A noble's rank is determined by his family name and is inherited across generations.
That is why lineage is so important to nobles.
The Office of Civil Affairs, one of eight administrative offices, manages the records of names and family registries that are so important to nobles.
CHATTER CHATTER
IS IT TRUE THAT A WELL-KNOWN DANCER IS COMING TO PERFORM...
Yes.
...AT THE CHIEF COUNCILOR'S BANQUET TONIGHT?
CHATTER CHATTER
YOU GUYS CAN TALK ABOUT ALL THAT STUFF LATER ON.
WE STILL HAVE A JOB TO DO, YOU KNOW.
LORD TAKA-MICHI ...

*SAKE IS JAPANESE RICE WINE. —ED

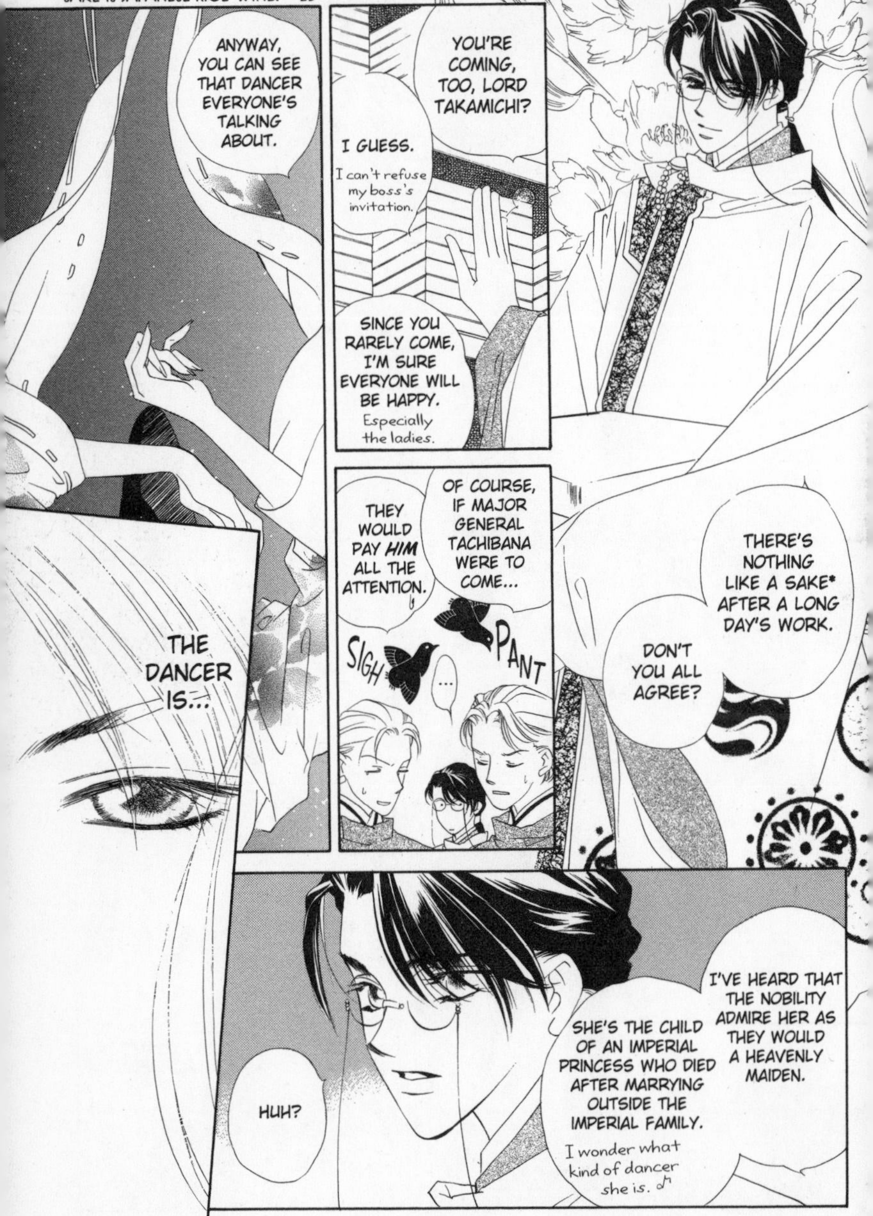

THERE'S NOTHING LIKE A SAKE* AFTER A LONG DAY'S WORK.
DON'T YOU ALL AGREE?
YOU'RE COMING, TOO, LORD TAKAMICHI?
I GUESS.
I can't refuse my boss's invitation.
SINCE YOU RARELY COME, I'M SURE EVERYONE WILL BE HAPPY.
Especially the ladies.
OF COURSE, IF MAJOR GENERAL TACHIBANA WERE TO COME...
THEY WOULD PAY *HIM* ALL THE ATTENTION.
PANT
SIGH
...
ANYWAY, YOU CAN SEE THAT DANCER EVERYONE'S TALKING ABOUT.
THE DANCER IS...
I'VE HEARD THAT THE NOBILITY ADMIRE HER AS THEY WOULD A HEAVENLY MAIDEN.
SHE'S THE CHILD OF AN IMPERIAL PRINCESS WHO DIED AFTER MARRYING OUTSIDE THE IMPERIAL FAMILY.
I wonder what kind of dancer she is.
HUH?

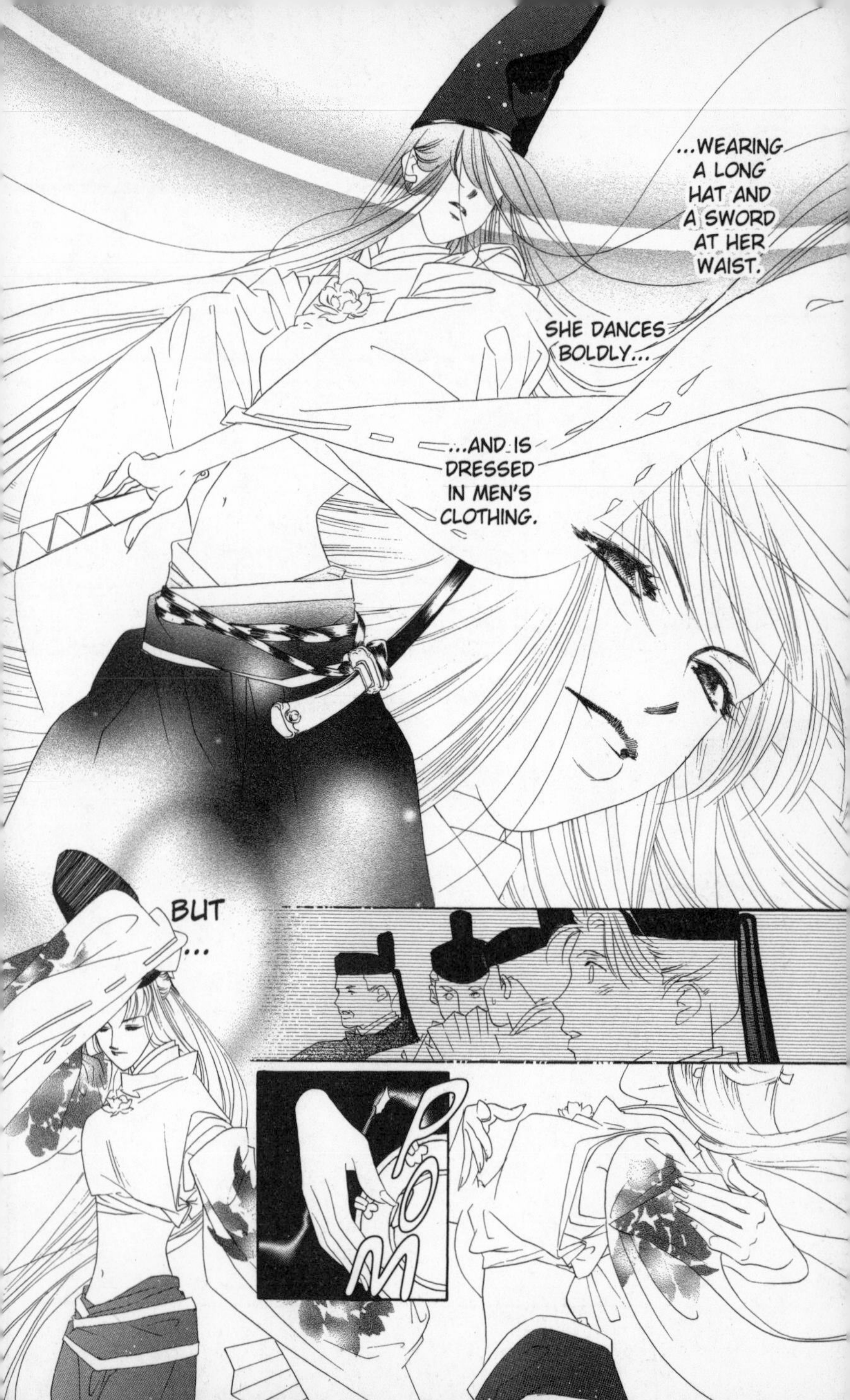
...WEARING A LONG HAT AND A SWORD AT HER WAIST.
SHE DANCES BOLDLY...
...AND IS DRESSED IN MEN'S CLOTHING.
POM
BUT...

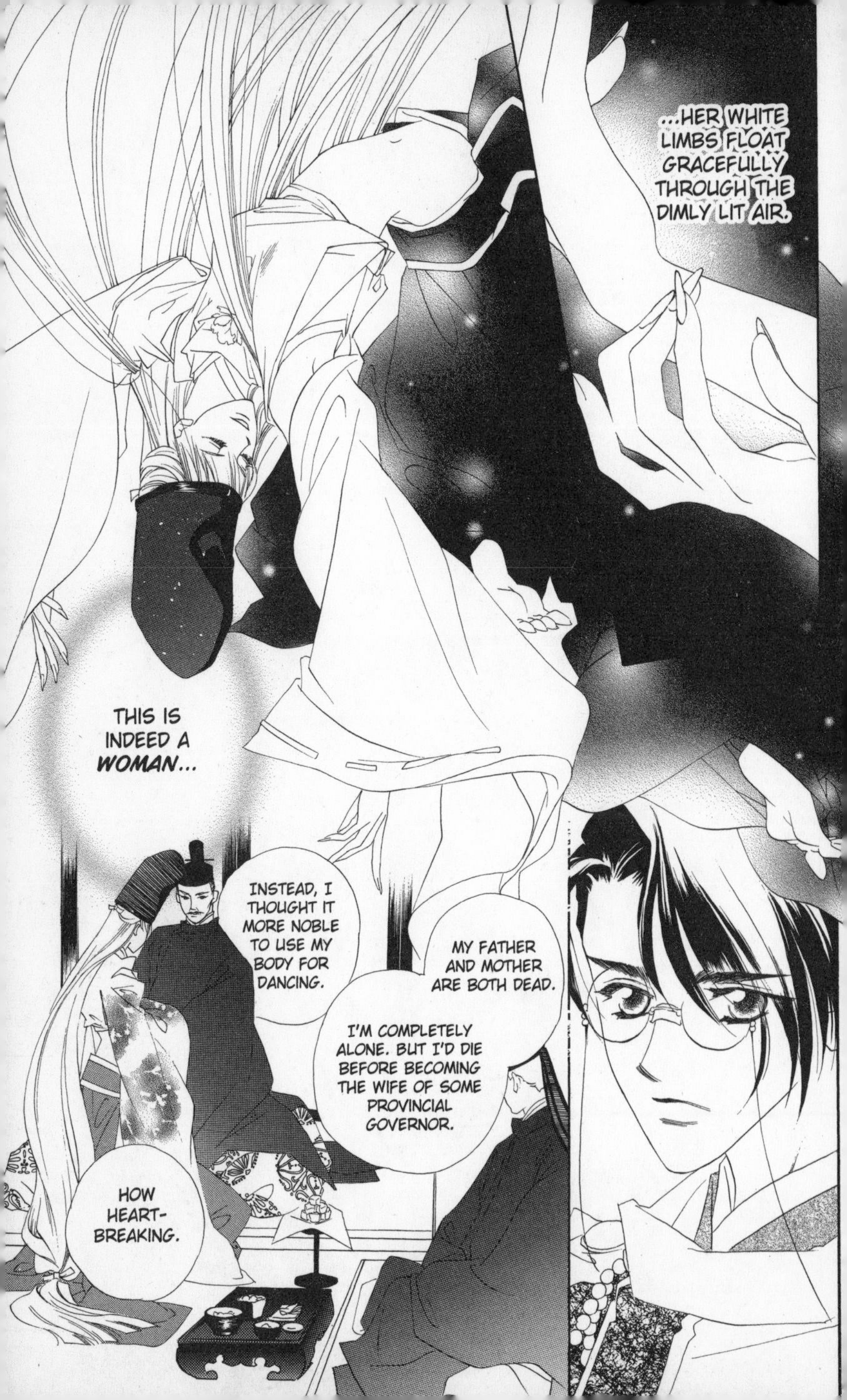
...HER WHITE LIMBS FLOAT GRACEFULLY THROUGH THE DIMLY LIT AIR.
THIS IS INDEED A *WOMAN*...
MY FATHER AND MOTHER ARE BOTH DEAD.
I'M COMPLETELY ALONE. BUT I'D DIE BEFORE BECOMING THE WIFE OF SOME PROVINCIAL GOVERNOR.
INSTEAD, I THOUGHT IT MORE NOBLE TO USE MY BODY FOR DANCING.
HOW HEART-BREAKING.

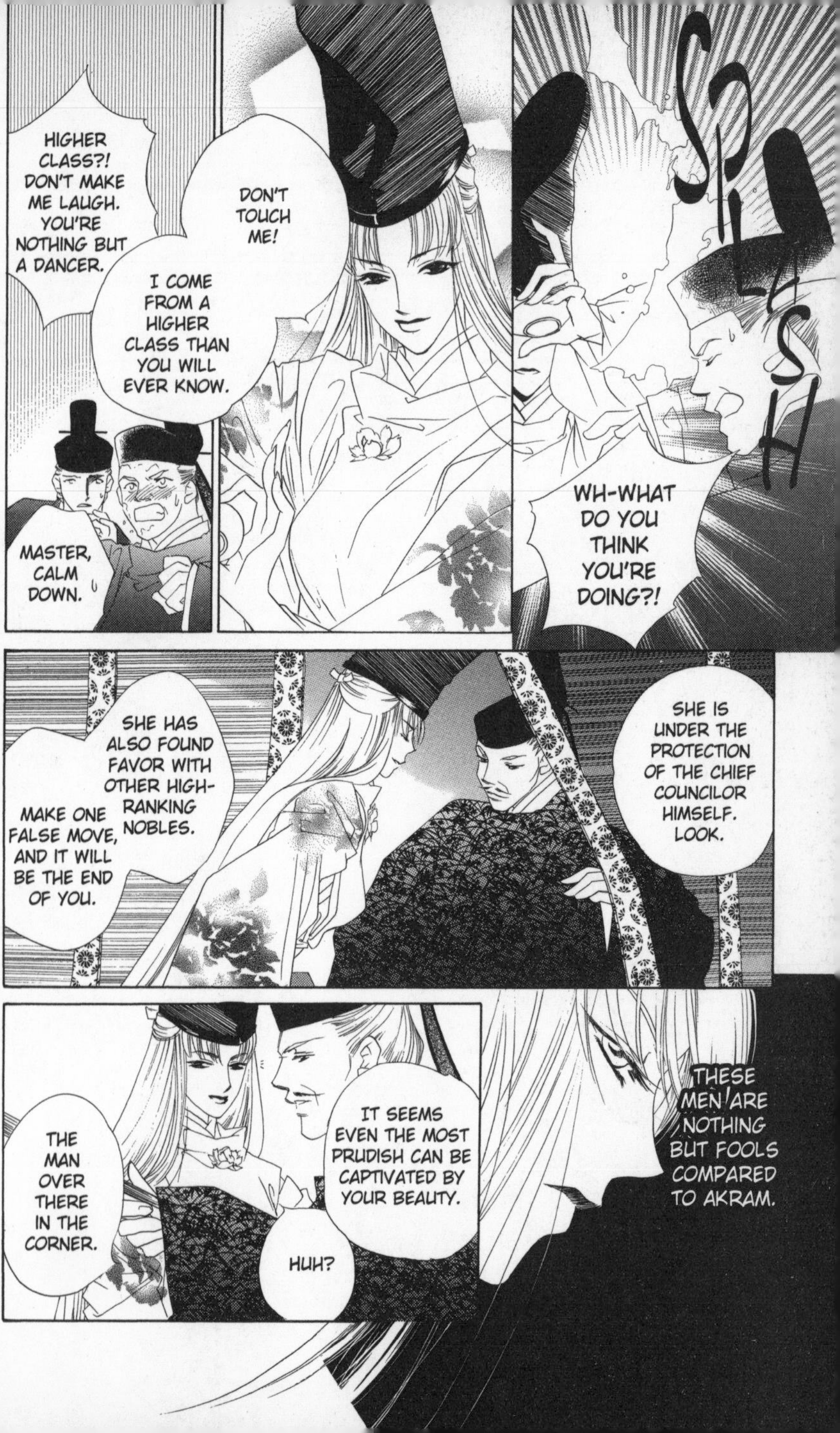
SPLASH
WH-WHAT DO YOU THINK YOU'RE DOING?!
DON'T TOUCH ME!
I COME FROM A HIGHER CLASS THAN YOU WILL EVER KNOW.
HIGHER CLASS?! DON'T MAKE ME LAUGH. YOU'RE NOTHING BUT A DANCER.
MASTER, CALM DOWN.
SHE IS UNDER THE PROTECTION OF THE CHIEF COUNCILOR HIMSELF. LOOK.
SHE HAS ALSO FOUND FAVOR WITH OTHER HIGH-RANKING NOBLES.
MAKE ONE FALSE MOVE, AND IT WILL BE THE END OF YOU.
THESE MEN ARE NOTHING BUT FOOLS COMPARED TO AKRAM.
IT SEEMS EVEN THE MOST PRUDISH CAN BE CAPTIVATED BY YOUR BEAUTY.
HUH?
THE MAN OVER THERE IN THE CORNER.

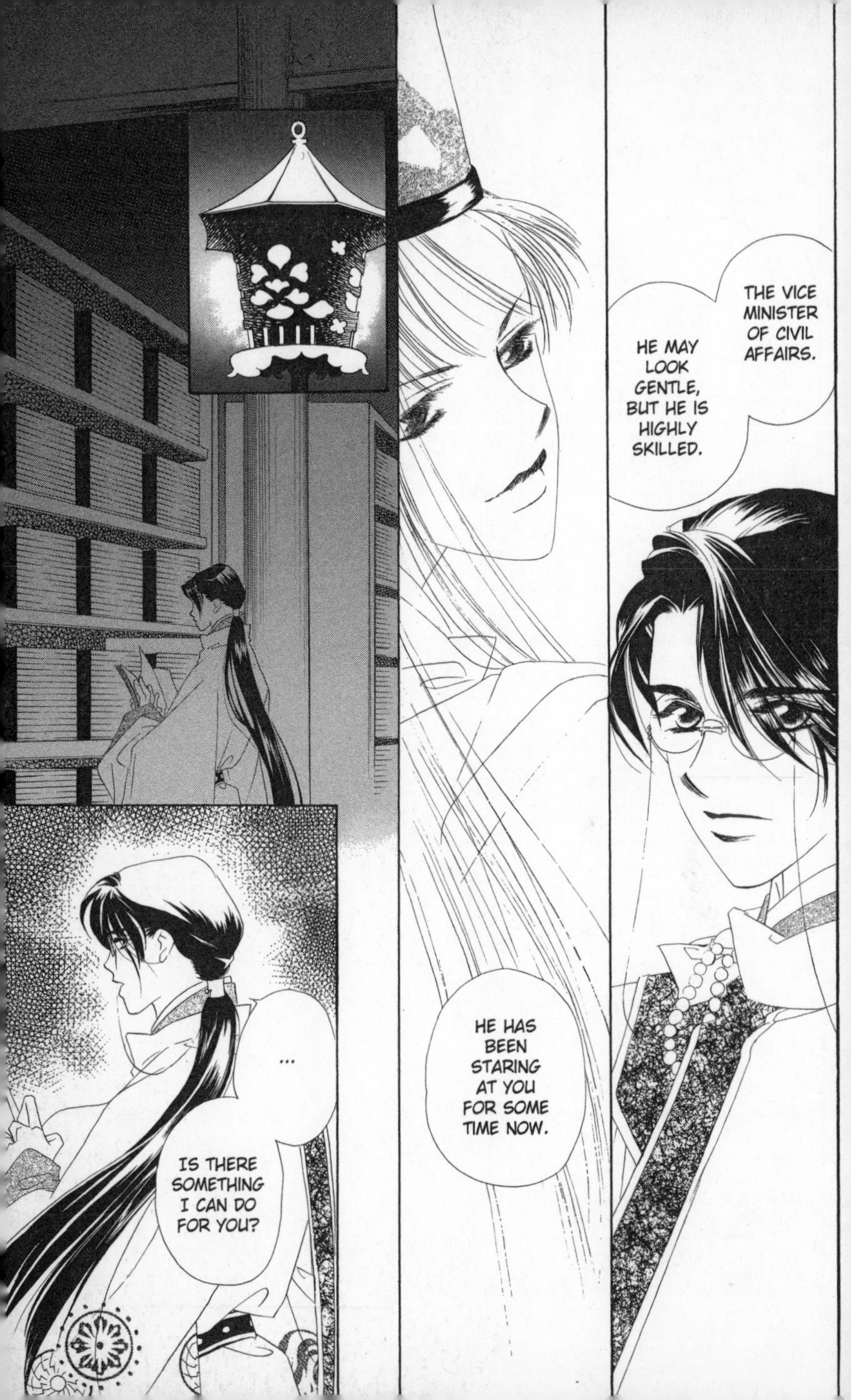
THE VICE MINISTER OF CIVIL AFFAIRS.
HE MAY LOOK GENTLE, BUT HE IS HIGHLY SKILLED.
HE HAS BEEN STARING AT YOU FOR SOME TIME NOW.
...
IS THERE SOMETHING I CAN DO FOR YOU?

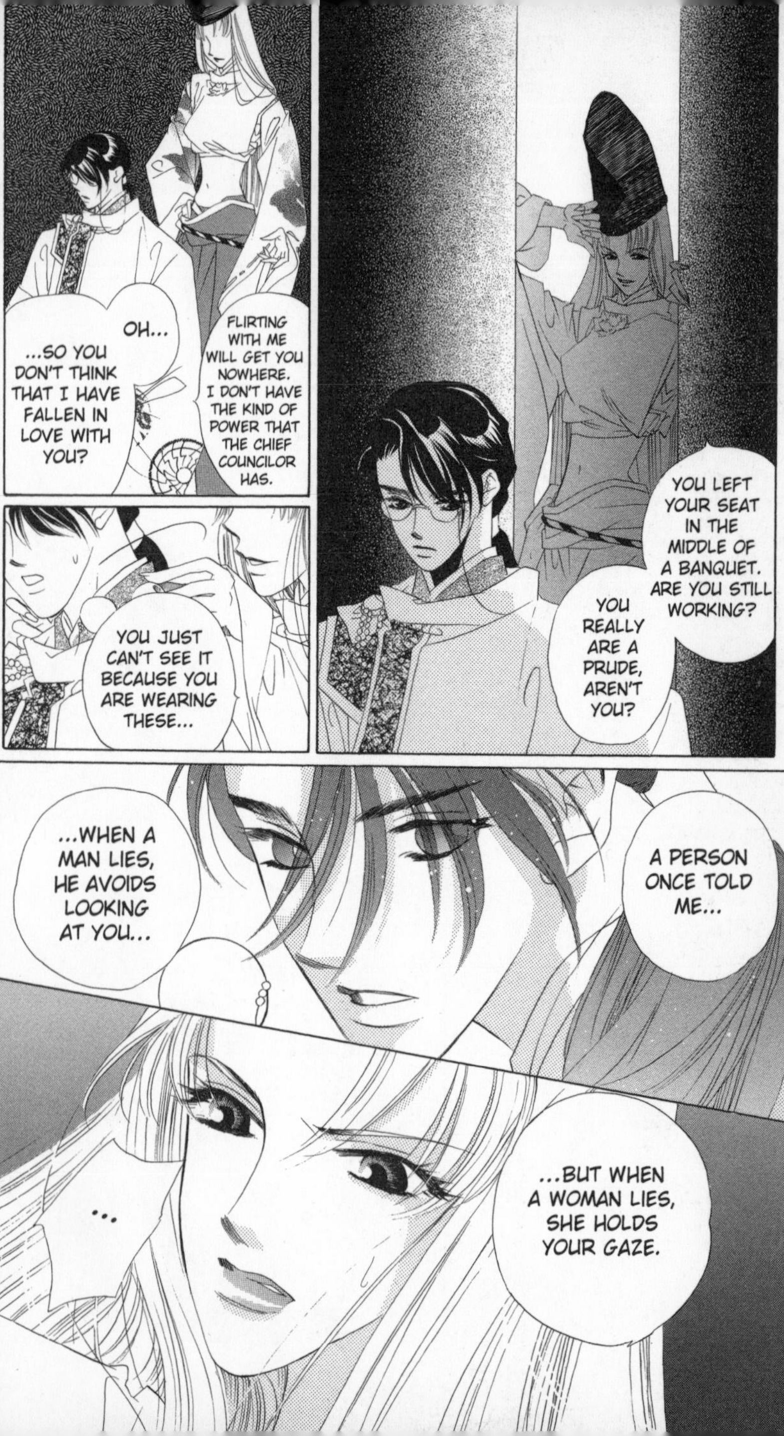
YOU LEFT YOUR SEAT IN THE MIDDLE OF A BANQUET. ARE YOU STILL WORKING?
YOU REALLY ARE A PRUDE, AREN'T YOU?
FLIRTING WITH ME WILL GET YOU NOWHERE. I DON'T HAVE THE KIND OF POWER THAT THE CHIEF COUNCILOR HAS.
OH...
...SO YOU DON'T THINK THAT I HAVE FALLEN IN LOVE WITH YOU?
YOU JUST CAN'T SEE IT BECAUSE YOU ARE WEARING THESE...
A PERSON ONCE TOLD ME...
...WHEN A MAN LIES, HE AVOIDS LOOKING AT YOU...
...BUT WHEN A WOMAN LIES, SHE HOLDS YOUR GAZE.
...

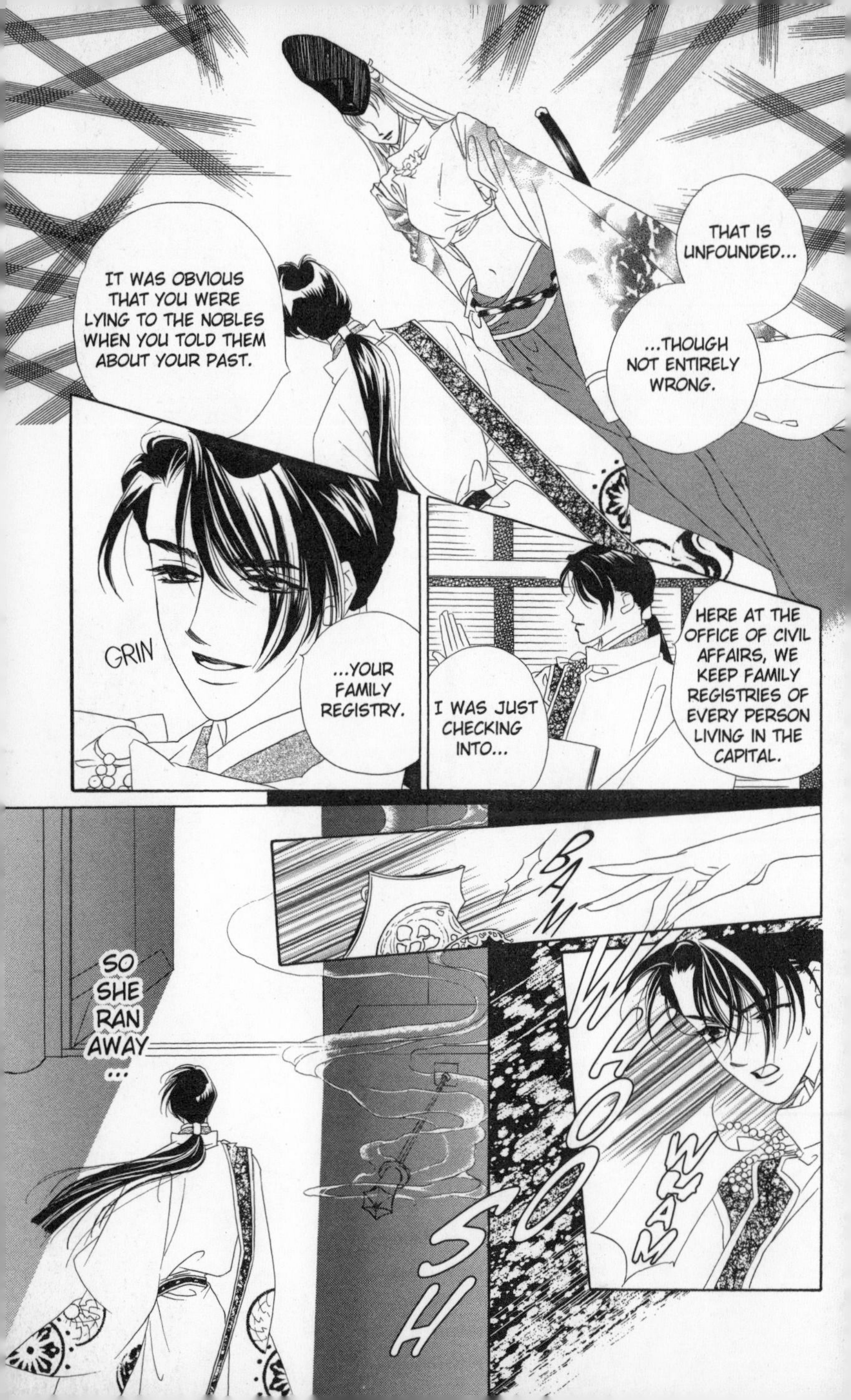
THAT IS UNFOUNDED...
...THOUGH NOT ENTIRELY WRONG.
IT WAS OBVIOUS THAT YOU WERE LYING TO THE NOBLES WHEN YOU TOLD THEM ABOUT YOUR PAST.
HERE AT THE OFFICE OF CIVIL AFFAIRS, WE KEEP FAMILY REGISTRIES OF EVERY PERSON LIVING IN THE CAPITAL.
I WAS JUST CHECKING INTO...
...YOUR FAMILY REGISTRY.
GRIN
BAM
WHOOOOSH
WHAM
SO SHE RAN AWAY...

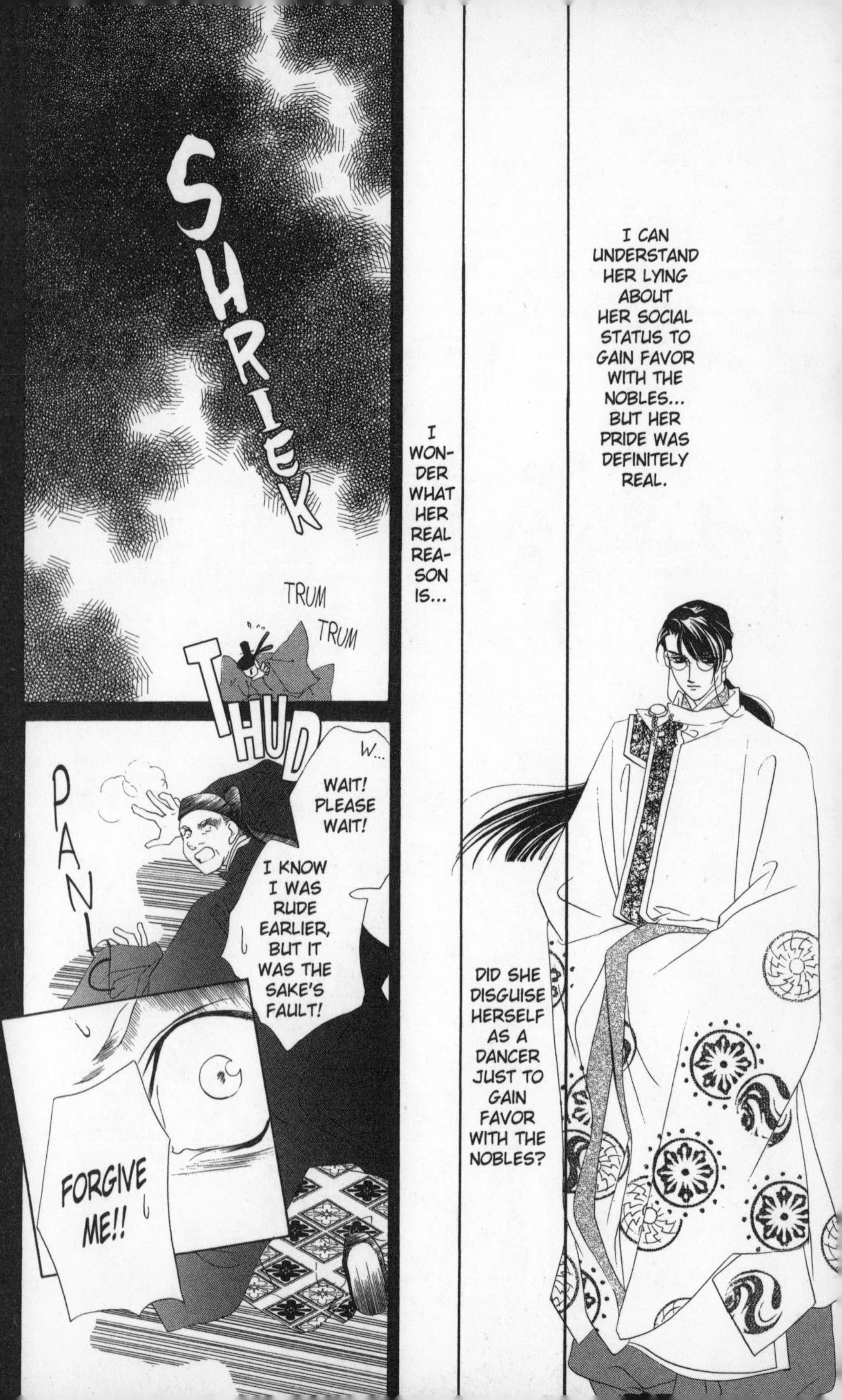
I CAN UNDERSTAND HER LYING ABOUT HER SOCIAL STATUS TO GAIN FAVOR WITH THE NOBLES... BUT HER PRIDE WAS DEFINITELY REAL.
DID SHE DISGUISE HERSELF AS A DANCER JUST TO GAIN FAVOR WITH THE NOBLES?
I WONDER WHAT HER REAL REASON IS...
SHRIEK
TRUM TRUM
THUD
W...
WAIT! PLEASE WAIT!
I KNOW I WAS RUDE EARLIER, BUT IT WAS THE SAKE'S FAULT!
PANIC
FORGIVE ME!!

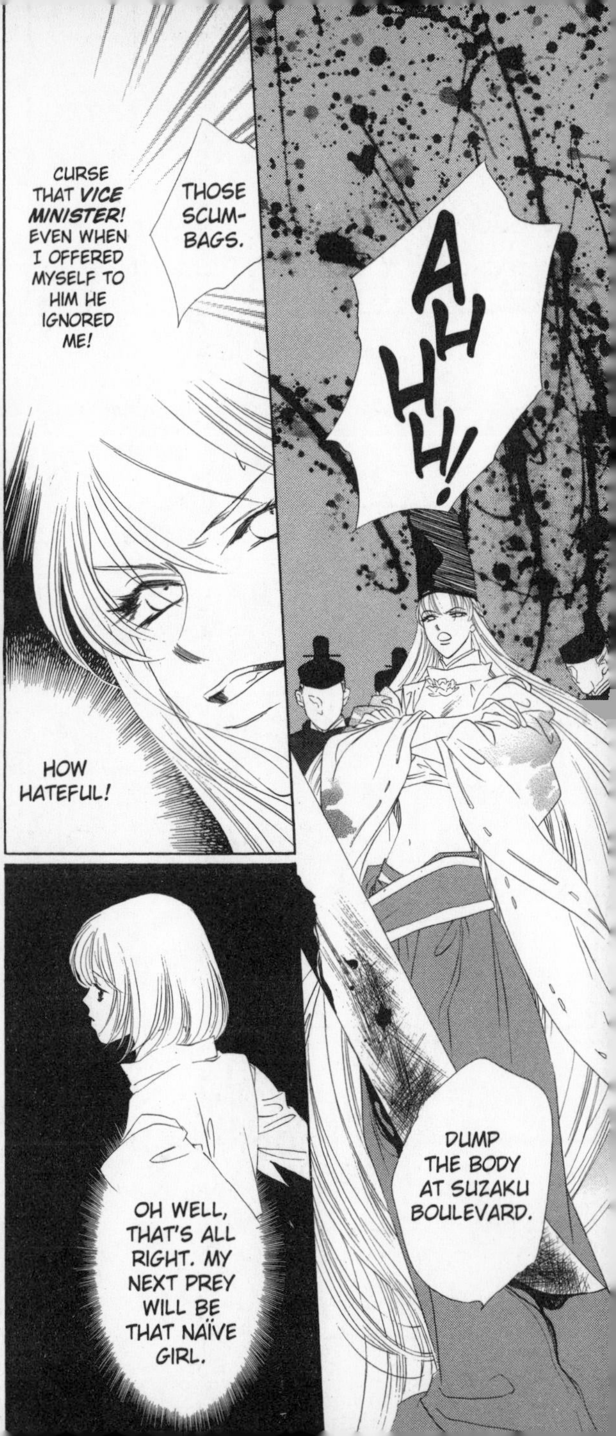
AHHHH!
DUMP THE BODY AT SUZAKU BOULEVARD.
THOSE SCUMBAGS.
CURSE THAT **VICE MINISTER!** EVEN WHEN I OFFERED MYSELF TO HIM HE IGNORED ME!
HOW HATEFUL!
OH WELL, THAT'S ALL RIGHT. MY NEXT PREY WILL BE THAT NAÏVE GIRL.

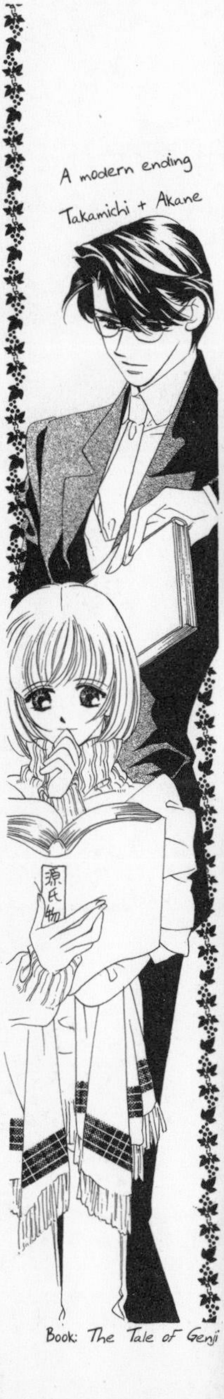
A modern ending
Takamichi + Akane
源氏物
Book: The Tale of Genji

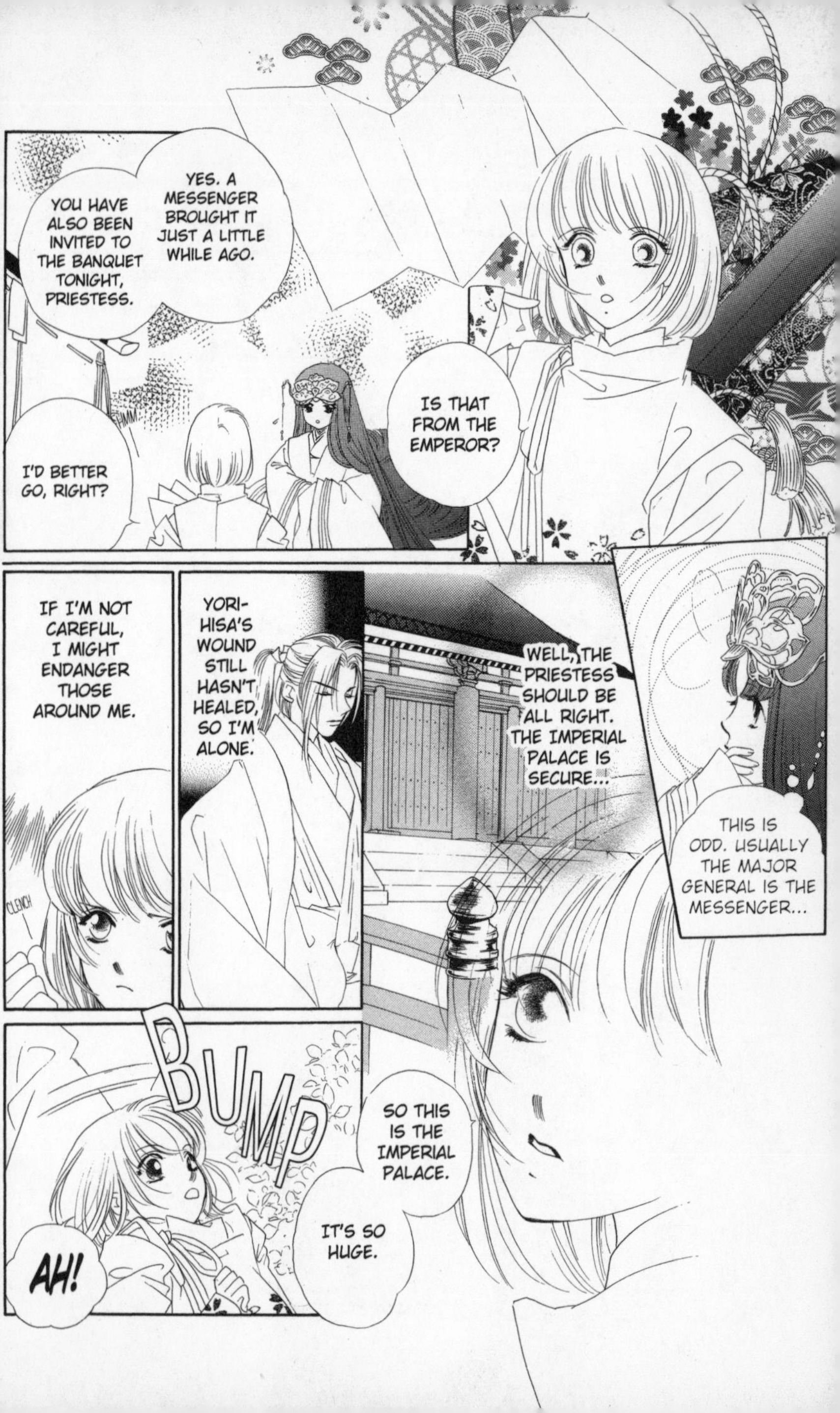
YES. A MESSENGER BROUGHT IT JUST A LITTLE WHILE AGO.
YOU HAVE ALSO BEEN INVITED TO THE BANQUET TONIGHT, PRIESTESS.
IS THAT FROM THE EMPEROR?
I'D BETTER GO, RIGHT?
THIS IS ODD. USUALLY THE MAJOR GENERAL IS THE MESSENGER...
WELL, THE PRIESTESS SHOULD BE ALL RIGHT. THE IMPERIAL PALACE IS SECURE...
YORI-HISA'S WOUND STILL HASN'T HEALED, SO I'M ALONE.
IF I'M NOT CAREFUL, I MIGHT ENDANGER THOSE AROUND ME.
CLENCH
SO THIS IS THE IMPERIAL PALACE.
IT'S SO HUGE.
BUMP
AH!

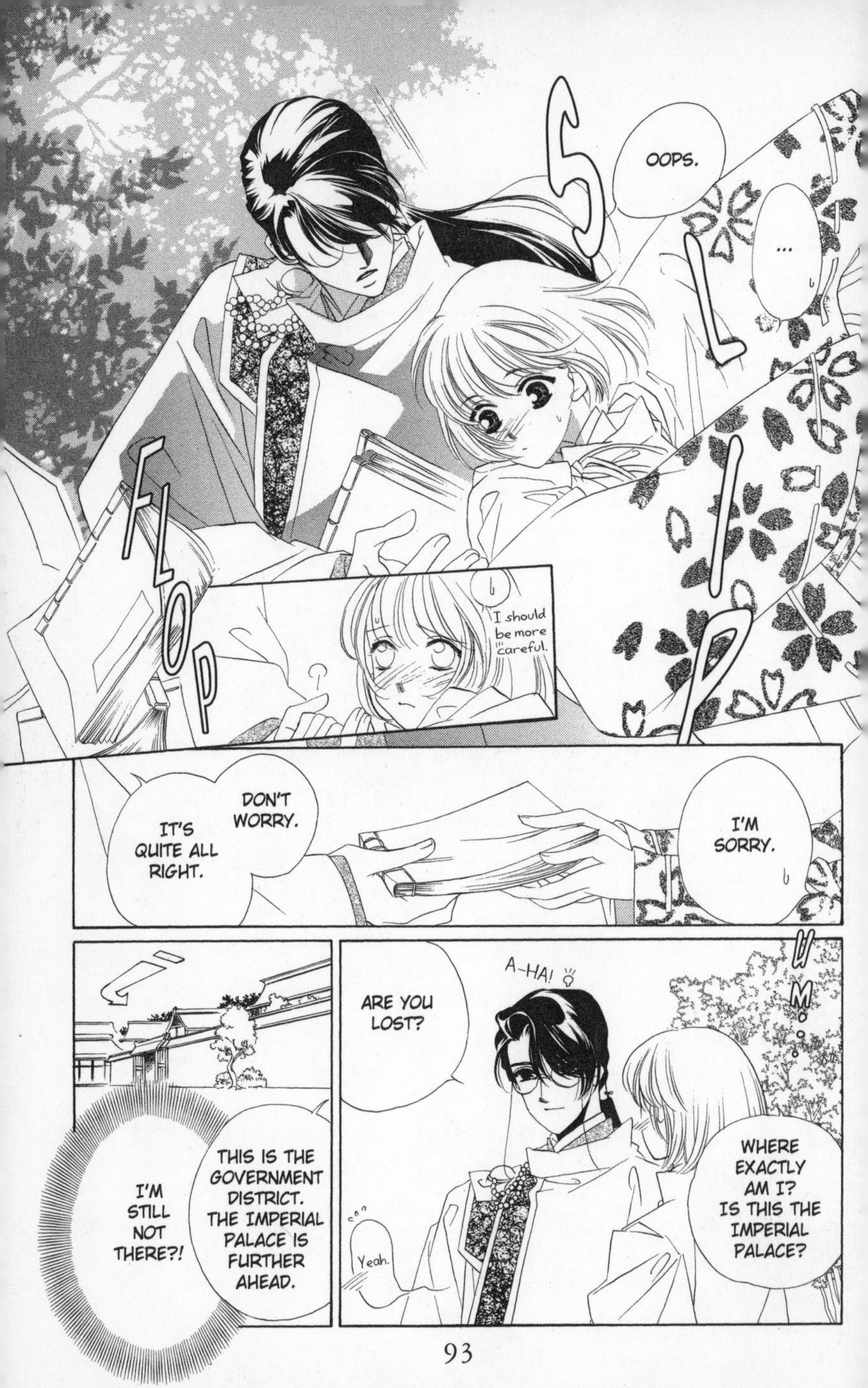
SLIP
OOPS.
...
I should be more careful.
FLOP
I'M SORRY.
DON'T WORRY.
IT'S QUITE ALL RIGHT.
UM...
A-HA!
ARE YOU LOST?
WHERE EXACTLY AM I? IS THIS THE IMPERIAL PALACE?
Yeah.
THIS IS THE GOVERNMENT DISTRICT. THE IMPERIAL PALACE IS FURTHER AHEAD.
I'M STILL NOT THERE?!

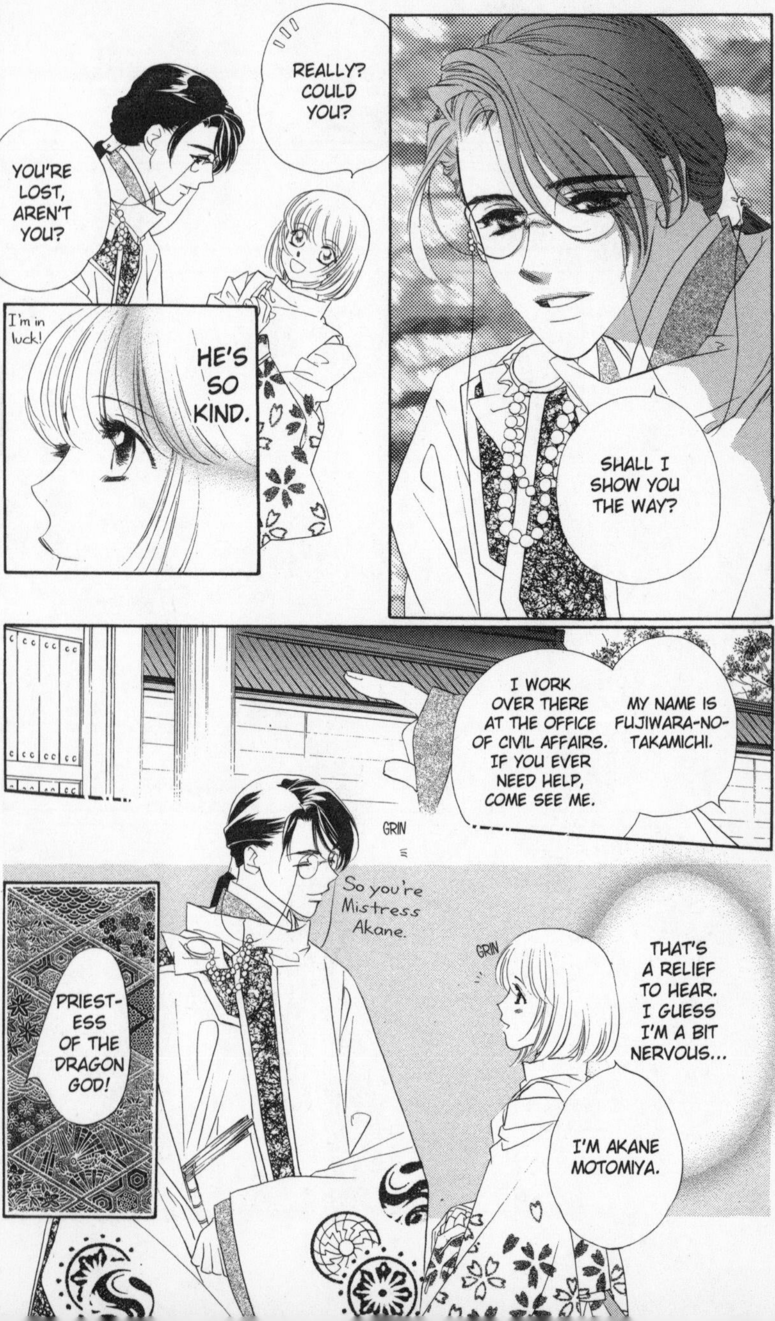
SHALL I SHOW YOU THE WAY?
REALLY? COULD YOU?
YOU'RE LOST, AREN'T YOU?
HE'S SO KIND.
I'm in luck!
MY NAME IS FUJIWARA-NO-TAKAMICHI.
I WORK OVER THERE AT THE OFFICE OF CIVIL AFFAIRS. IF YOU EVER NEED HELP, COME SEE ME.
GRIN
THAT'S A RELIEF TO HEAR. I GUESS I'M A BIT NERVOUS...
I'M AKANE MOTOMIYA.
GRIN
So you're Mistress Akane.
PRIEST-ESS OF THE DRAGON GOD!

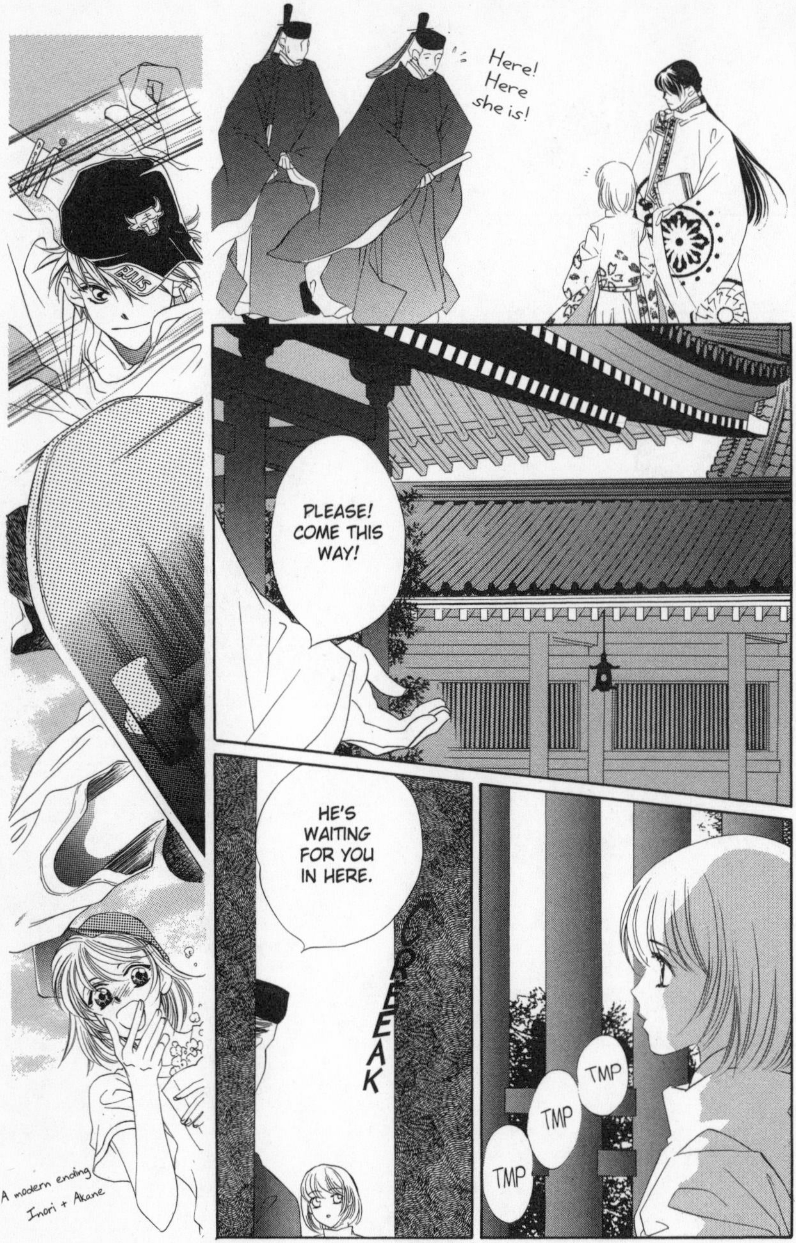
Here! Here she is!
PLEASE! COME THIS WAY!
TMP
TMP
TMP
HE'S WAITING FOR YOU IN HERE.
CREEEAK
A modern ending
Inori + Akane

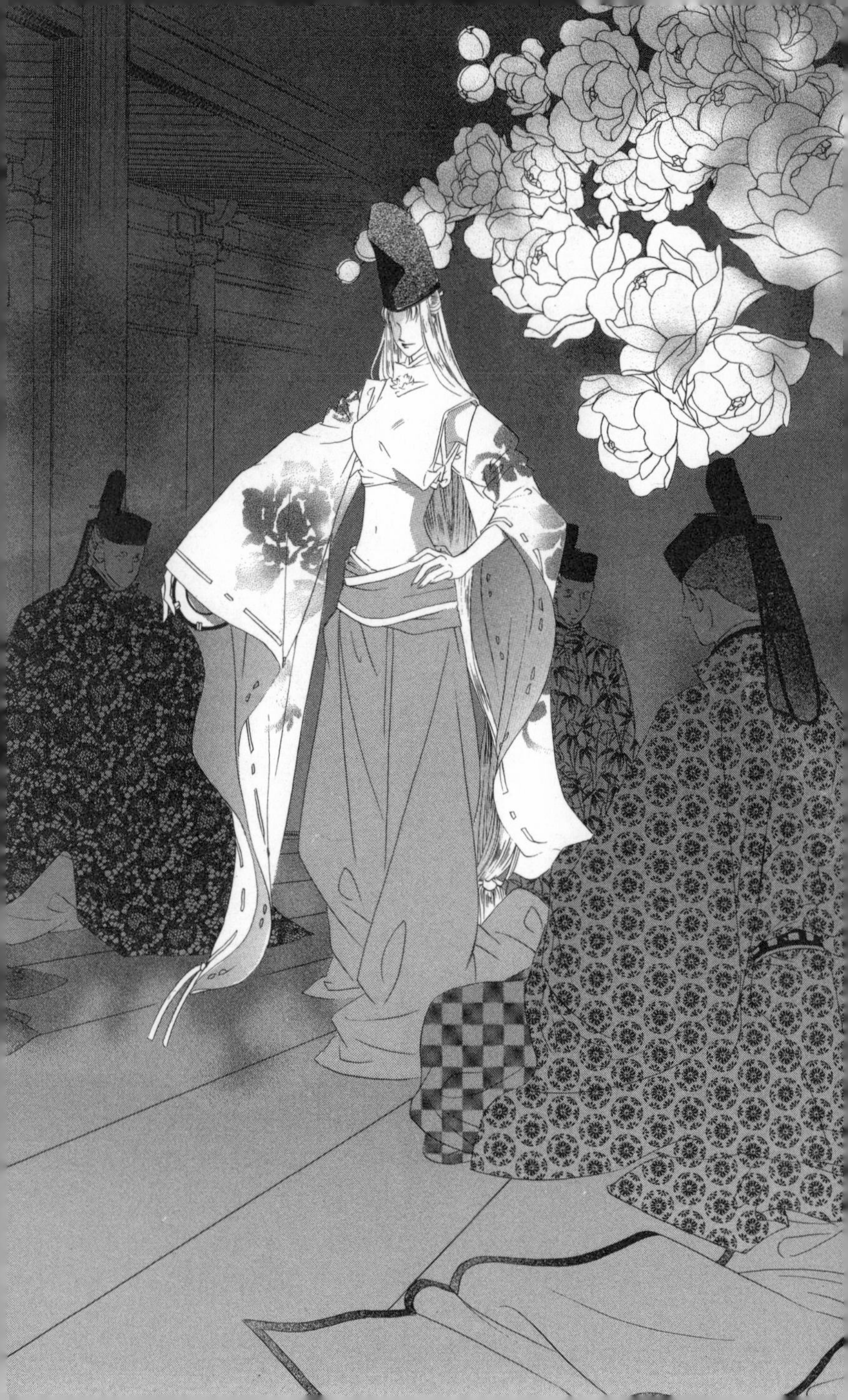

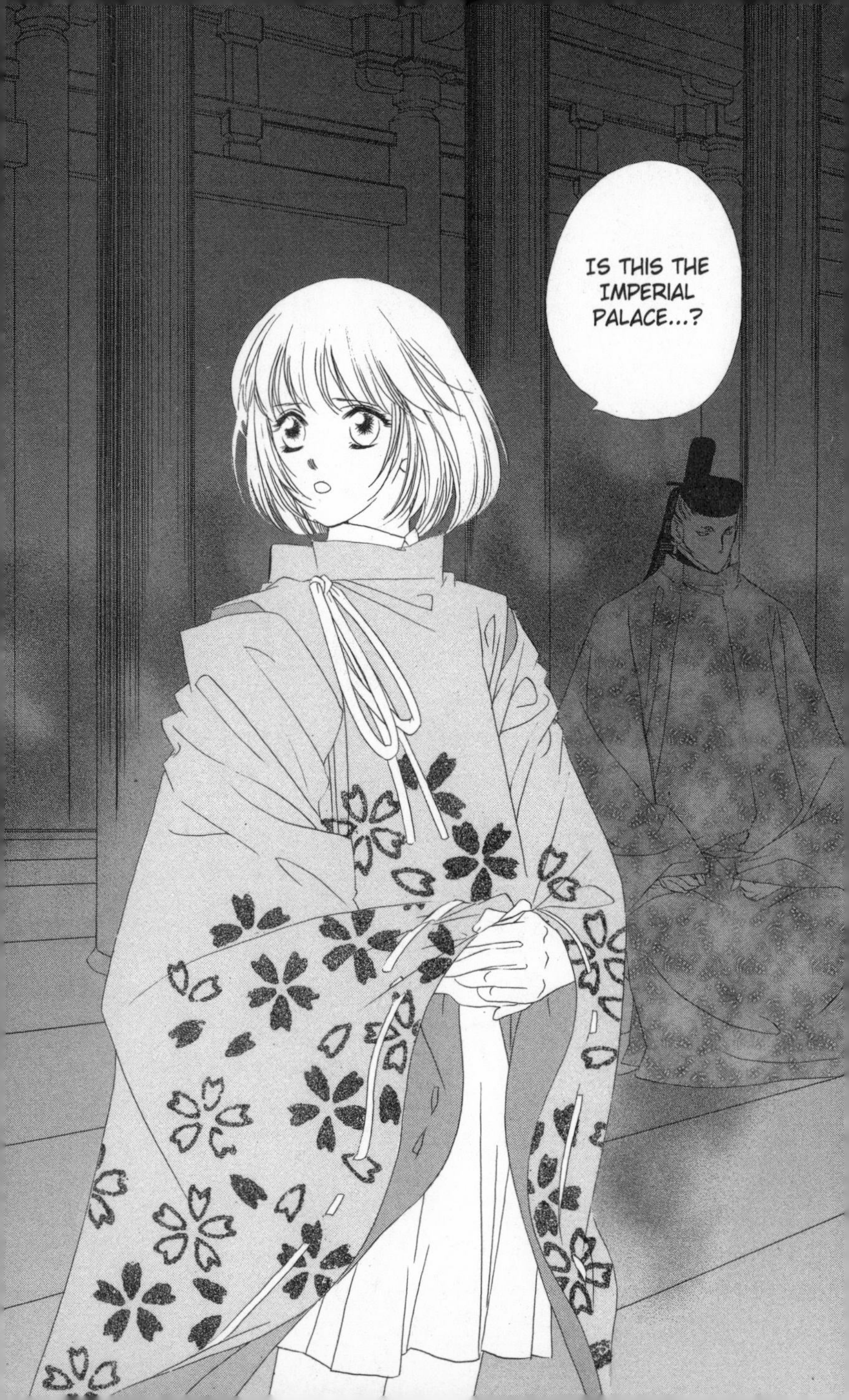
IS THIS THE IMPERIAL PALACE...?

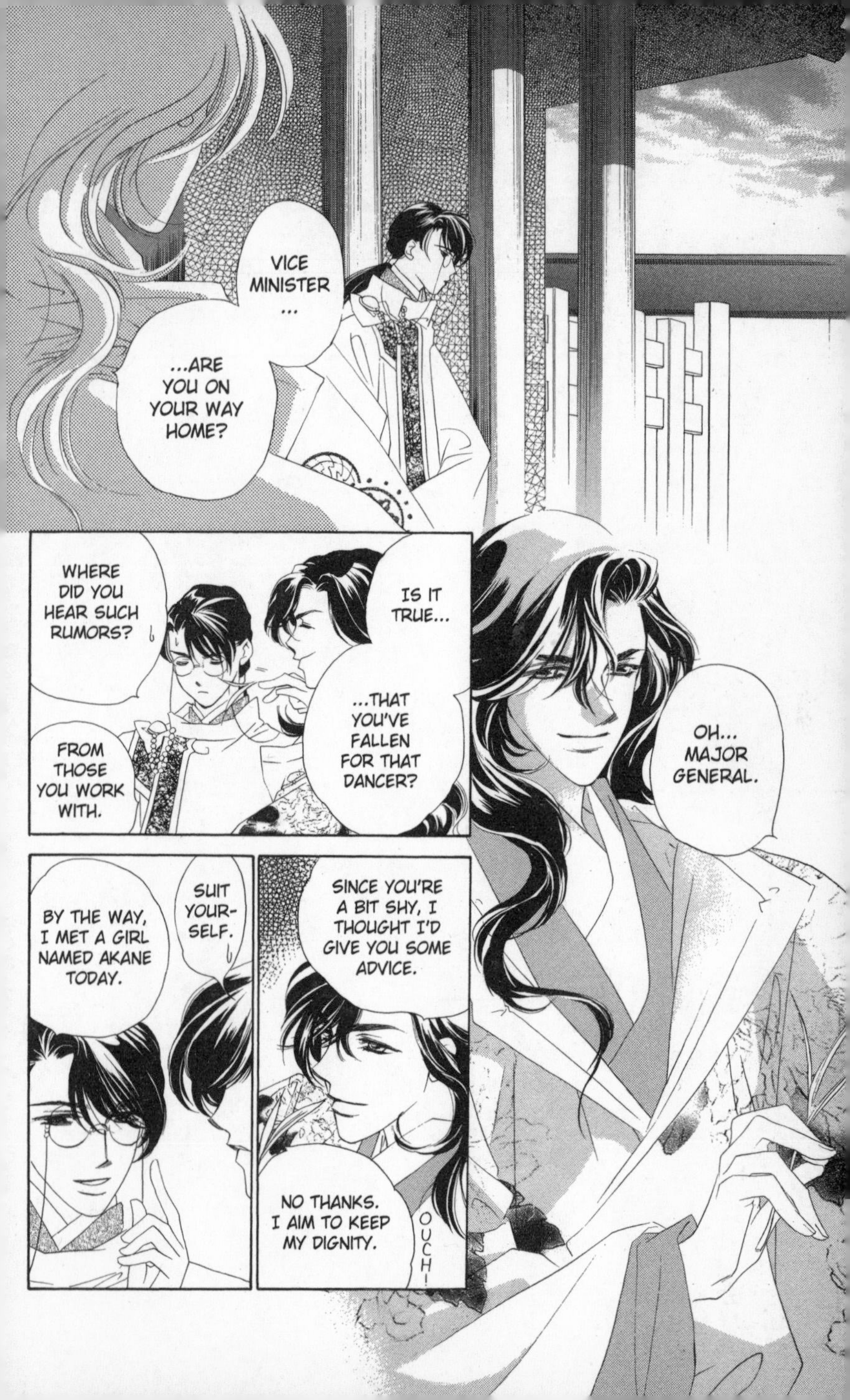

VICE MINISTER ...
...ARE YOU ON YOUR WAY HOME?
OH... MAJOR GENERAL.
IS IT TRUE...
...THAT YOU'VE FALLEN FOR THAT DANCER?
WHERE DID YOU HEAR SUCH RUMORS?
FROM THOSE YOU WORK WITH.
SINCE YOU'RE A BIT SHY, I THOUGHT I'D GIVE YOU SOME ADVICE.
NO THANKS. I AIM TO KEEP MY DIGNITY.
OUCH!
SUIT YOURSELF.
BY THE WAY, I MET A GIRL NAMED AKANE TODAY.

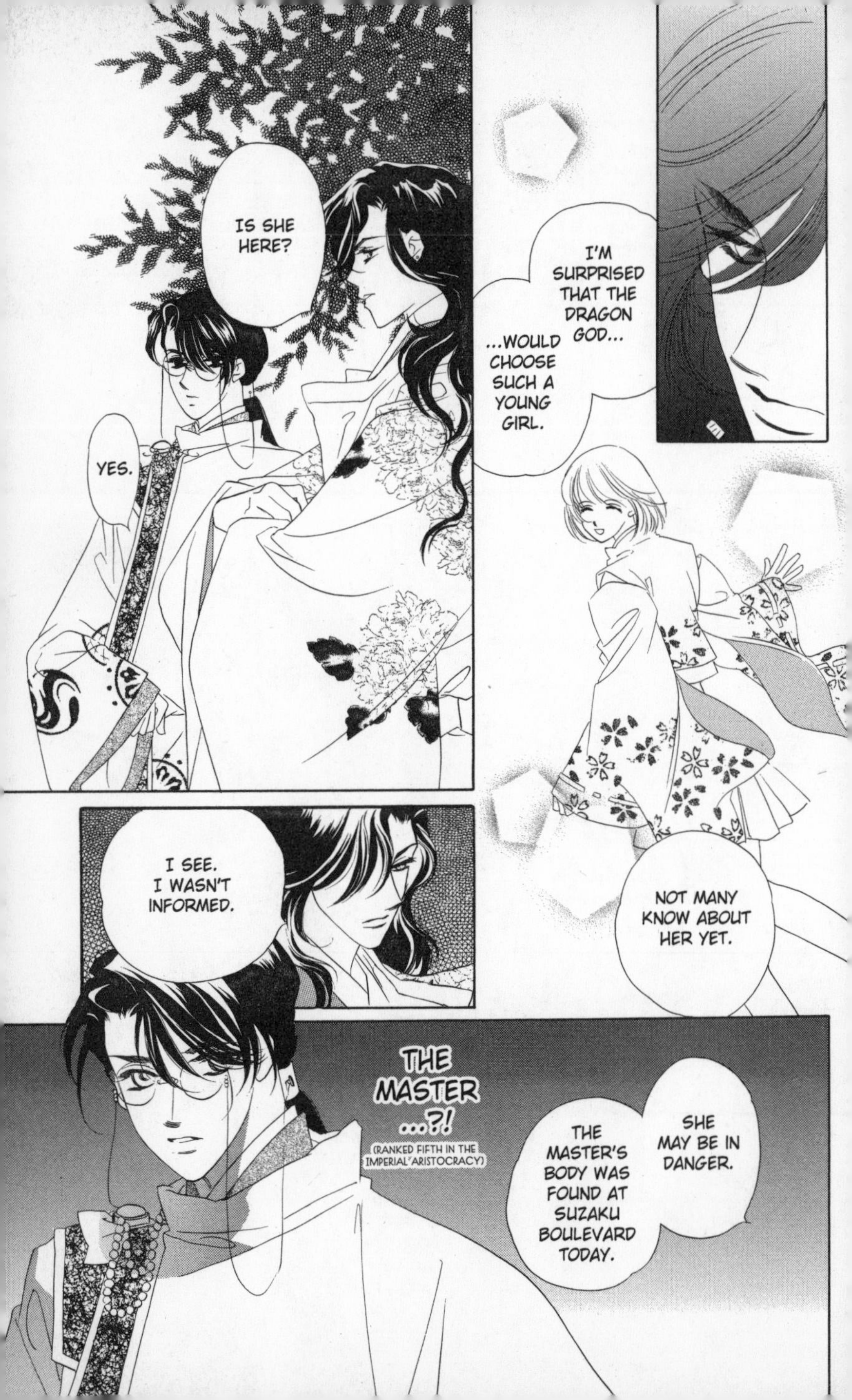
I'M SURPRISED THAT THE DRAGON GOD...
...WOULD CHOOSE SUCH A YOUNG GIRL.
NOT MANY KNOW ABOUT HER YET.
IS SHE HERE?
YES.
I SEE. I WASN'T INFORMED.
SHE MAY BE IN DANGER.
THE MASTER'S BODY WAS FOUND AT SUZAKU BOULEVARD TODAY.
THE MASTER ...?!
(RANKED FIFTH IN THE IMPERIAL ARISTOCRACY)

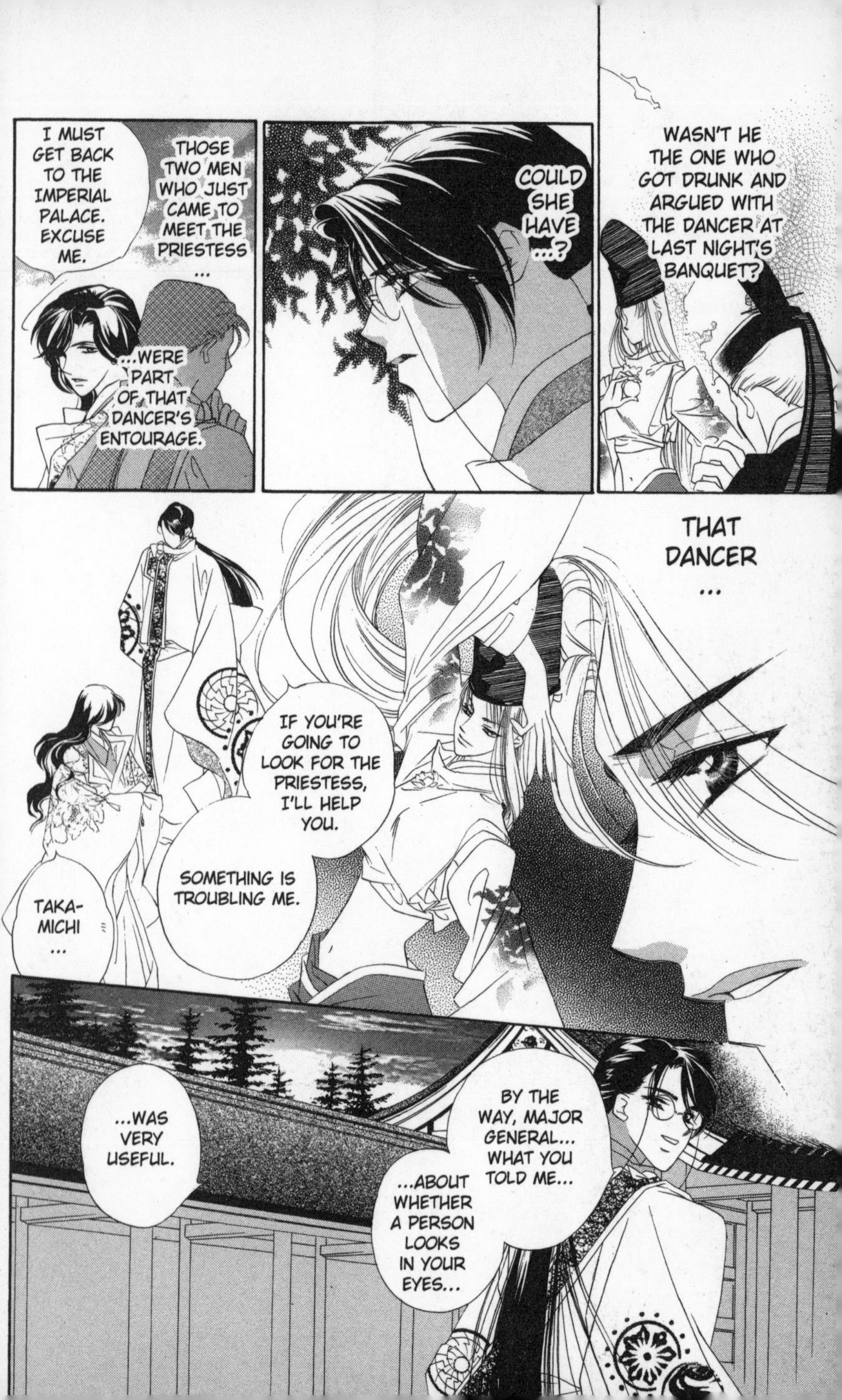
WASN'T HE THE ONE WHO GOT DRUNK AND ARGUED WITH THE DANCER AT LAST NIGHT'S BANQUET?
COULD SHE HAVE ...?
THOSE TWO MEN WHO JUST CAME TO MEET THE PRIESTESS ...
...WERE PART OF THAT DANCER'S ENTOURAGE.
I MUST GET BACK TO THE IMPERIAL PALACE. EXCUSE ME.
THAT DANCER ...
IF YOU'RE GOING TO LOOK FOR THE PRIESTESS, I'LL HELP YOU.
SOMETHING IS TROUBLING ME.
TAKA-MICHI ...
BY THE WAY, MAJOR GENERAL... WHAT YOU TOLD ME...
...ABOUT WHETHER A PERSON LOOKS IN YOUR EYES...
...WAS VERY USEFUL.

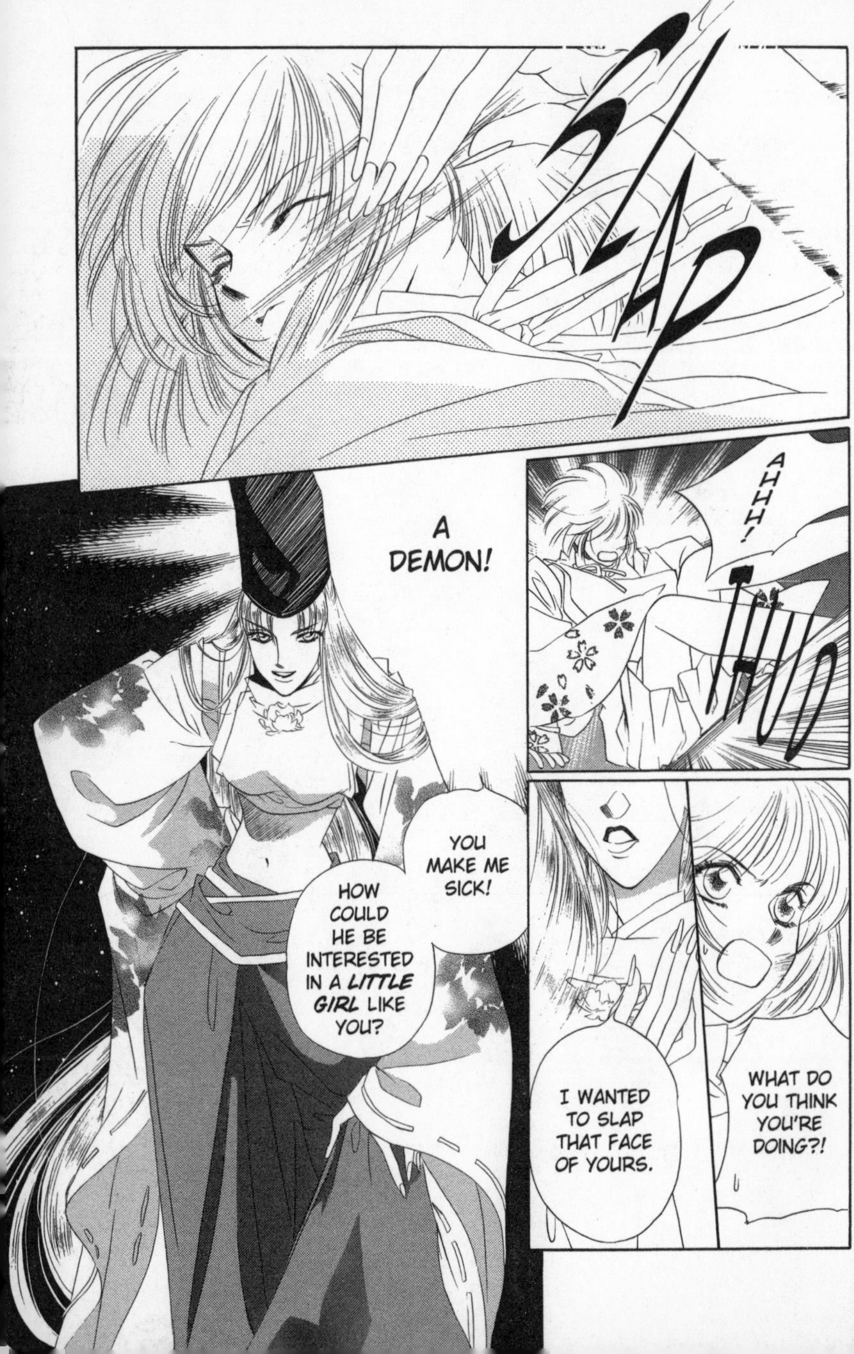
SLAP
AHHH!
THUD
WHAT DO YOU THINK YOU'RE DOING?!
I WANTED TO SLAP THAT FACE OF YOURS.
A DEMON!
YOU MAKE ME SICK!
HOW COULD HE BE INTERESTED IN A *LITTLE GIRL* LIKE YOU?

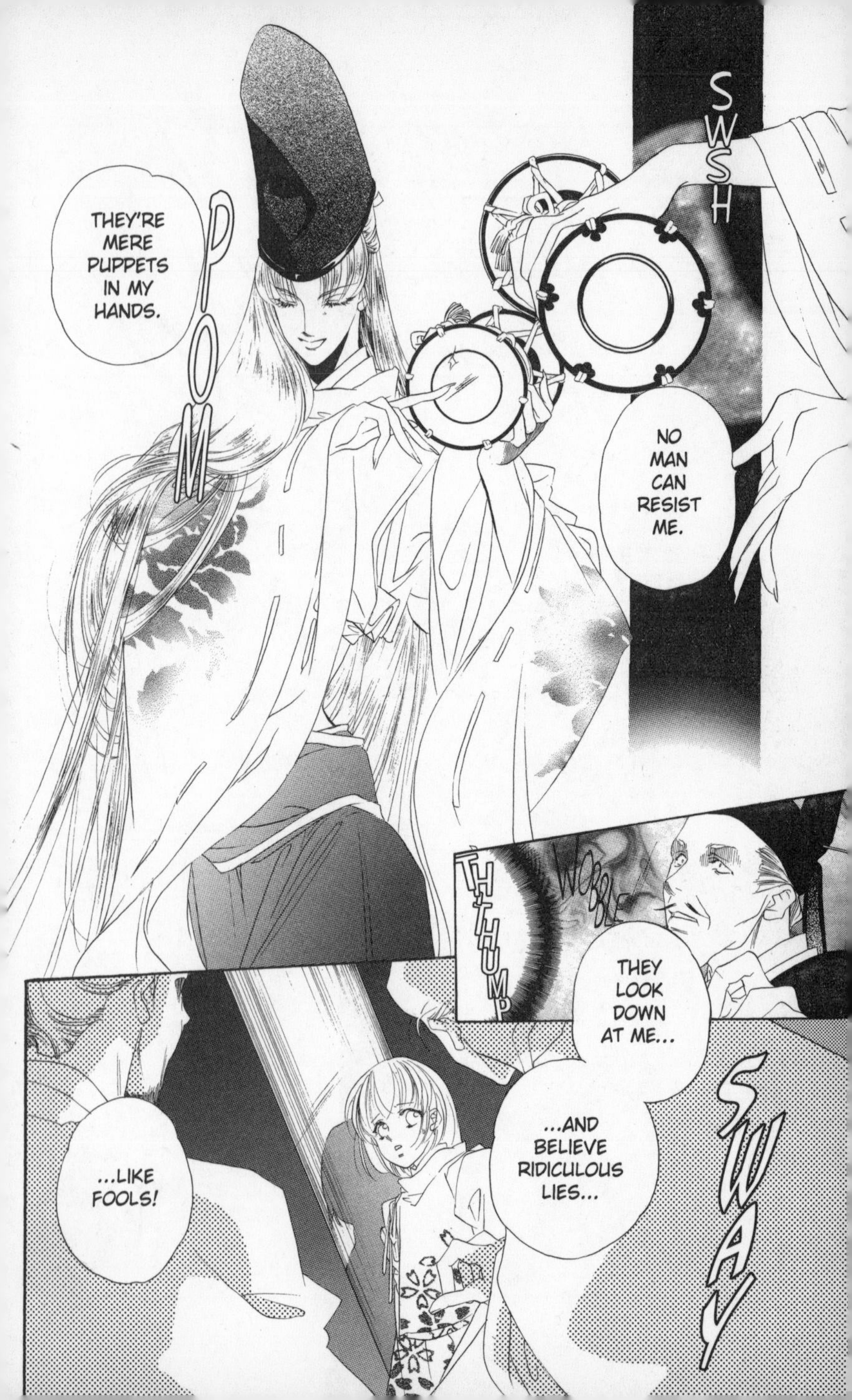
SWSH
NO MAN CAN RESIST ME.
POM
THEY'RE MERE PUPPETS IN MY HANDS.
WOBBLE
THTHUMP
THEY LOOK DOWN AT ME...
...AND BELIEVE RIDICULOUS LIES...
SWAY
...LIKE FOOLS!

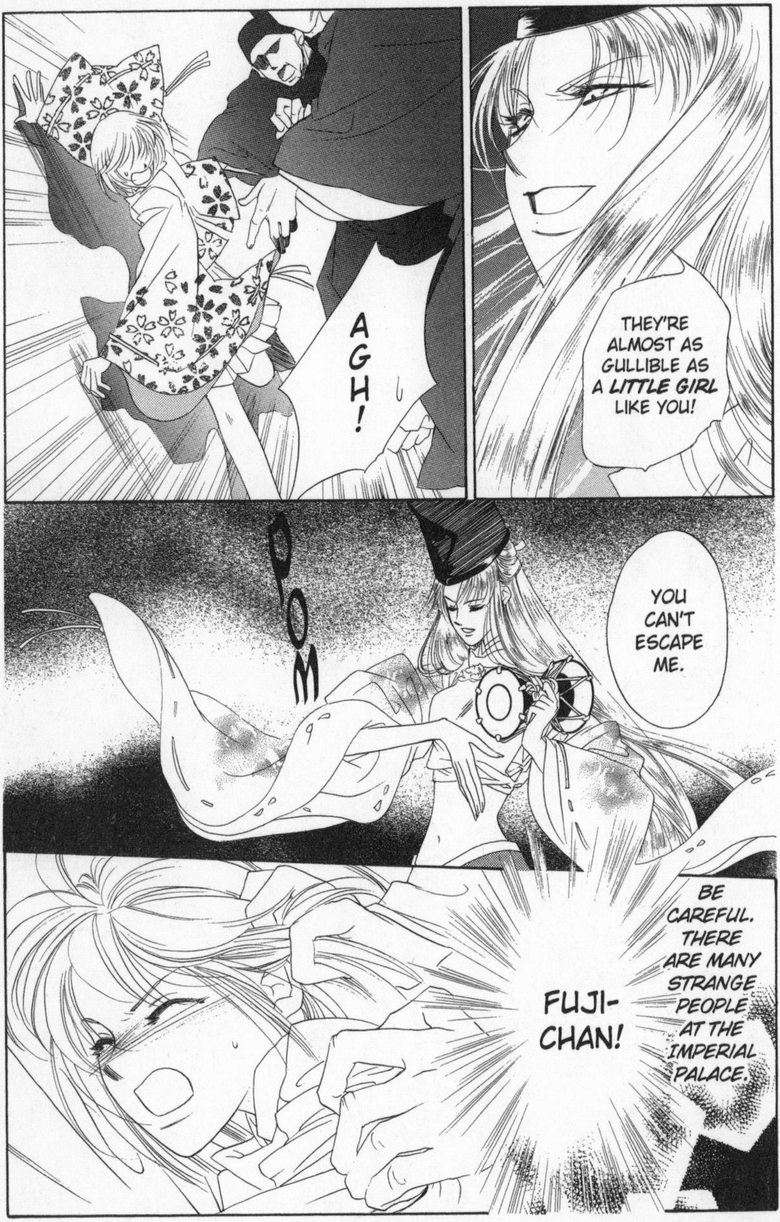
THEY'RE ALMOST AS GULLIBLE AS A *LITTLE GIRL* LIKE YOU!
AGH!
YOU CAN'T ESCAPE ME.
POM
BE CAREFUL. THERE ARE MANY STRANGE PEOPLE AT THE IMPERIAL PALACE.
FUJI-CHAN!

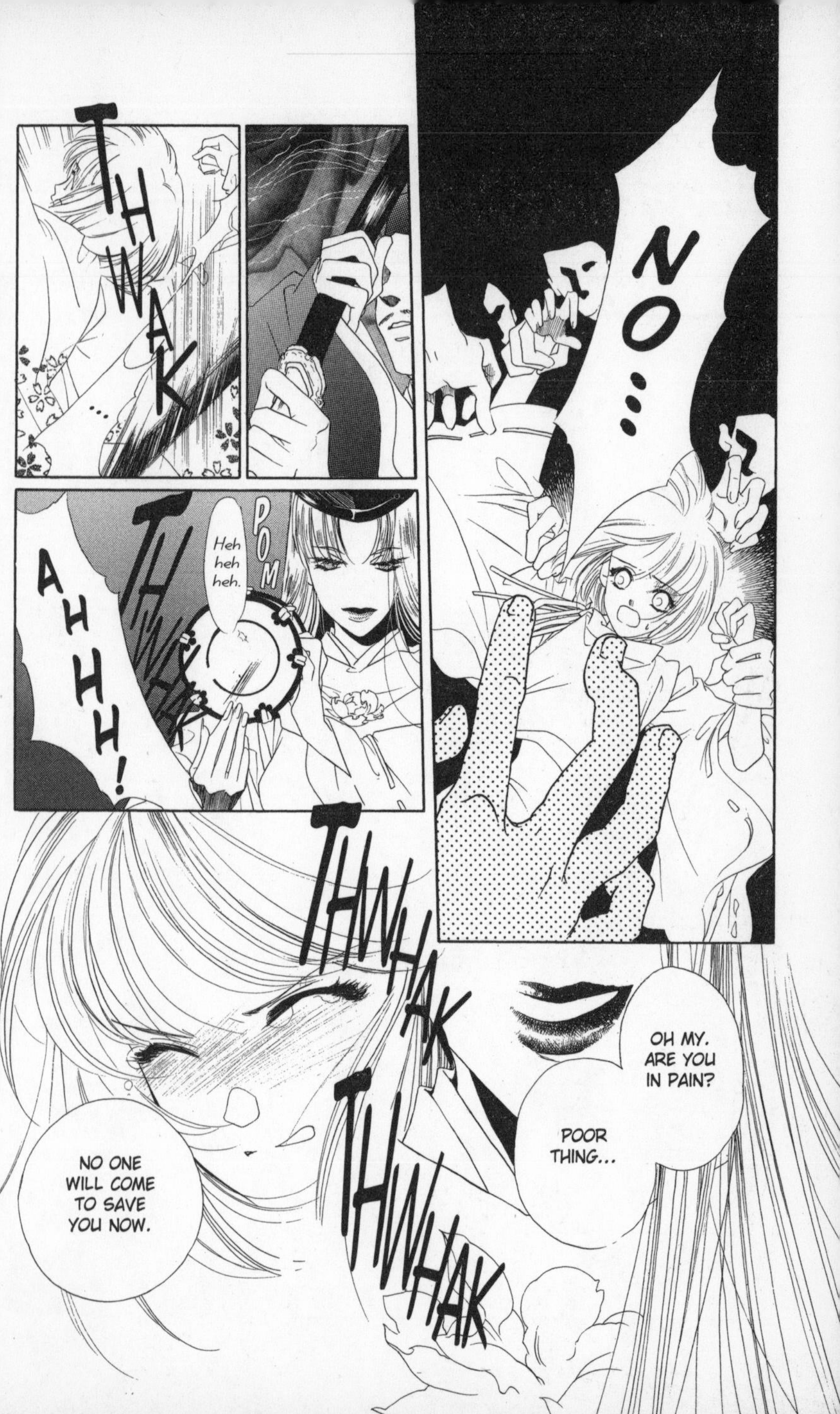
NO...
THWAK
...
Heh heh heh.
POM
THWAK
AHHHH!
THWHAK
OH MY. ARE YOU IN PAIN?
POOR THING...
THWHAK
NO ONE WILL COME TO SAVE YOU NOW.

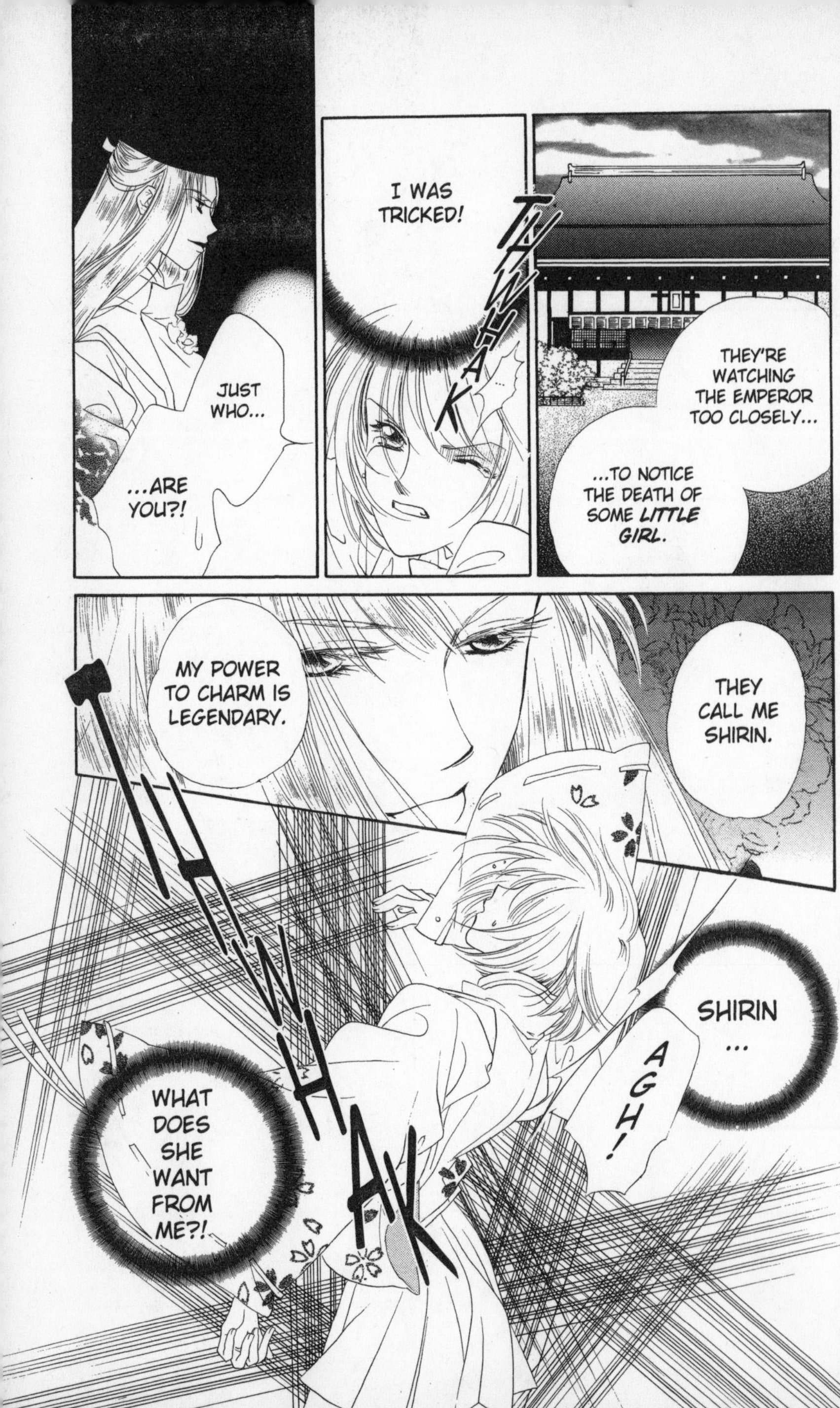
THEY'RE WATCHING THE EMPEROR TOO CLOSELY...
...TO NOTICE THE DEATH OF SOME *LITTLE GIRL*.
I WAS TRICKED!
THWHAK
JUST WHO...
...ARE YOU?!
THEY CALL ME SHIRIN.
MY POWER TO CHARM IS LEGENDARY.
SHIRIN ...
AGH!
WHAT DOES SHE WANT FROM ME?!
THWHAK

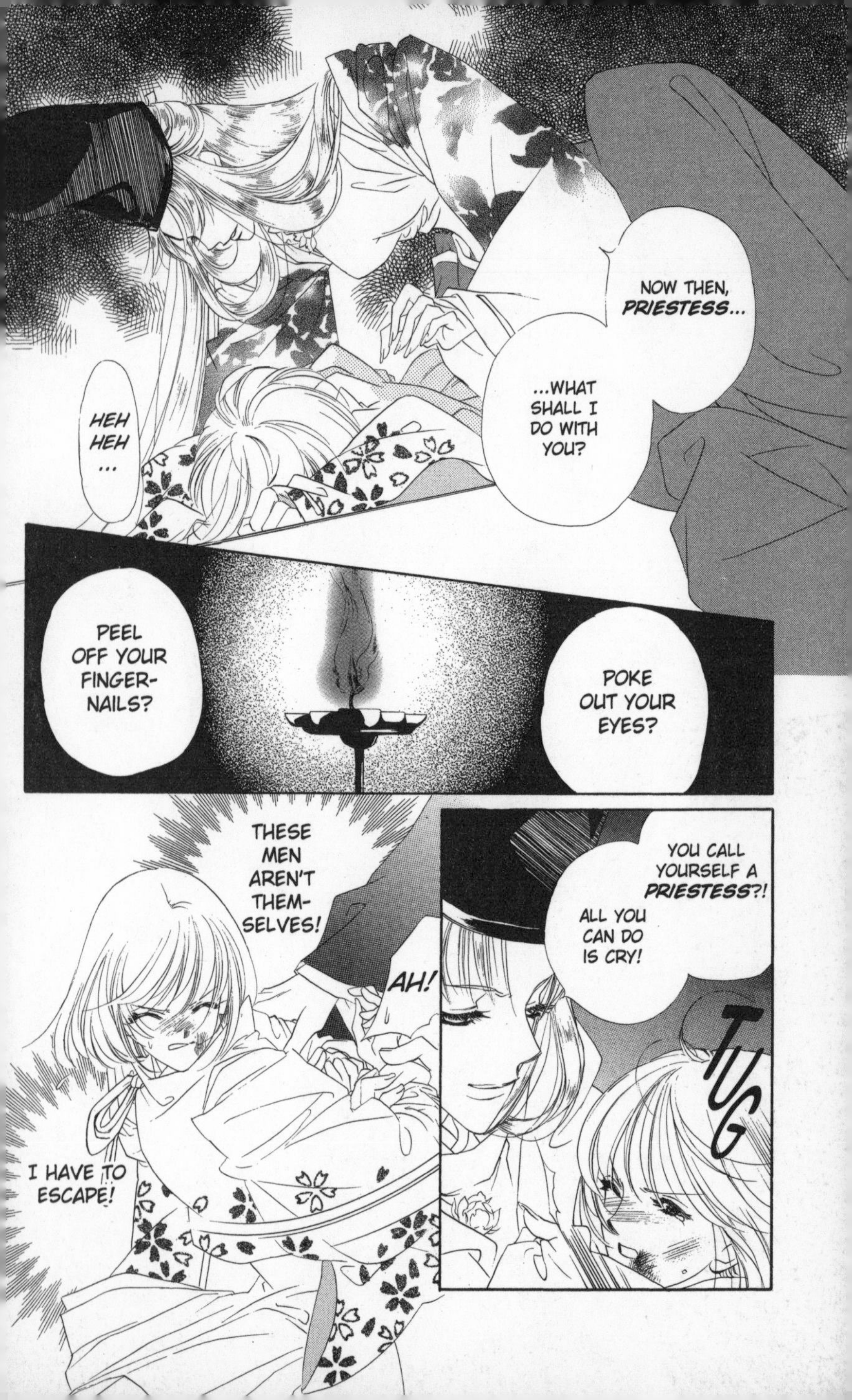
NOW THEN, **PRIESTESS...**
...WHAT SHALL I DO WITH YOU?
HEH HEH ...
POKE OUT YOUR EYES?
PEEL OFF YOUR FINGER-NAILS?
YOU CALL YOURSELF A **PRIESTESS**?!
ALL YOU CAN DO IS CRY!
TUG
AH!
THESE MEN AREN'T THEM-SELVES!
I HAVE TO ESCAPE!

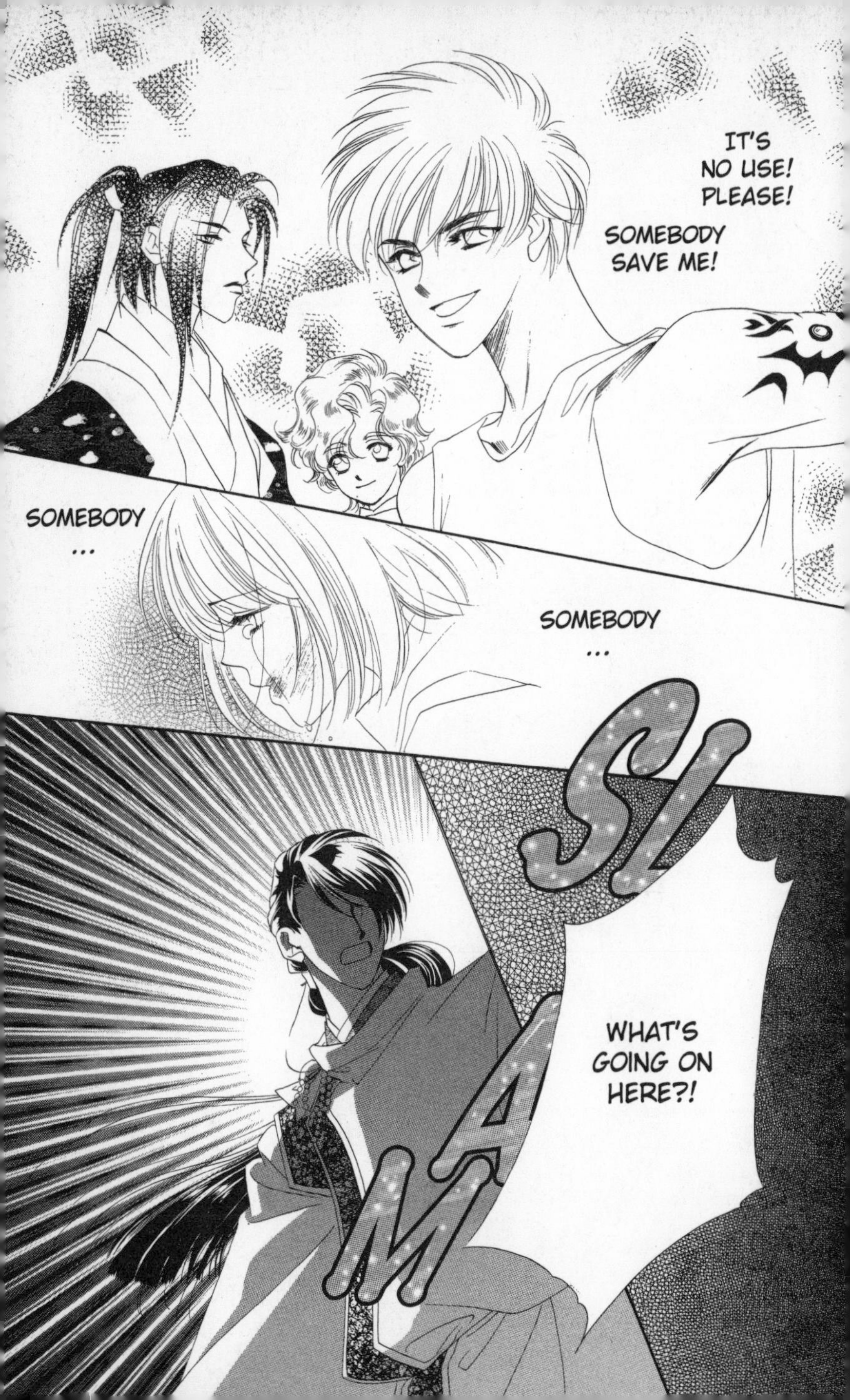
IT'S NO USE! PLEASE!
SOMEBODY SAVE ME!
SOMEBODY ...
SOMEBODY ...
SLAM
WHAT'S GOING ON HERE?!

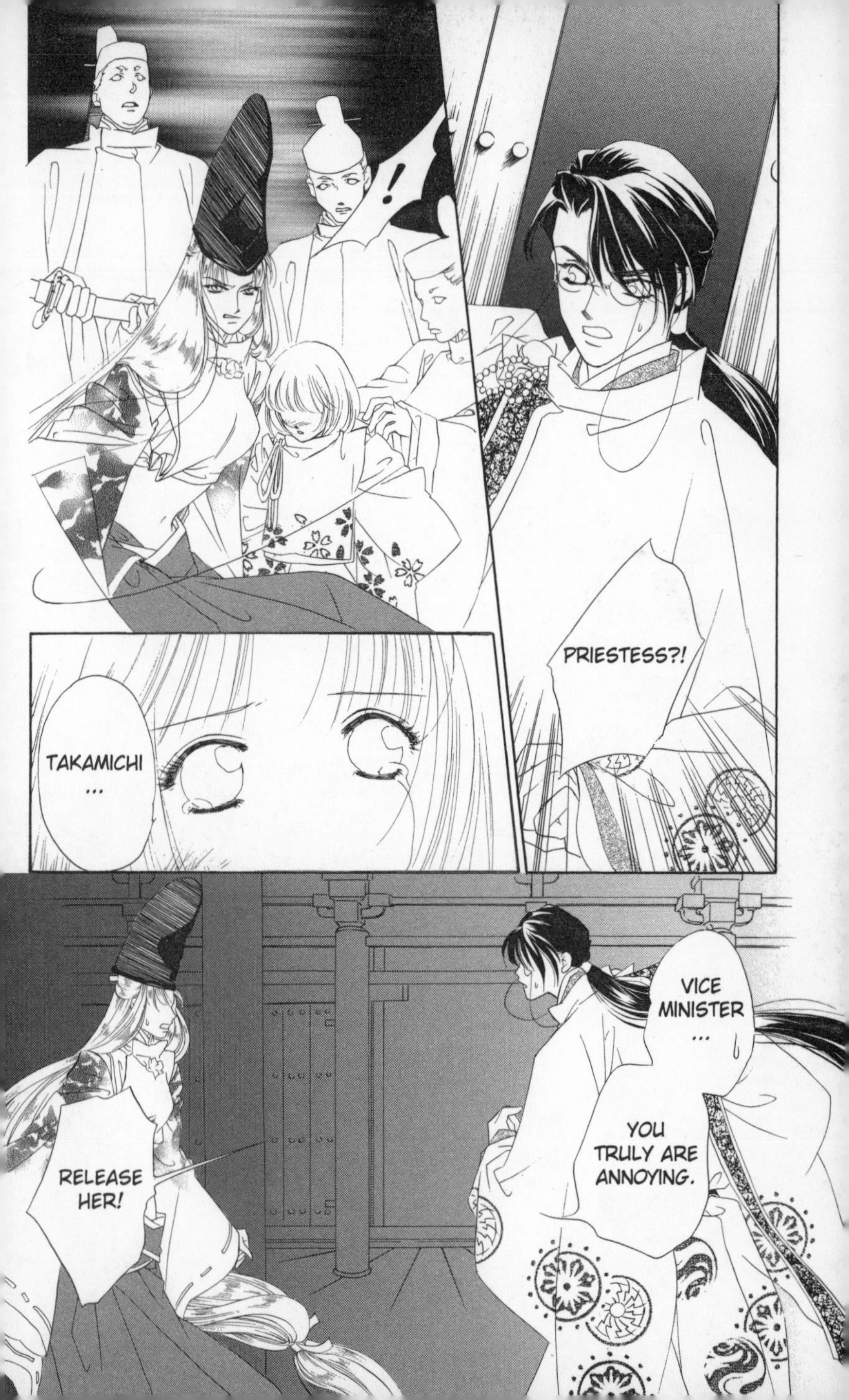
PRIESTESS?!
!
TAKAMICHI ...
VICE MINISTER ...
YOU TRULY ARE ANNOYING.
RELEASE HER!

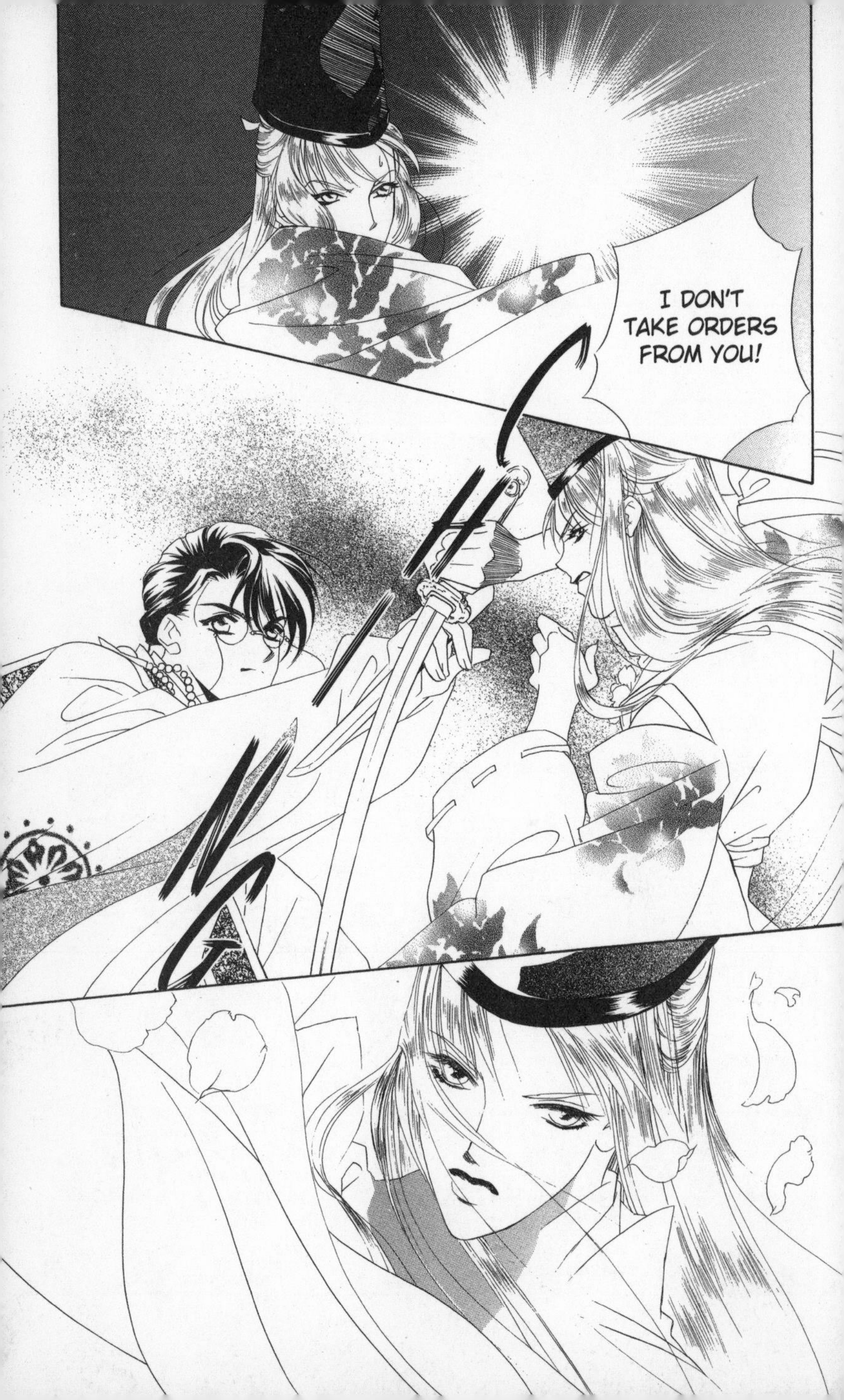
I DON'T TAKE ORDERS FROM YOU!

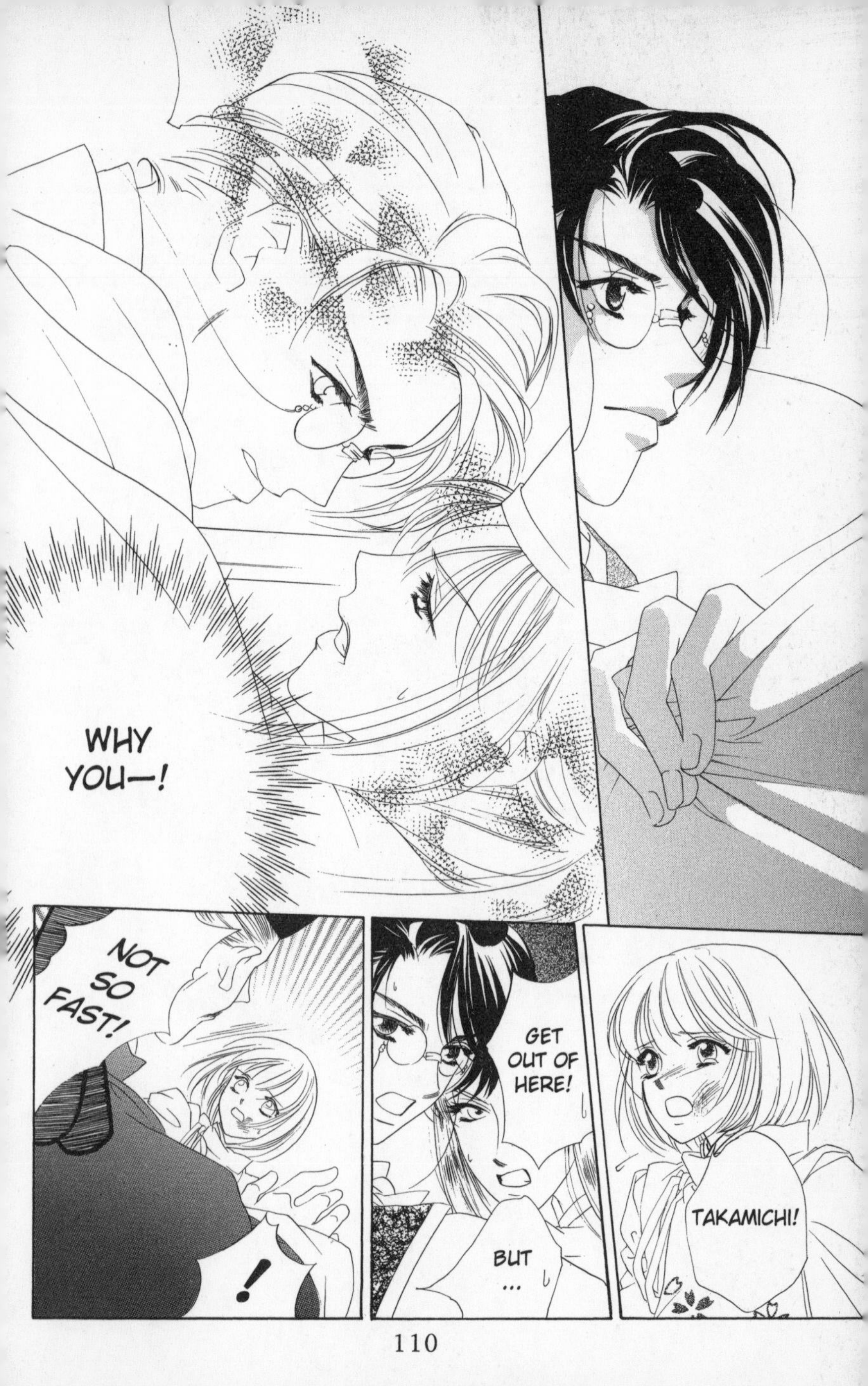
WHY YOU—!
TAKAMICHI!
GET OUT OF HERE!
BUT ...
NOT SO FAST!
!

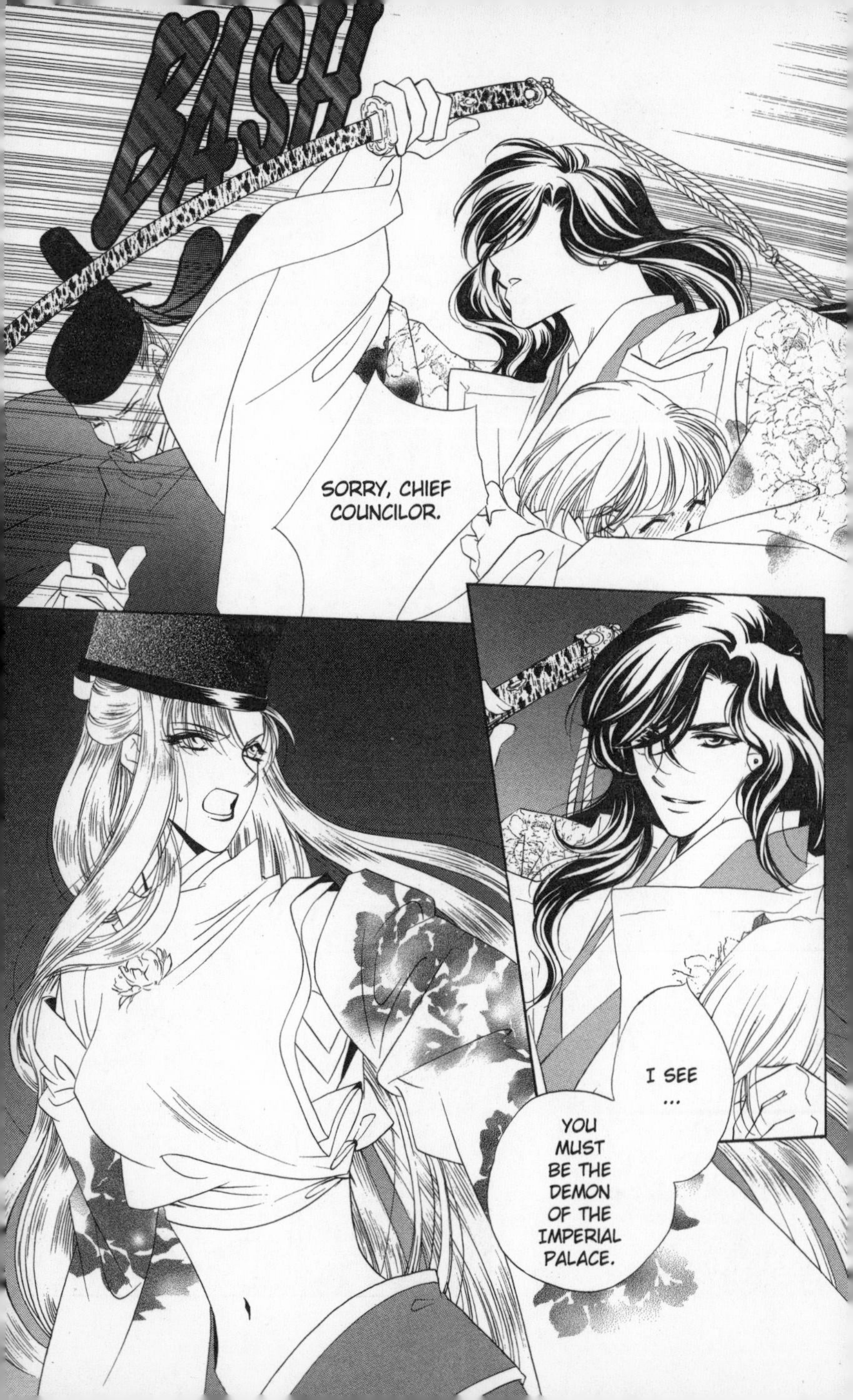
BASH
SORRY, CHIEF COUNCILOR.
I SEE ...
YOU MUST BE THE DEMON OF THE IMPERIAL PALACE.

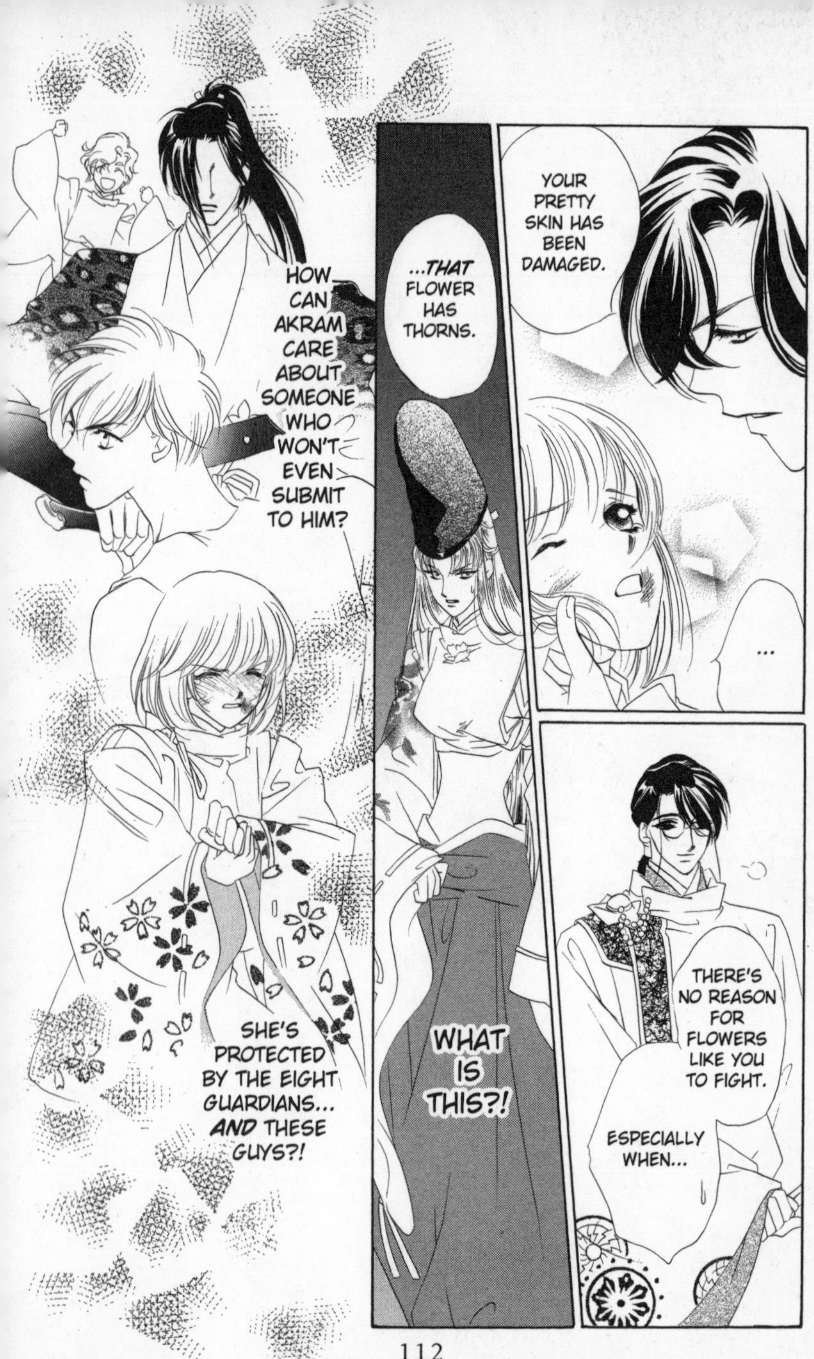
YOUR PRETTY SKIN HAS BEEN DAMAGED.
...
THERE'S NO REASON FOR FLOWERS LIKE YOU TO FIGHT.
ESPECIALLY WHEN...
...*THAT* FLOWER HAS THORNS.
WHAT IS THIS?!
HOW CAN AKRAM CARE ABOUT SOMEONE WHO WON'T EVEN SUBMIT TO HIM?
SHE'S PROTECTED BY THE EIGHT GUARDIANS... *AND* THESE GUYS?!

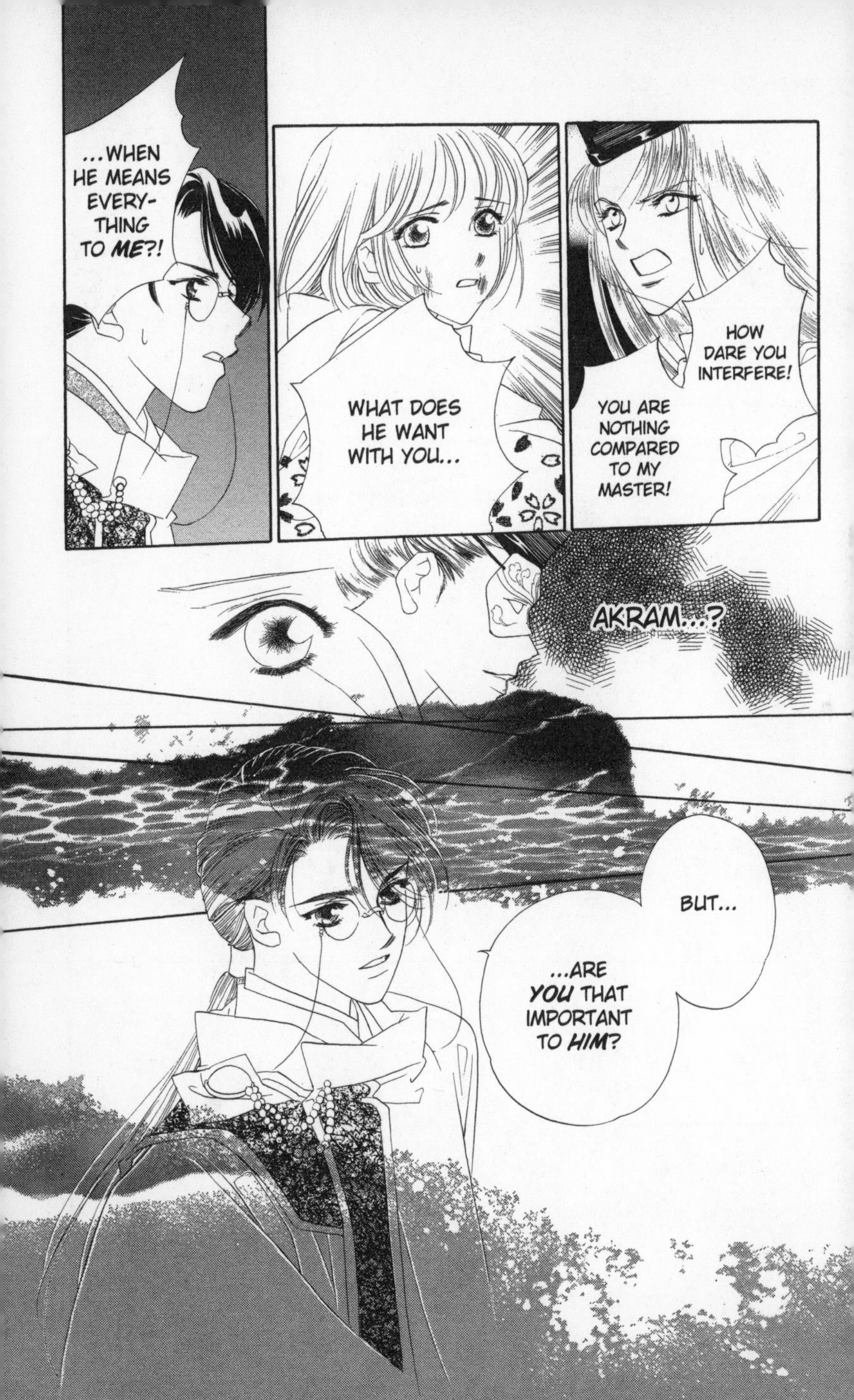
HOW DARE YOU INTERFERE!
YOU ARE NOTHING COMPARED TO MY MASTER!
WHAT DOES HE WANT WITH YOU...
...WHEN HE MEANS EVERYTHING TO *ME*?!
AKRAM...?
BUT...
...ARE *YOU* THAT IMPORTANT TO *HIM*?

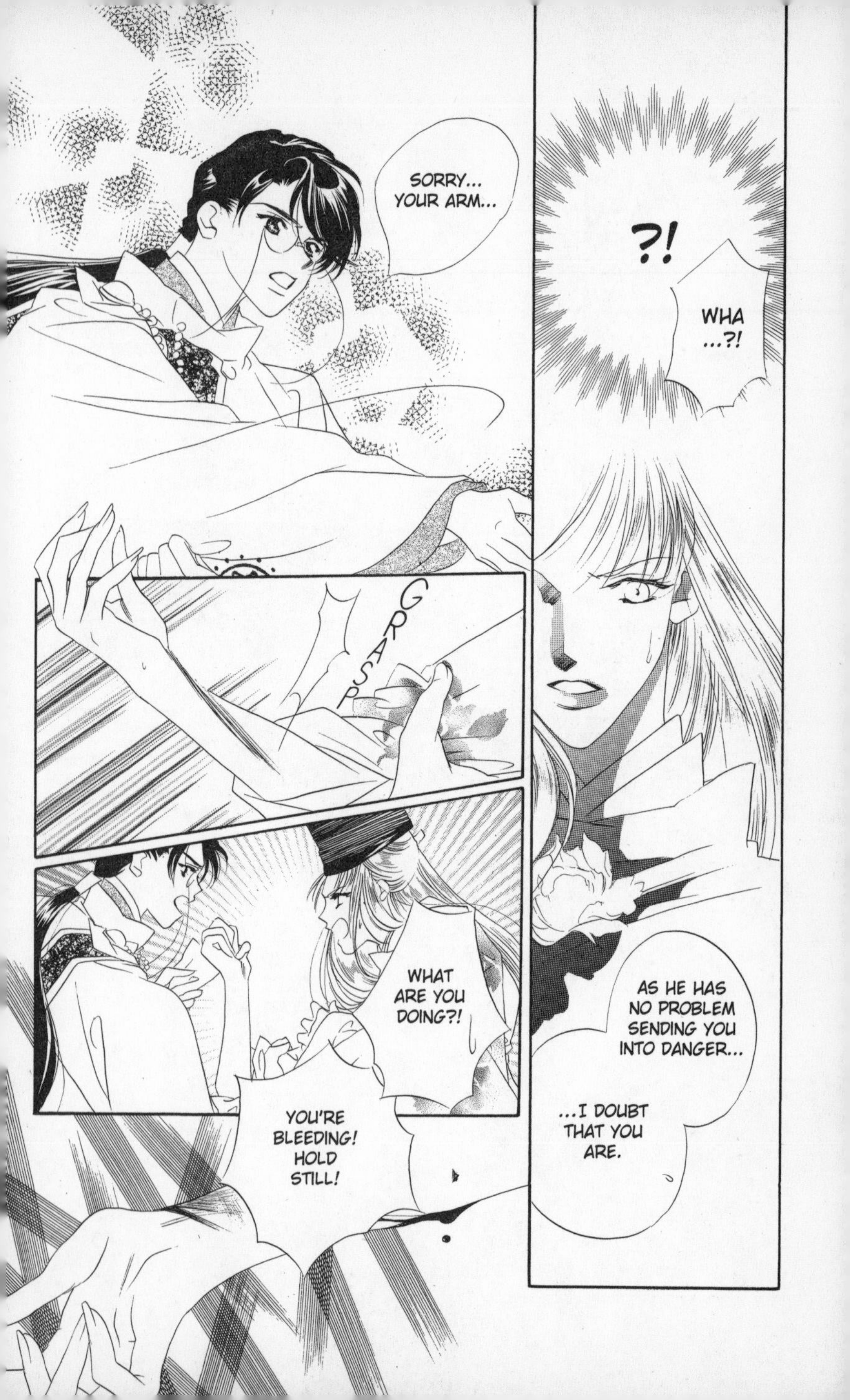
?!
WHA ...?!
AS HE HAS NO PROBLEM SENDING YOU INTO DANGER...
...I DOUBT THAT YOU ARE.
SORRY... YOUR ARM...
GRASP
WHAT ARE YOU DOING?!
YOU'RE BLEEDING! HOLD STILL!

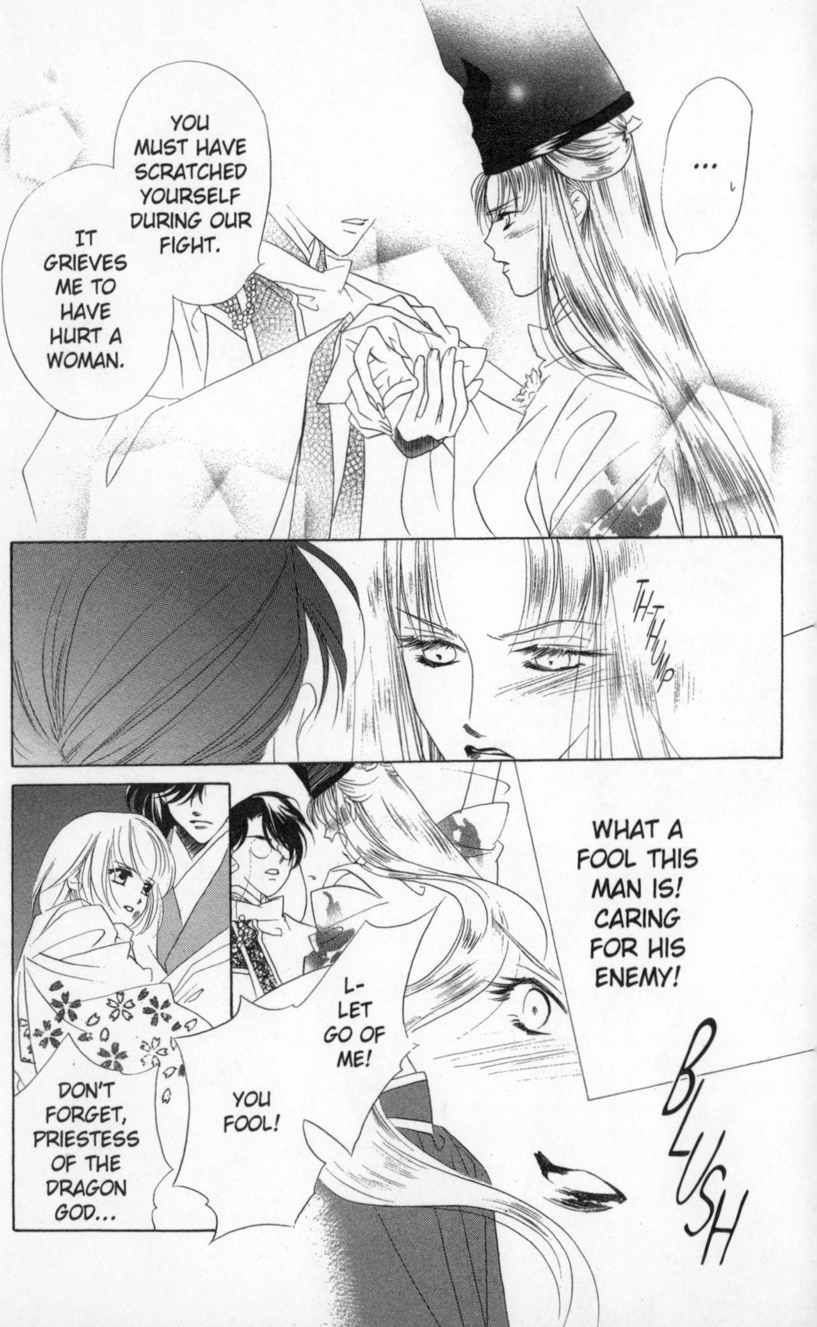
...
YOU MUST HAVE SCRATCHED YOURSELF DURING OUR FIGHT.
IT GRIEVES ME TO HAVE HURT A WOMAN.
TH-THUMP
WHAT A FOOL THIS MAN IS! CARING FOR HIS ENEMY!
BLUSH
L-LET GO OF ME!
YOU FOOL!
DON'T FORGET, PRIESTESS OF THE DRAGON GOD...

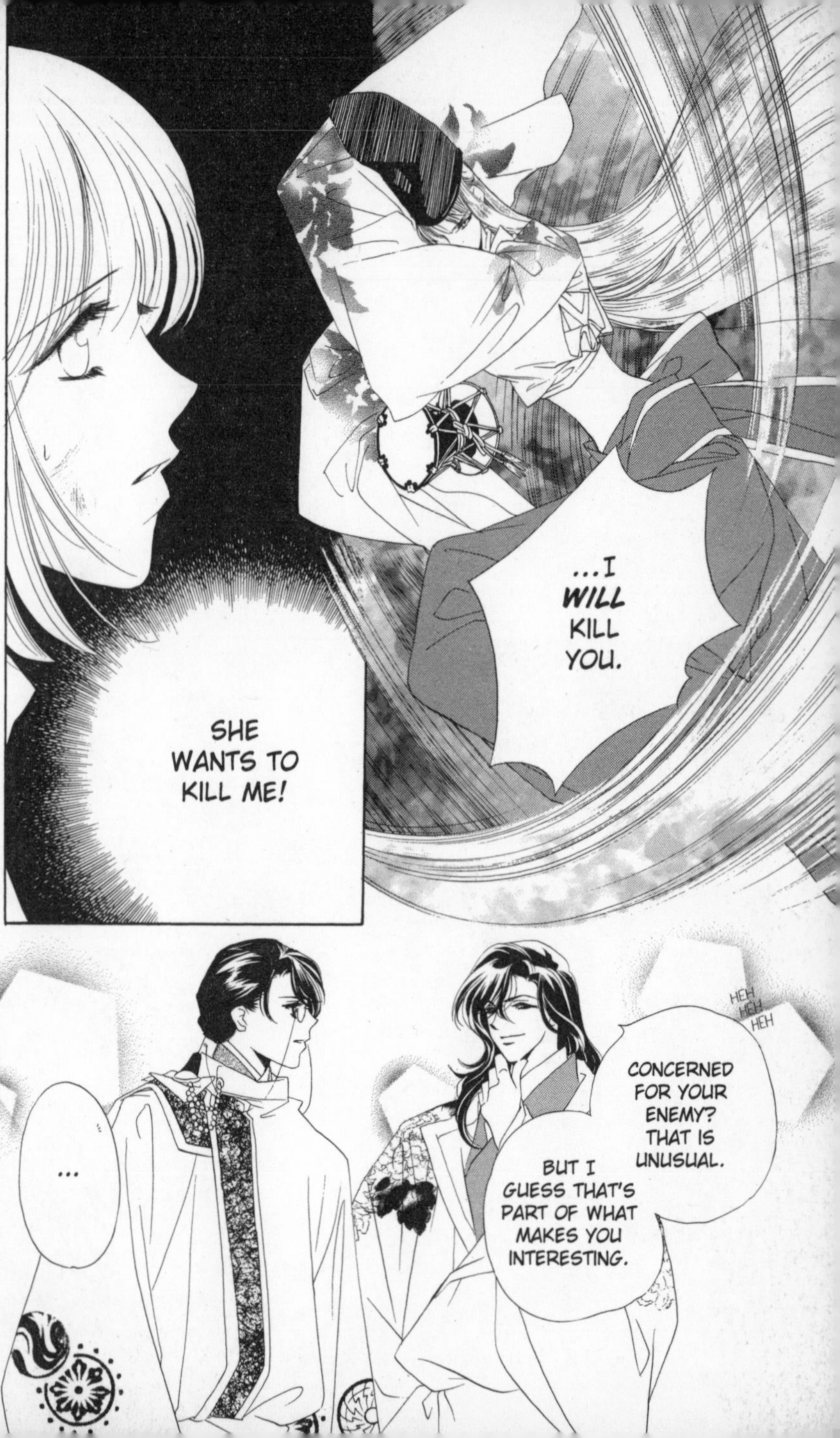
...I WILL KILL YOU.
SHE WANTS TO KILL ME!
HEH HEH HEH
CONCERNED FOR YOUR ENEMY? THAT IS UNUSUAL.
BUT I GUESS THAT'S PART OF WHAT MAKES YOU INTERESTING.
...

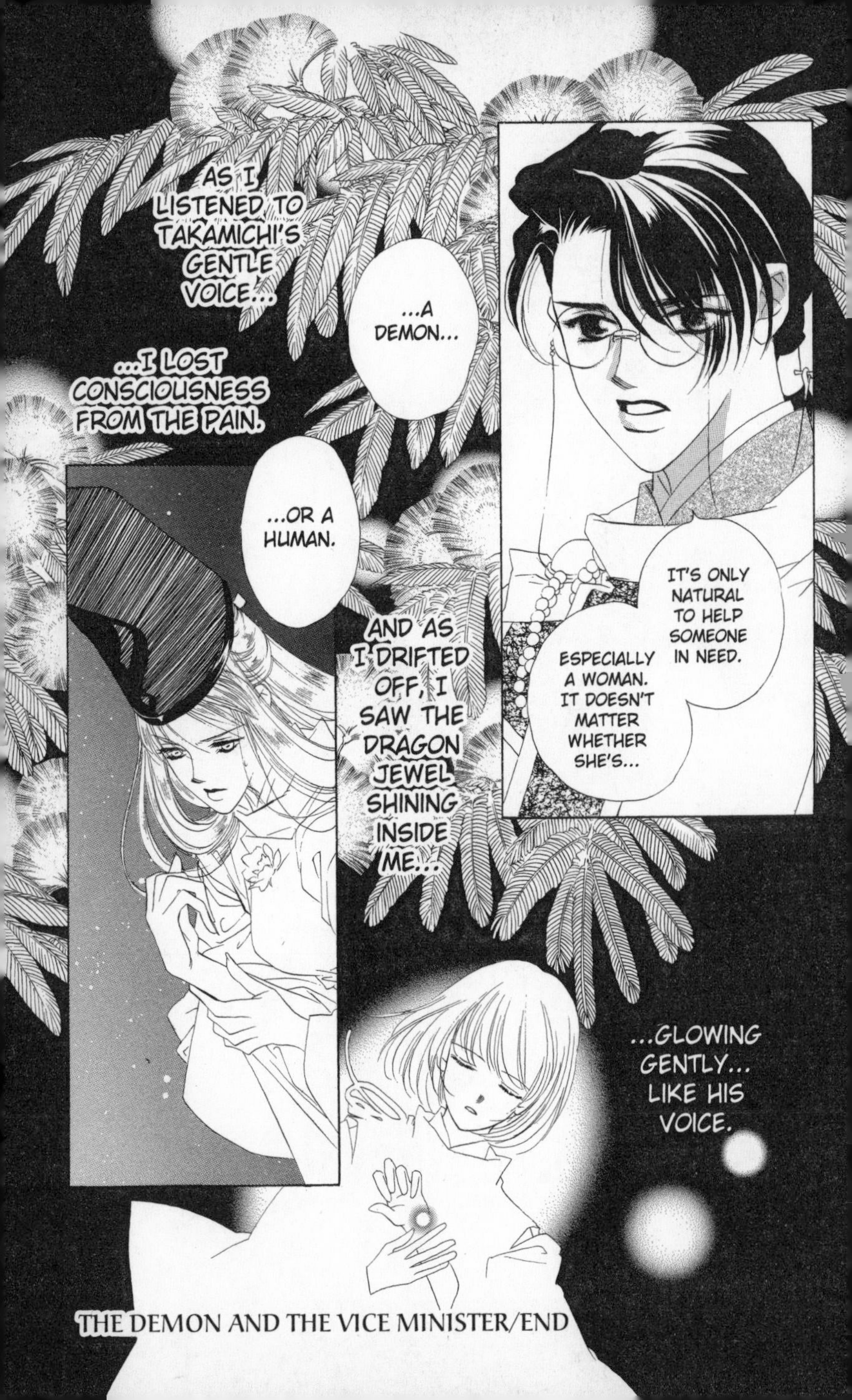
IT'S ONLY NATURAL TO HELP SOMEONE IN NEED.
ESPECIALLY A WOMAN. IT DOESN'T MATTER WHETHER SHE'S...
...A DEMON...
...OR A HUMAN.
AS I LISTENED TO TAKAMICHI'S GENTLE VOICE...
...I LOST CONSCIOUSNESS FROM THE PAIN.
AND AS I DRIFTED OFF, I SAW THE DRAGON JEWEL SHINING INSIDE ME...
...GLOWING GENTLY... LIKE HIS VOICE.
THE DEMON AND THE VICE MINISTER/END

THE EIGHT GUARDIANS: WHAT YOU WISH THEY'D SAY

<Minamoto-no-Yorihisa>

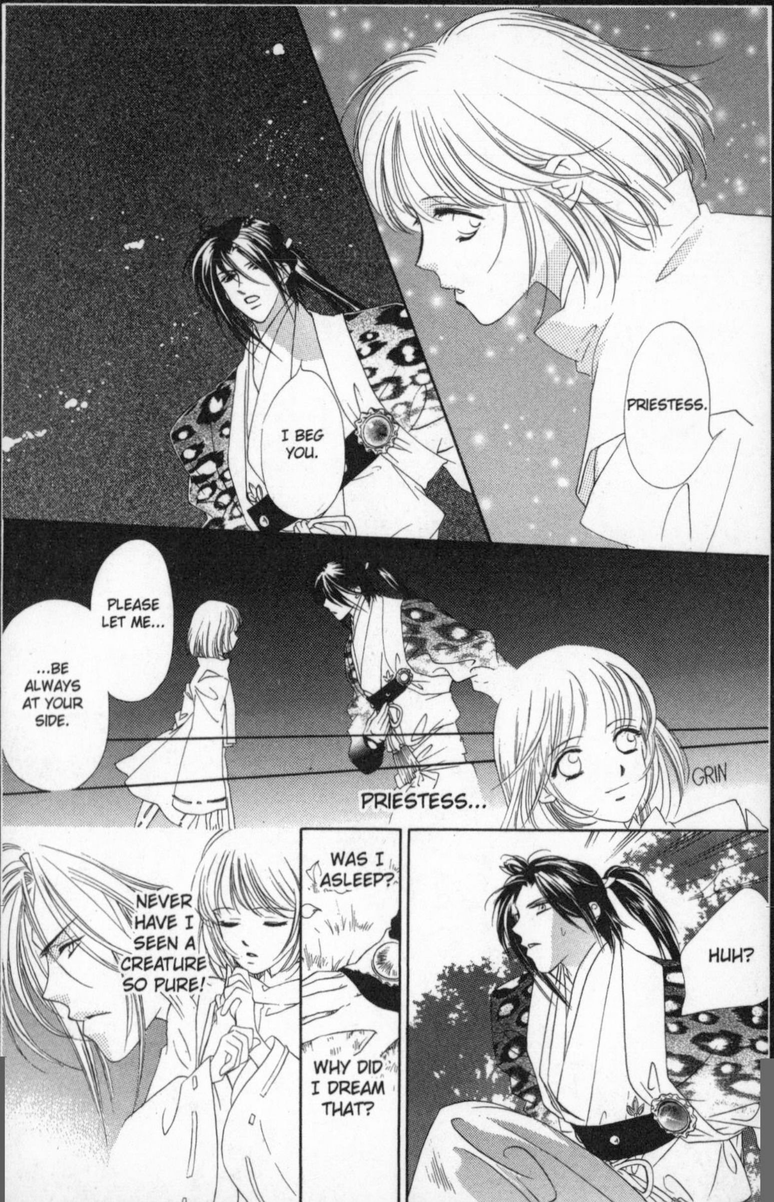
PRIESTESS.
I BEG YOU.
GRIN
PRIESTESS...
PLEASE LET ME...
...BE ALWAYS AT YOUR SIDE.
HUH?
WAS I ASLEEP?
WHY DID I DREAM THAT?
NEVER HAVE I SEEN A CREATURE SO PURE!

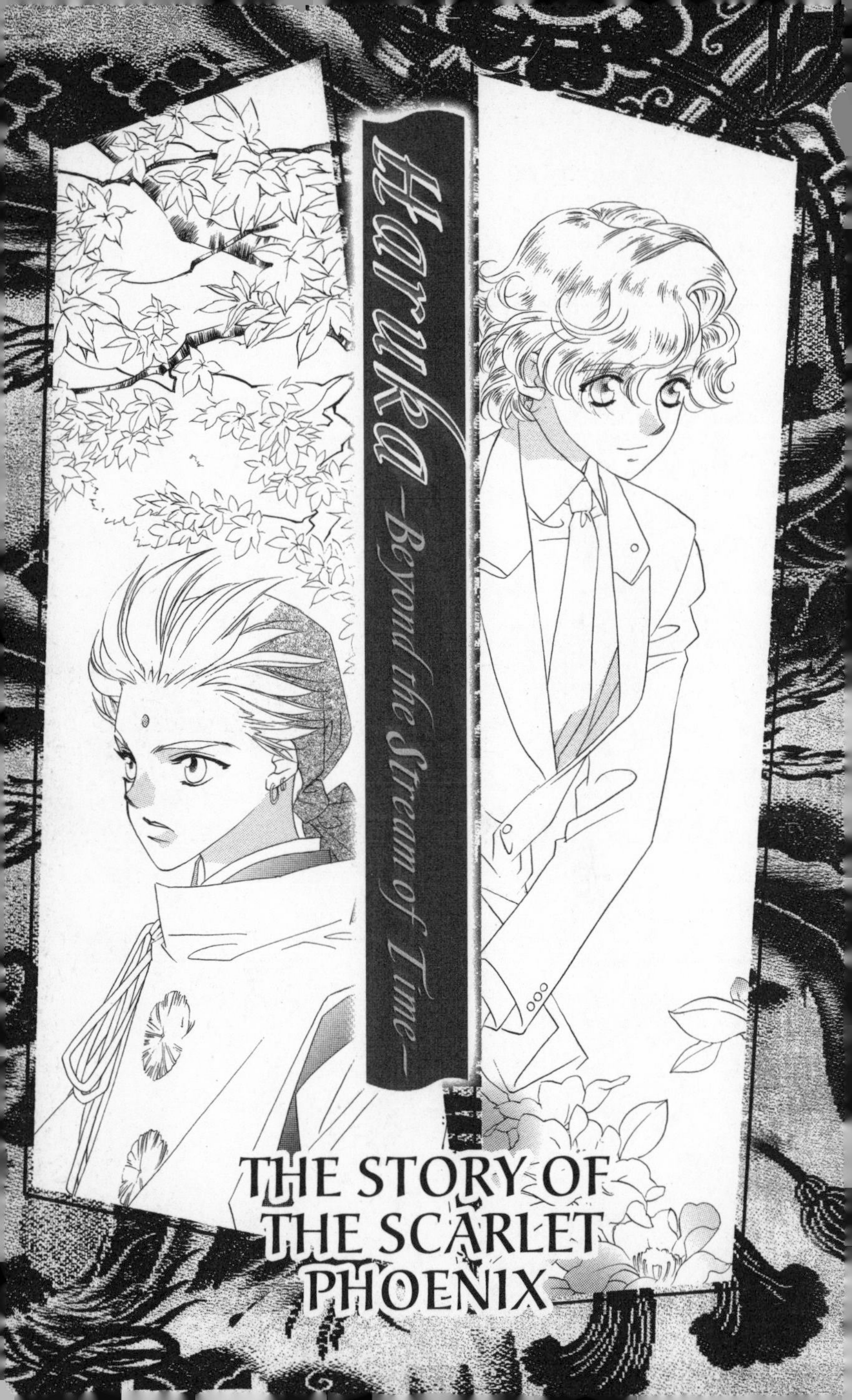
Haruka -Beyond the Stream of Time-
THE STORY OF THE SCARLET PHOENIX

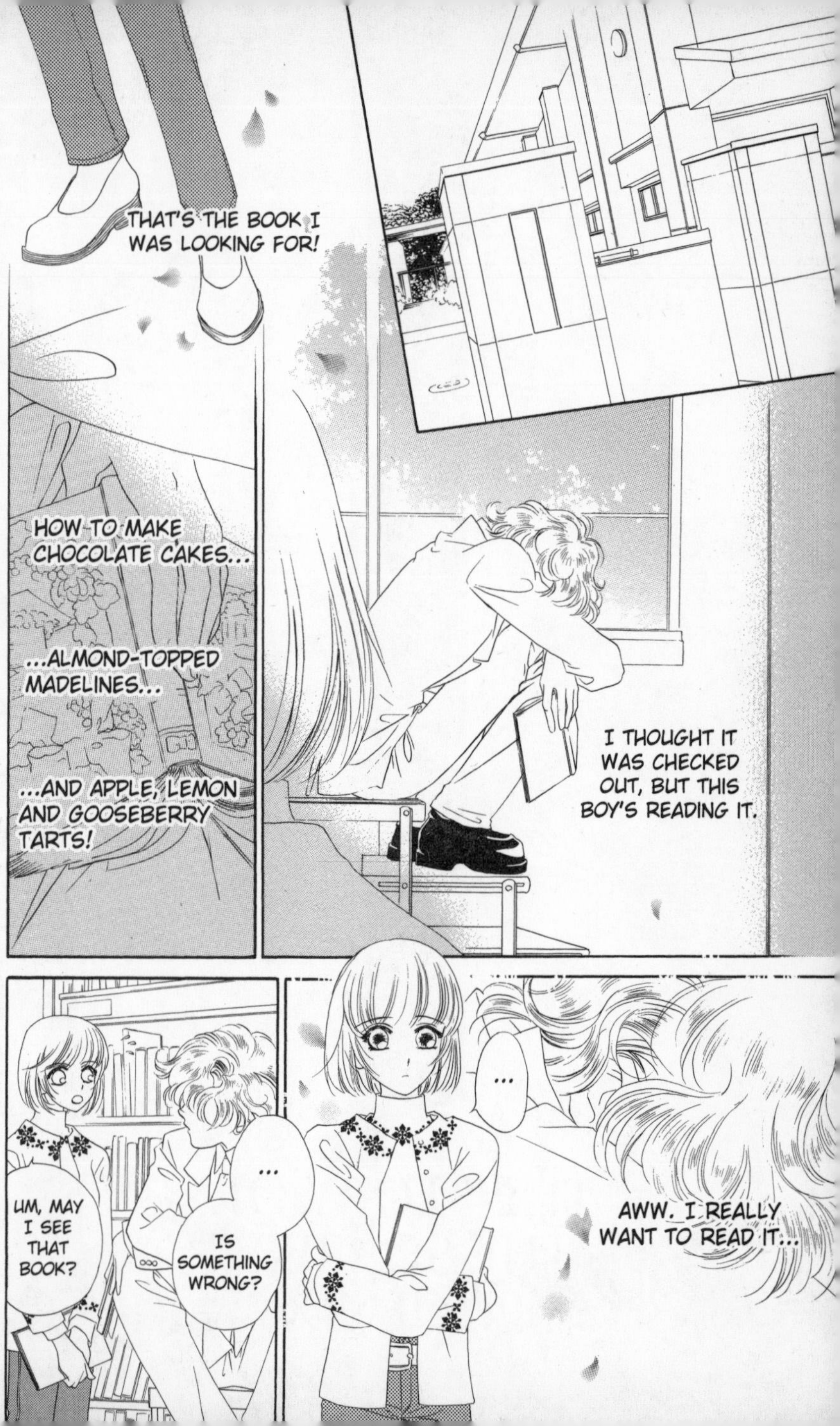
THAT'S THE BOOK I WAS LOOKING FOR!
I THOUGHT IT WAS CHECKED OUT, BUT THIS BOY'S READING IT.
HOW TO MAKE CHOCOLATE CAKES...
...ALMOND-TOPPED MADELINES...
...AND APPLE, LEMON AND GOOSEBERRY TARTS!
...
AWW. I REALLY WANT TO READ IT...
...
IS SOMETHING WRONG?
UM, MAY I SEE THAT BOOK?

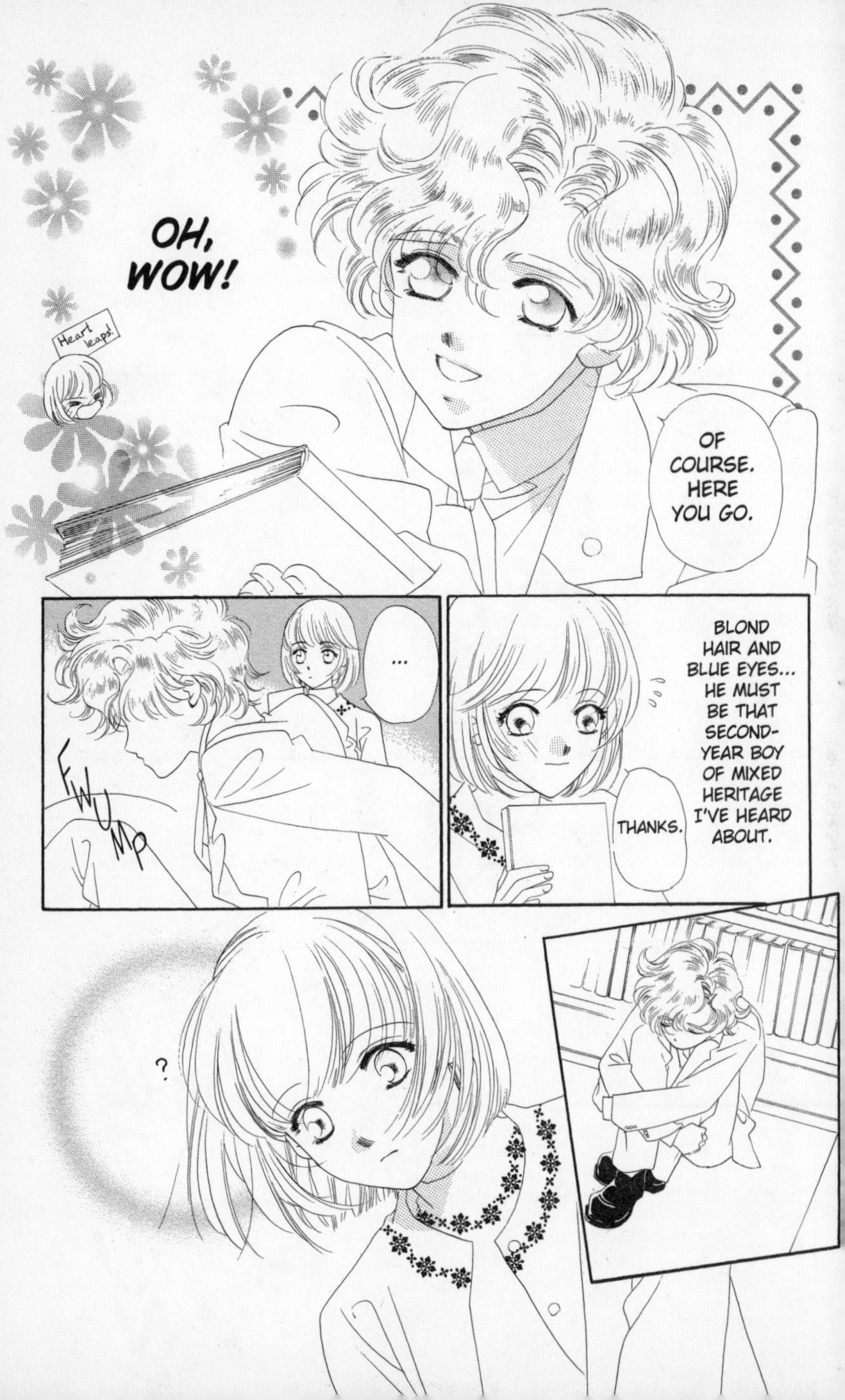
OF COURSE. HERE YOU GO.
OH, WOW!
Heart leaps!
BLOND HAIR AND BLUE EYES... HE MUST BE THAT SECOND-YEAR BOY OF MIXED HERITAGE I'VE HEARD ABOUT.
THANKS.
...
FWUMP
?

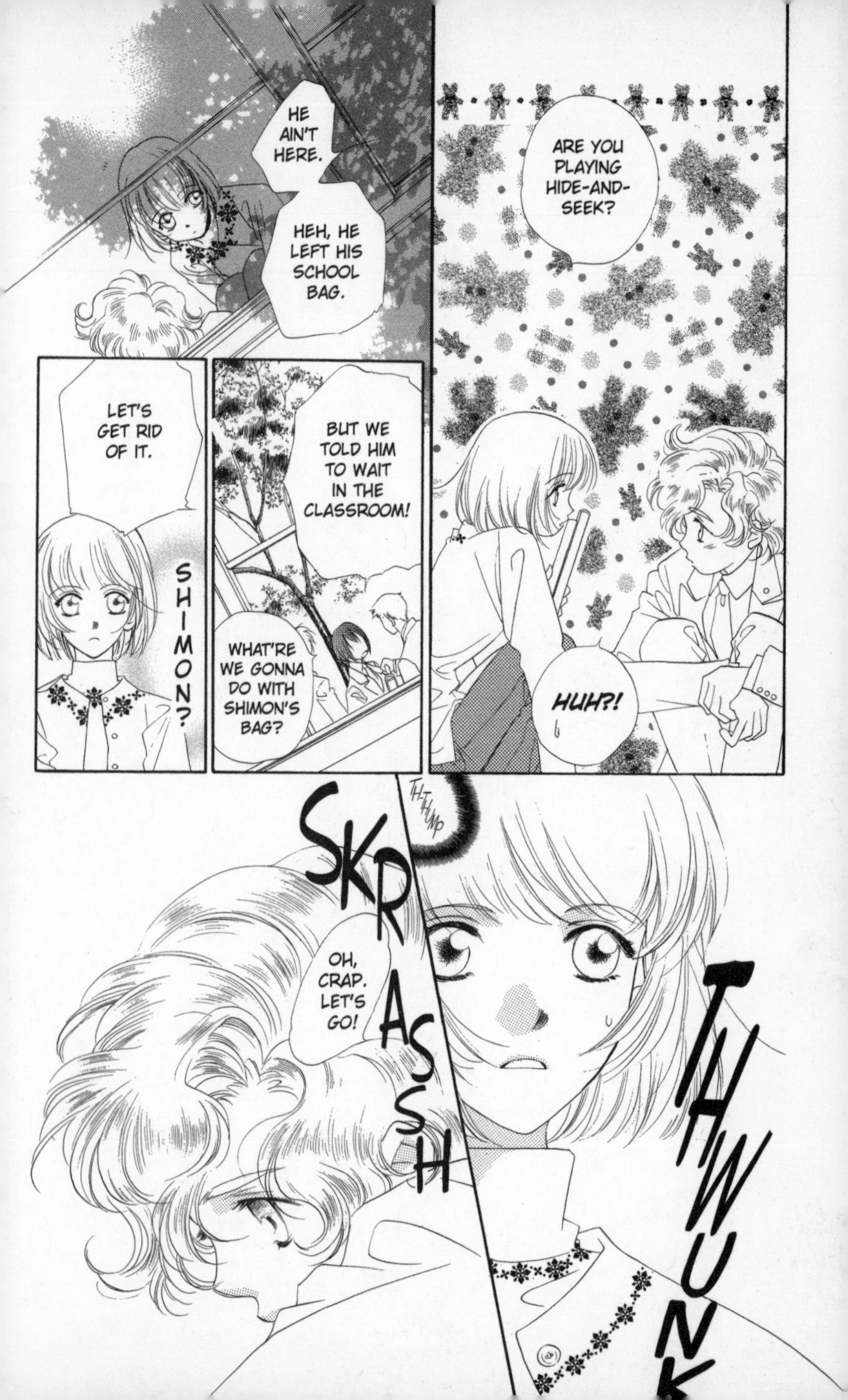
ARE YOU PLAYING HIDE-AND-SEEK?
HUH?!
HE AIN'T HERE.
HEH, HE LEFT HIS SCHOOL BAG.
BUT WE TOLD HIM TO WAIT IN THE CLASSROOM!
WHAT'RE WE GONNA DO WITH SHIMON'S BAG?
LET'S GET RID OF IT.
SHIMON?
TH-THUMP
SKRASH
THWUNK
OH, CRAP. LET'S GO!

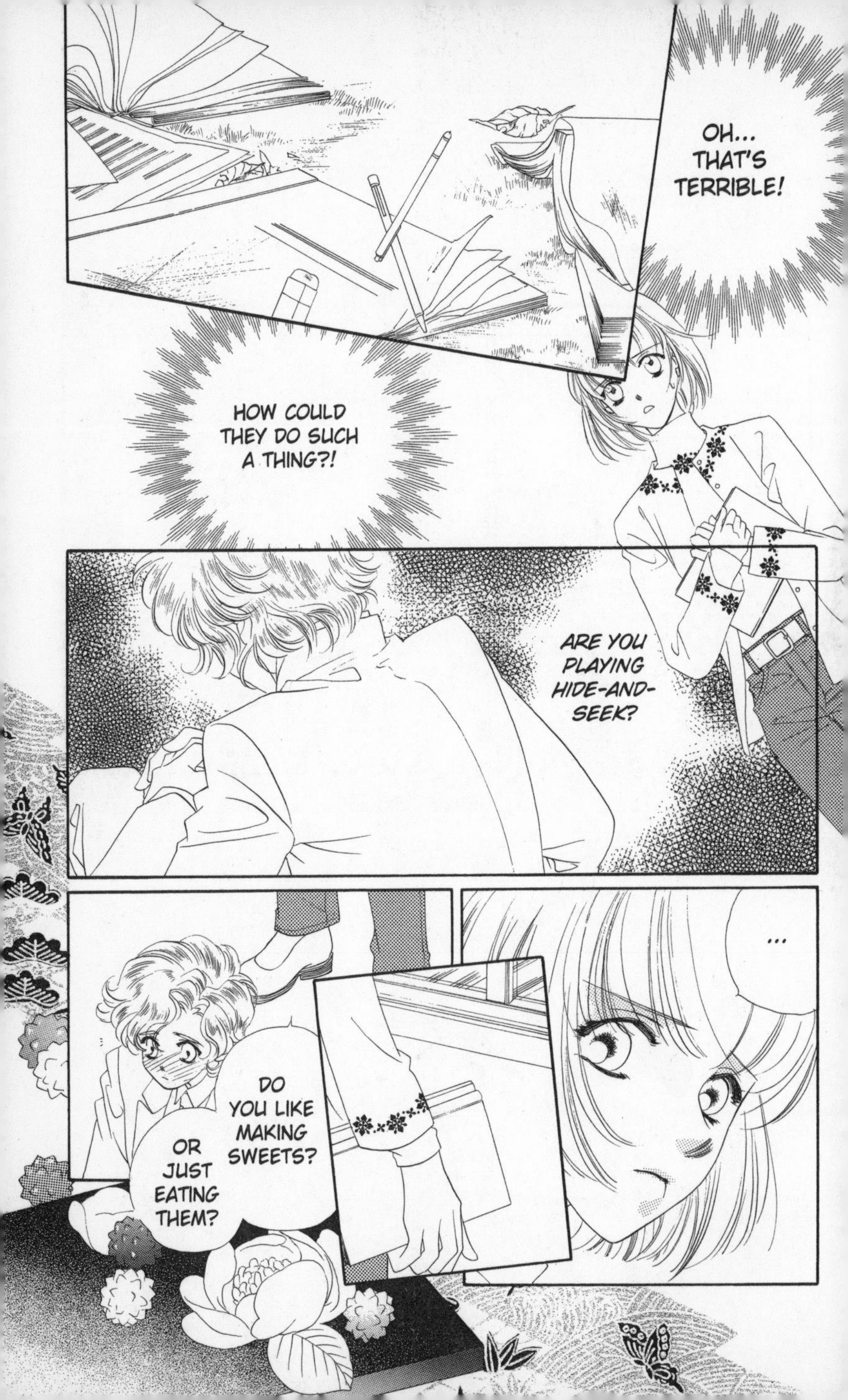
OH... THAT'S TERRIBLE!
HOW COULD THEY DO SUCH A THING?!
ARE YOU PLAYING HIDE-AND-SEEK?
...
DO YOU LIKE MAKING SWEETS?
OR JUST EATING THEM?

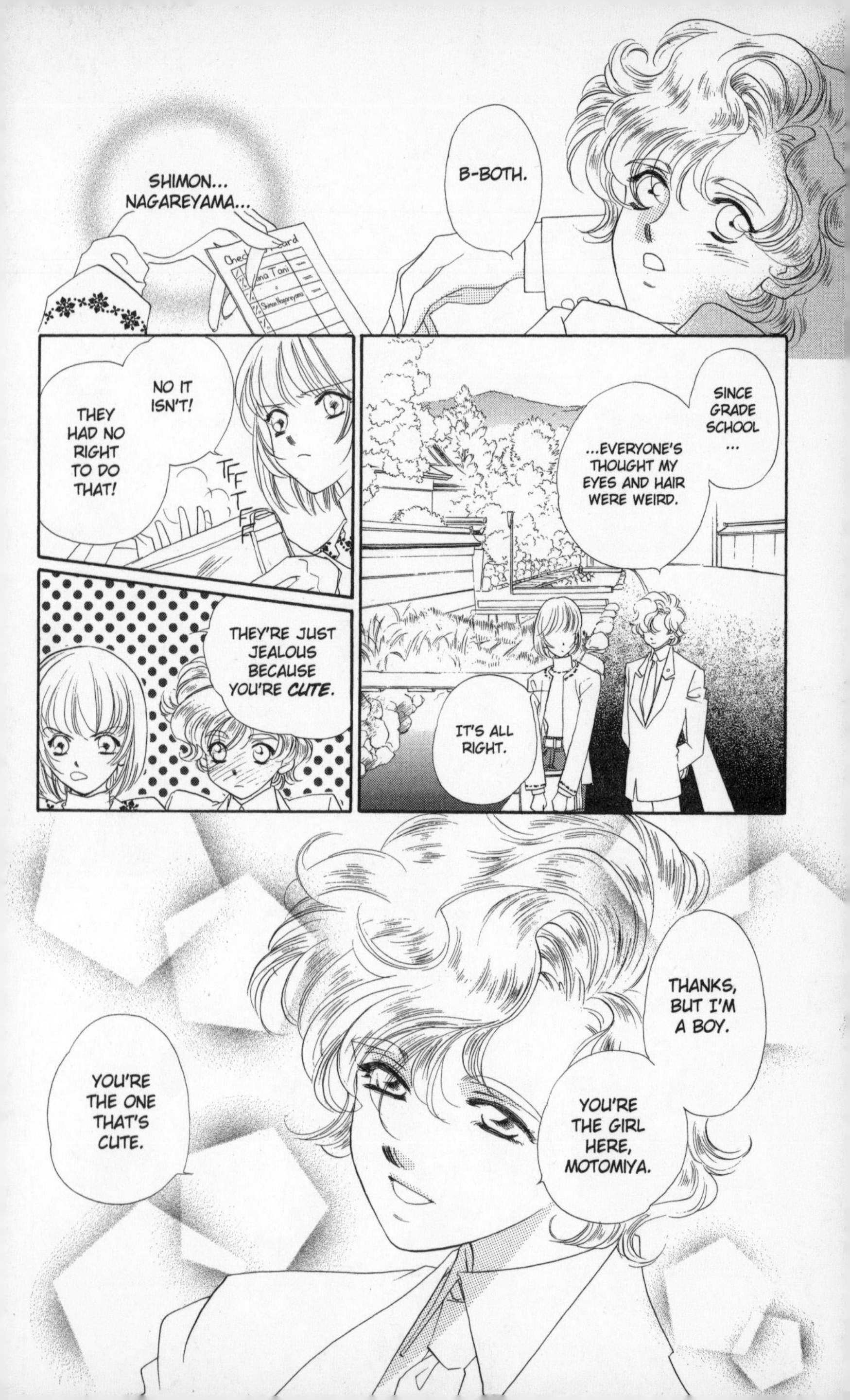
B-BOTH.
SHIMON... NAGAREYAMA...
SINCE GRADE SCHOOL ...
...EVERYONE'S THOUGHT MY EYES AND HAIR WERE WEIRD.
IT'S ALL RIGHT.
NO IT ISN'T!
THEY HAD NO RIGHT TO DO THAT!
TFF TFF
THEY'RE JUST JEALOUS BECAUSE YOU'RE *CUTE*.
THANKS, BUT I'M A BOY.
YOU'RE THE GIRL HERE, MOTOMIYA.
YOU'RE THE ONE THAT'S CUTE.

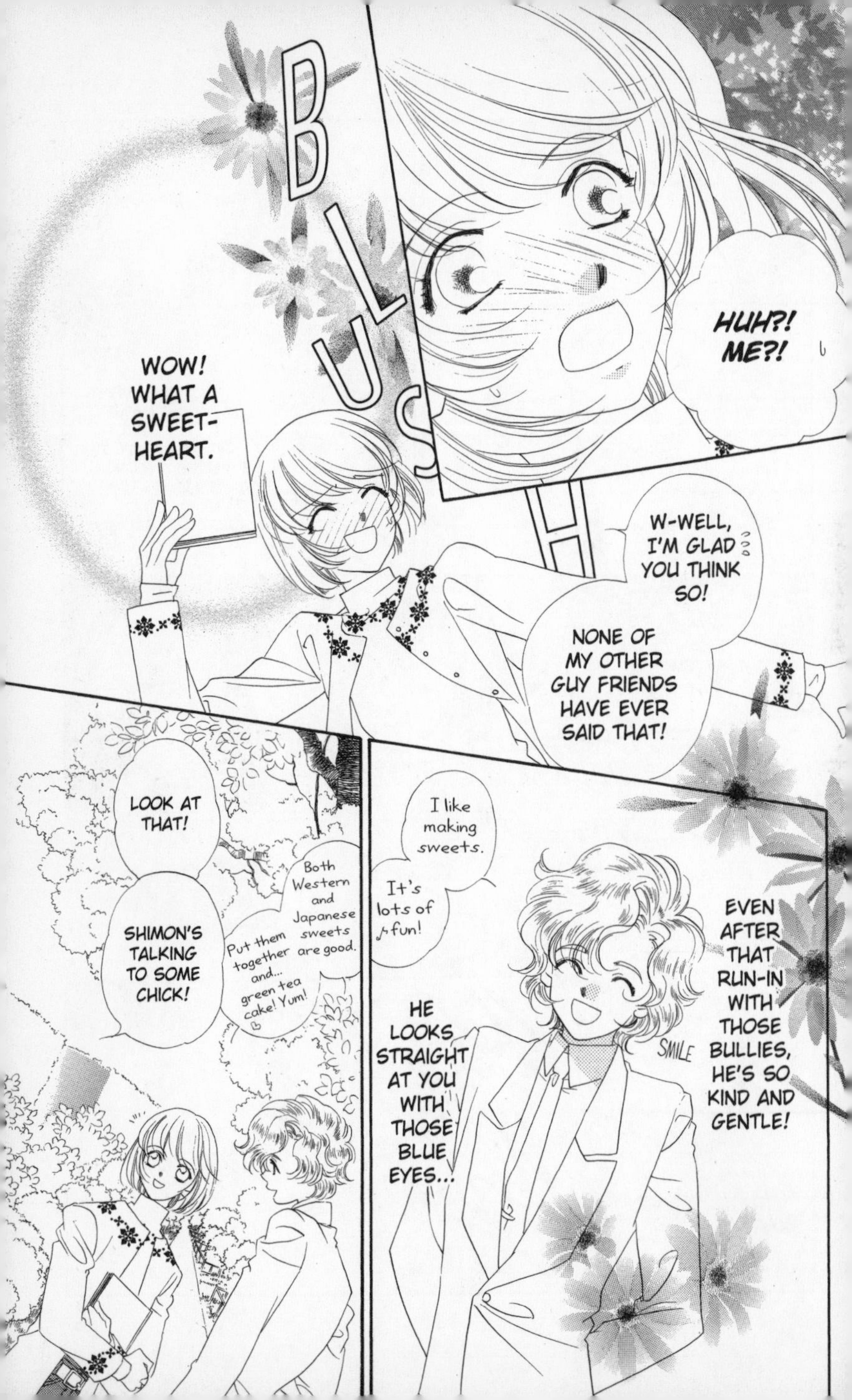
HUH?! ME?!
BLUSH
WOW! WHAT A SWEET-HEART.
W-WELL, I'M GLAD YOU THINK SO!
NONE OF MY OTHER GUY FRIENDS HAVE EVER SAID THAT!
I like making sweets.
It's lots of fun!
EVEN AFTER THAT RUN-IN WITH THOSE BULLIES, HE'S SO KIND AND GENTLE!
SMILE
HE LOOKS STRAIGHT AT YOU WITH THOSE BLUE EYES...
Both Western and Japanese sweets are good.
Put them together and... green tea cake! Yum!
LOOK AT THAT!
SHIMON'S TALKING TO SOME CHICK!

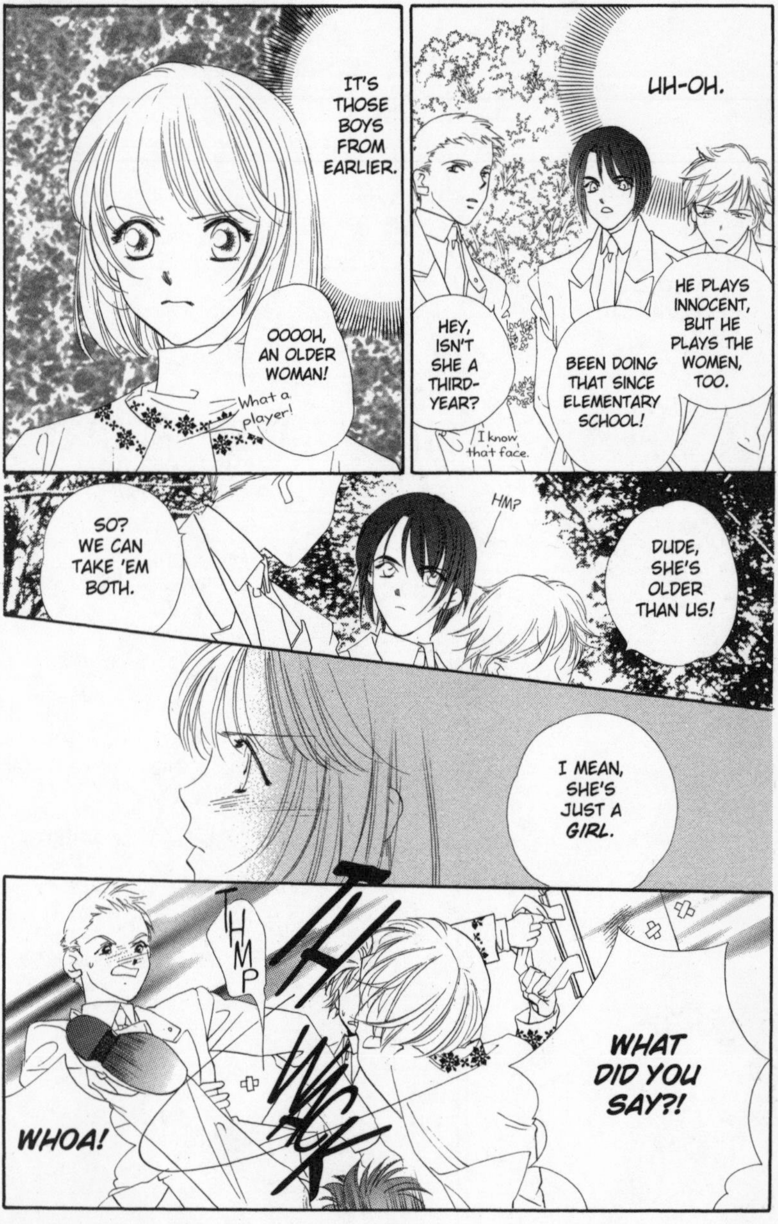
UH-OH.
HE PLAYS INNOCENT, BUT HE PLAYS THE WOMEN, TOO.
BEEN DOING THAT SINCE ELEMENTARY SCHOOL!
HEY, ISN'T SHE A THIRD-YEAR?
I know that face.
IT'S THOSE BOYS FROM EARLIER.
OOOOH, AN OLDER WOMAN!
What a player!
DUDE, SHE'S OLDER THAN US!
HM?
SO? WE CAN TAKE 'EM BOTH.
I MEAN, SHE'S JUST A GIRL.
WHAT DID YOU SAY?!
THWACK
THMP
WHOA!

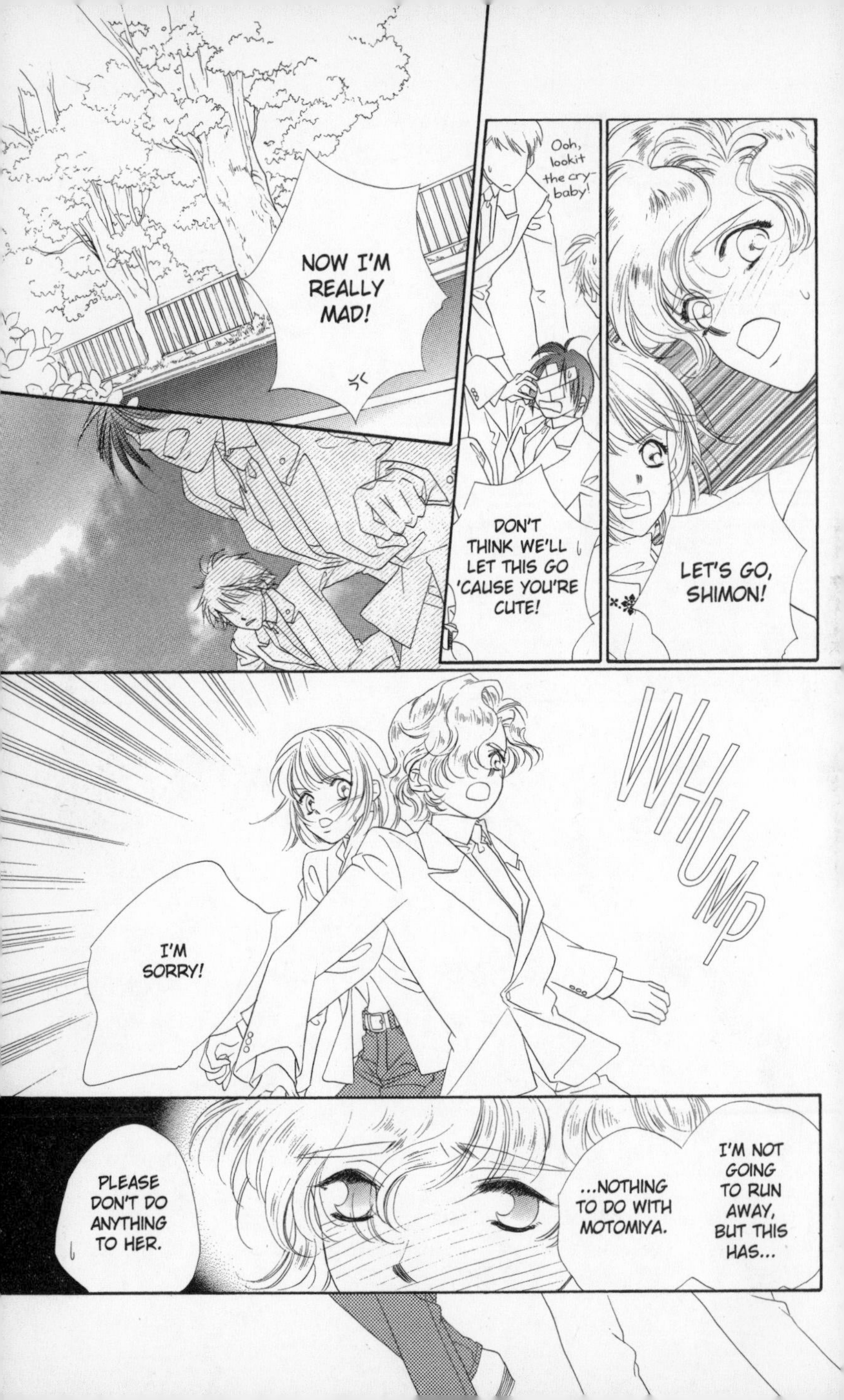
LET'S GO, SHIMON!
Ooh, lookit the cry-baby!
DON'T THINK WE'LL LET THIS GO 'CAUSE YOU'RE CUTE!
NOW I'M REALLY MAD!
WHUMP
I'M SORRY!
I'M NOT GOING TO RUN AWAY, BUT THIS HAS...
...NOTHING TO DO WITH MOTOMIYA.
PLEASE DON'T DO ANYTHING TO HER.

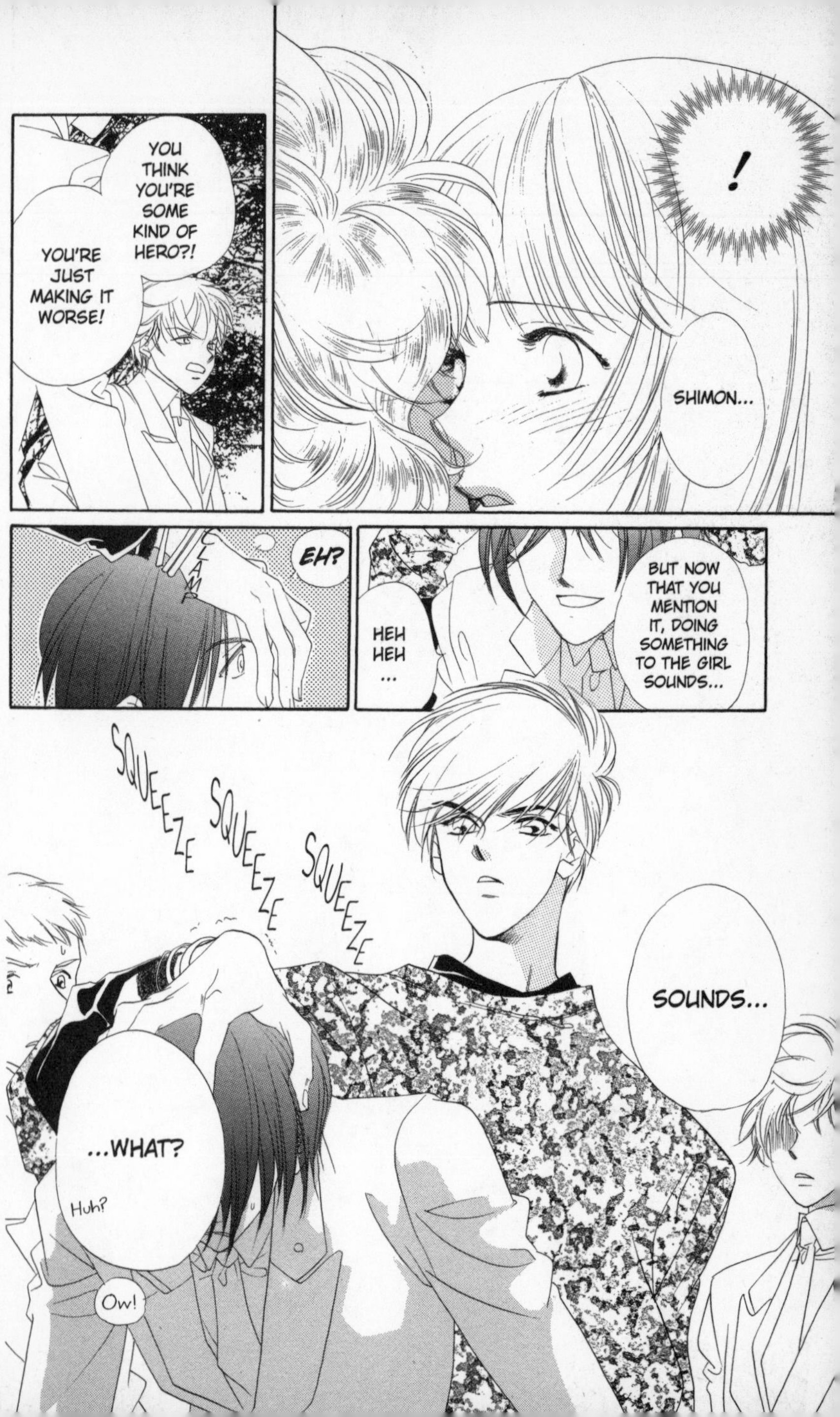
!
SHIMON...
YOU THINK YOU'RE SOME KIND OF HERO?!
YOU'RE JUST MAKING IT WORSE!
BUT NOW THAT YOU MENTION IT, DOING SOMETHING TO THE GIRL SOUNDS...
HEH HEH ...
EH?
CLAMP
SQUEEZE
SQUEEZE
SQUEEZE
SOUNDS...
...WHAT?
Huh?
Ow!

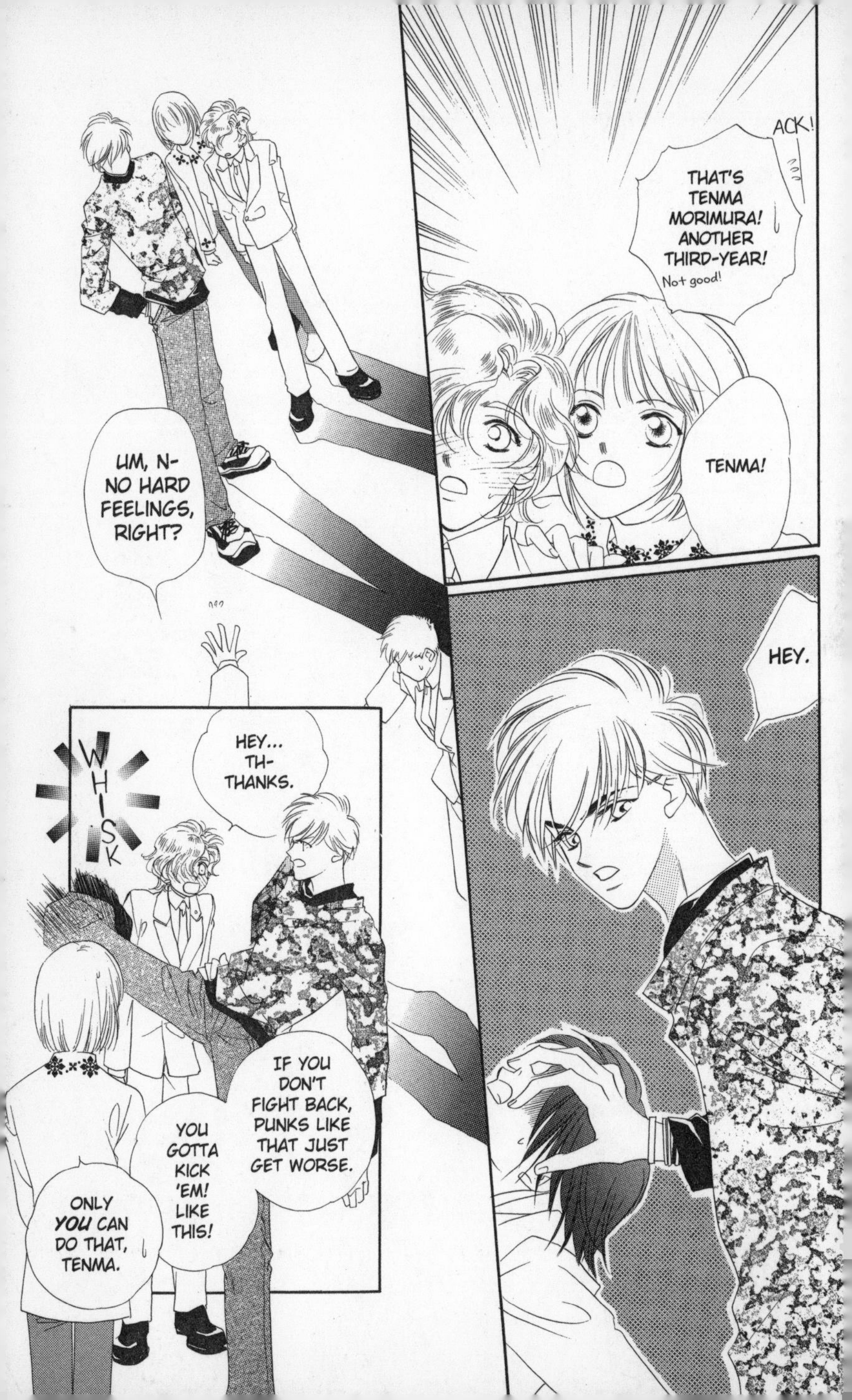
ACK!
THAT'S TENMA MORIMURA! ANOTHER THIRD-YEAR!
Not good!
TENMA!
HEY.
UM, N-NO HARD FEELINGS, RIGHT?
HEY... TH-THANKS.
WHISK
IF YOU DON'T FIGHT BACK, PUNKS LIKE THAT JUST GET WORSE.
YOU GOTTA KICK 'EM! LIKE THIS!
ONLY *YOU* CAN DO THAT, TENMA.

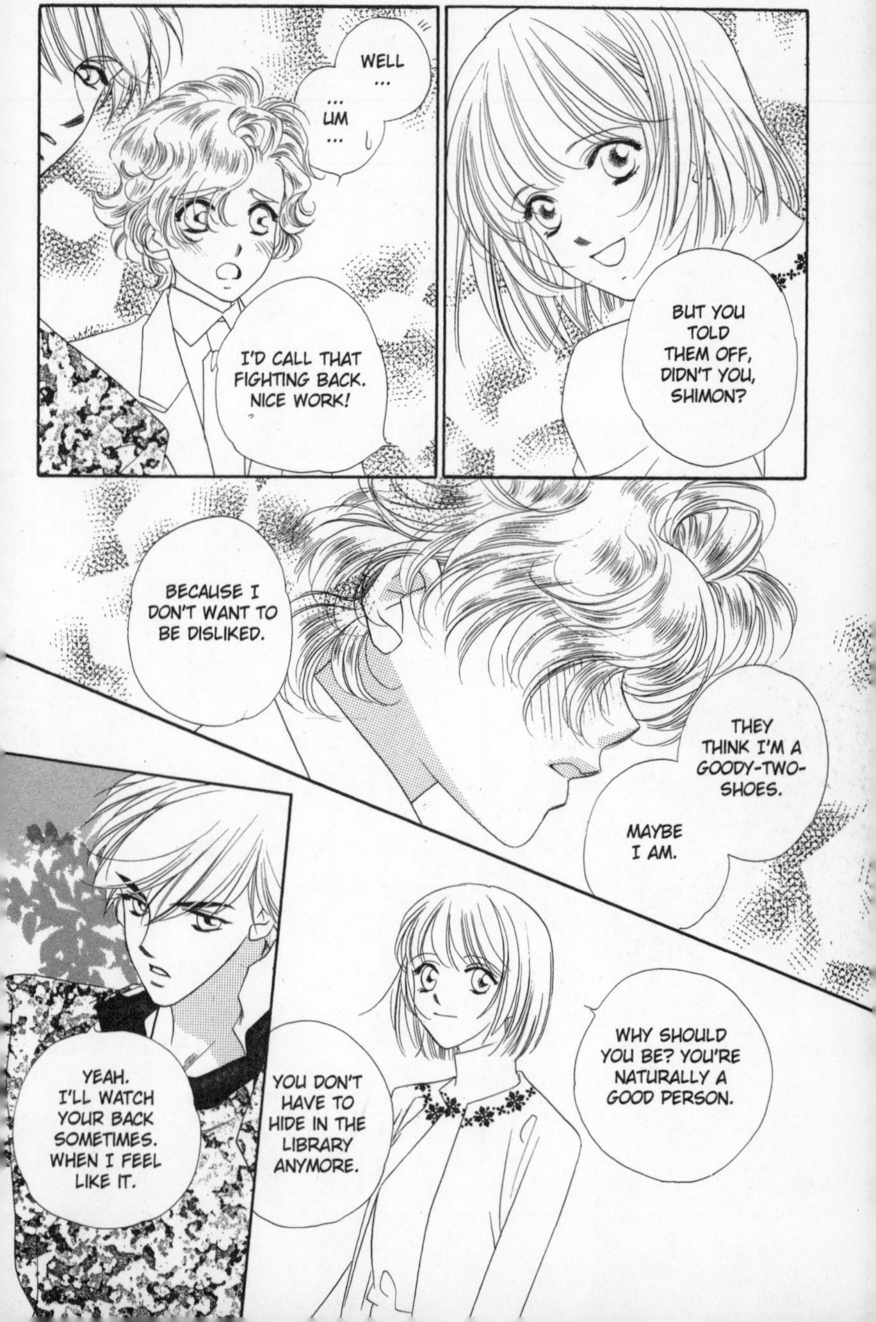
BUT YOU TOLD THEM OFF, DIDN'T YOU, SHIMON?
WELL ...
... UM ...
I'D CALL THAT FIGHTING BACK. NICE WORK!
BECAUSE I DON'T WANT TO BE DISLIKED.
THEY THINK I'M A GOODY-TWO-SHOES.
MAYBE I AM.
WHY SHOULD YOU BE? YOU'RE NATURALLY A GOOD PERSON.
YOU DON'T HAVE TO HIDE IN THE LIBRARY ANYMORE.
YEAH. I'LL WATCH YOUR BACK SOMETIMES. WHEN I FEEL LIKE IT.

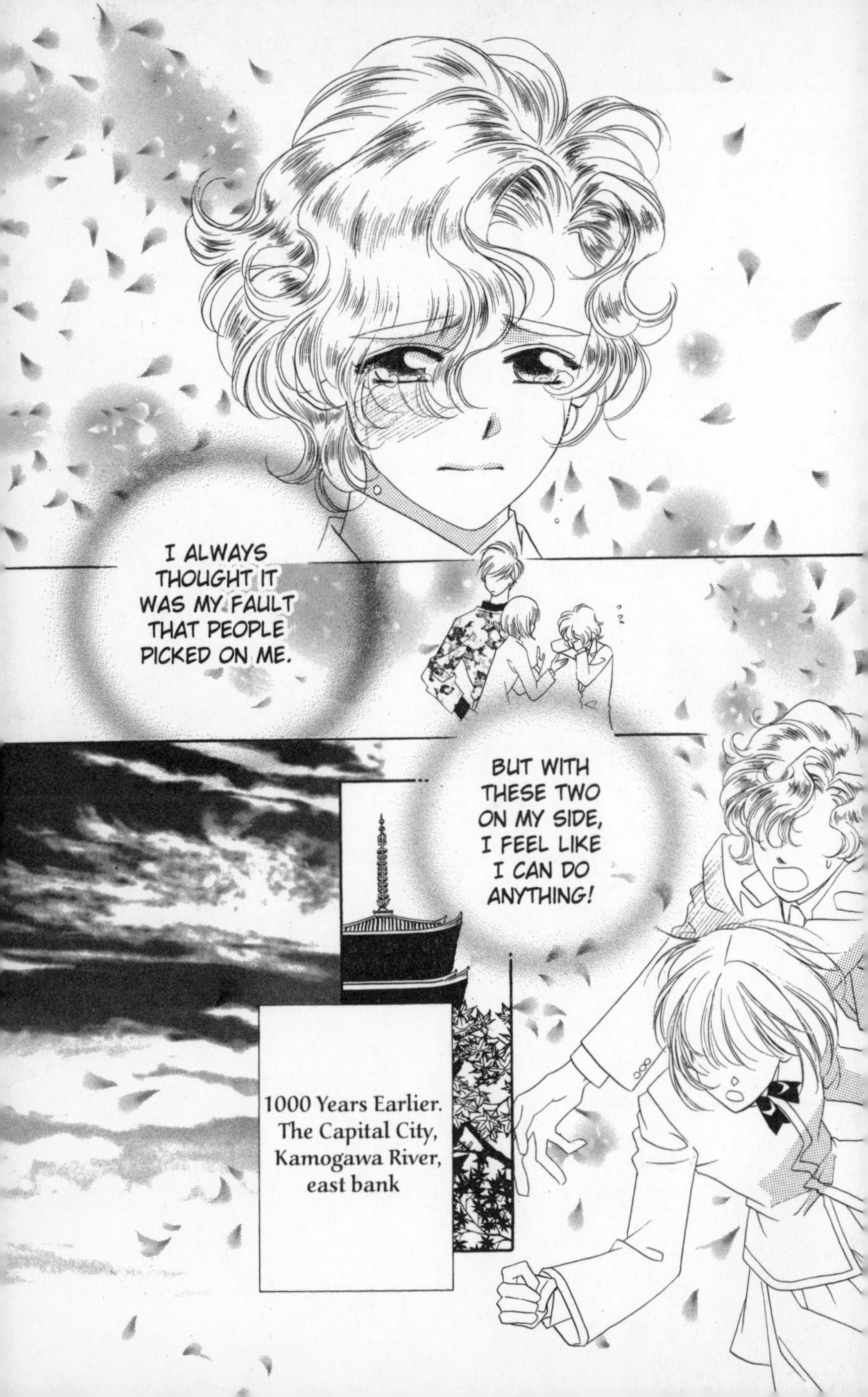
I ALWAYS THOUGHT IT WAS MY FAULT THAT PEOPLE PICKED ON ME.
BUT WITH THESE TWO ON MY SIDE, I FEEL LIKE I CAN DO ANYTHING!
1000 Years Earlier. The Capital City, Kamogawa River, east bank

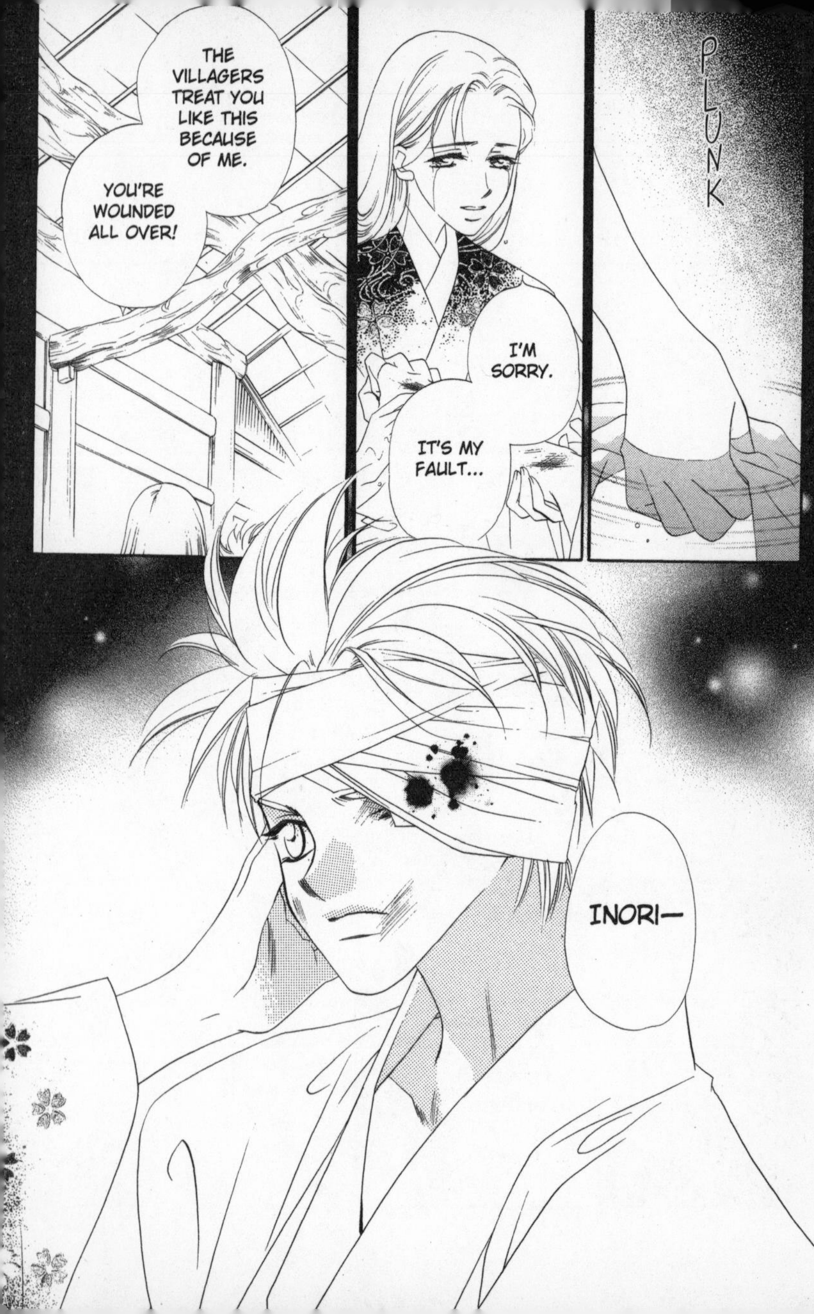
PLUNK
I'M SORRY.
IT'S MY FAULT...
THE VILLAGERS TREAT YOU LIKE THIS BECAUSE OF ME.
YOU'RE WOUNDED ALL OVER!
INORI—

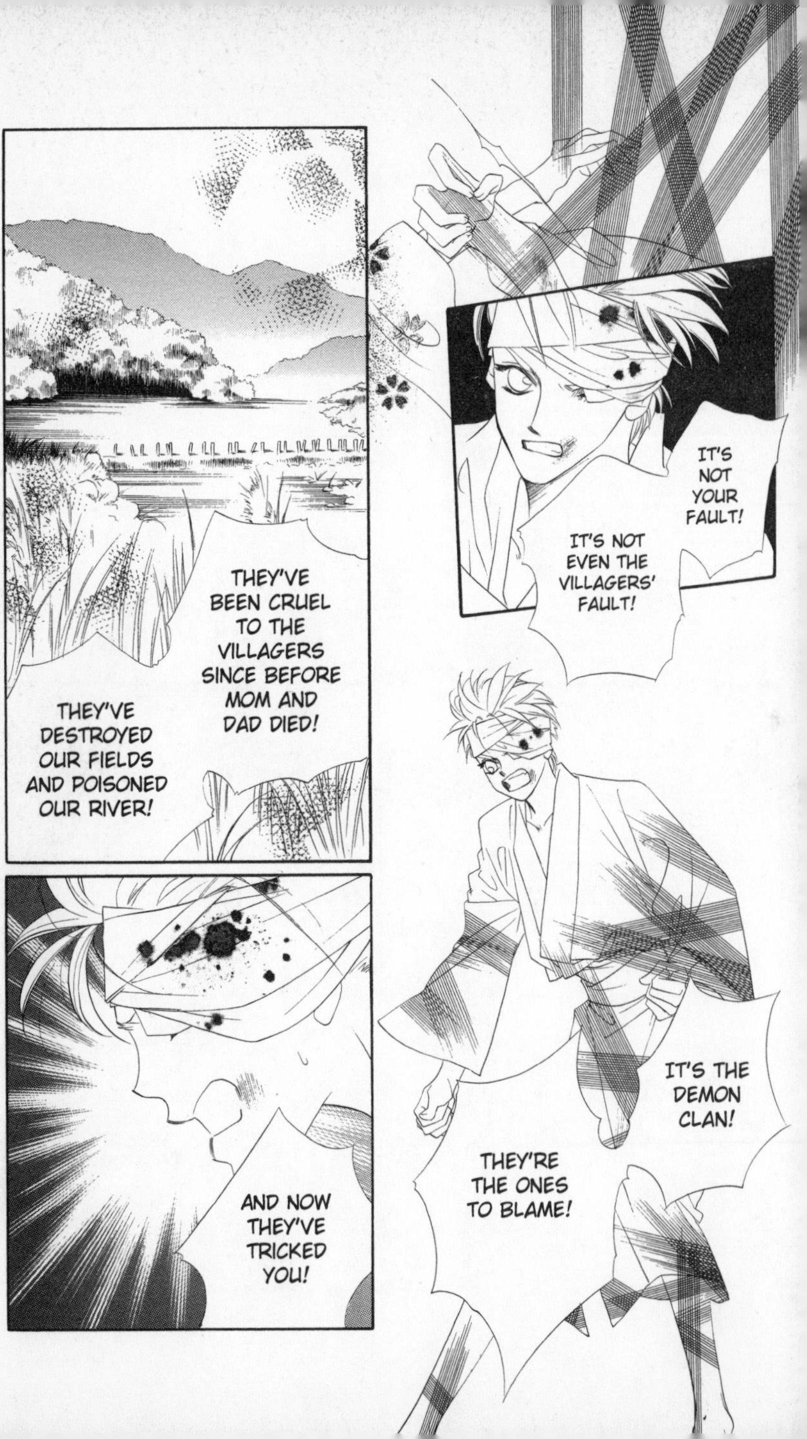
IT'S NOT YOUR FAULT!
IT'S NOT EVEN THE VILLAGERS' FAULT!
IT'S THE DEMON CLAN!
THEY'RE THE ONES TO BLAME!
THEY'VE BEEN CRUEL TO THE VILLAGERS SINCE BEFORE MOM AND DAD DIED!
THEY'VE DESTROYED OUR FIELDS AND POISONED OUR RIVER!
AND NOW THEY'VE TRICKED YOU!

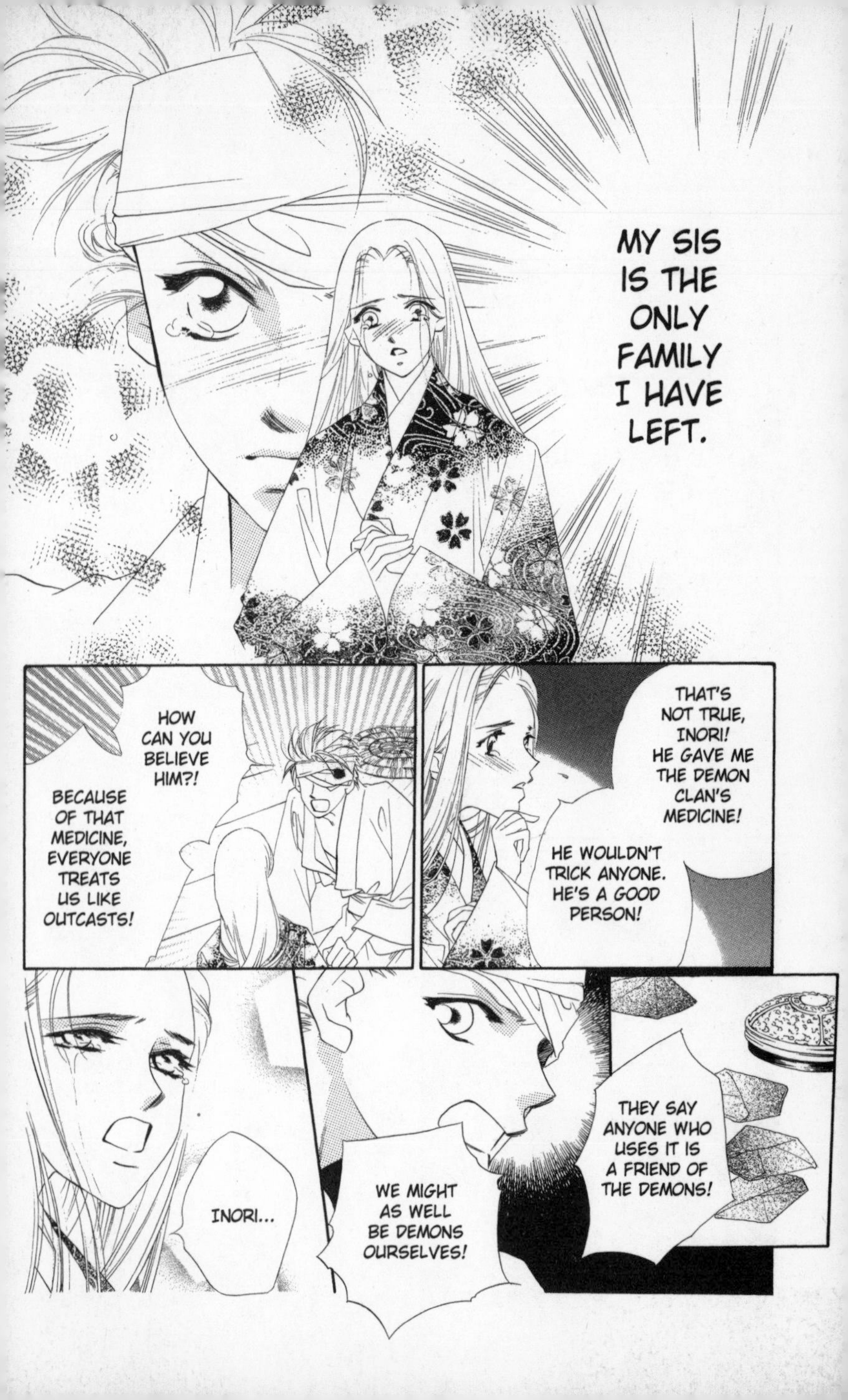
MY SIS IS THE ONLY FAMILY I HAVE LEFT.
THAT'S NOT TRUE, INORI! HE GAVE ME THE DEMON CLAN'S MEDICINE!
HE WOULDN'T TRICK ANYONE. HE'S A GOOD PERSON!
HOW CAN YOU BELIEVE HIM?!
BECAUSE OF THAT MEDICINE, EVERYONE TREATS US LIKE OUTCASTS!
THEY SAY ANYONE WHO USES IT IS A FRIEND OF THE DEMONS!
WE MIGHT AS WELL BE DEMONS OURSELVES!
INORI...

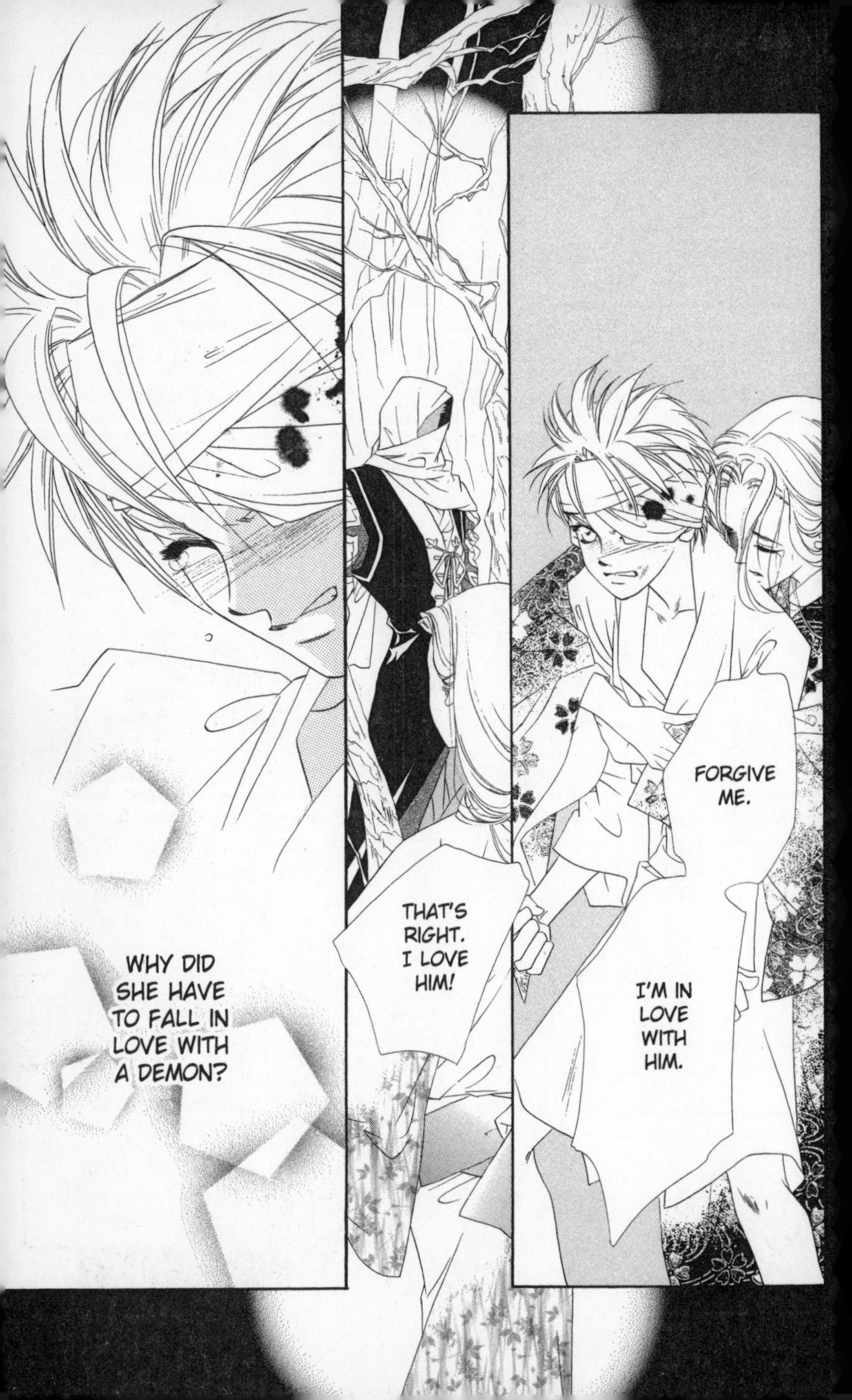
FORGIVE ME.
I'M IN LOVE WITH HIM.
THAT'S RIGHT. I LOVE HIM!
WHY DID SHE HAVE TO FALL IN LOVE WITH A DEMON?

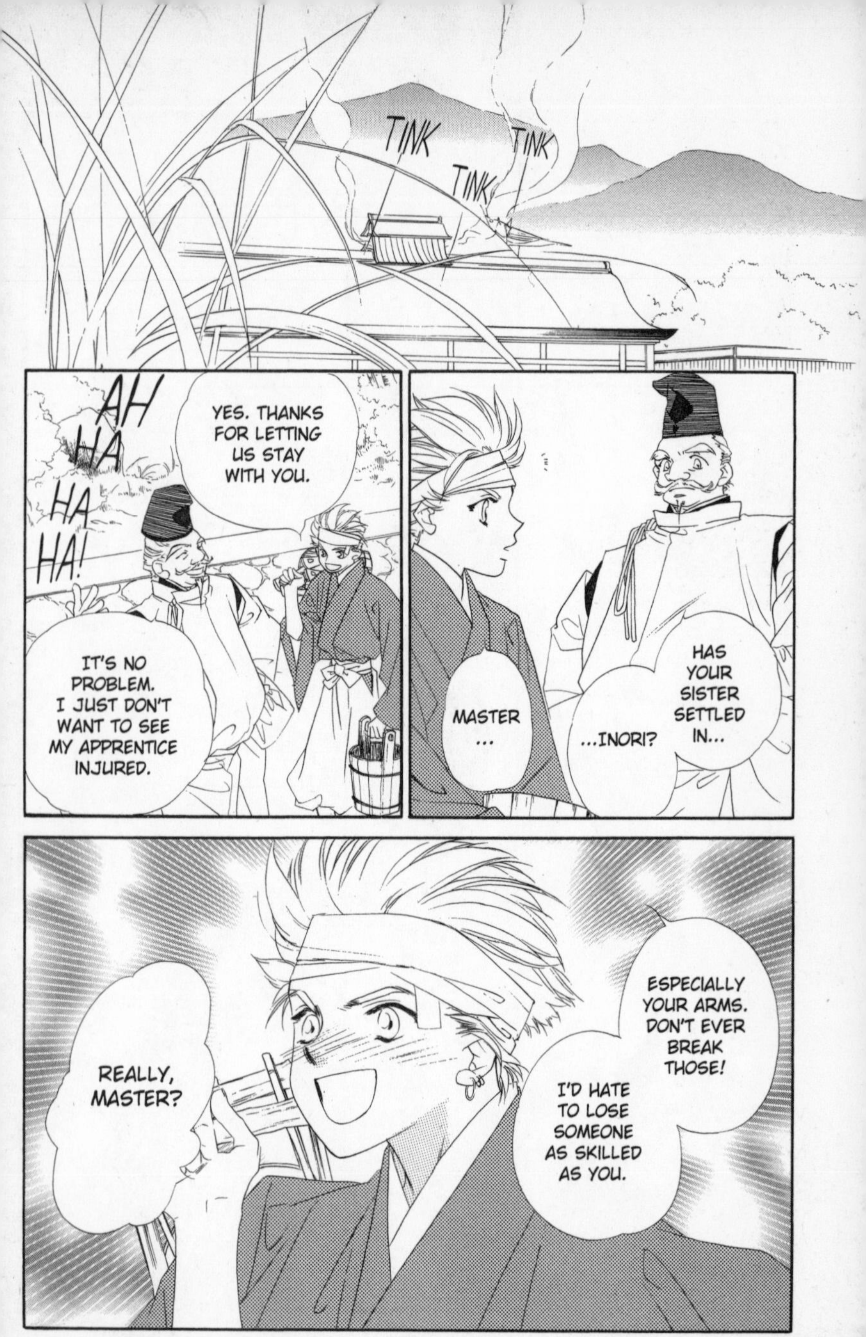
TINK
TINK
TINK
HAS YOUR SISTER SETTLED IN...
...INORI?
MASTER ...
YES. THANKS FOR LETTING US STAY WITH YOU.
AH HA HA HA!
IT'S NO PROBLEM. I JUST DON'T WANT TO SEE MY APPRENTICE INJURED.
ESPECIALLY YOUR ARMS. DON'T EVER BREAK THOSE!
I'D HATE TO LOSE SOMEONE AS SKILLED AS YOU.
REALLY, MASTER?

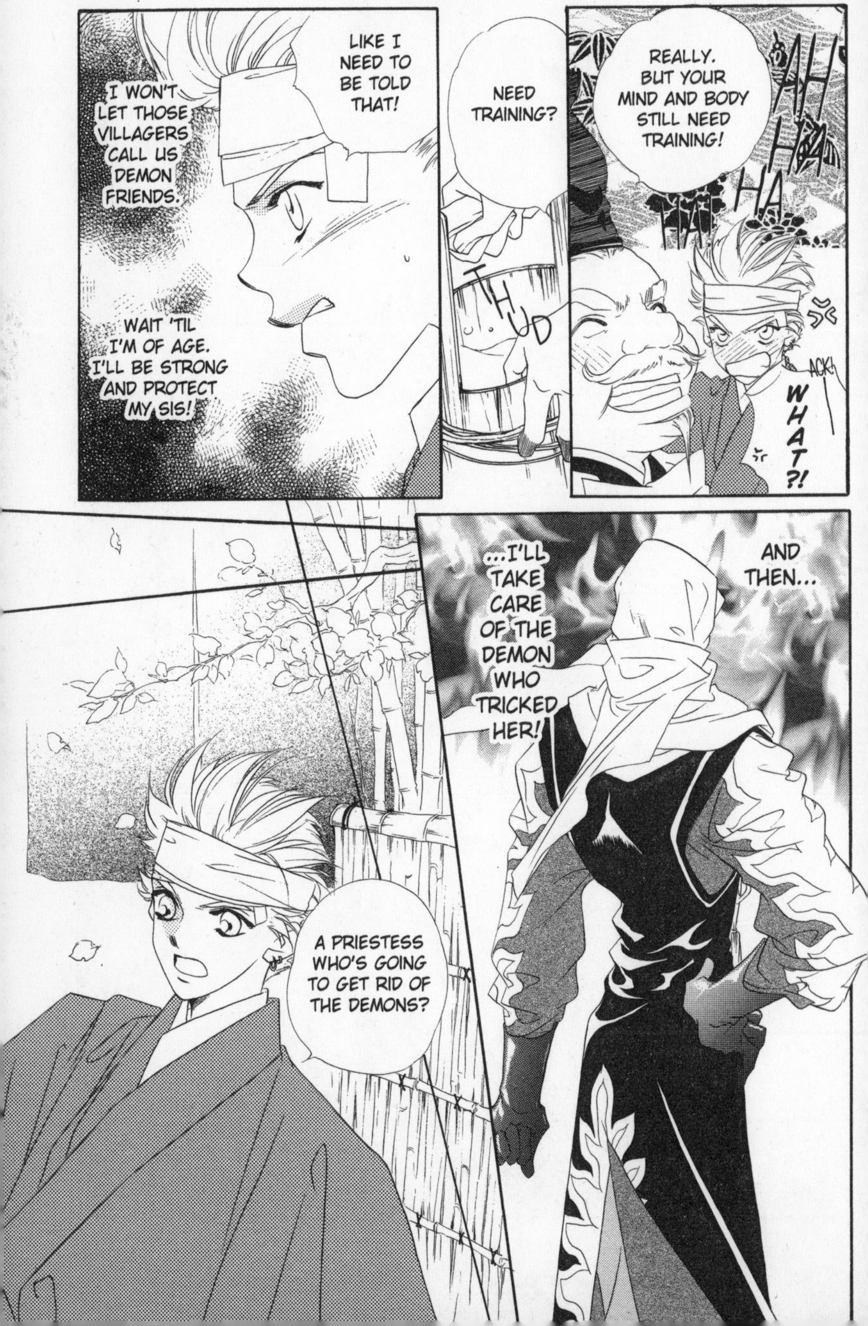
REALLY. BUT YOUR MIND AND BODY STILL NEED TRAINING!
AH HA HA HA
ACK!
WHAT?!
NEED TRAINING?
THUD
LIKE I NEED TO BE TOLD THAT!
I WON'T LET THOSE VILLAGERS CALL US DEMON FRIENDS.
WAIT 'TIL I'M OF AGE. I'LL BE STRONG AND PROTECT MY SIS!
AND THEN...
...I'LL TAKE CARE OF THE DEMON WHO TRICKED HER!
A PRIESTESS WHO'S GOING TO GET RID OF THE DEMONS?

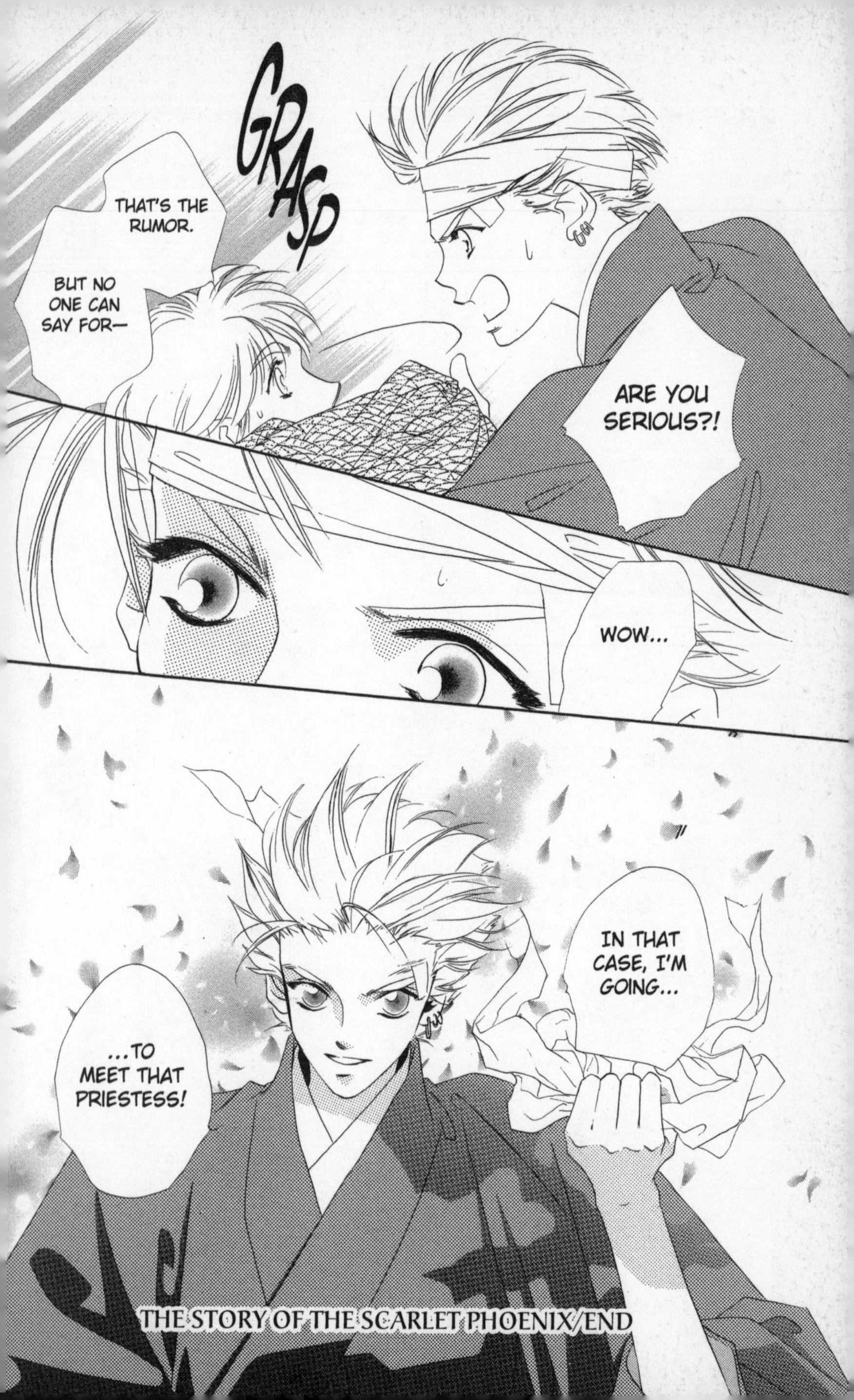
THAT'S THE RUMOR.
BUT NO ONE CAN SAY FOR—
GRASP
ARE YOU SERIOUS?!
WOW...
IN THAT CASE, I'M GOING...
...TO MEET THAT PRIESTESS!
THE STORY OF THE SCARLET PHOENIX/END

THE EIGHT GUARDIANS: WHAT YOU WISH THEY'D SAY

<Abe-no-Yasuaki>

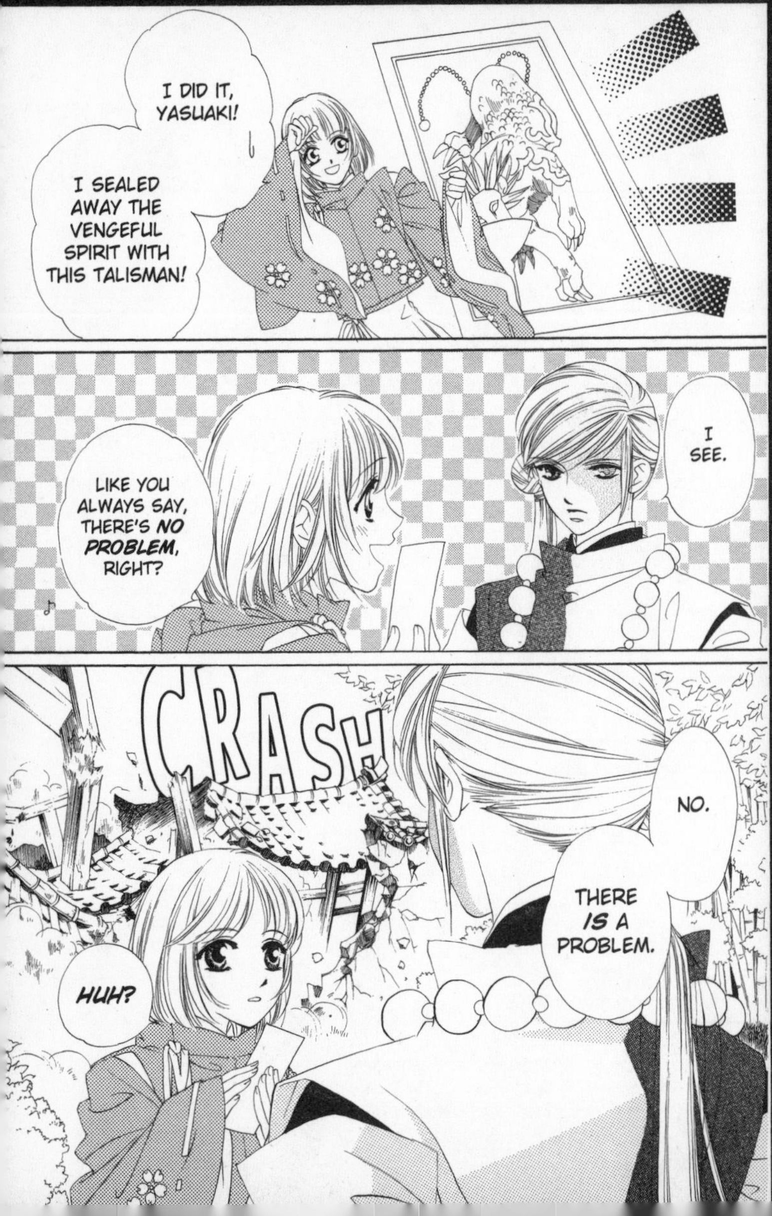

I DID IT, YASUAKI!
I SEALED AWAY THE VENGEFUL SPIRIT WITH THIS TALISMAN!
I SEE.
LIKE YOU ALWAYS SAY, THERE'S NO PROBLEM, RIGHT?
CRASH
NO.
THERE IS A PROBLEM.
HUH?

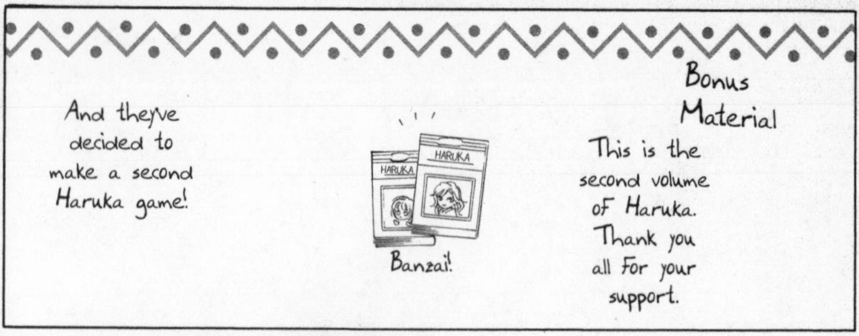
Bonus Material
This is the second volume of Haruka. Thank you all for your support.
HARUKA
HARUKA
And they've decided to make a second Haruka game!
Banzai!

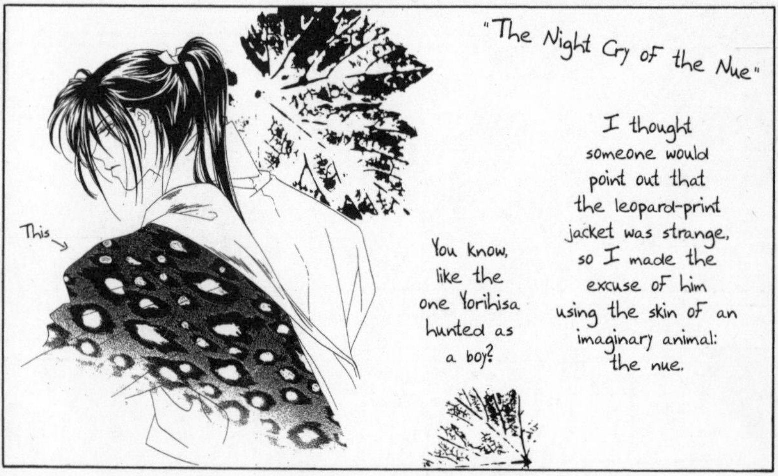
"The Night Cry of the Nue"
I thought someone would point out that the leopard-print jacket was strange, so I made the excuse of him using the skin of an imaginary animal: the nue.
You know, like the one Yorihisa hunted as a boy?
This

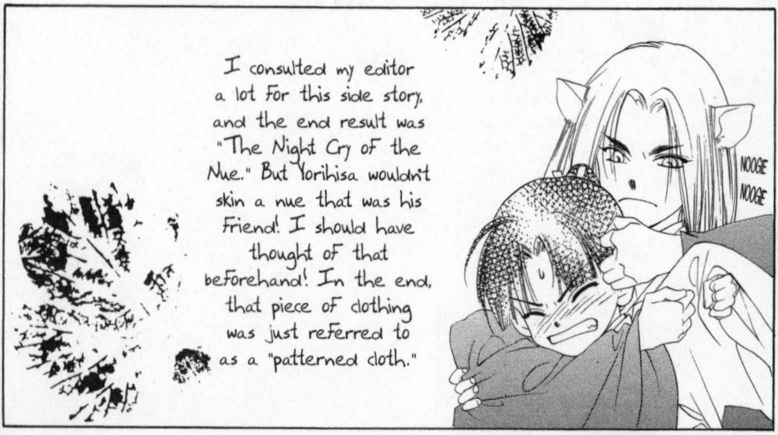
NOOGIE NOOGIE
I consulted my editor a lot for this side story, and the end result was "The Night Cry of the Nue." But Yorihisa wouldn't skin a nue that was his friend! I should have thought of that beforehand! In the end, that piece of clothing was just referred to as a "patterned cloth."

"Tachibana's Fondness For Fuji"

In the game's very First scene, Princess Fuji was going to be in the arms of either Tachibana or Takamichi when the Eight Guardians appeared. I thought the idea of a little princess like Fuji having a crush on a grown-up like Tachibana was cute, so that's how this story came to be.

In the end, that scene was never used in the game, so the pairing seems a bit strange now.

Since the manga unfolds differently from the game, some of the characters' personalities in here might seem inconsistent from those in the game.

This is most often said of Tenma and Yasuaki. Since Yorihisa hardly ever talks, it's much more difficult to compare him with the game version (laugh)

Personality Test
Place your favorite Guardians or Demons around yourself.

①	②	③
④	YOU	⑤
⑥	⑦	⑧

This was in a letter I received. I thought it was fun-
you should give it a try, too!

Thank you, Y.Y.!

Hey, everyone, which character do you think is the hardest to draw? You probably think it's one of the characters that don't appear much, like Shimon or Eisen... but actually it's Akane, the main character!
I hadn't played the game yet when I got the Haruka character design job, so I never knew that Akane, who is the main character controlled by the player, would have so few defined personality traits.
By contrast, Shimon and Eisen have clearly defined characters in the game: plenty of dialogue, background information, etc.
Akane's in the most scenes, so she definitely caused me the most trouble!
I'll have to work harder on her...
2000.12

My Answers to the Personality Test

The One You Respect the Most	The One Who's Closest to Perfect	Your Ideal Match
The One You Love Most Deeply	YOU	The One You Most Want to Love You
The One You Consider the Best Friend	The One You Don't Consider Male	The One You Think Is Most Strange

As for my results:

① Yorihisa ② Eisen ③ Tenma ④ Inori
⑤ Takamichi ⑥ Shimon ⑦ Yasuaki ⑧ Secret!

P.S.

Thank you, everyone, for your letters! I think I'll respond to them by sending out summer greeting cards.

That reminds me...in the thank-you letters I received for last summer's greeting cards, quite a few of you mentioned that the postmark was over Yasuaki's face. I'm not sure why the postmark was on that side of the card to begin with!*

*USUALLY THE POSTMARK IS ON THE SIDE WHERE THE ADDRESS IS WRITTEN, NOT THE SIDE THAT WOULD HAVE HAD THE PICTURE ON IT. ED

BONUS/END

MS. TOHKO MIZUNO'S SPECIAL PROJECT!

THE EIGHT GUARDIANS: WHAT YOU WISH THEY'D SAY

★ Did you read pages 6, 76, 78, 118 and 139 of this book? We put an ad in the December 2000 edition of *LaLa* magazine for readers to participate in our special project: The Eight Guardians: What You Wish They'd Say. We received tons of entries from fans all over Japan requesting lines that they would like their favorite Guardians to say. Due to the wide variety and large amount of entries, Mizuno-sensei had to choose the lines that would be easiest for her to draw. The postcards that were used are presented below.

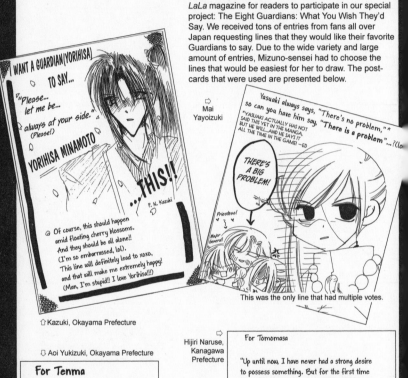

I WANT A GUARDIAN (YORIHISA) TO SAY...

"Please... let me be... always at your side."
(Please!)

YORIHISA MINAMOTO

...THIS!!

P. N. Kazuki

○ Of course, this should happen amid floating cherry blossoms. And they should be all alone!! (I'm so embarrassed, lol). This line will definitely lead to xoxo, and that will make me extremely happy! (Man, I'm stupid!! I love Yorihisa!!!)

⇧ Kazuki, Okayama Prefecture

⇨ Mai Yayoizuki

Yasuaki always says, "There's no problem,"* so can you have him say, "There is a problem"...? (lo
*YASUAKI ACTUALLY HAS NOT SAID THIS YET IN THE MANGA, BUT HE WILL...AND HE SAYS IT ALL THE TIME IN THE GAME! —ED

THERE'S A BIG PROBLEM!

Priestess!

Major General!

This was the only line that had multiple votes.

⇨ Hijiri Naruse, Kanagawa Prefecture

For Tomomasa

"Up until now, I have never had a strong desire to possess something. But for the first time in my life, I have found something I desire at any cost. Now then, what do you think it is?"

⇩ Aoi Yukizuki, Okayama Prefecture

For Tenma

"Just stay by my side."

⇩ Aoimaru, Niigata Prefecture

A line for Inori
"I just don't get women." Inori gets into an argument with the girl he likes, which bothers him. It would be even better if Inori could say the line while pushing back his hair... ← Even though his hair already sticks up! (lol)

~The Judging is Finished!~

Because of the overwhelming response, I picked the lines that could be most easily used in manga. I got plenty of other requests: Akane murmuring, Takamichi's glasses, and all kinds of cute lines! The one with all Eight Guardians saying "Hiya!" at once was especially funny. Thank you all so much!   (comments by Mizuno-sensei)

An alien who speaks in outdated slang!

Wazzap?!

La la la!

←NEXT

An odd, unbalanced love story.

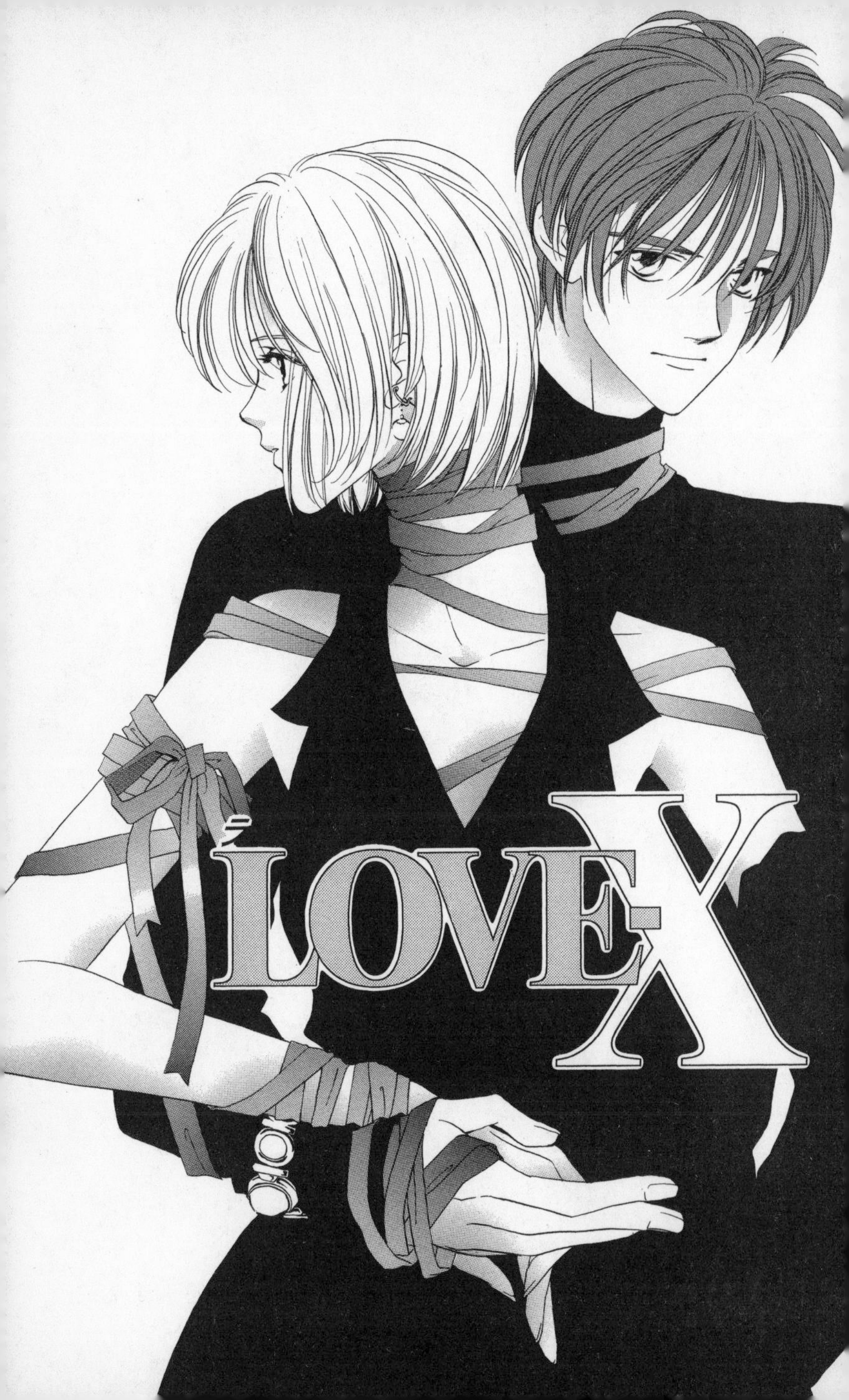
LOVE-X

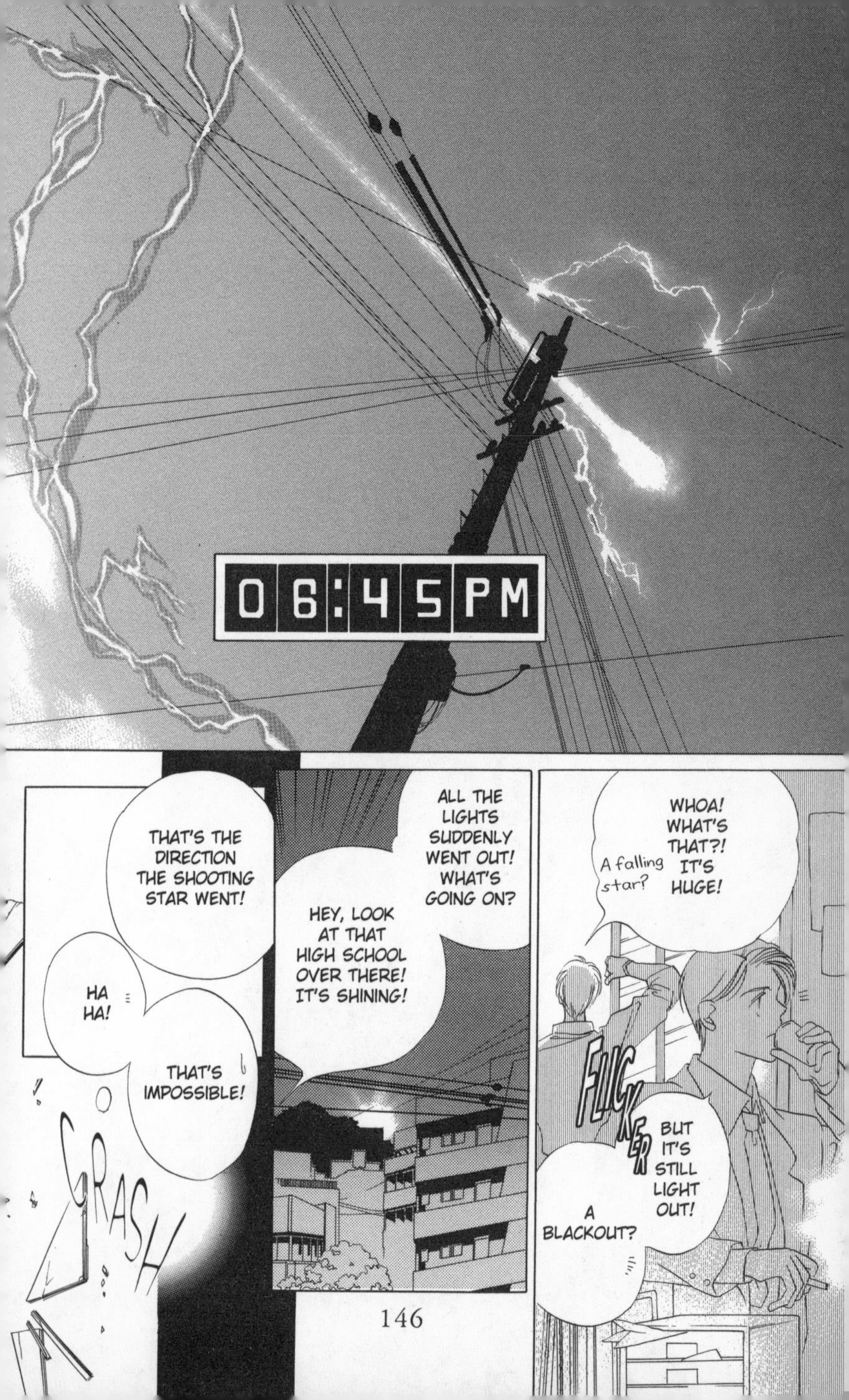
06:45PM
WHOA! WHAT'S THAT?! IT'S HUGE!
A falling star?
FLICKER
BUT IT'S STILL LIGHT OUT!
A BLACKOUT?
ALL THE LIGHTS SUDDENLY WENT OUT! WHAT'S GOING ON?
HEY, LOOK AT THAT HIGH SCHOOL OVER THERE! IT'S SHINING!
THAT'S THE DIRECTION THE SHOOTING STAR WENT!
HA HA!
THAT'S IMPOSSIBLE!
CRASH

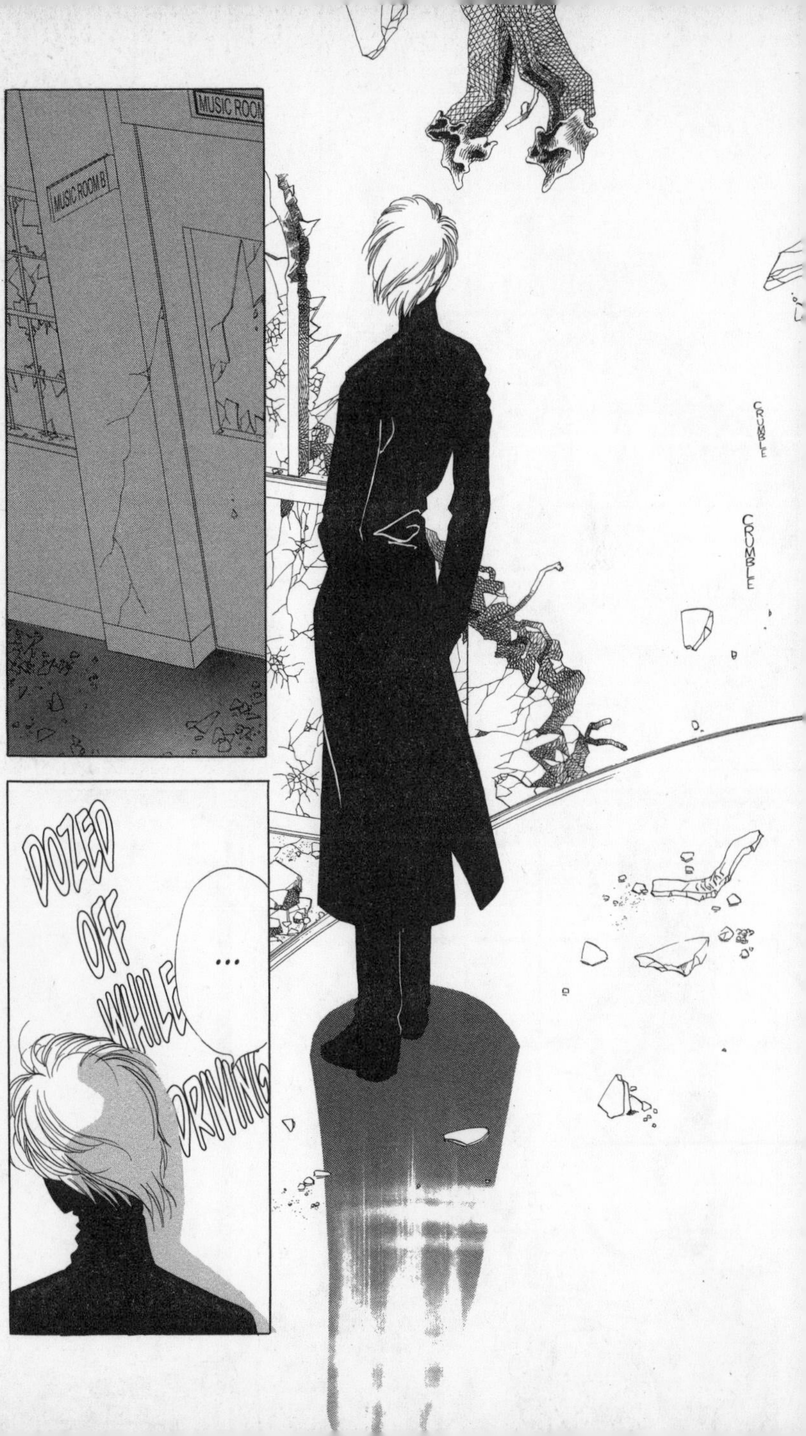
CRUMBLE
CRUMBLE
MUSIC ROOM
MUSIC ROOM B
...
DOZED OFF WHILE DRIVING

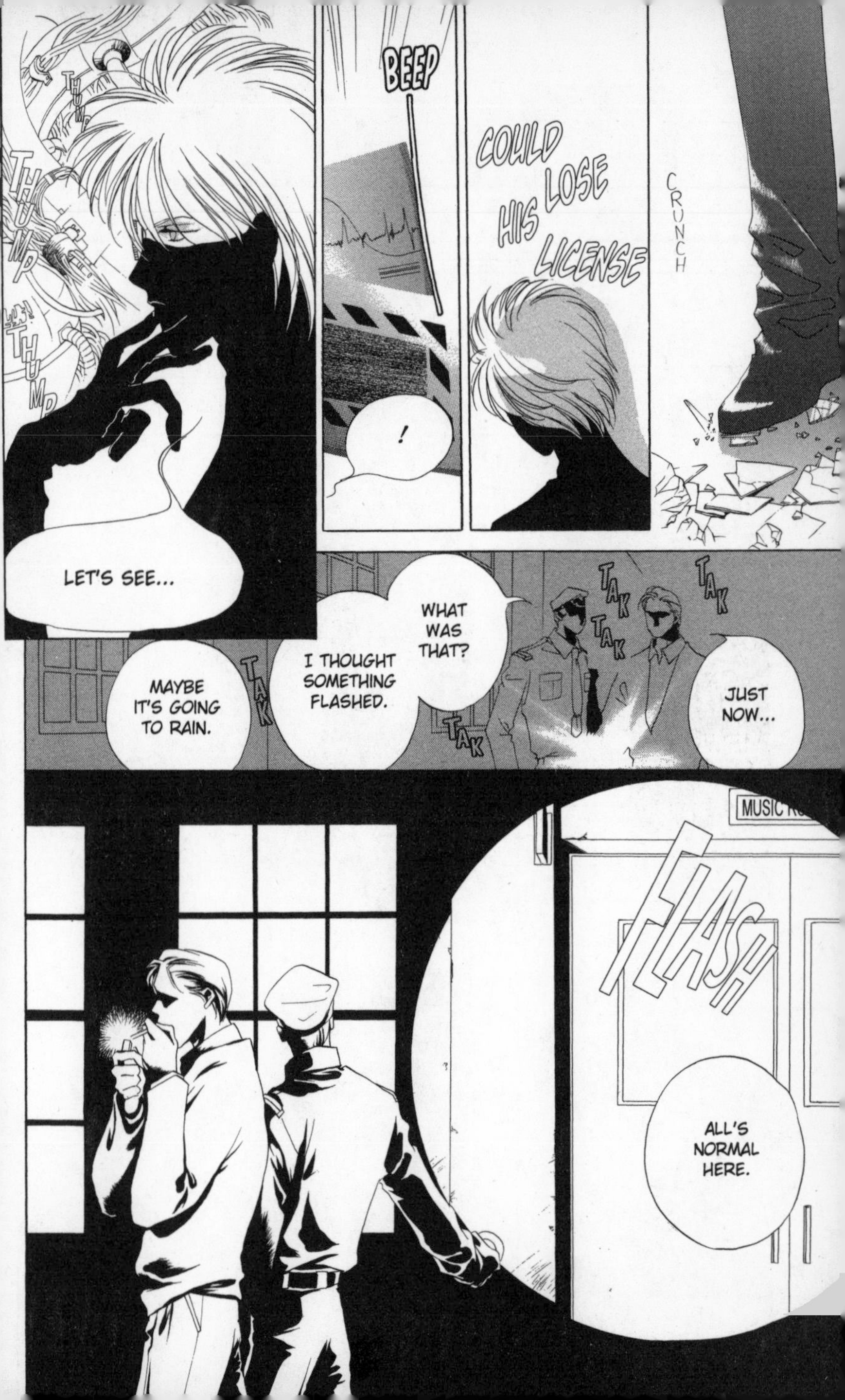
CRUNCH
COULD
HIS LOSE
LICENSE
BEEP
!
THUMP
THUMP
THUMP
THUMP
LET'S SEE...
TAK
TAK
TAK
JUST NOW...
WHAT WAS THAT?
I THOUGHT SOMETHING FLASHED.
TAK
TAK
MAYBE IT'S GOING TO RAIN.
MUSIC RO
FLASH
ALL'S NORMAL HERE.

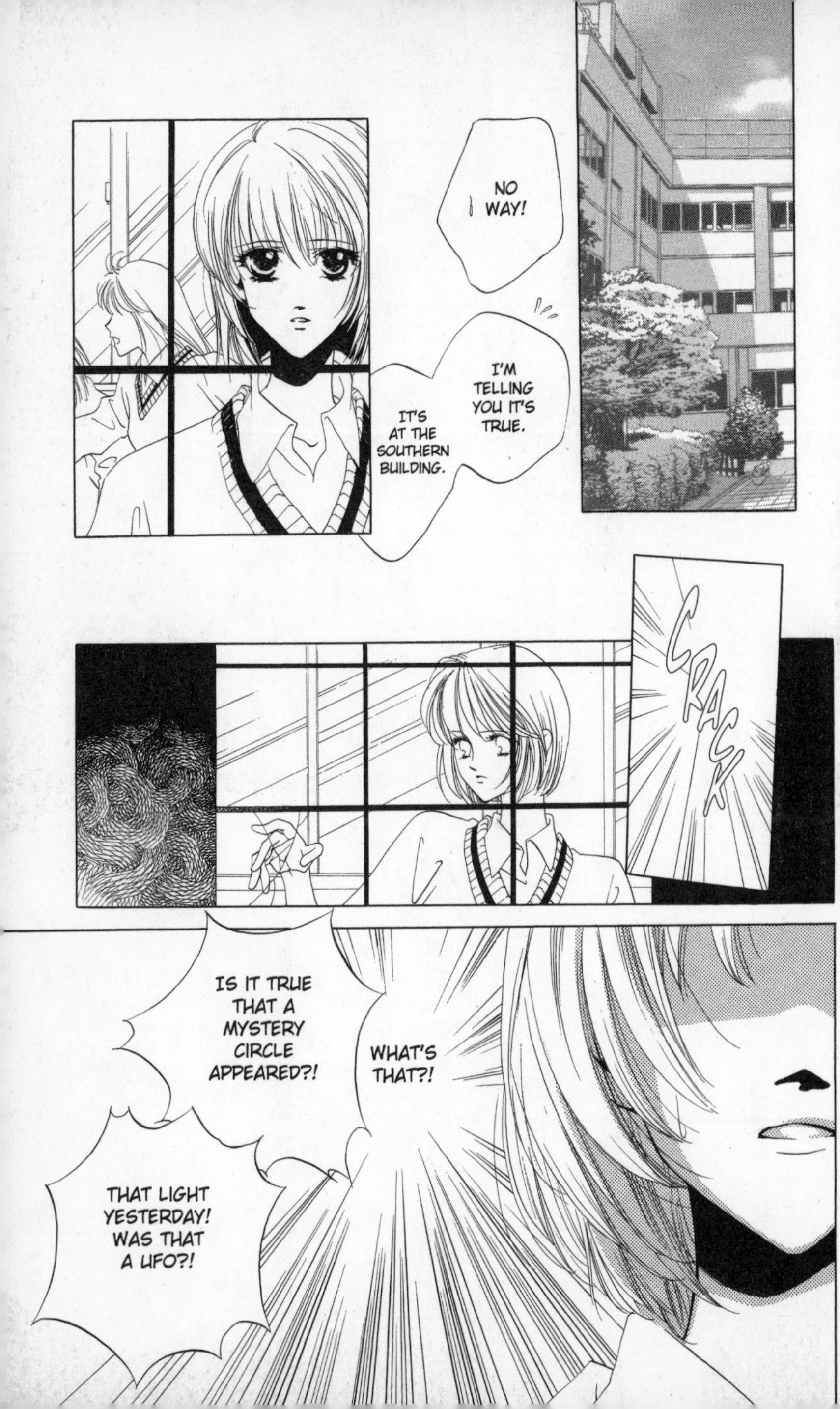
NO WAY!
I'M TELLING YOU IT'S TRUE.
IT'S AT THE SOUTHERN BUILDING.
CRACK
WHAT'S THAT?!
IS IT TRUE THAT A MYSTERY CIRCLE APPEARED?!
THAT LIGHT YESTERDAY! WAS THAT A UFO?!

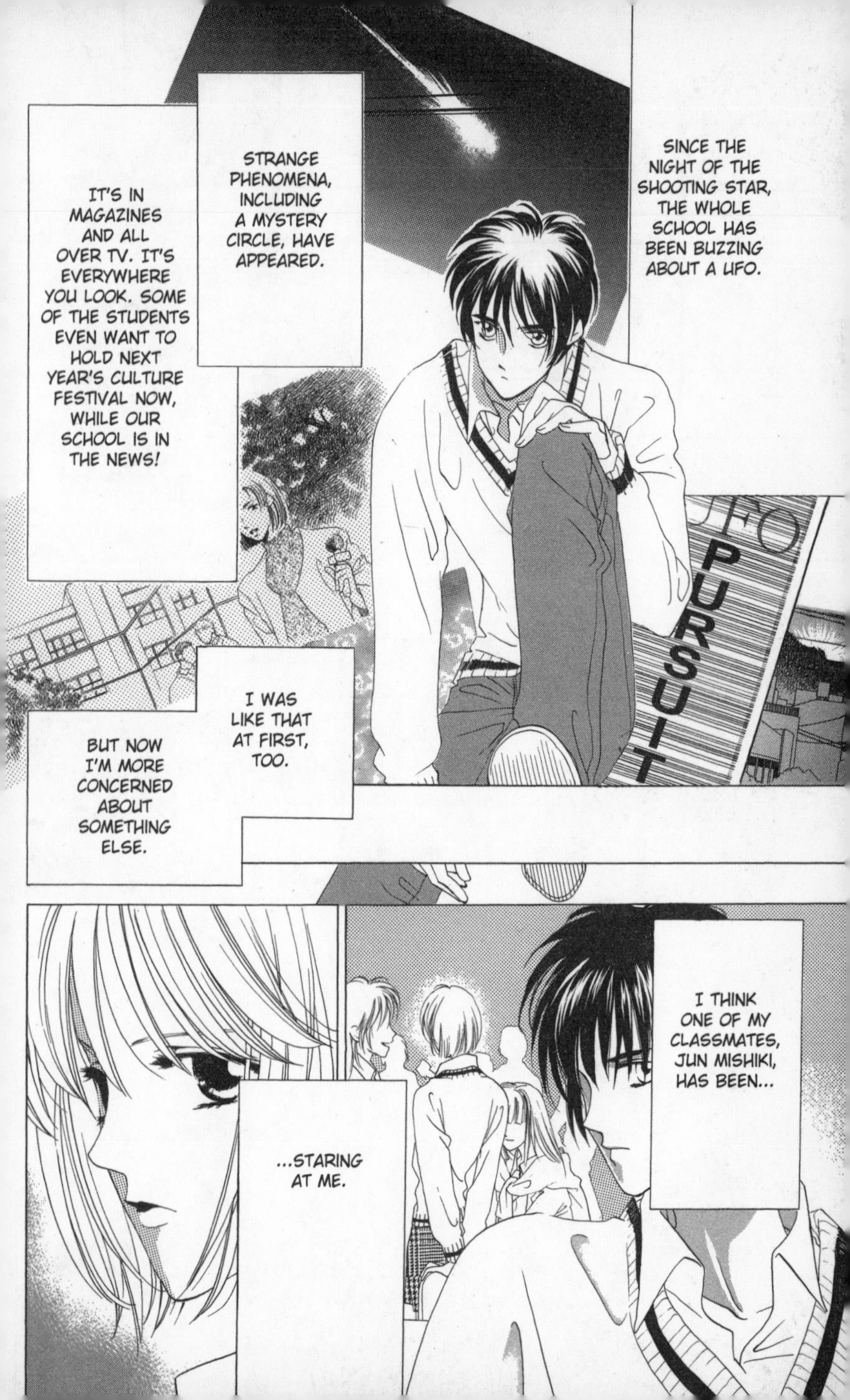
SINCE THE NIGHT OF THE SHOOTING STAR, THE WHOLE SCHOOL HAS BEEN BUZZING ABOUT A UFO.
UFO PURSUIT
STRANGE PHENOMENA, INCLUDING A MYSTERY CIRCLE, HAVE APPEARED.
IT'S IN MAGAZINES AND ALL OVER TV. IT'S EVERYWHERE YOU LOOK. SOME OF THE STUDENTS EVEN WANT TO HOLD NEXT YEAR'S CULTURE FESTIVAL NOW, WHILE OUR SCHOOL IS IN THE NEWS!
I WAS LIKE THAT AT FIRST, TOO.
BUT NOW I'M MORE CONCERNED ABOUT SOMETHING ELSE.
I THINK ONE OF MY CLASSMATES, JUN MISHIKI, HAS BEEN...
...STARING AT ME.

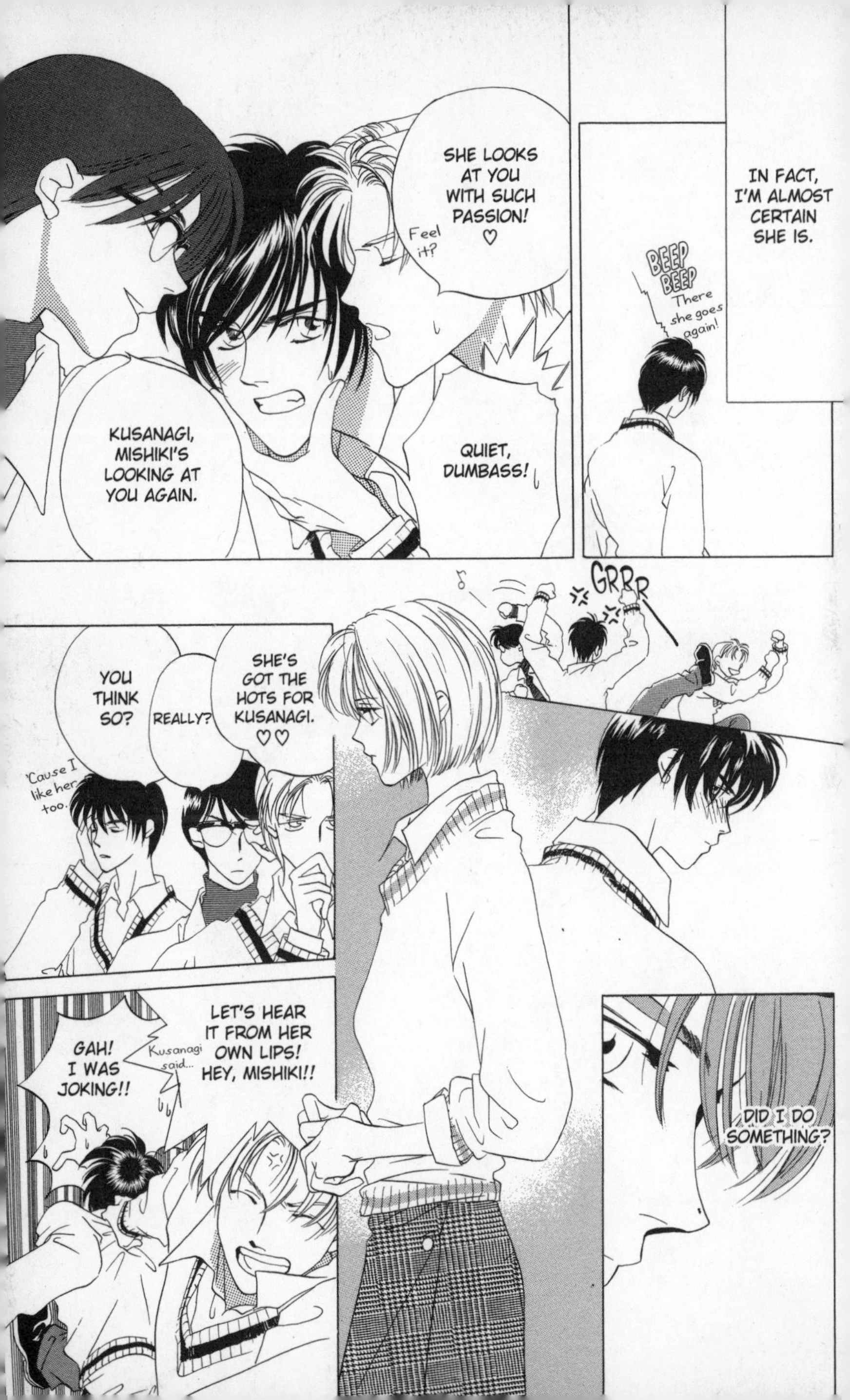
IN FACT, I'M ALMOST CERTAIN SHE IS.
BEEP BEEP
There she goes again!
SHE LOOKS AT YOU WITH SUCH PASSION! ♡
Feel it?
QUIET, DUMBASS!
KUSANAGI, MISHIKI'S LOOKING AT YOU AGAIN.
GRRR
SHE'S GOT THE HOTS FOR KUSANAGI. ♡♡
REALLY?
YOU THINK SO?
'Cause I like her too.
LET'S HEAR IT FROM HER OWN LIPS! HEY, MISHIKI!!
Kusanagi said...
GAH! I WAS JOKING!!
DID I DO SOMETHING?

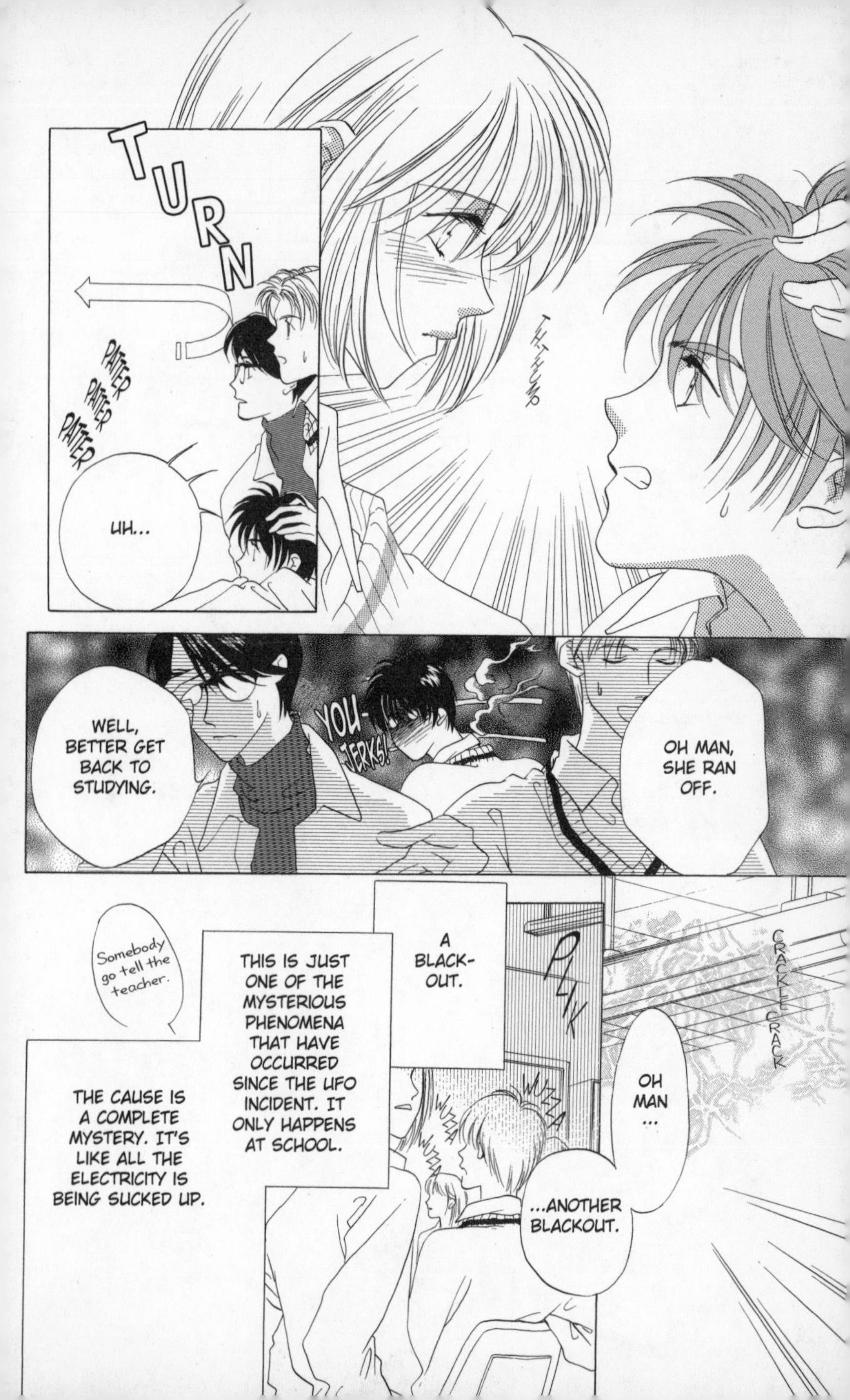
TH-THUMP
TURN
PATTER PATTER PATTER
UH...
OH MAN, SHE RAN OFF.
YOU- JERKS!
WELL, BETTER GET BACK TO STUDYING.
CRACKLE CRACK
OH MAN ...
...ANOTHER BLACKOUT.
PLINK
WUZZA WUZZA WUZZA
A BLACK-OUT.
THIS IS JUST ONE OF THE MYSTERIOUS PHENOMENA THAT HAVE OCCURRED SINCE THE UFO INCIDENT. IT ONLY HAPPENS AT SCHOOL.
Somebody go tell the teacher.
THE CAUSE IS A COMPLETE MYSTERY. IT'S LIKE ALL THE ELECTRICITY IS BEING SUCKED UP.

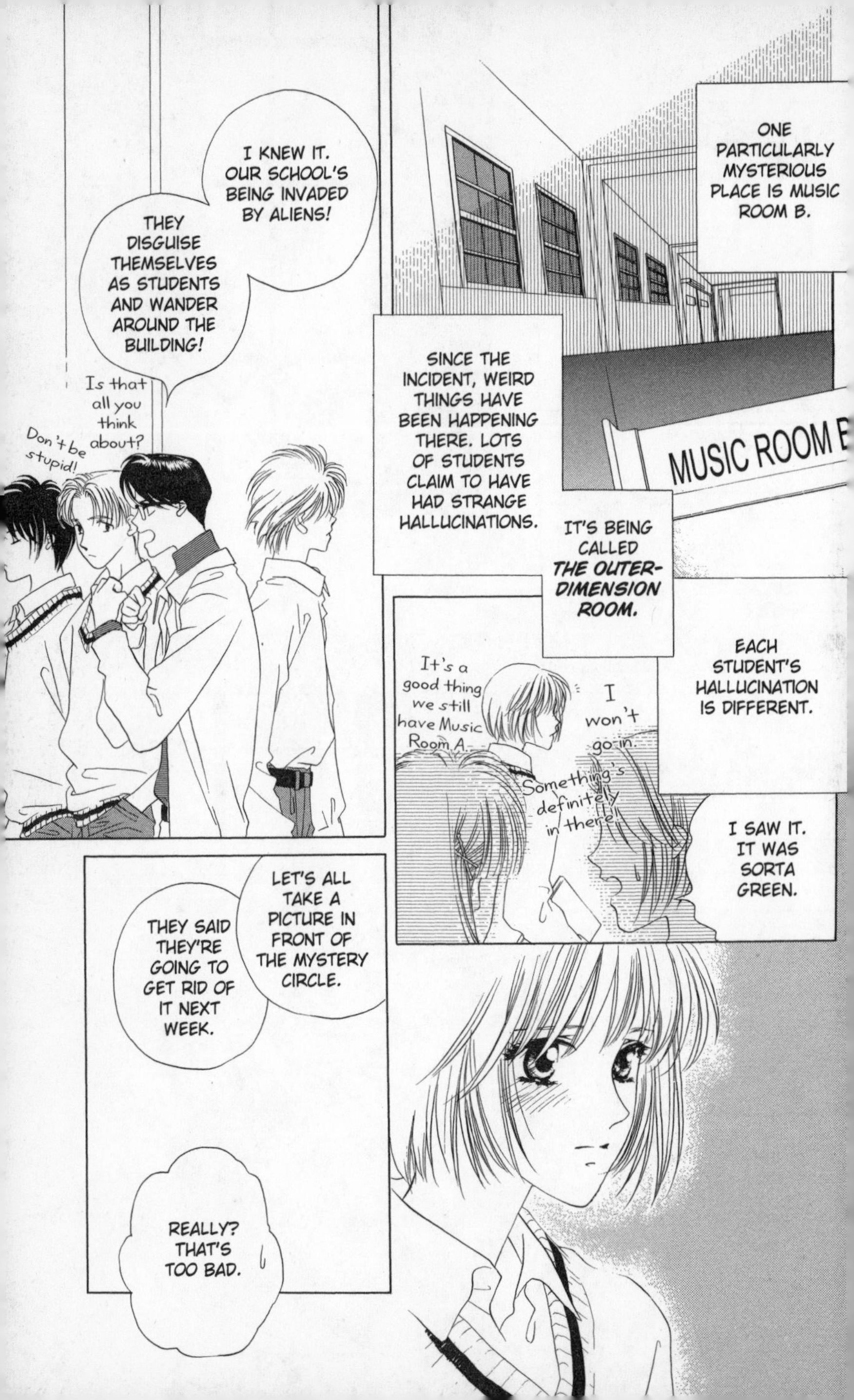

ONE PARTICULARLY MYSTERIOUS PLACE IS MUSIC ROOM B.
MUSIC ROOM B
SINCE THE INCIDENT, WEIRD THINGS HAVE BEEN HAPPENING THERE. LOTS OF STUDENTS CLAIM TO HAVE HAD STRANGE HALLUCINATIONS.
IT'S BEING CALLED *THE OUTER-DIMENSION ROOM.*
EACH STUDENT'S HALLUCINATION IS DIFFERENT.
I won't go in.
It's a good thing we still have Music Room A.
Something's definitely in there!
I SAW IT. IT WAS SORTA GREEN.
I KNEW IT. OUR SCHOOL'S BEING INVADED BY ALIENS!
THEY DISGUISE THEMSELVES AS STUDENTS AND WANDER AROUND THE BUILDING!
Is that all you think about?
Don't be stupid!
LET'S ALL TAKE A PICTURE IN FRONT OF THE MYSTERY CIRCLE.
THEY SAID THEY'RE GOING TO GET RID OF IT NEXT WEEK.
REALLY? THAT'S TOO BAD.

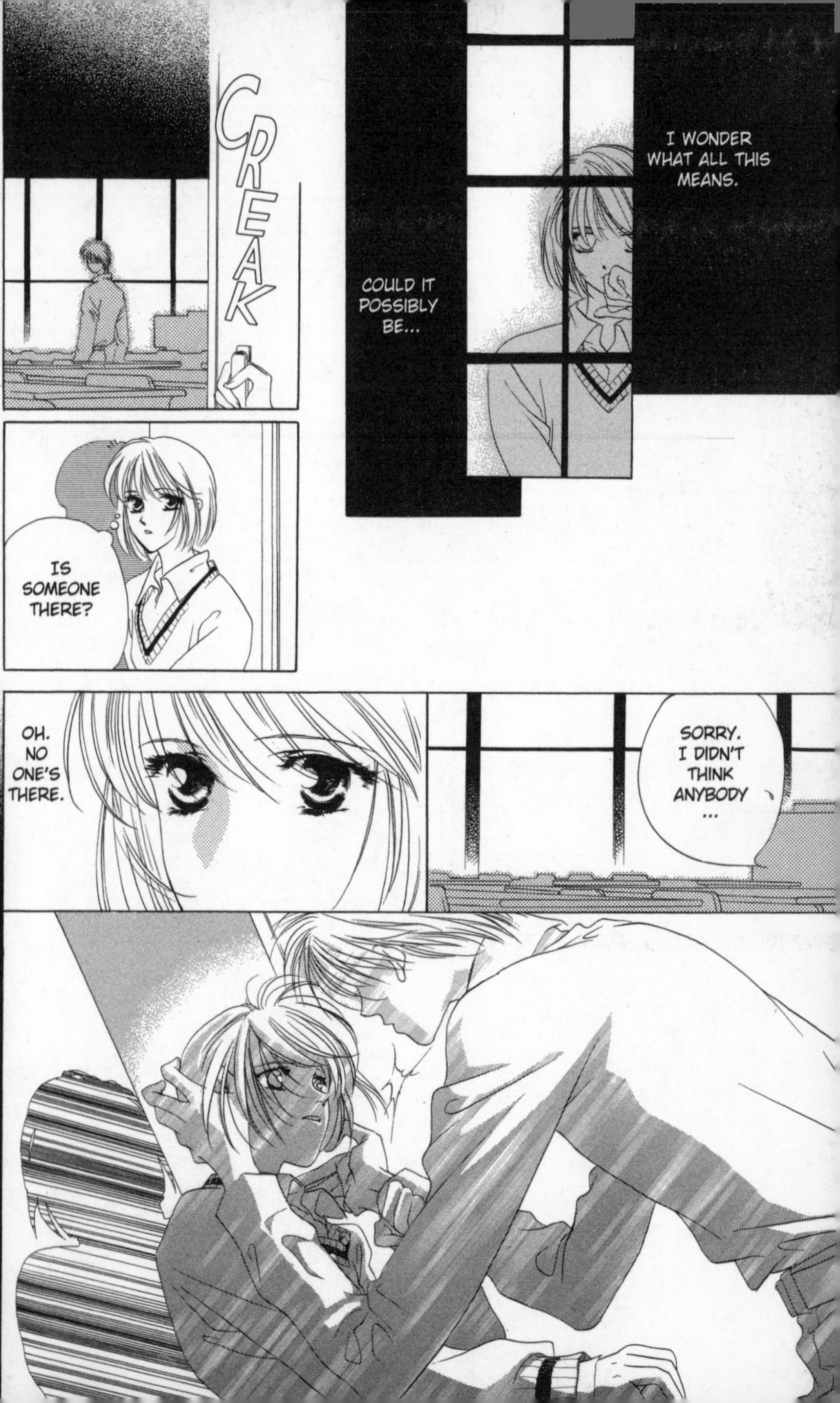
I WONDER WHAT ALL THIS MEANS.
COULD IT POSSIBLY BE...
CREAK
IS SOMEONE THERE?
SORRY. I DIDN'T THINK ANYBODY ...
OH. NO ONE'S THERE.

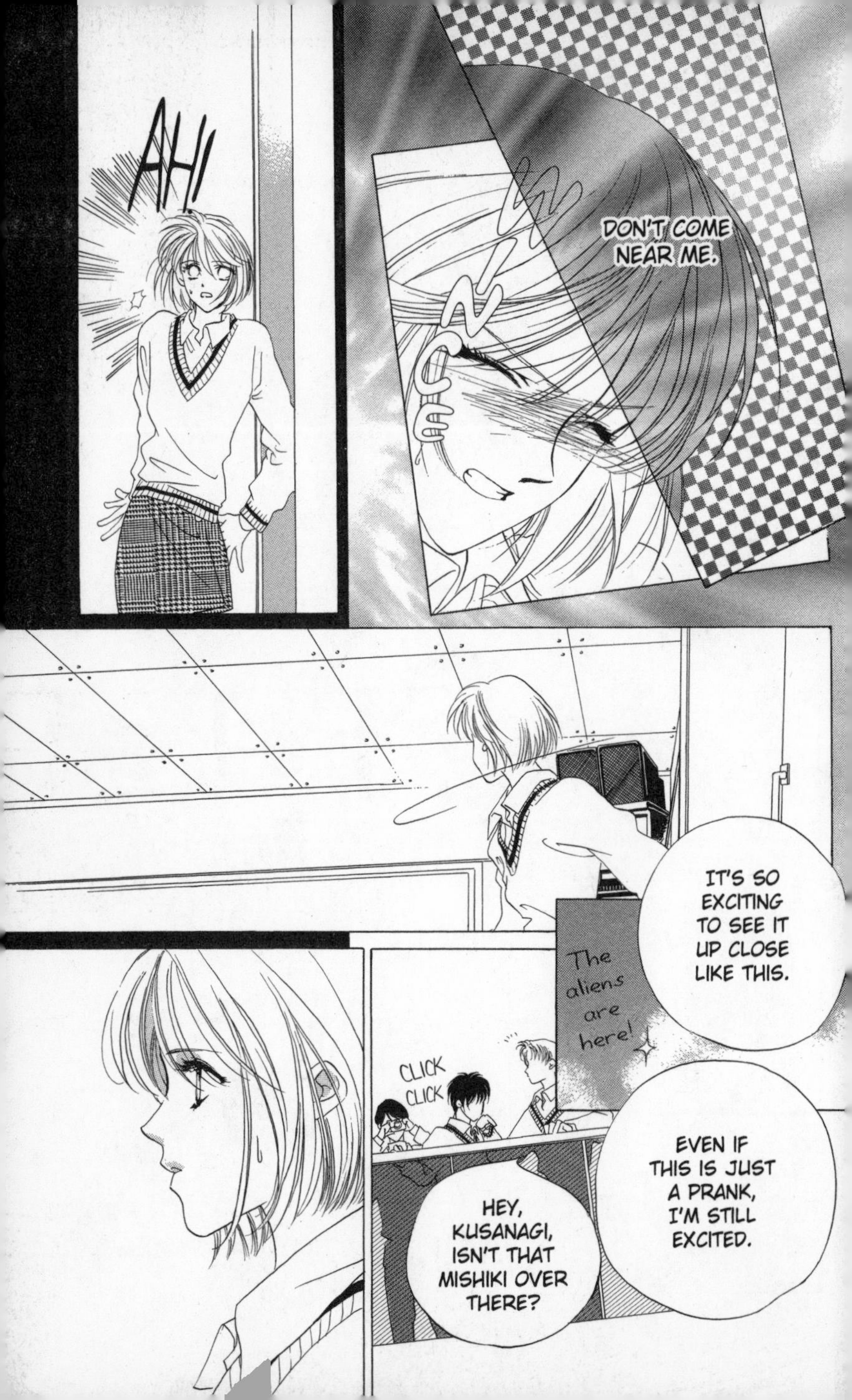
DON'T COME NEAR ME.
WINCE
AH!
IT'S SO EXCITING TO SEE IT UP CLOSE LIKE THIS.
The aliens are here!
EVEN IF THIS IS JUST A PRANK, I'M STILL EXCITED.
CLICK CLICK
HEY, KUSANAGI, ISN'T THAT MISHIKI OVER THERE?

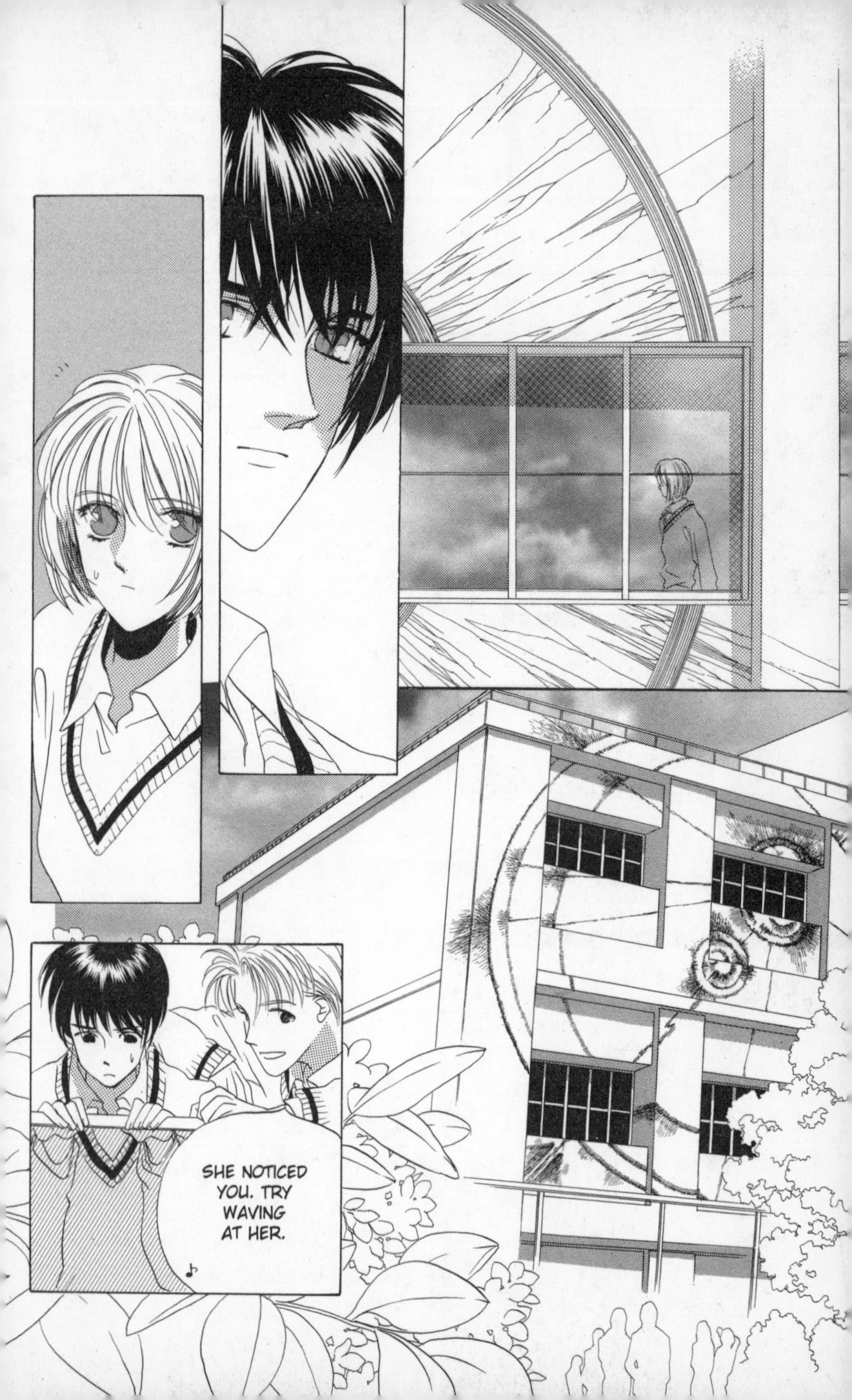
SHE NOTICED YOU. TRY WAVING AT HER.

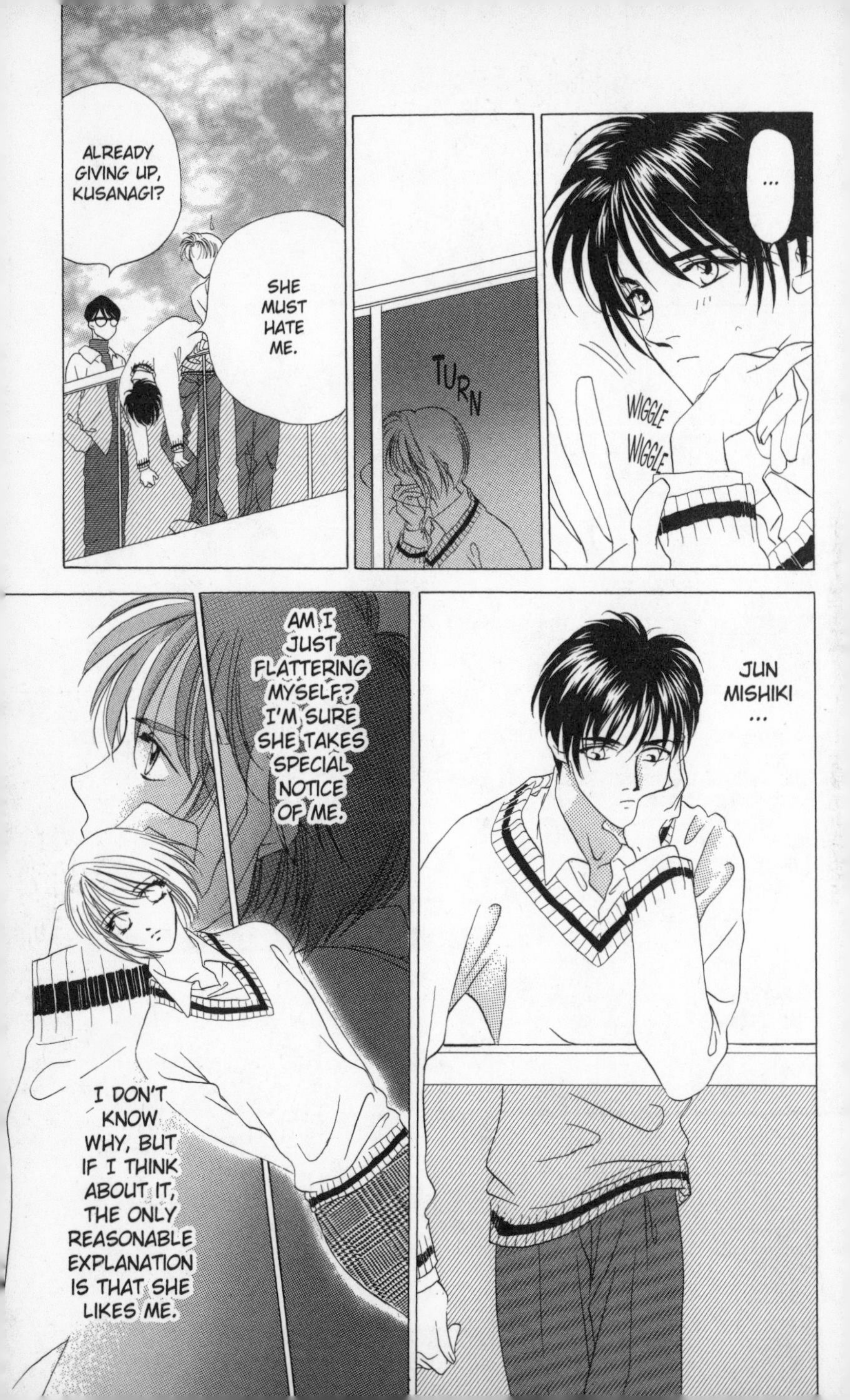
...
WIGGLE WIGGLE
TURN
ALREADY GIVING UP, KUSANAGI?
SHE MUST HATE ME.
JUN MISHIKI ...
AM I JUST FLATTERING MYSELF? I'M SURE SHE TAKES SPECIAL NOTICE OF ME.
I DON'T KNOW WHY, BUT IF I THINK ABOUT IT, THE ONLY REASONABLE EXPLANATION IS THAT SHE LIKES ME.

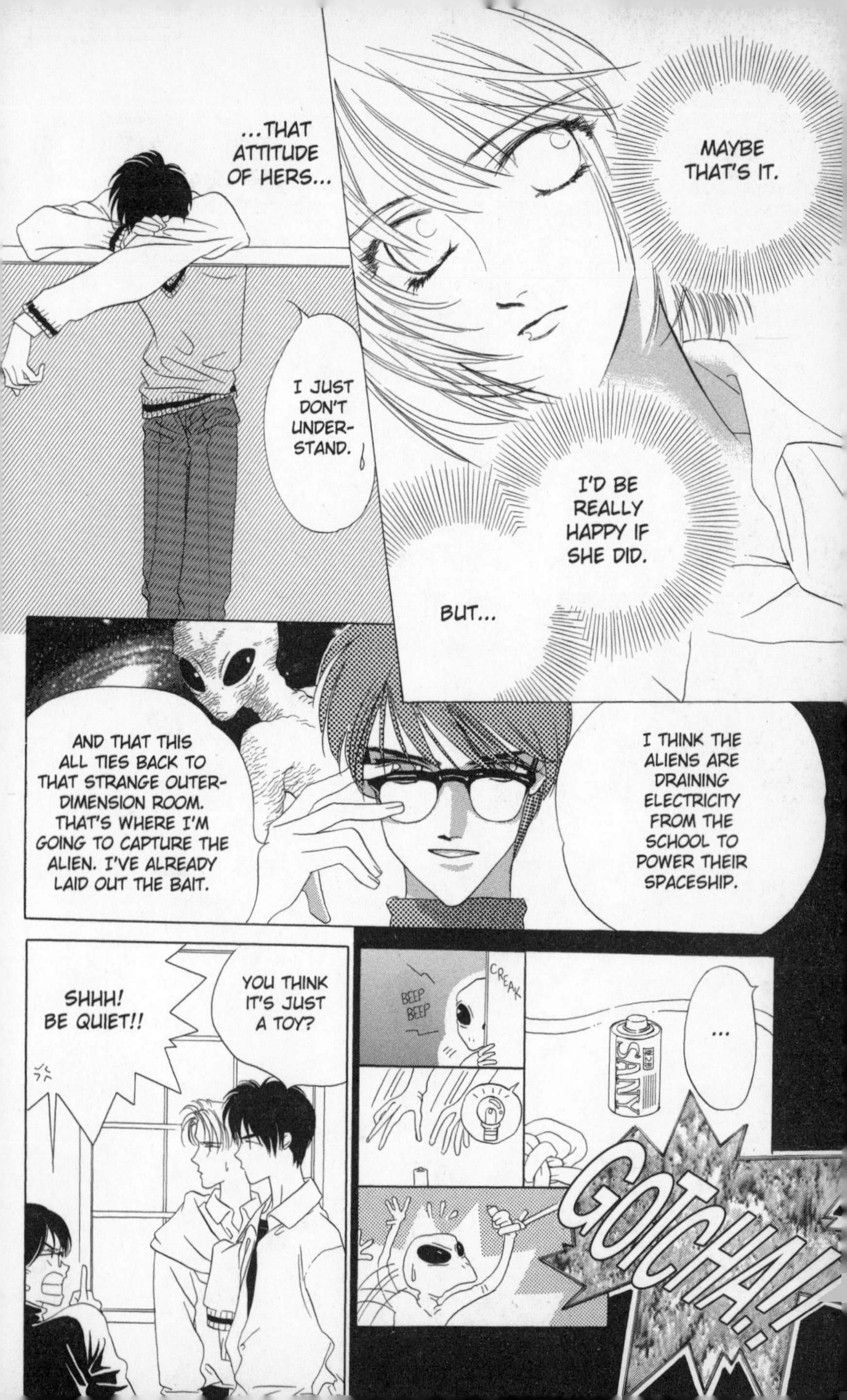
MAYBE THAT'S IT.
I'D BE REALLY HAPPY IF SHE DID.
BUT...
...THAT ATTITUDE OF HERS...
I JUST DON'T UNDER-STAND.
I THINK THE ALIENS ARE DRAINING ELECTRICITY FROM THE SCHOOL TO POWER THEIR SPACESHIP.
AND THAT THIS ALL TIES BACK TO THAT STRANGE OUTER-DIMENSION ROOM. THAT'S WHERE I'M GOING TO CAPTURE THE ALIEN. I'VE ALREADY LAID OUT THE BAIT.
...
CREAK
BEEP BEEP
SANY
GOTCHA!!
YOU THINK IT'S JUST A TOY?
SHHH! BE QUIET!!

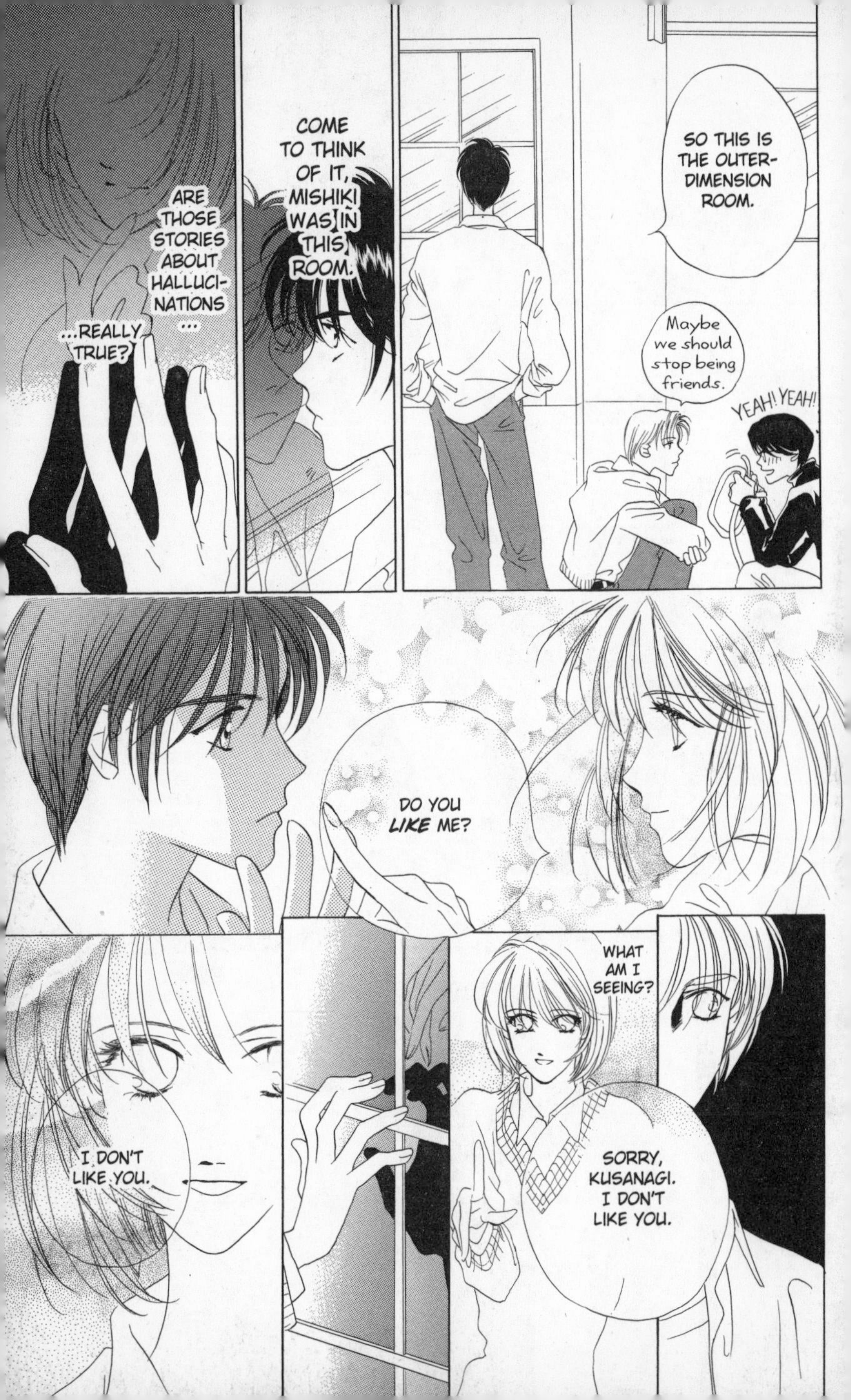
SO THIS IS THE OUTER-DIMENSION ROOM.
Maybe we should stop being friends.
YEAH! YEAH!
COME TO THINK OF IT, MISHIKI WAS IN THIS ROOM.
ARE THOSE STORIES ABOUT HALLUCINATIONS ...
...REALLY TRUE?
DO YOU *LIKE* ME?
WHAT AM I SEEING?
SORRY, KUSANAGI. I DON'T LIKE YOU.
I DON'T LIKE YOU.

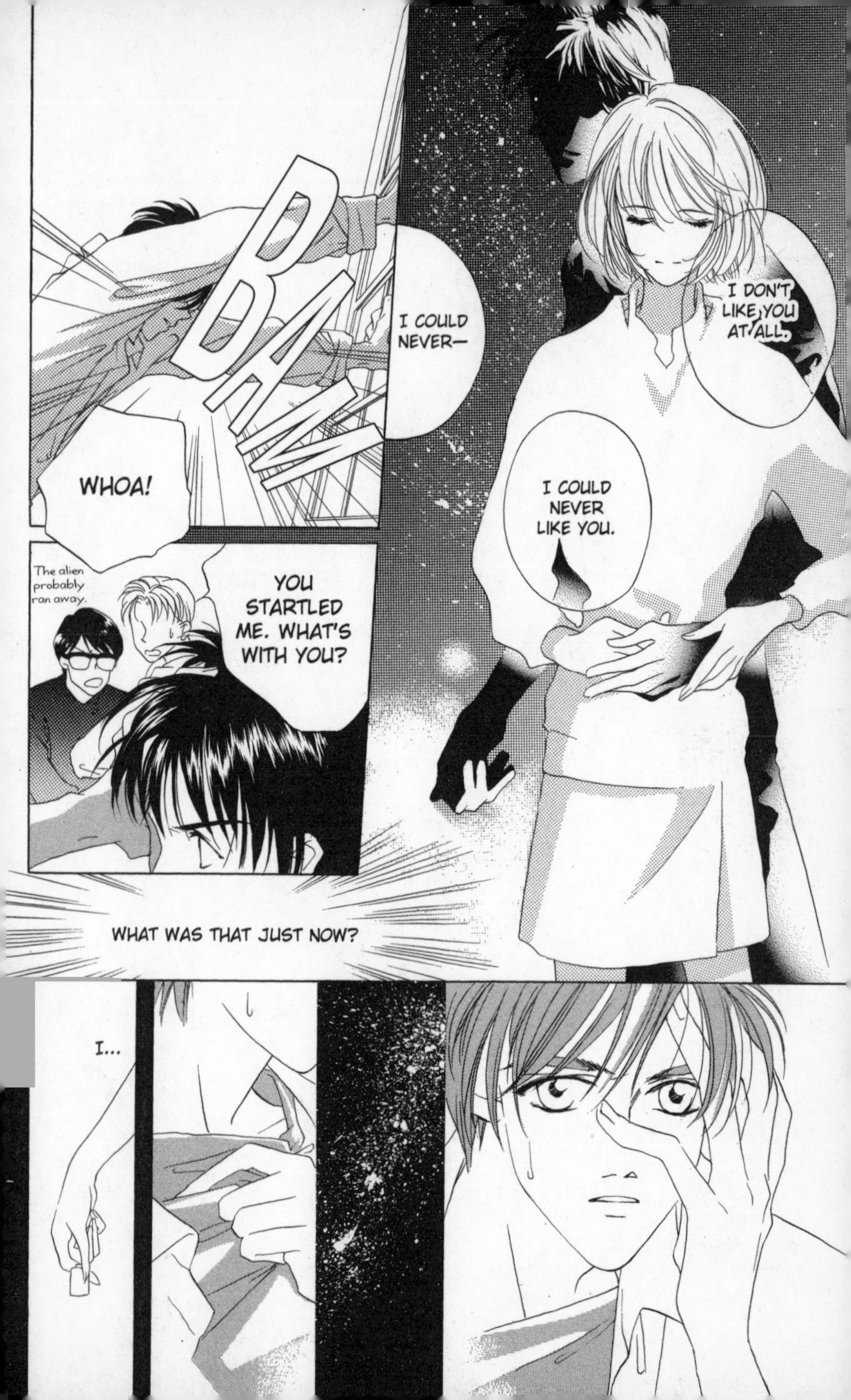
I DON'T LIKE YOU AT ALL.
I COULD NEVER—
I COULD NEVER LIKE YOU.
BAM
WHOA!
YOU STARTLED ME. WHAT'S WITH YOU?
The alien probably ran away.
WHAT WAS THAT JUST NOW?
I...

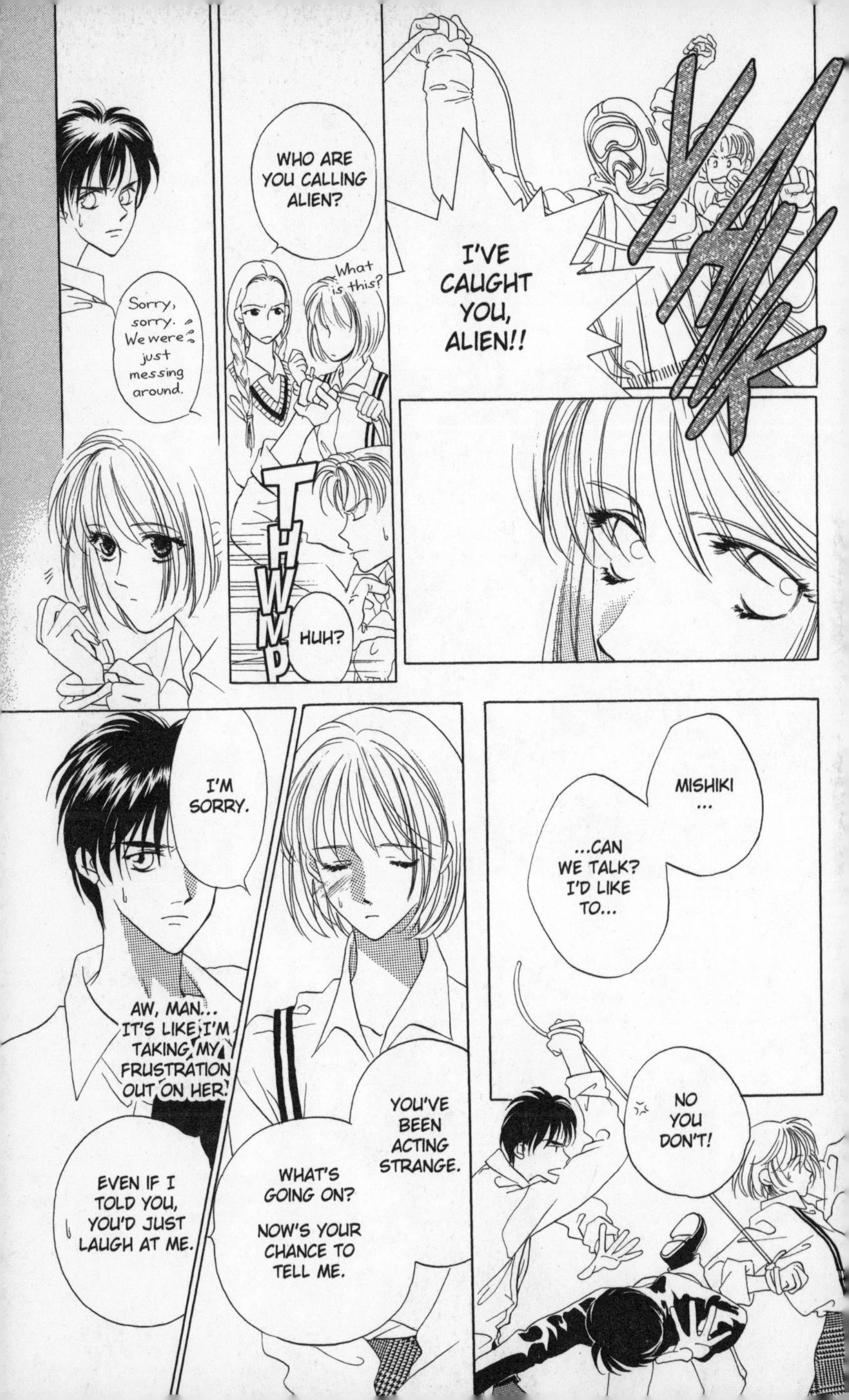
I'VE CAUGHT YOU, ALIEN!!
WHO ARE YOU CALLING ALIEN?
What is this?
THWMP
HUH?
Sorry, sorry. We were just messing around.
MISHIKI ...
...CAN WE TALK? I'D LIKE TO...
NO YOU DON'T!
YOU'VE BEEN ACTING STRANGE.
WHAT'S GOING ON?
NOW'S YOUR CHANCE TO TELL ME.
I'M SORRY.
AW, MAN... IT'S LIKE I'M TAKING MY FRUSTRATION OUT ON HER.
EVEN IF I TOLD YOU, YOU'D JUST LAUGH AT ME.

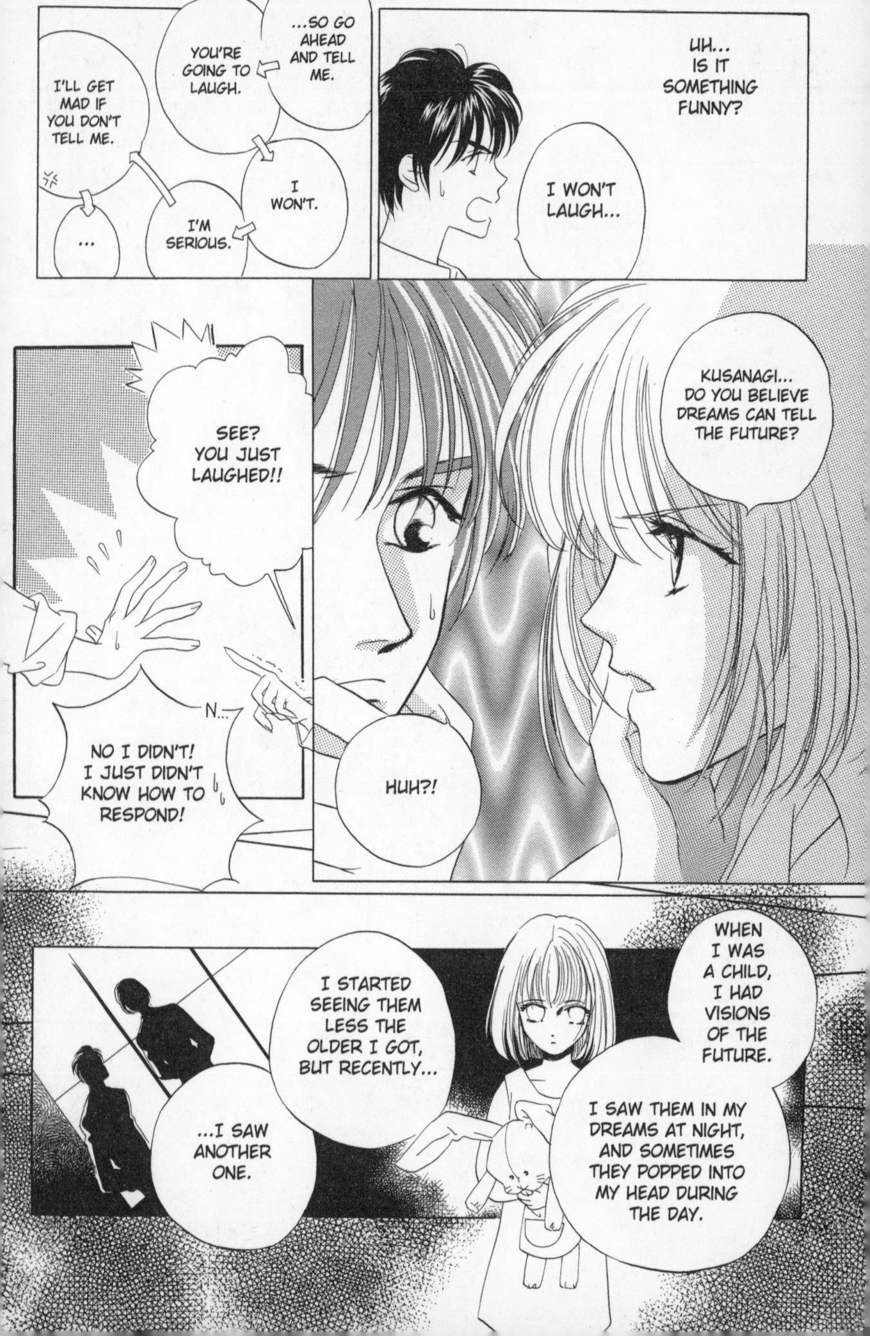
UH... IS IT SOMETHING FUNNY?
I WON'T LAUGH...
...SO GO AHEAD AND TELL ME.
YOU'RE GOING TO LAUGH.
I WON'T.
I'M SERIOUS.
I'LL GET MAD IF YOU DON'T TELL ME.
...
KUSANAGI... DO YOU BELIEVE DREAMS CAN TELL THE FUTURE?
HUH?!
SEE? YOU JUST LAUGHED!!
N...
NO I DIDN'T! I JUST DIDN'T KNOW HOW TO RESPOND!
WHEN I WAS A CHILD, I HAD VISIONS OF THE FUTURE.
I SAW THEM IN MY DREAMS AT NIGHT, AND SOMETIMES THEY POPPED INTO MY HEAD DURING THE DAY.
I STARTED SEEING THEM LESS THE OLDER I GOT, BUT RECENTLY...
...I SAW ANOTHER ONE.

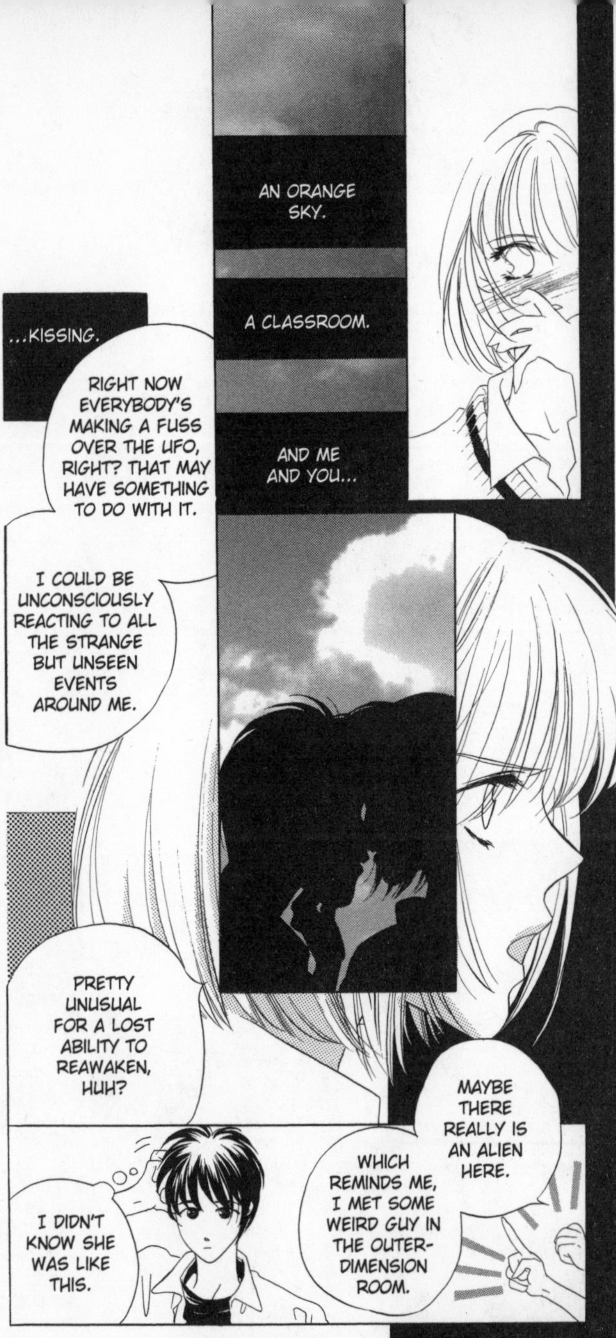
AN ORANGE SKY.
A CLASSROOM.
AND ME AND YOU...
...KISSING.
RIGHT NOW EVERYBODY'S MAKING A FUSS OVER THE UFO, RIGHT? THAT MAY HAVE SOMETHING TO DO WITH IT.
I COULD BE UNCONSCIOUSLY REACTING TO ALL THE STRANGE BUT UNSEEN EVENTS AROUND ME.
PRETTY UNUSUAL FOR A LOST ABILITY TO REAWAKEN, HUH?
MAYBE THERE REALLY IS AN ALIEN HERE.
WHICH REMINDS ME, I MET SOME WEIRD GUY IN THE OUTER-DIMENSION ROOM.
I DIDN'T KNOW SHE WAS LIKE THIS.

Okay, time to Fill up space!

• In the summer of 2000 I sprained my hip. I was lying down and my nephew flumped down on my back with a loud thud. I didn't think anything of it at First, but as the days passed, I Found myself unable to stand up straight. My hip would hurt whenever I stretched the muscles there. Even though it was summer, I would pull out my electric heater to warm up my hip...

Since there was nothing I could do, I went to see an osteopath. He explained everything to me using a bunch of medical jargon and then laughed at me, saying, "In layman's terms, you've sprained your hip." Then I started to laugh too.

☆☆☆

• Love-X

I made this a long time ago so I'm really embarrassed by it. There really isn't anything else I can say about it. Read one...if you dare!

Mizuno

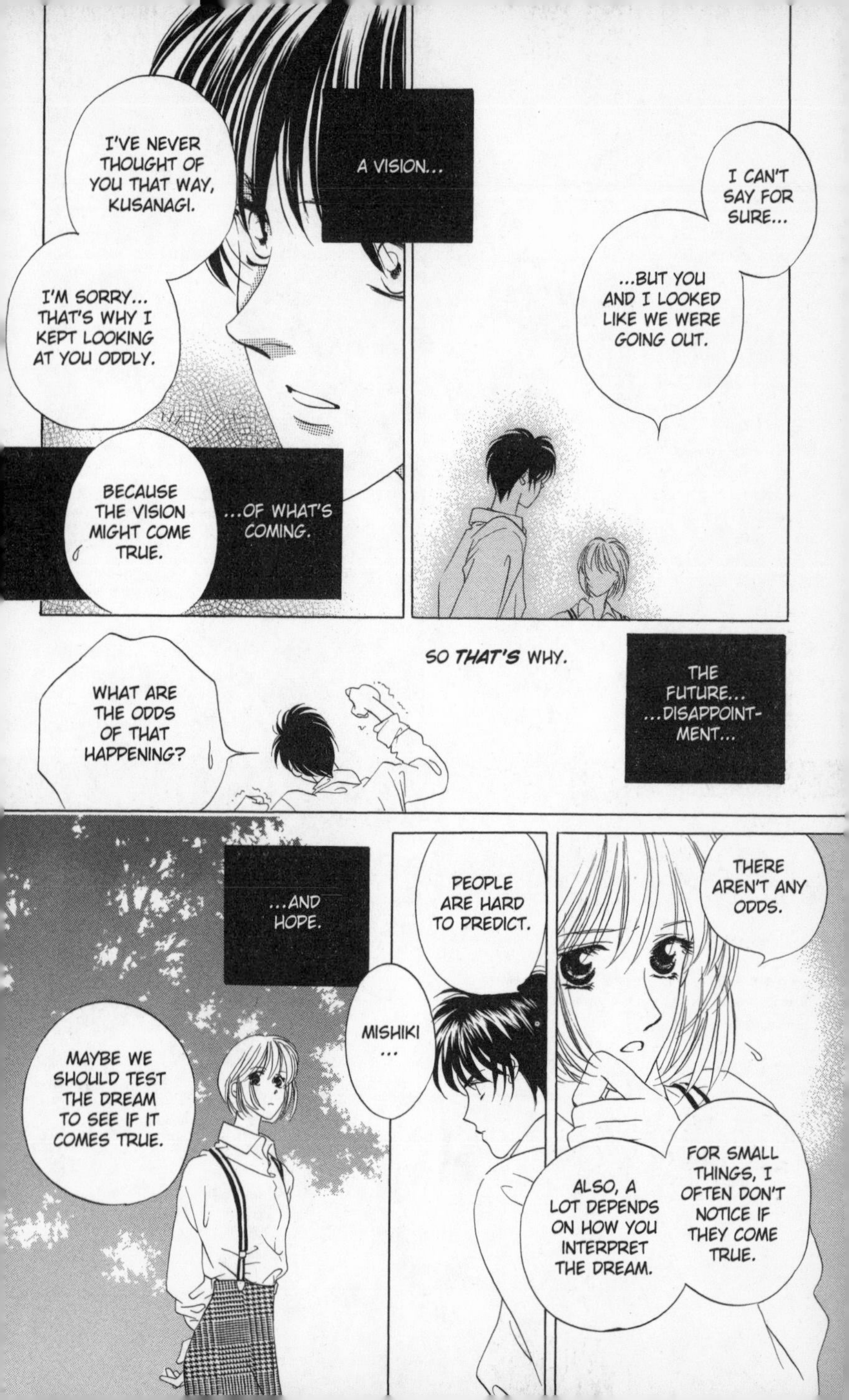
I CAN'T SAY FOR SURE...
...BUT YOU AND I LOOKED LIKE WE WERE GOING OUT.
A VISION...
I'VE NEVER THOUGHT OF YOU THAT WAY, KUSANAGI.
I'M SORRY... THAT'S WHY I KEPT LOOKING AT YOU ODDLY.
...OF WHAT'S COMING.
BECAUSE THE VISION MIGHT COME TRUE.
THE FUTURE... ...DISAPPOINT-MENT...
SO *THAT'S* WHY.
WHAT ARE THE ODDS OF THAT HAPPENING?
THERE AREN'T ANY ODDS.
FOR SMALL THINGS, I OFTEN DON'T NOTICE IF THEY COME TRUE.
ALSO, A LOT DEPENDS ON HOW YOU INTERPRET THE DREAM.
PEOPLE ARE HARD TO PREDICT.
MISHIKI ...
...AND HOPE.
MAYBE WE SHOULD TEST THE DREAM TO SEE IF IT COMES TRUE.

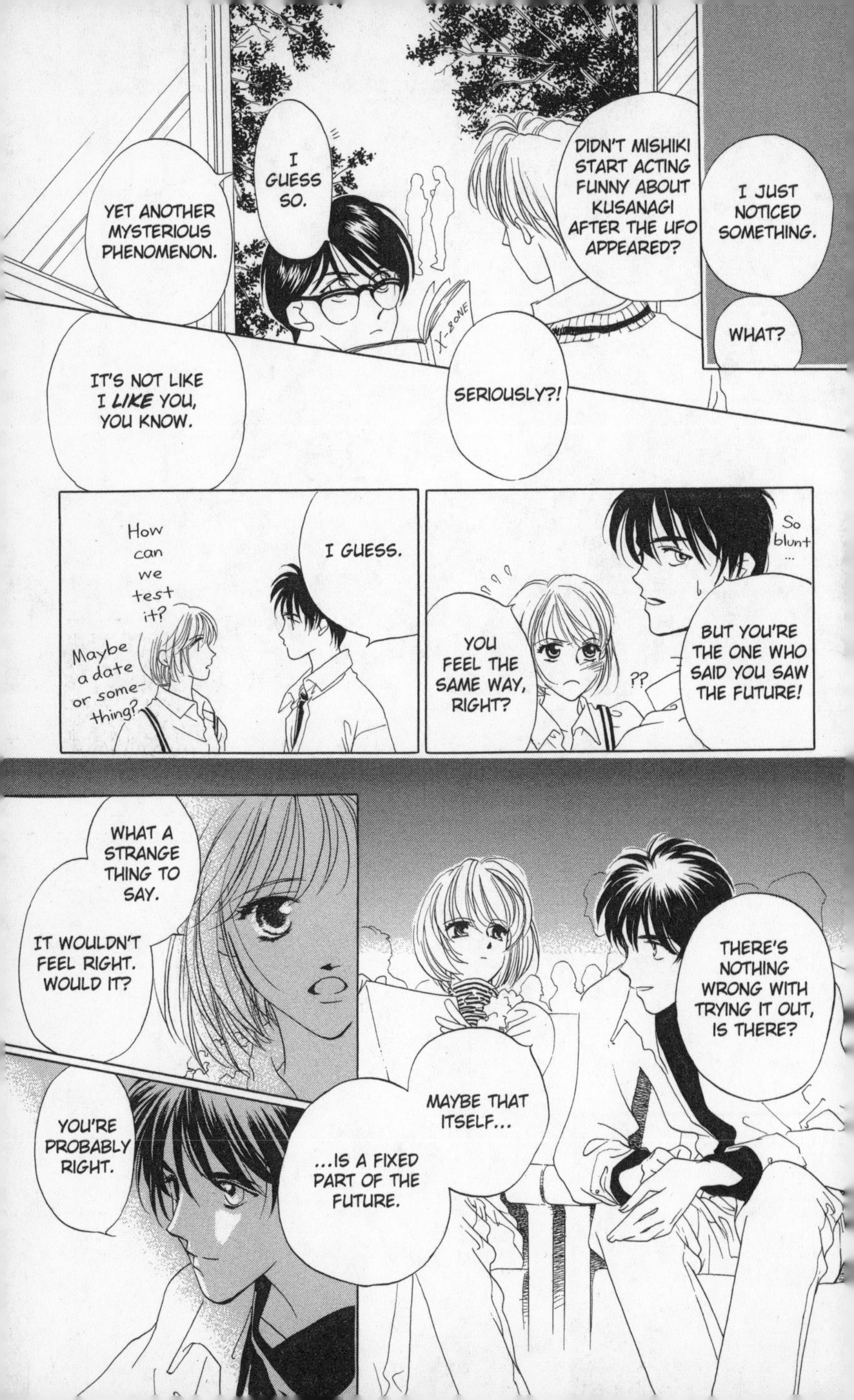
I JUST NOTICED SOMETHING.
WHAT?
DIDN'T MISHIKI START ACTING FUNNY ABOUT KUSANAGI AFTER THE UFO APPEARED?
I GUESS SO.
YET ANOTHER MYSTERIOUS PHENOMENON.
SERIOUSLY?!
IT'S NOT LIKE I *LIKE* YOU, YOU KNOW.
So blunt...
BUT YOU'RE THE ONE WHO SAID YOU SAW THE FUTURE!
??
YOU FEEL THE SAME WAY, RIGHT?
I GUESS.
How can we test it?
Maybe a date or something?
THERE'S NOTHING WRONG WITH TRYING IT OUT, IS THERE?
WHAT A STRANGE THING TO SAY.
IT WOULDN'T FEEL RIGHT. WOULD IT?
MAYBE THAT ITSELF...
...IS A FIXED PART OF THE FUTURE.
YOU'RE PROBABLY RIGHT.

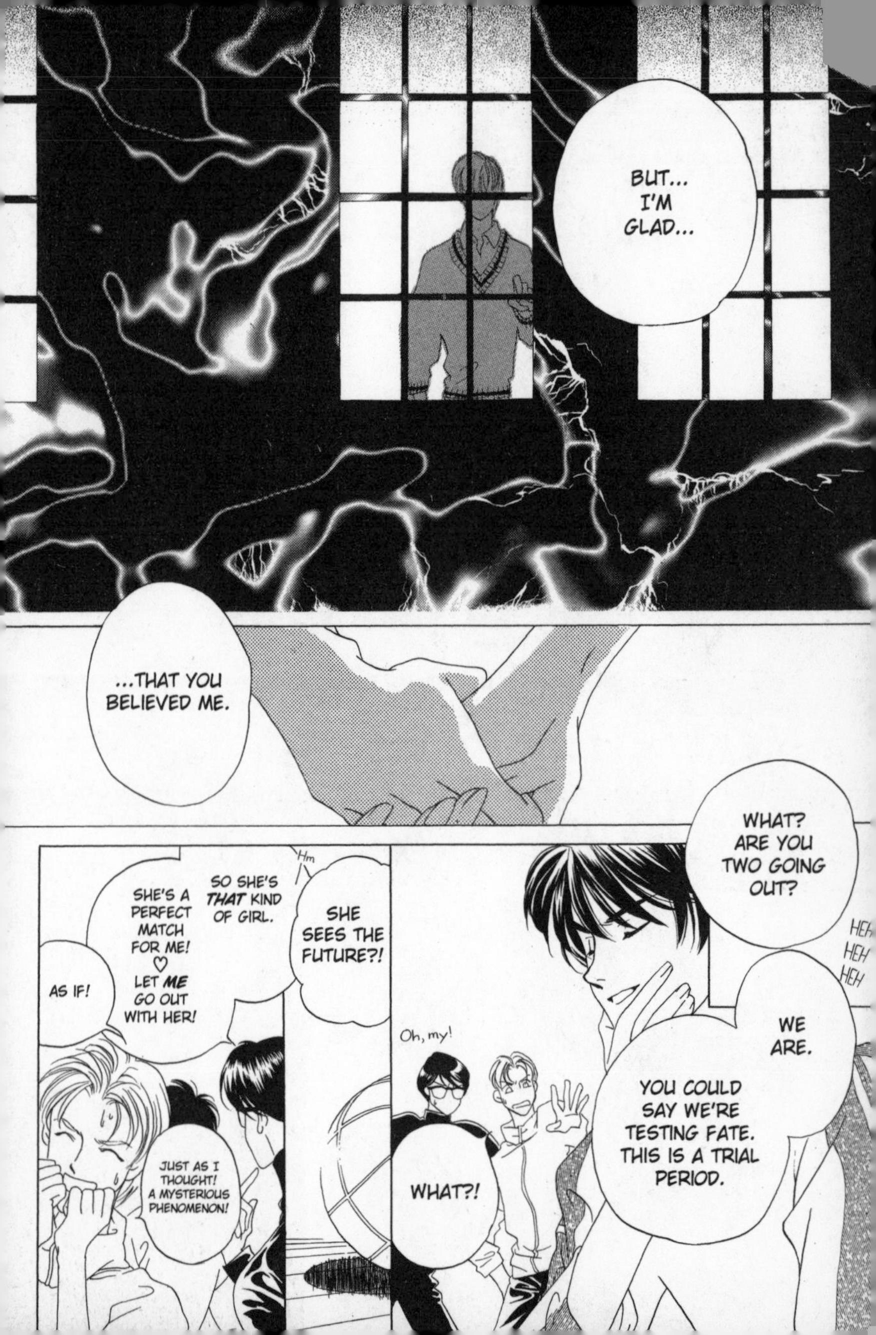
BUT... I'M GLAD...
...THAT YOU BELIEVED ME.
WHAT? ARE YOU TWO GOING OUT?
HEH HEH HEH
WE ARE.
YOU COULD SAY WE'RE TESTING FATE. THIS IS A TRIAL PERIOD.
Oh, my!
WHAT?!
Hm
SHE SEES THE FUTURE?!
SO SHE'S *THAT* KIND OF GIRL.
SHE'S A PERFECT MATCH FOR ME! ♡ LET *ME* GO OUT WITH HER!
AS IF!
JUST AS I THOUGHT! A MYSTERIOUS PHENOMENON!

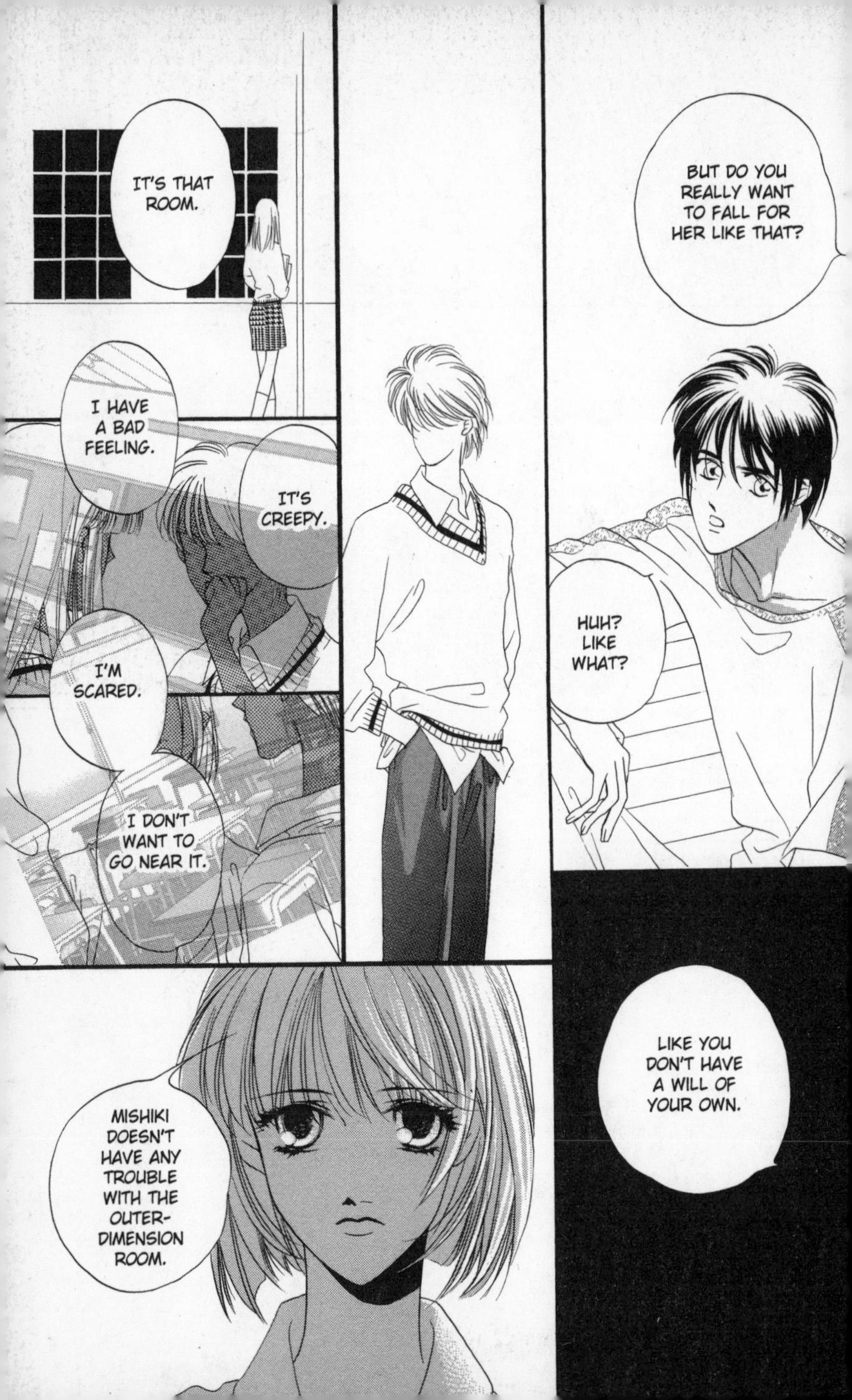
BUT DO YOU REALLY WANT TO FALL FOR HER LIKE THAT?
HUH? LIKE WHAT?
IT'S THAT ROOM.
I HAVE A BAD FEELING.
IT'S CREEPY.
I'M SCARED.
I DON'T WANT TO GO NEAR IT.
LIKE YOU DON'T HAVE A WILL OF YOUR OWN.
MISHIKI DOESN'T HAVE ANY TROUBLE WITH THE OUTER-DIMENSION ROOM.

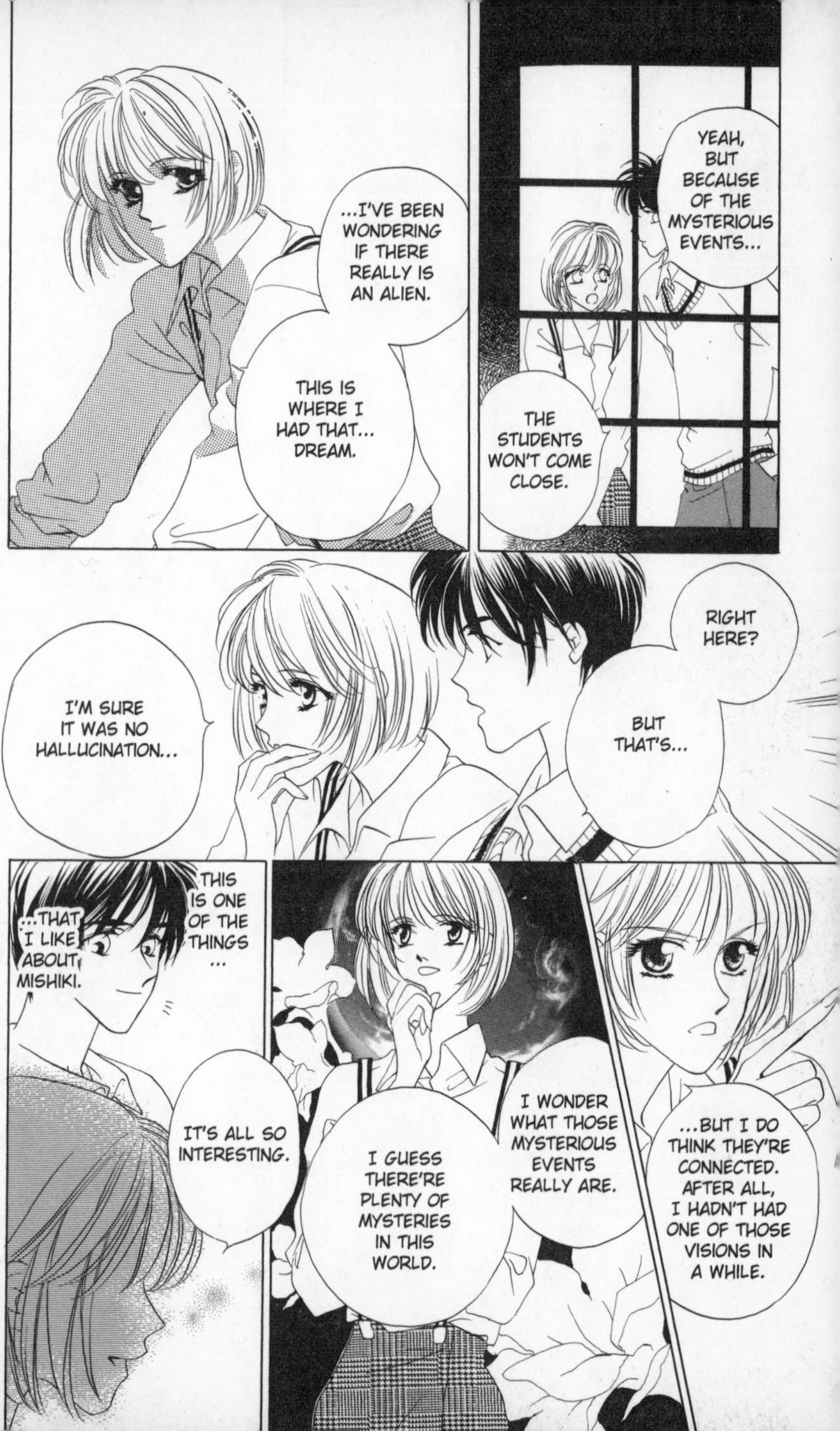
YEAH, BUT BECAUSE OF THE MYSTERIOUS EVENTS...
THE STUDENTS WON'T COME CLOSE.
...I'VE BEEN WONDERING IF THERE REALLY IS AN ALIEN.
THIS IS WHERE I HAD THAT... DREAM.
RIGHT HERE?
BUT THAT'S...
I'M SURE IT WAS NO HALLUCINATION...
...BUT I DO THINK THEY'RE CONNECTED. AFTER ALL, I HADN'T HAD ONE OF THOSE VISIONS IN A WHILE.
I WONDER WHAT THOSE MYSTERIOUS EVENTS REALLY ARE.
I GUESS THERE'RE PLENTY OF MYSTERIES IN THIS WORLD.
IT'S ALL SO INTERESTING.
THIS IS ONE OF THE THINGS...
...THAT I LIKE ABOUT MISHIKI.

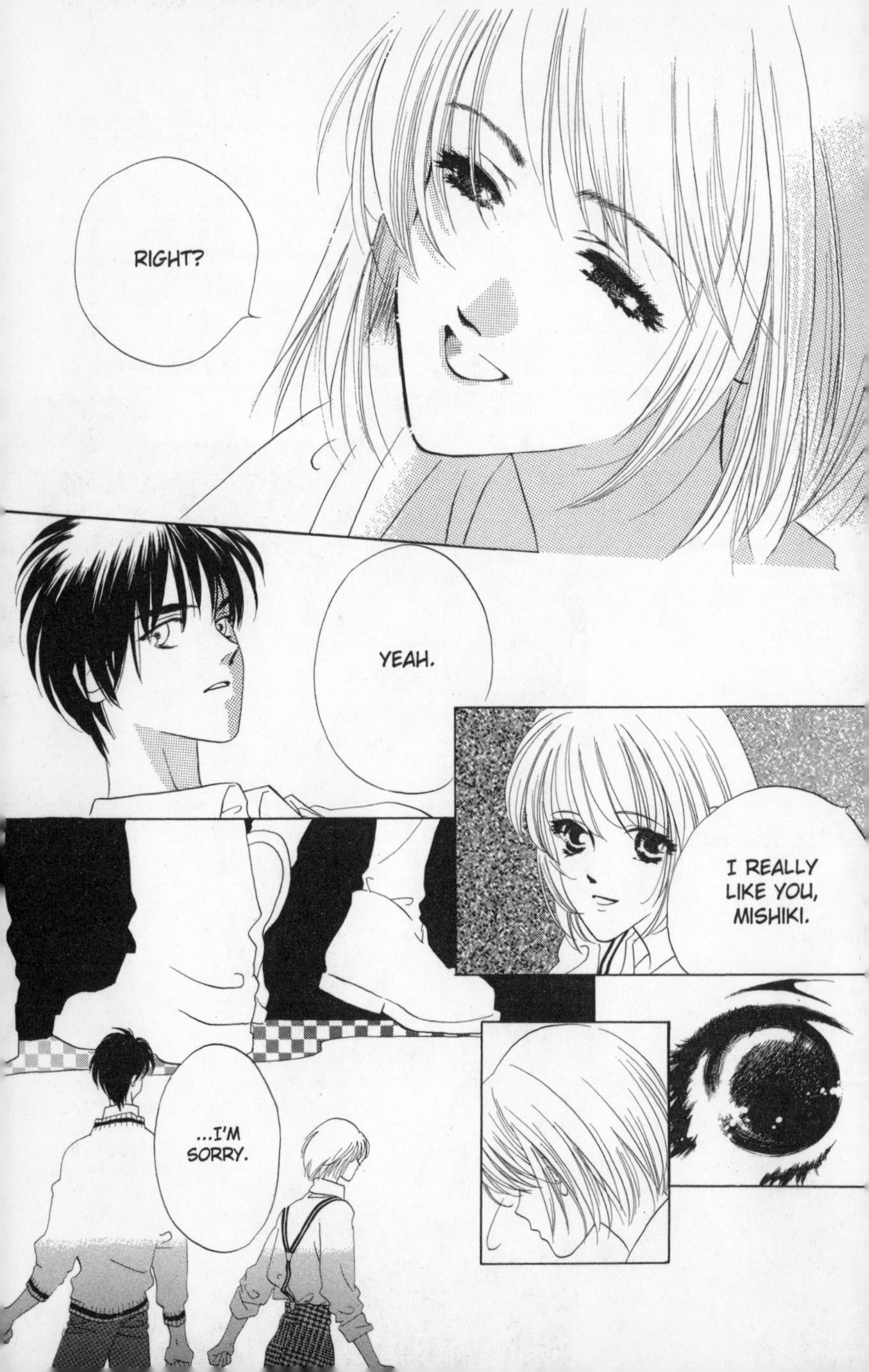
RIGHT?
YEAH.
I REALLY LIKE YOU, MISHIKI.
...I'M SORRY.

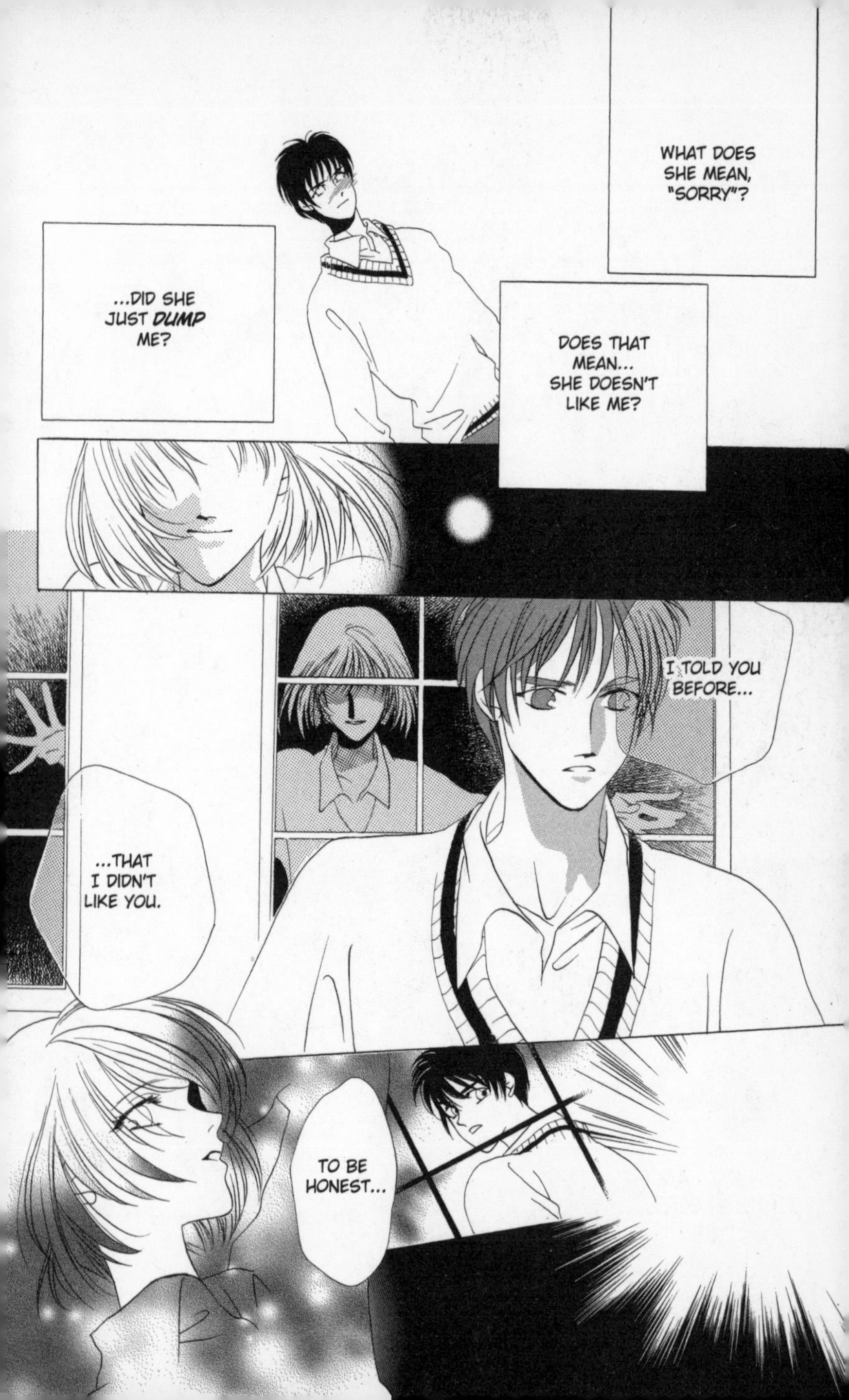
WHAT DOES SHE MEAN, "SORRY"?
DOES THAT MEAN... SHE DOESN'T LIKE ME?
...DID SHE JUST *DUMP* ME?
I TOLD YOU BEFORE...
...THAT I DIDN'T LIKE YOU.
TO BE HONEST...

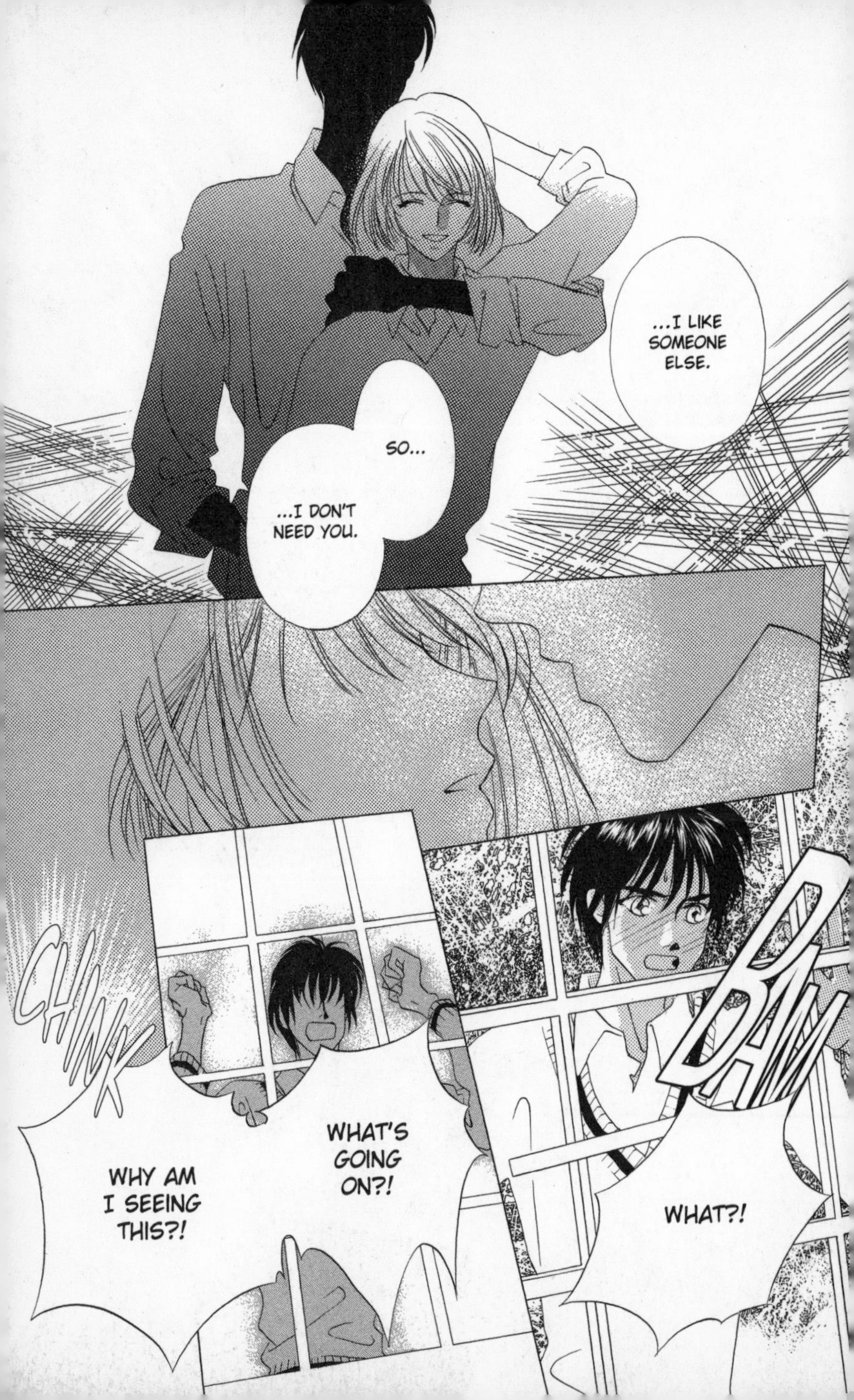
...I LIKE SOMEONE ELSE.
SO...
...I DON'T NEED YOU.
BAM
WHAT?!
CHINK
WHAT'S GOING ON?!
WHY AM I SEEING THIS?!

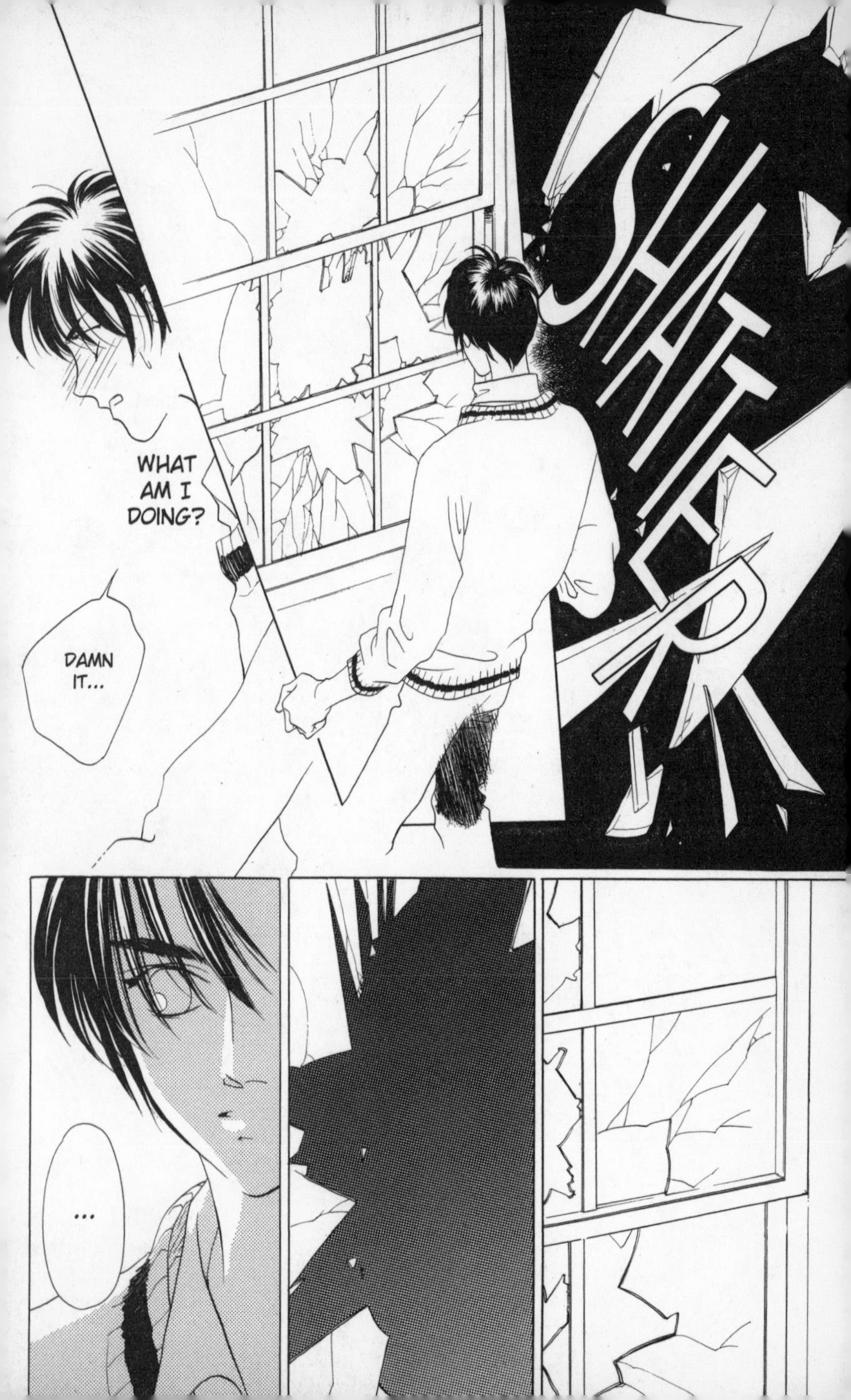
SHATTER
WHAT AM I DOING?
DAMN IT...
...

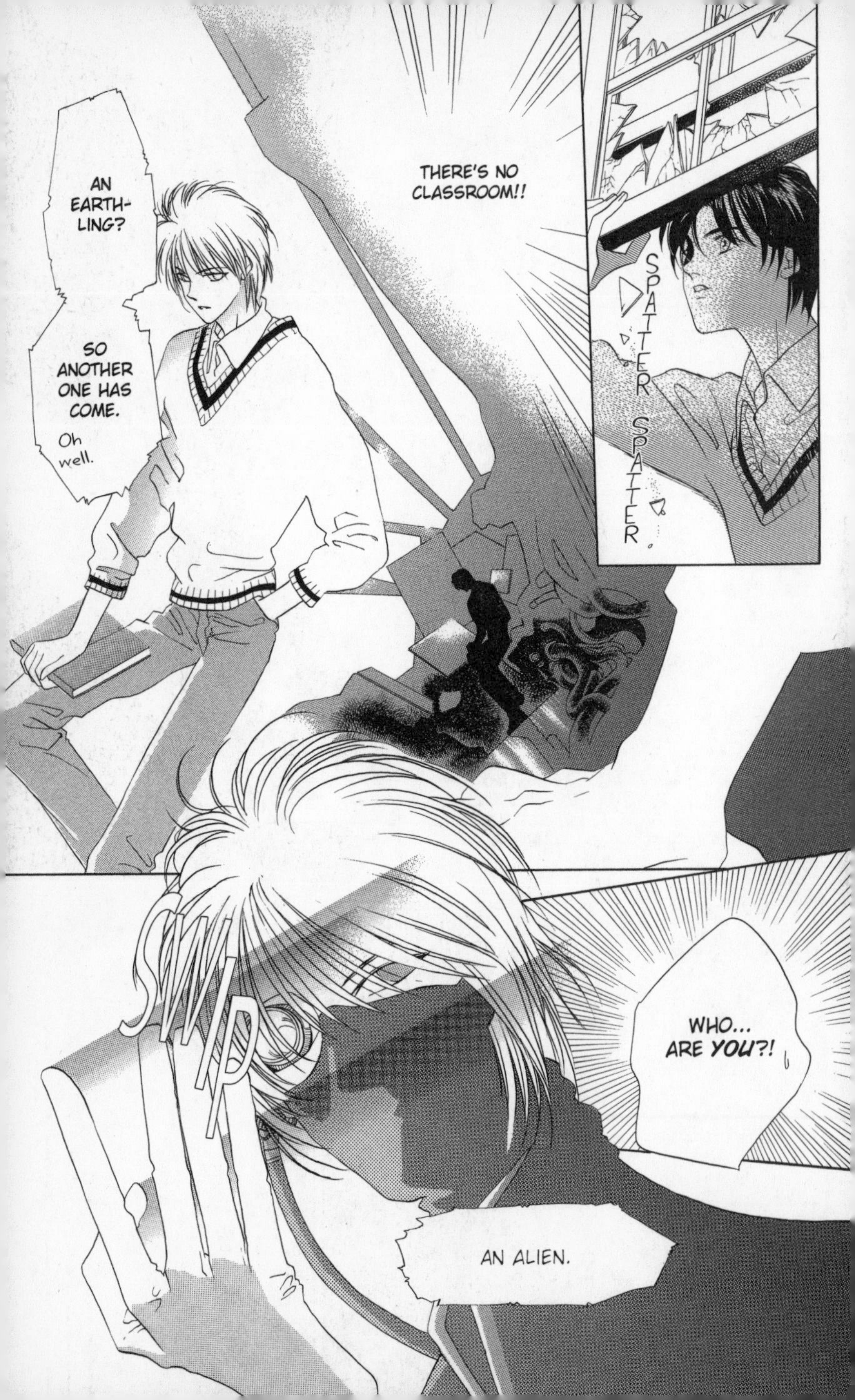

SPATTER SPATTER
THERE'S NO CLASSROOM!!
AN EARTHLING?
SO ANOTHER ONE HAS COME.
Oh well.
WHO... ARE *YOU*?!
SNIP
AN ALIEN.

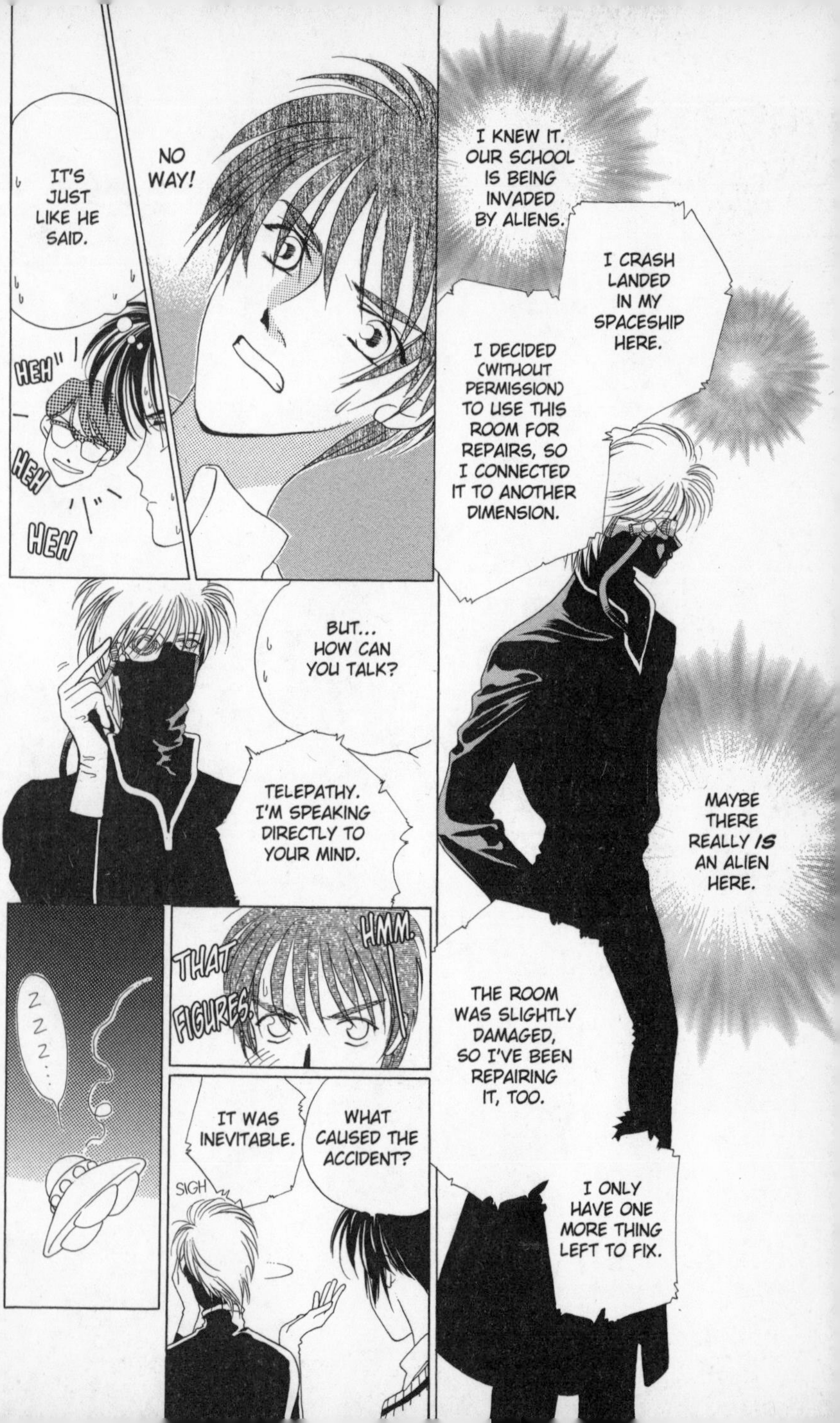
I KNEW IT. OUR SCHOOL IS BEING INVADED BY ALIENS.
I CRASH LANDED IN MY SPACESHIP HERE.
I DECIDED (WITHOUT PERMISSION) TO USE THIS ROOM FOR REPAIRS, SO I CONNECTED IT TO ANOTHER DIMENSION.
MAYBE THERE REALLY *IS* AN ALIEN HERE.
THE ROOM WAS SLIGHTLY DAMAGED, SO I'VE BEEN REPAIRING IT, TOO.
I ONLY HAVE ONE MORE THING LEFT TO FIX.
NO WAY!
IT'S JUST LIKE HE SAID.
HEH
HEH
HEH
BUT... HOW CAN YOU TALK?
TELEPATHY. I'M SPEAKING DIRECTLY TO YOUR MIND.
HMM.
THAT FIGURES.
WHAT CAUSED THE ACCIDENT?
IT WAS INEVITABLE.
SIGH
ZZZ...

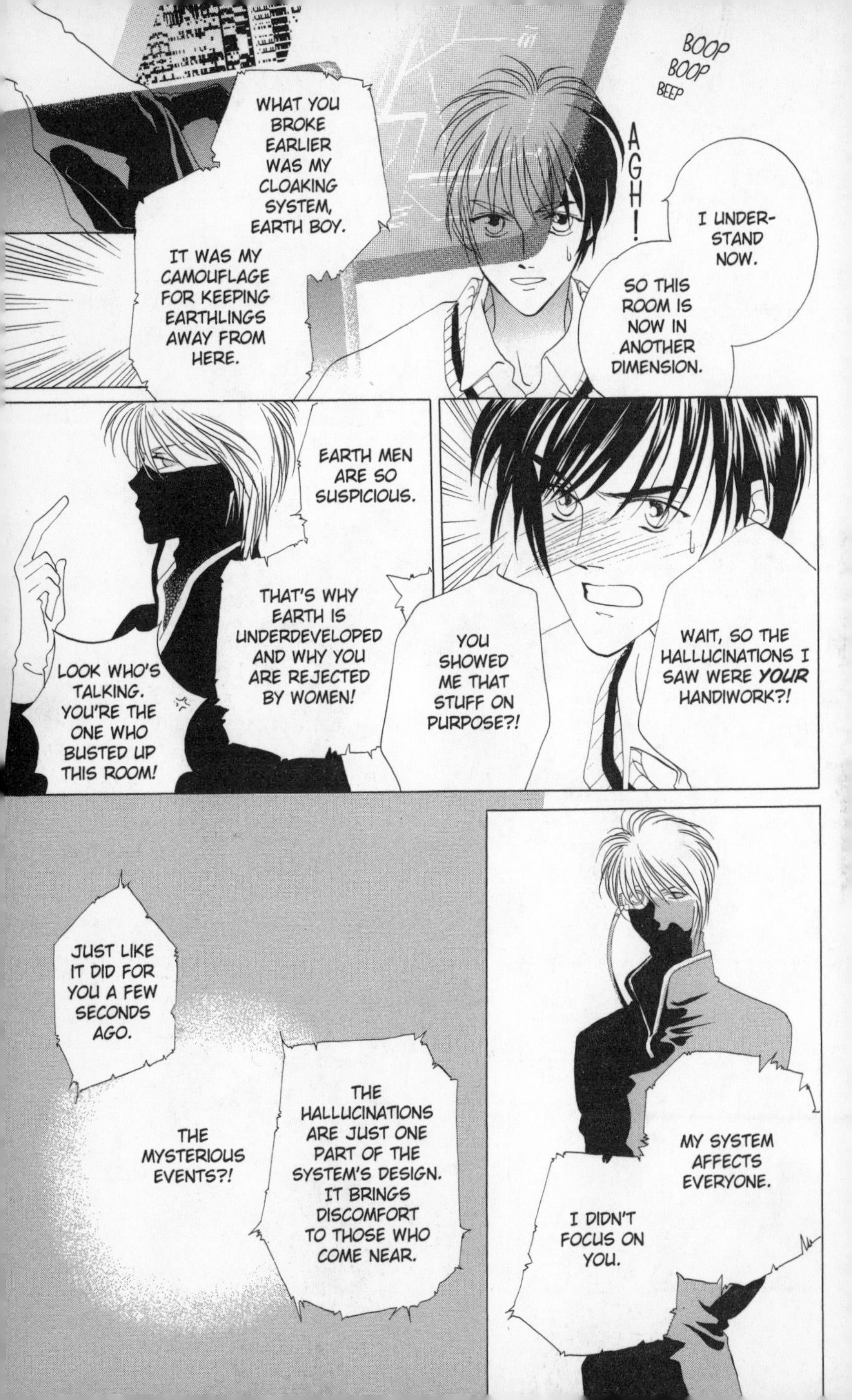
BOOP BOOP BEEP
AGH!
I UNDER-STAND NOW.
SO THIS ROOM IS NOW IN ANOTHER DIMENSION.
WHAT YOU BROKE EARLIER WAS MY CLOAKING SYSTEM, EARTH BOY.
IT WAS MY CAMOUFLAGE FOR KEEPING EARTHLINGS AWAY FROM HERE.
WAIT, SO THE HALLUCINATIONS I SAW WERE *YOUR* HANDIWORK?!
YOU SHOWED ME THAT STUFF ON PURPOSE?!
EARTH MEN ARE SO SUSPICIOUS.
THAT'S WHY EARTH IS UNDERDEVELOPED AND WHY YOU ARE REJECTED BY WOMEN!
LOOK WHO'S TALKING. YOU'RE THE ONE WHO BUSTED UP THIS ROOM!
MY SYSTEM AFFECTS EVERYONE.
I DIDN'T FOCUS ON YOU.
THE HALLUCINATIONS ARE JUST ONE PART OF THE SYSTEM'S DESIGN. IT BRINGS DISCOMFORT TO THOSE WHO COME NEAR.
THE MYSTERIOUS EVENTS?!
JUST LIKE IT DID FOR YOU A FEW SECONDS AGO.

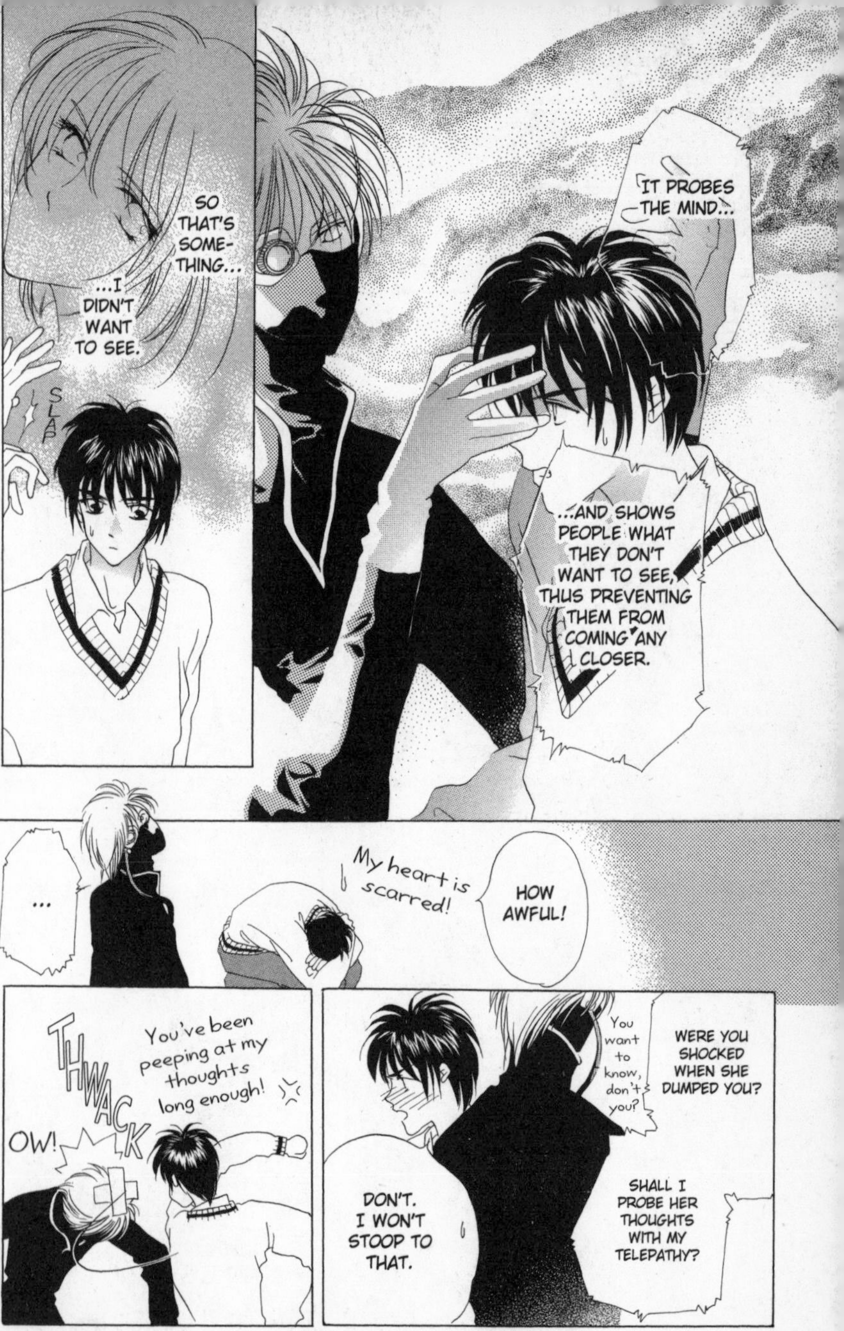
IT PROBES THE MIND...
...AND SHOWS PEOPLE WHAT THEY DON'T WANT TO SEE, THUS PREVENTING THEM FROM COMING ANY CLOSER.
SO THAT'S SOMETHING...
...I DIDN'T WANT TO SEE.
SLAP
HOW AWFUL!
My heart is scarred!
...
WERE YOU SHOCKED WHEN SHE DUMPED YOU?
You want to know, don't you?
SHALL I PROBE HER THOUGHTS WITH MY TELEPATHY?
DON'T. I WON'T STOOP TO THAT.
You've been peeping at my thoughts long enough!
THWACK
OW!

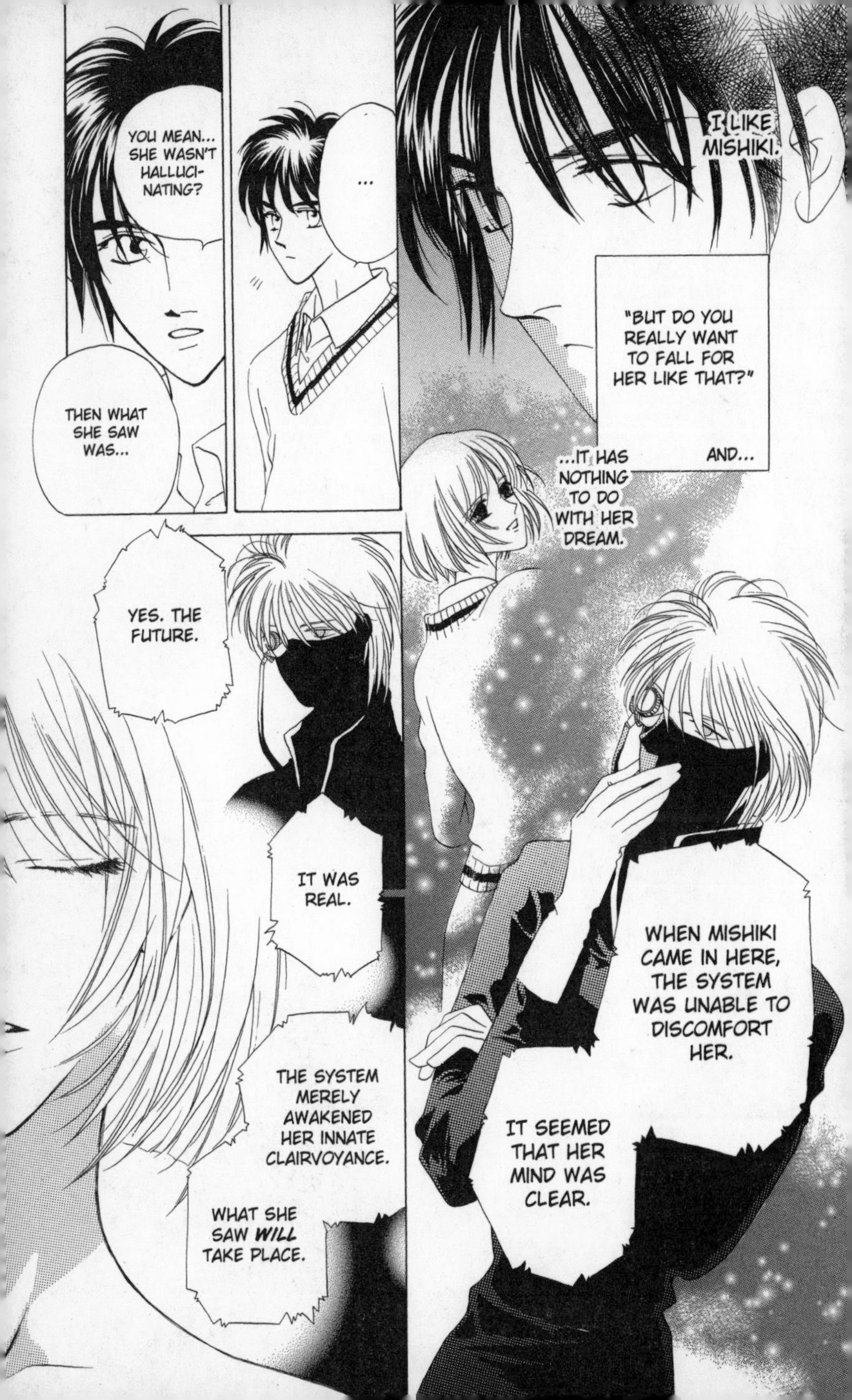
...
YOU MEAN... SHE WASN'T HALLUCI-NATING?
THEN WHAT SHE SAW WAS...
YES. THE FUTURE.
IT WAS REAL.
THE SYSTEM MERELY AWAKENED HER INNATE CLAIRVOYANCE.
WHAT SHE SAW *WILL* TAKE PLACE.
I LIKE MISHIKI.
"BUT DO YOU REALLY WANT TO FALL FOR HER LIKE THAT?"
AND...
...IT HAS NOTHING TO DO WITH HER DREAM.
WHEN MISHIKI CAME IN HERE, THE SYSTEM WAS UNABLE TO DISCOMFORT HER.
IT SEEMED THAT HER MIND WAS CLEAR.

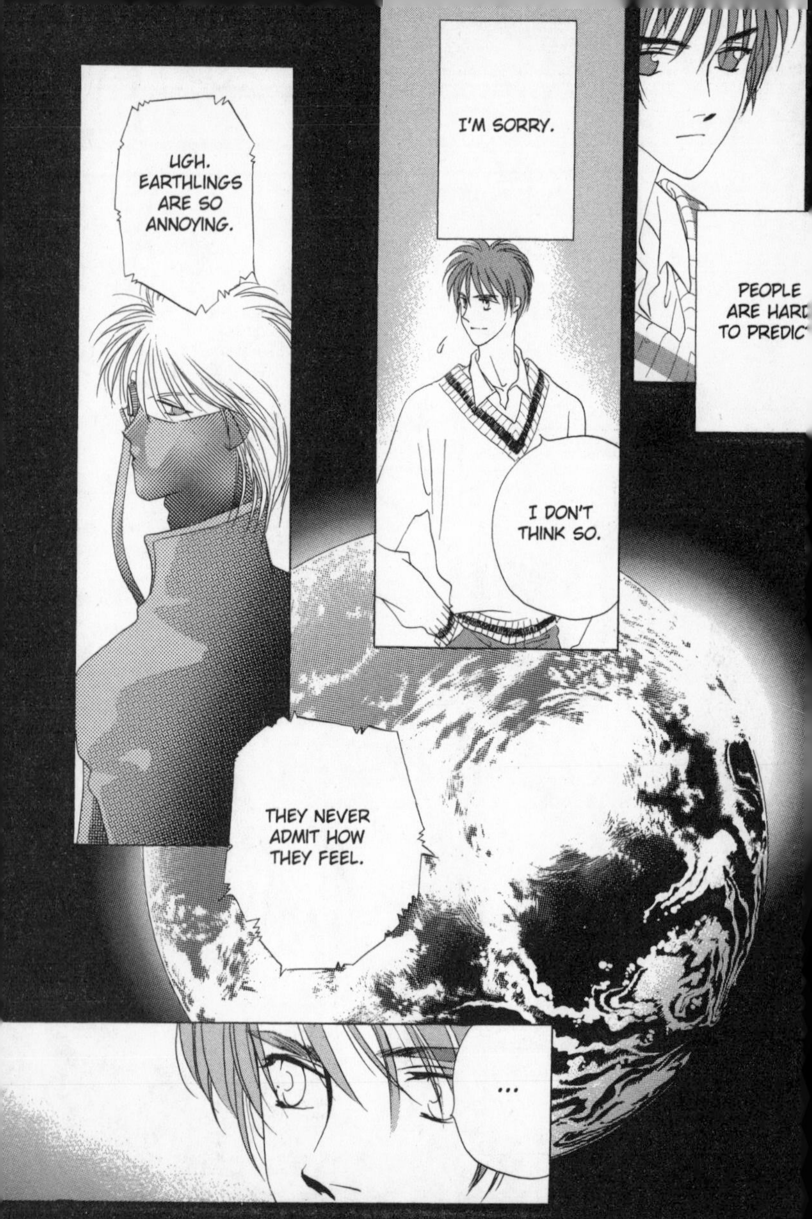
PEOPLE ARE HARD TO PREDICT
I'M SORRY.
I DON'T THINK SO.
UGH. EARTHLINGS ARE SO ANNOYING.
THEY NEVER ADMIT HOW THEY FEEL.
...

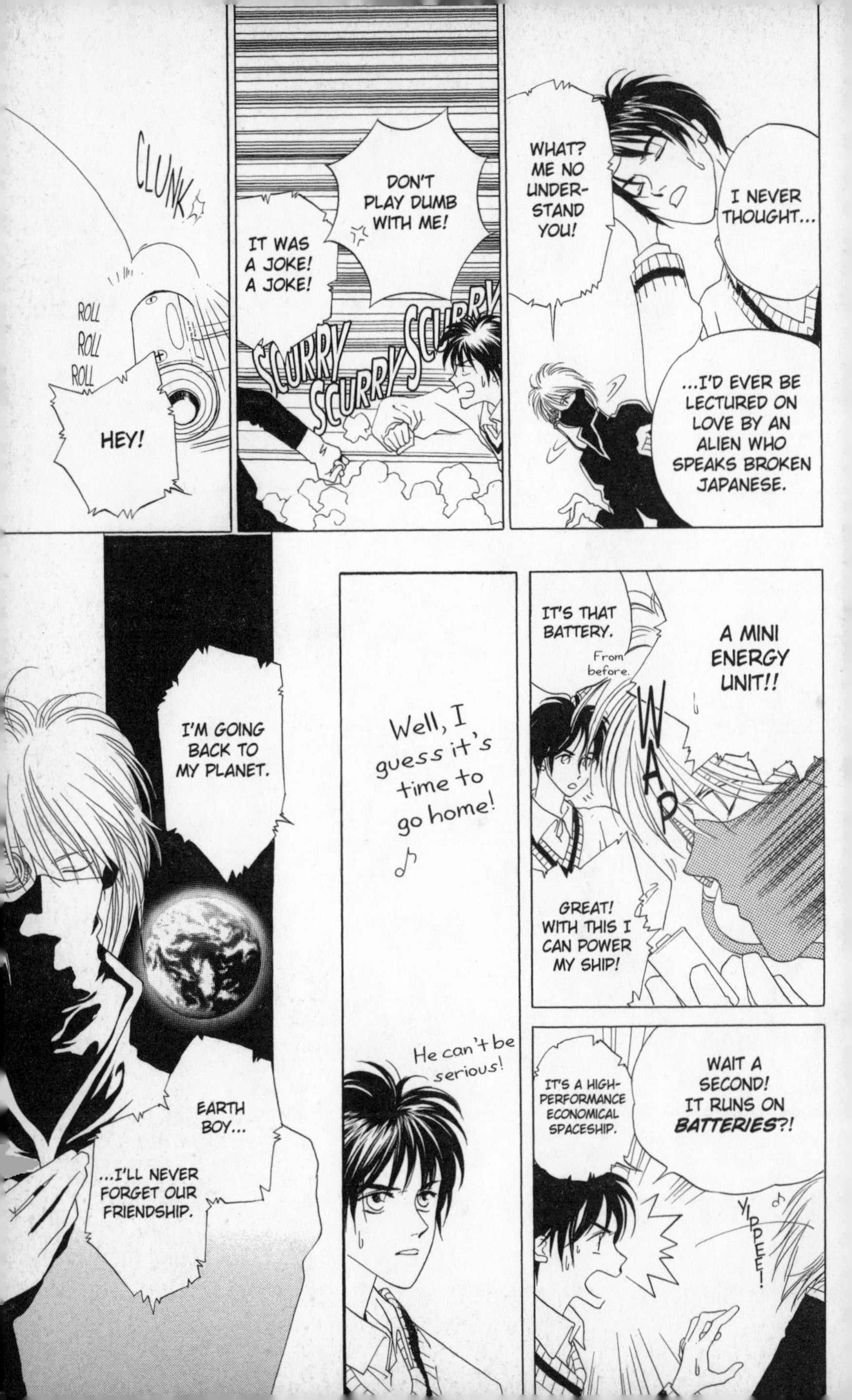
I NEVER THOUGHT...
...I'D EVER BE LECTURED ON LOVE BY AN ALIEN WHO SPEAKS BROKEN JAPANESE.
WHAT? ME NO UNDER-STAND YOU!
DON'T PLAY DUMB WITH ME!
IT WAS A JOKE! A JOKE!
SCURRY SCURRY SCURRY
CLUNK
ROLL ROLL ROLL
HEY!
A MINI ENERGY UNIT!!
IT'S THAT BATTERY.
From before.
WAP
GREAT! WITH THIS I CAN POWER MY SHIP!
WAIT A SECOND! IT RUNS ON BATTERIES?!
IT'S A HIGH-PERFORMANCE ECONOMICAL SPACESHIP.
YIPPEE!
Well, I guess it's time to go home!
He can't be serious!
I'M GOING BACK TO MY PLANET.
EARTH BOY...
...I'LL NEVER FORGET OUR FRIENDSHIP.

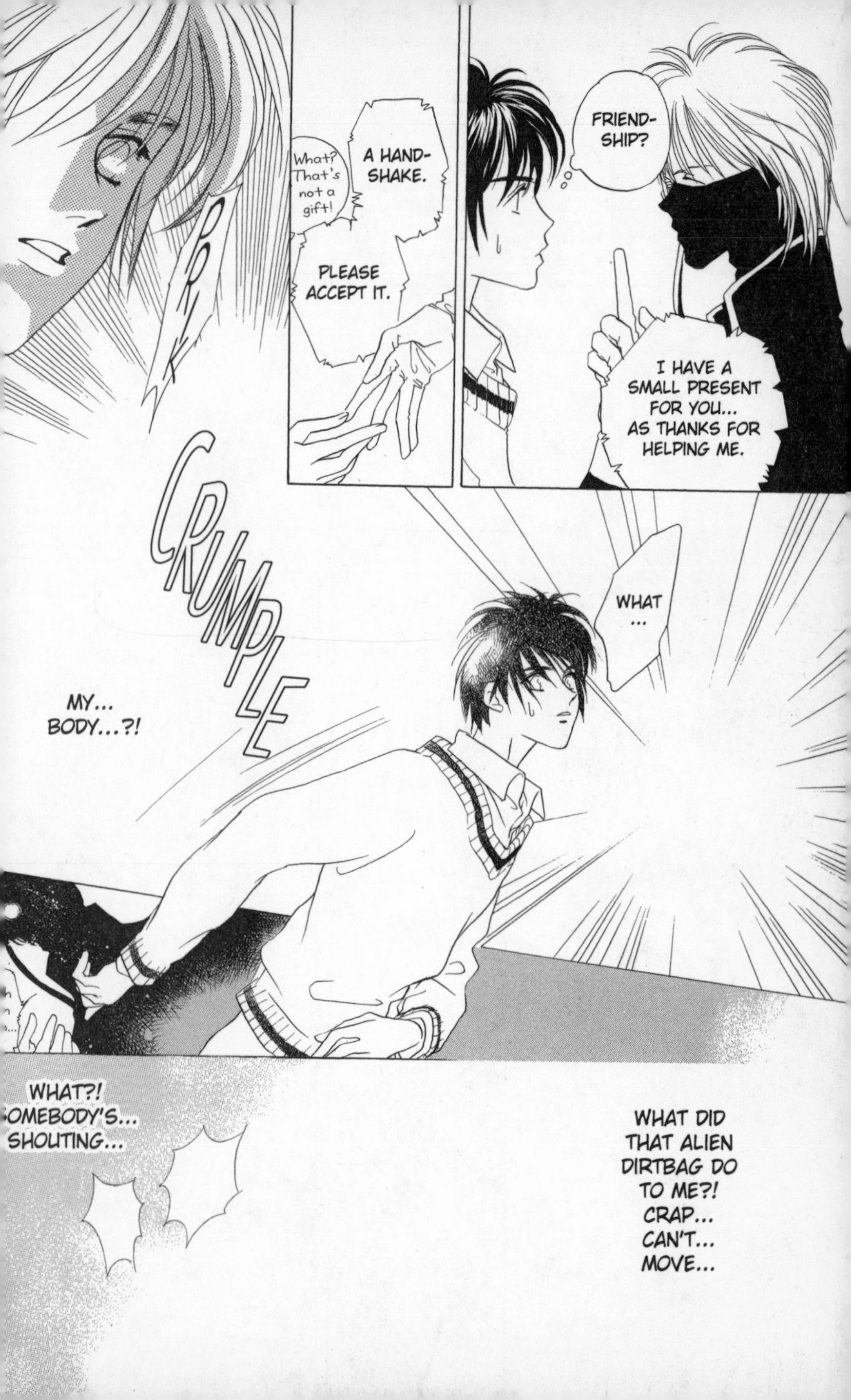

I HAVE A SMALL PRESENT FOR YOU... AS THANKS FOR HELPING ME.
FRIEND-SHIP?
A HAND-SHAKE.
What? That's not a gift!
PLEASE ACCEPT IT.
CRUMPLE
MY... BODY...?!
WHAT...
WHAT DID THAT ALIEN DIRTBAG DO TO ME?! CRAP... CAN'T... MOVE...
WHAT?! OMEBODY'S... SHOUTING...

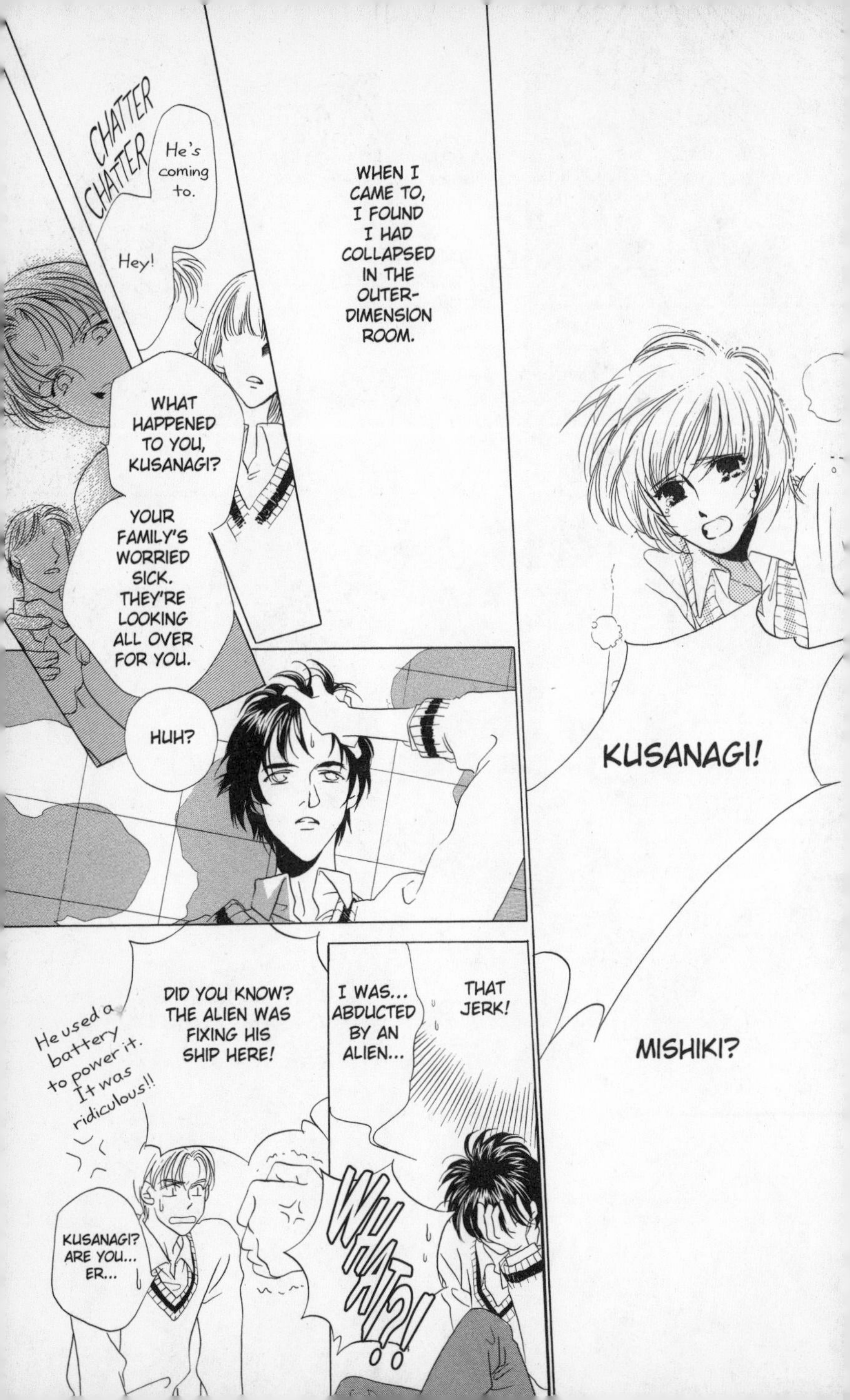
KUSANAGI!
MISHIKI?
WHEN I CAME TO, I FOUND I HAD COLLAPSED IN THE OUTER-DIMENSION ROOM.
CHATTER CHATTER
He's coming to.
Hey!
WHAT HAPPENED TO YOU, KUSANAGI?
YOUR FAMILY'S WORRIED SICK. THEY'RE LOOKING ALL OVER FOR YOU.
HUH?
THAT JERK!
I WAS... ABDUCTED BY AN ALIEN...
WHAT?!
DID YOU KNOW? THE ALIEN WAS FIXING HIS SHIP HERE!
He used a battery to power it. It was ridiculous!!
KUSANAGI? ARE YOU... ER...

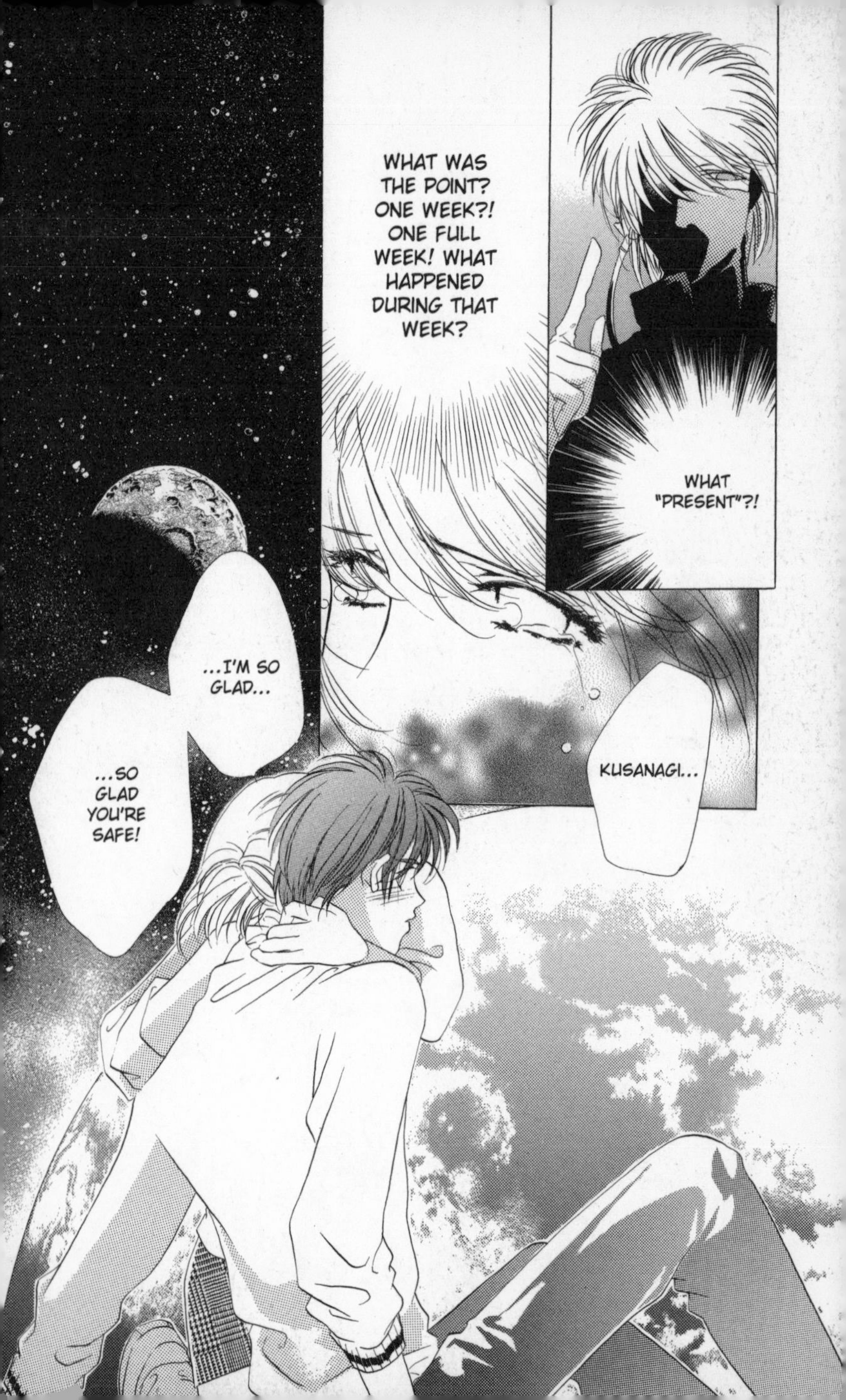
WHAT "PRESENT"?!
WHAT WAS THE POINT? ONE WEEK?! ONE FULL WEEK! WHAT HAPPENED DURING THAT WEEK?
KUSANAGI...
...I'M SO GLAD...
...SO GLAD YOU'RE SAFE!

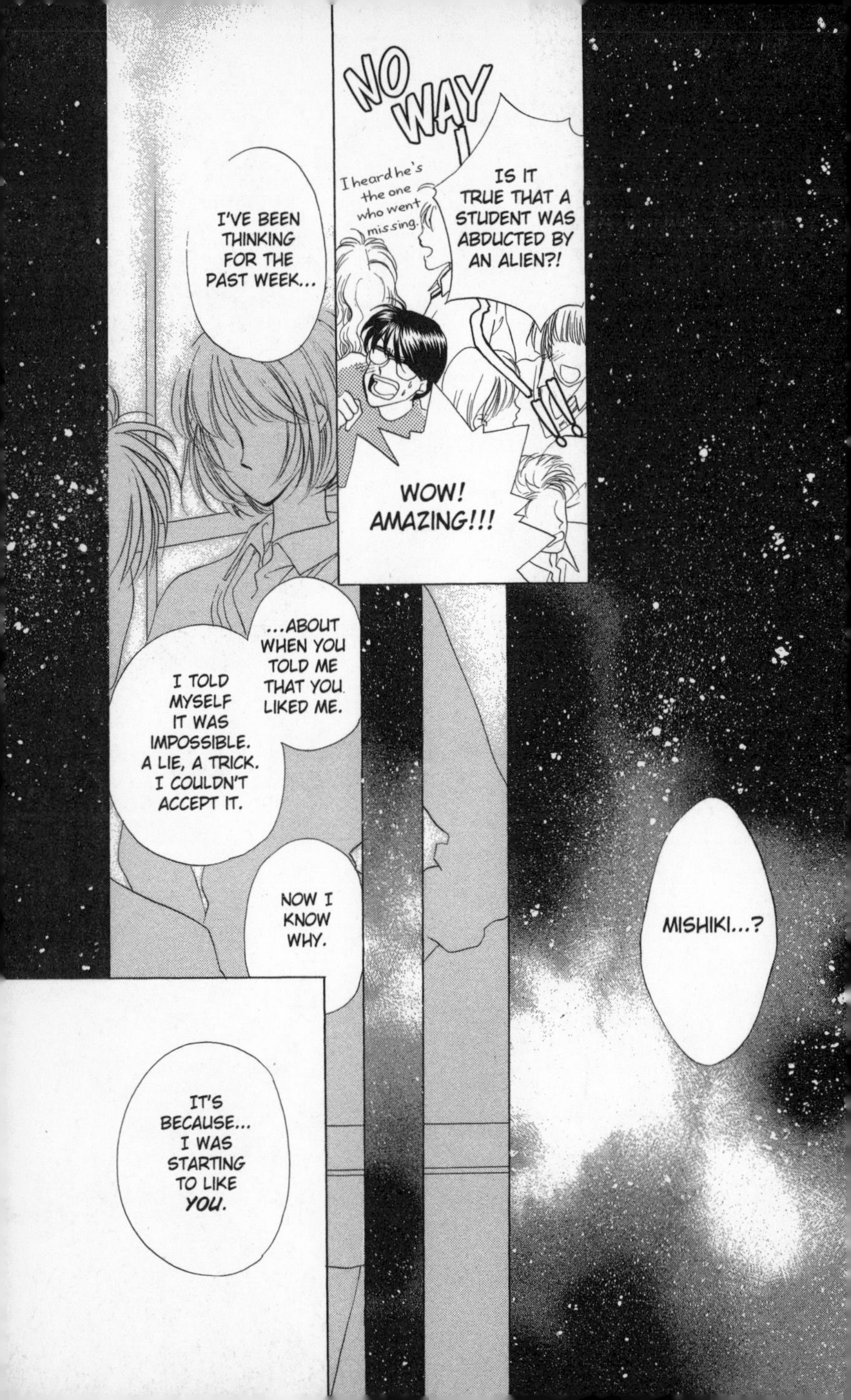
NO WAY
IS IT TRUE THAT A STUDENT WAS ABDUCTED BY AN ALIEN?!
I heard he's the one who went missing.
WOW! AMAZING!!!
I'VE BEEN THINKING FOR THE PAST WEEK...
...ABOUT WHEN YOU TOLD ME THAT YOU LIKED ME.
I TOLD MYSELF IT WAS IMPOSSIBLE. A LIE, A TRICK. I COULDN'T ACCEPT IT.
NOW I KNOW WHY.
MISHIKI...?
IT'S BECAUSE... I WAS STARTING TO LIKE YOU.

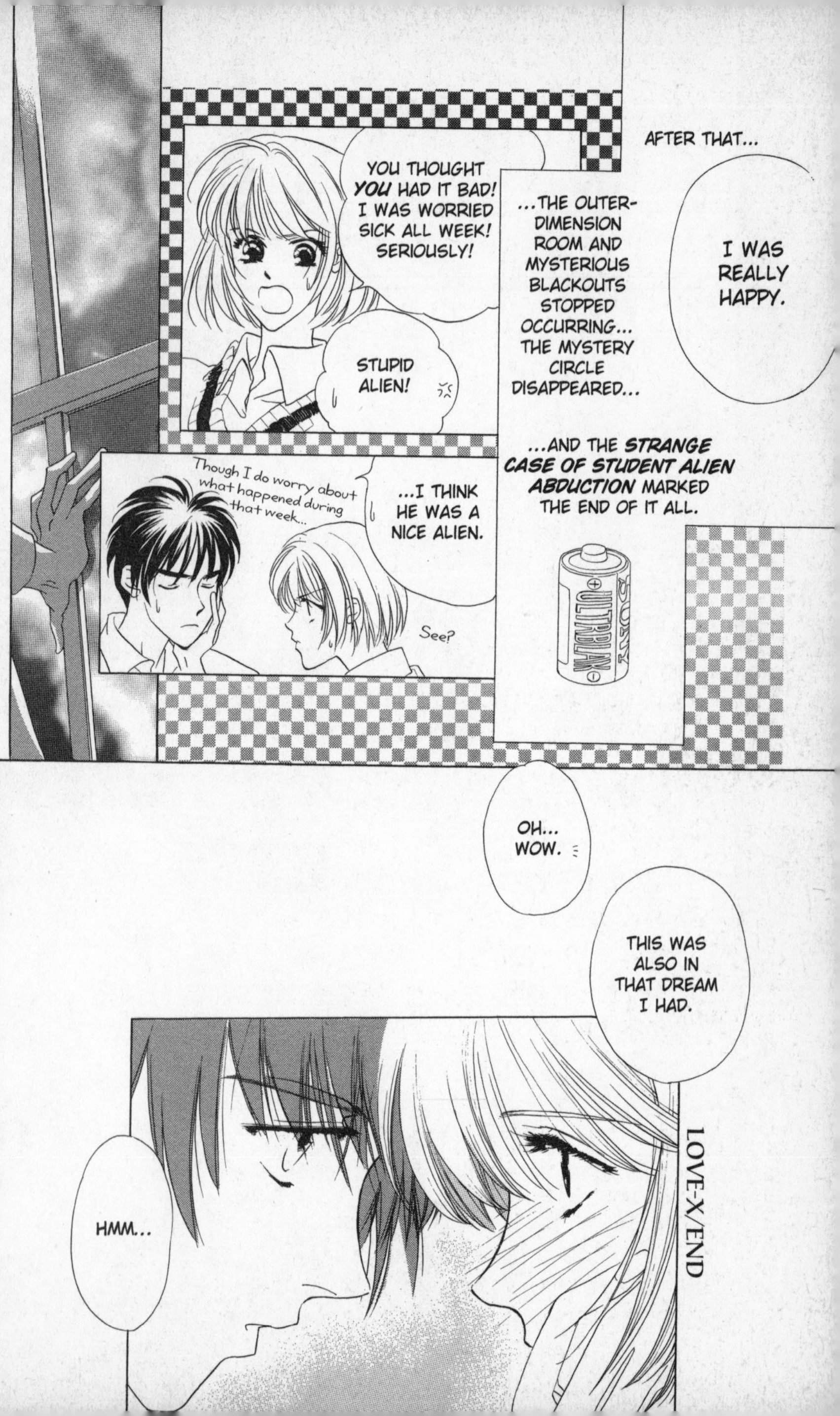
AFTER THAT...
I WAS REALLY HAPPY.
...THE OUTER-DIMENSION ROOM AND MYSTERIOUS BLACKOUTS STOPPED OCCURRING... THE MYSTERY CIRCLE DISAPPEARED...
YOU THOUGHT YOU HAD IT BAD! I WAS WORRIED SICK ALL WEEK! SERIOUSLY!
STUPID ALIEN!
...AND THE STRANGE CASE OF STUDENT ALIEN ABDUCTION MARKED THE END OF IT ALL.
SONY
ULTRABLAK
...I THINK HE WAS A NICE ALIEN.
Though I do worry about what happened during that week...
See?
OH... WOW.
THIS WAS ALSO IN THAT DREAM I HAD.
LOVE-X/END
HMM...

Tohko Mizuno made her mangaka debut with *Night Walk*, which ran in *Lunatic LaLa* magazine in 1995. Showcasing her delicate line work and use of rich textures and patterns, the quasi-historical *Haruka* is Mizuno's first serialized manga and is based on a video game of the same name. It has spawned several books, including a fanbook, a super guidebook, and a collection of illustrations. Mizuno is also the author of *Mukashi, Oboronaru Otoko Arikeri* (Once Upon a Time, There Was a Hazy Man).

HARUKA
VOL. 2
The Shojo Beat Manga Edition

STORY AND ART BY
TOHKO MIZUNO
ORIGINAL CONCEPT BY RUBY PARTY

Translation/Stanley Floyd, HC Language Solutions
Touch-up Art & Lettering/James Gaubatz
Cover Design/Hidemi Dunn
Interior Design/Yuki Ameda
Editor/Carol Fox

Editor in Chief, Books/Alvin Lu
Editor in Chief, Magazines/Marc Weidenbaum
VP of Publishing Licensing/Rika Inouye
VP of Sales/Gonzalo Ferreyra
Sr. VP of Marketing/Liza Coppola
Publisher/Hyoe Narita

Harukanaru Toki no Nakade by Tohko Mizuno
© Tohko Mizuno, KOEI Co., Ltd. 1997.
All rights reserved.
First published in Japan in 2001 by HAKUSENSHA, Inc., Tokyo.
English language translation rights arranged
with HAKUSENSHA, Inc., Tokyo.
The stories, characters and incidents mentioned
in this publication are entirely fictional.

Printed in Canada

Published by VIZ Media, LLC
P.O. Box 77010
San Francisco, CA 94107

Shojo Beat Manga Edition
10 9 8 7 6 5 4 3 2 1
First printing, August 2008

www.viz.com

store.viz.com

RATED

PARENTAL ADVISORY
HARUKA is rated T+ for Older
Teen and is recommended for
ages 16 and up.
ratings.viz.com

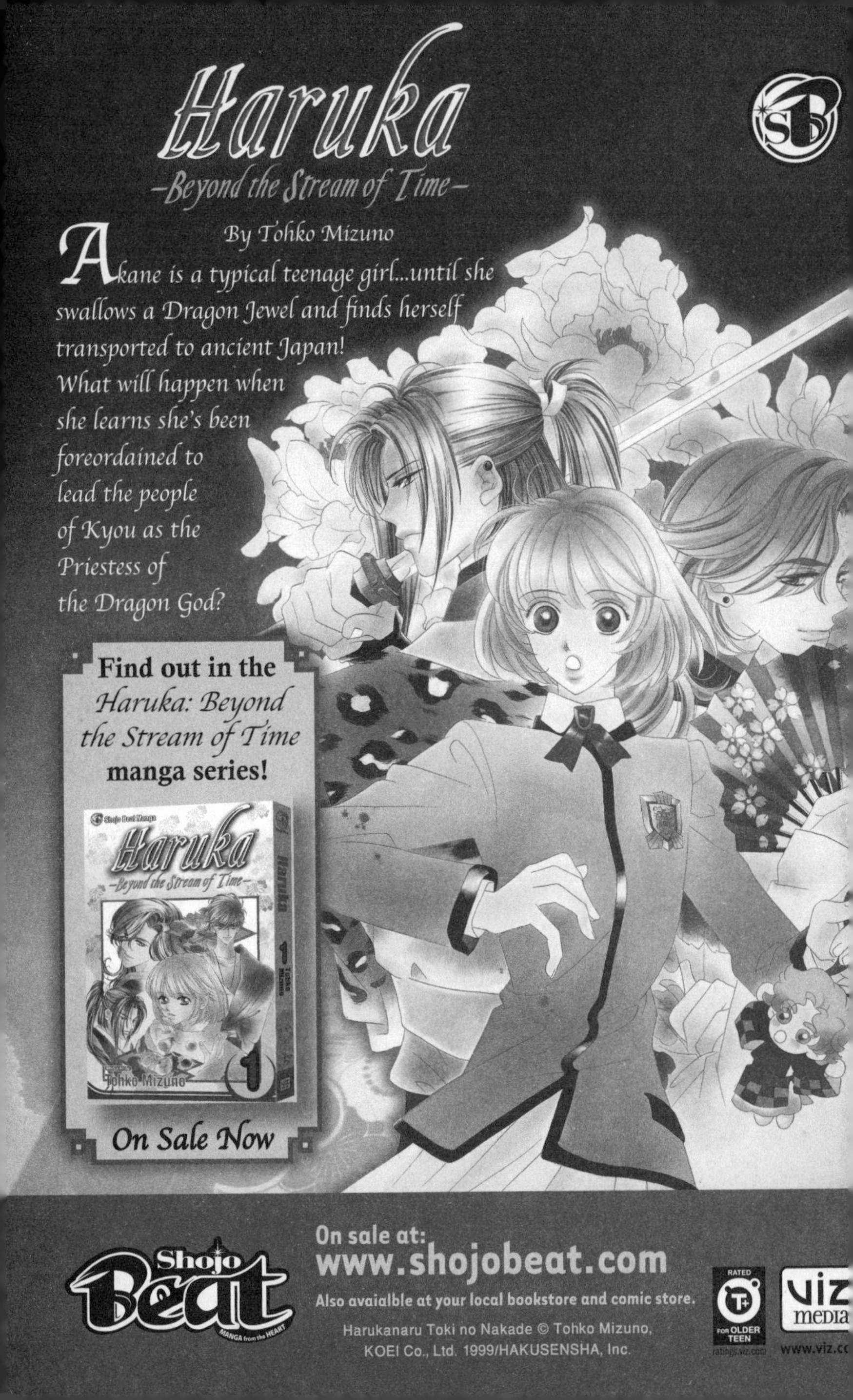
Haruka
-Beyond the Stream of Time-
By Tohko Mizuno
Akane is a typical teenage girl...until she swallows a Dragon Jewel and finds herself transported to ancient Japan! What will happen when she learns she's been foreordained to lead the people of Kyou as the Priestess of the Dragon God?
Find out in the Haruka: Beyond the Stream of Time manga series!
Shojo Beat Manga
Haruka
-Beyond the Stream of Time-
Tohko Mizuno
1
On Sale Now
Shojo Beat
MANGA from the HEART
On sale at:
www.shojobeat.com
Also avaialble at your local bookstore and comic store.
Harukanaru Toki no Nakade © Tohko Mizuno, KOEI Co., Ltd. 1999/HAKUSENSHA, Inc.
RATED
T+
FOR OLDER TEEN
ratings.viz.com
viz media

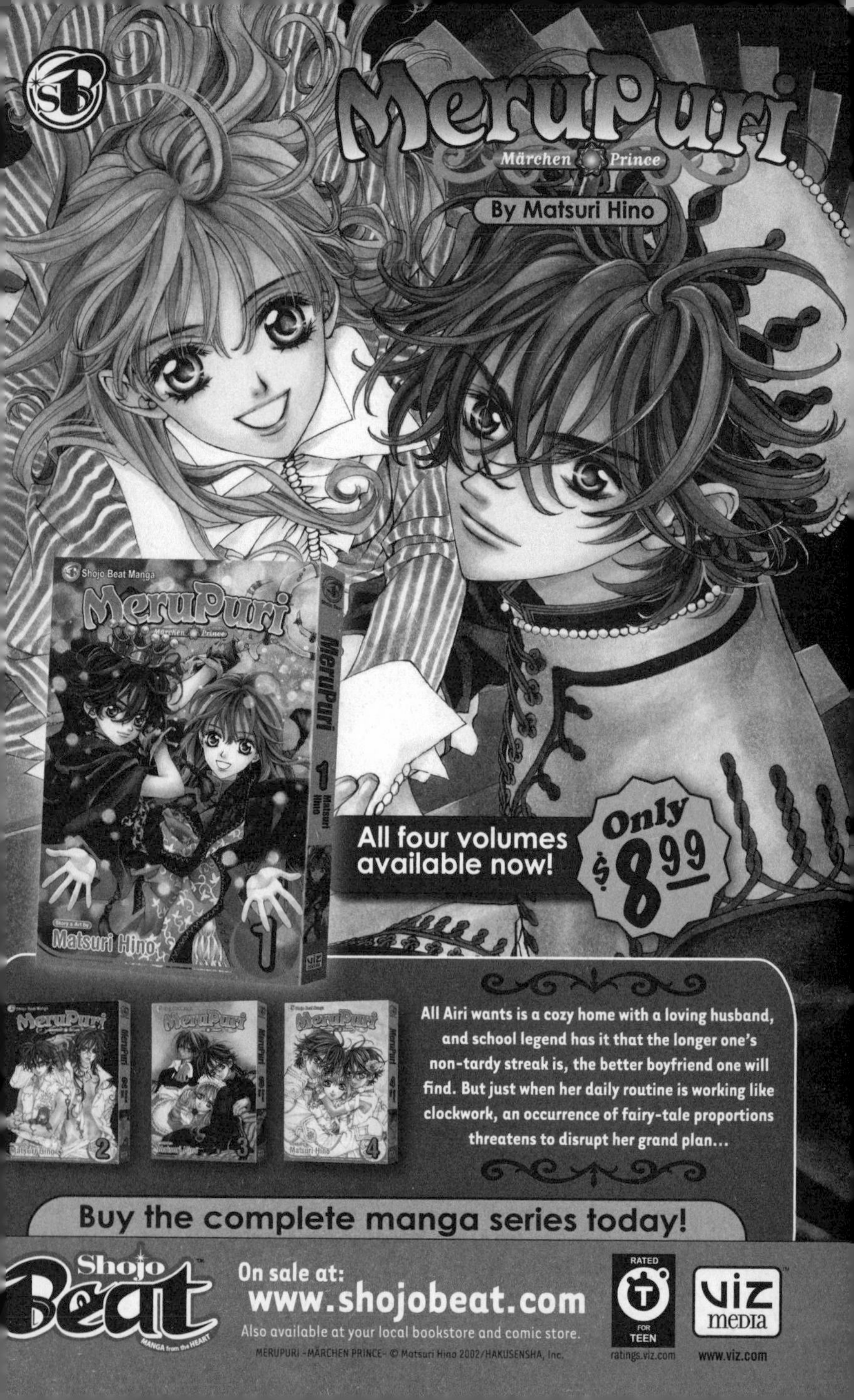
MeruPuri
Märchen Prince
By Matsuri Hino
Shojo Beat Manga
MeruPuri
Märchen Prince
Matsuri Hino
1
All four volumes available now!
Only $8.99
All Airi wants is a cozy home with a loving husband, and school legend has it that the longer one's non-tardy streak is, the better boyfriend one will find. But just when her daily routine is working like clockwork, an occurrence of fairy-tale proportions threatens to disrupt her grand plan...
Buy the complete manga series today!
Shojo Beat
MANGA from the HEART
On sale at:
www.shojobeat.com
Also available at your local bookstore and comic store.
MERUPURI -MÄRCHEN PRINCE- © Matsuri Hino 2002/HAKUSENSHA, Inc.
RATED T FOR TEEN
ratings.viz.com
VIZ MEDIA
www.viz.com

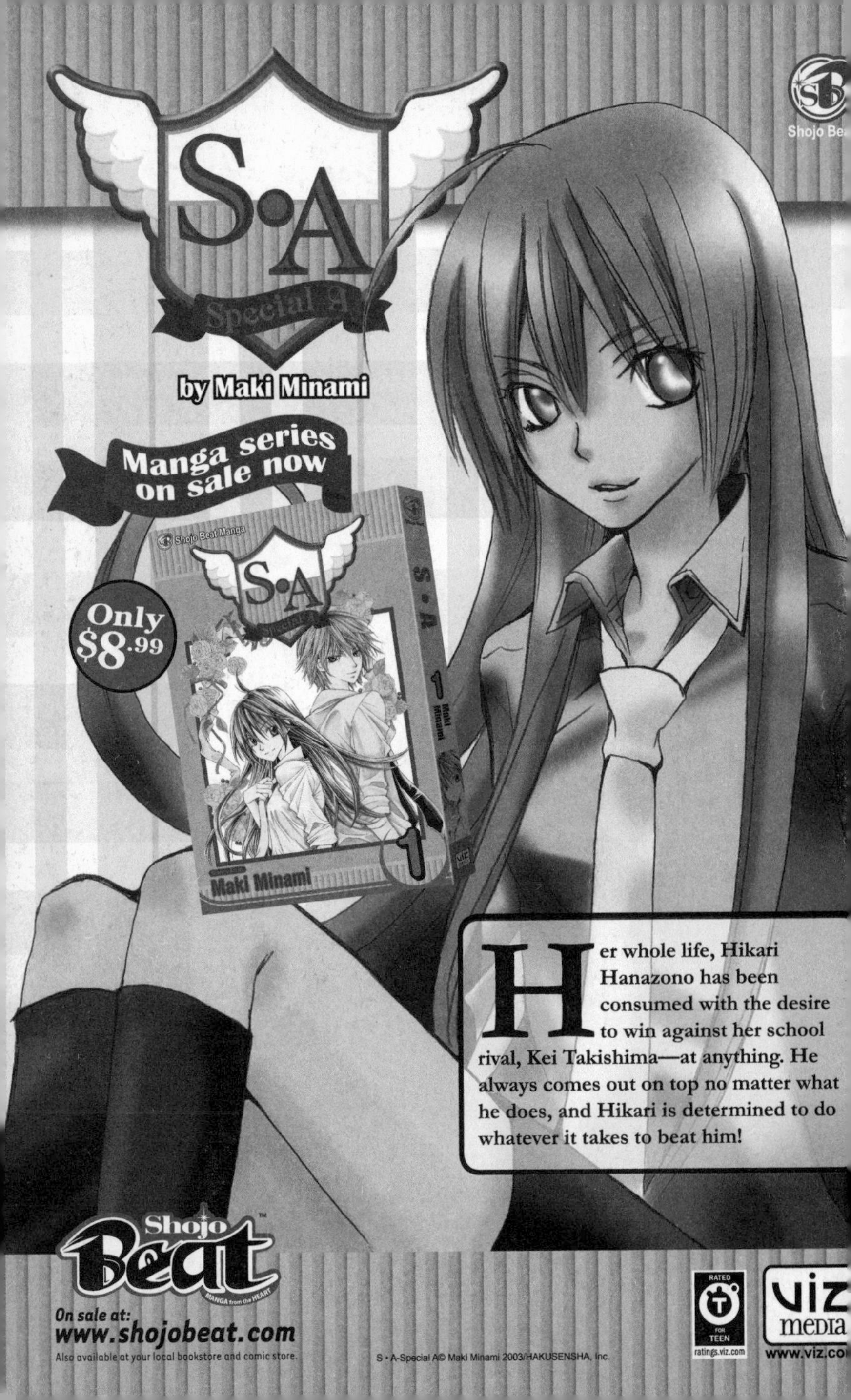

S•A
Special A
by Maki Minami
Manga series on sale now
Only $8.99
Shojo Beat Manga
S•A
1
Maki Minami
Her whole life, Hikari Hanazono has been consumed with the desire to win against her school rival, Kei Takishima—at anything. He always comes out on top no matter what he does, and Hikari is determined to do whatever it takes to beat him!
Shojo Beat
MANGA from the HEART
On sale at:
www.shojobeat.com
Also available at your local bookstore and comic store.
S • A-Special A© Maki Minami 2003/HAKUSENSHA, Inc.
RATED T FOR TEEN
ratings.viz.com
VIZ MEDIA
www.viz.co

Shojo Beat™

MANGA from the HEART

HAYNER PLD/ALTON SQUARE